1/84

# Summerfolk

# Summerfolk

*A History of the Dacha, 1710–2000*

S T E P H E N   L O V E L L

Cornell University Press

ITHACA AND LONDON

First published 2003 by Cornell University Press

Printed in the United States of America

Library of Congress Cataloging-in-Publication Data

Lovell, Stephen, 1972–
Summerfolk : a history of the dacha, 1710–2000 / Stephen Lovell.
p. cm.
Includes bibliographical references and index.
ISBN 0–8014–4071–8
1. Country homes—Russia.  2. Country homes—Soviet Union.  3. Country homes—Russia (Federation)  4. Russia—Social life and customs—1533–1917.  5. Soviet Union—Social life and customs.  6. Russia (Federation)—Social life and customs.  I. Title.
DK32.L79 2003
643.2—DC21
2002012234

Cornell University Press strives to use environmentally responsible suppliers and materials to the fullest extent possible in the publishing of its books. Such materials include vegetable-based, low-VOC inks and acid-free papers that are recycled, totally chlorine-free, or partly composed of nonwood fibers. For further information, visit our website at www.cornellpress.cornell.edu.

1 3 5 7 9 cloth printing 10 8 6 4 2

*For my parents*

# Contents

# Illustrations

# Acknowledgments

This book would probably not have been written without the award of a Junior Research Fellowship by St. John's College, Oxford. I thank that enlightened and generous institution for support both financial and intellectual.

Institutional assistance of a different kind has been provided by Cornell University Press, where Bernhard Kendler has been a courteous and efficient editor, and Karen Laun and Barbara Salazar have done excellent work on the manuscript.

My research has been made possible by the staff of several libraries and archives. In Oxford, I thank especially Mrs. Menzies at the Bodleian and the delightful and expert personnel at the Slavonic annex of the Taylor Institute. In Helsinki, Irina Lukka has been unfailingly helpful with illustrations and bibliographical queries. Librarians and archivists in Moscow and St. Petersburg, although not invariably charming, have been much more obliging than their abysmal salaries and working conditions give me any right to expect.

Several friends and colleagues have made my stays in Russia more pleasant and productive. I am especially grateful to Konstantin Barsht, Daniel Beer, Irina Chekhovskikh, Ol'ga Egoshina and Vladimir Spiridonov, Al'bin Konechnyi and Ksana Kumpan, Sergei and Ol'ga Parkhomovskii, Natal'ia Poltavtseva, and Ol'ga Sevan.

I gratefully acknowledge the helpful information I have received from Jana Howlett, David Moon, and Andrei Rogachevskii.

Several people have given me the benefit of their brainpower by reading various pieces of work in draft form. For this help I thank Charles Hachten, Steven Harris, Barbara Heldt, Julie Hessler, Geoffrey Hosking, Judith Pallot, David Saunders, and Gerry Smith.

Catriona Kelly has contributed to this book in more ways than I have space to enumerate here.

Liz Leach took time away from her own work to join me on trips to Russia, and her intelligent interest in the summerfolk was surprisingly undiminished by the experience; she has also taught me more about domesticity than any dachnik ever will.

A FEW sections of this book have already been published elsewhere. Some passages in Chapters 3 and 4 appeared in "Between Arcadia and Suburbia: Dachas in Late Imperial Russia," *Slavic Review* 61 (Spring 2002); despite its title, this article is quite different from Chapter 4 here. About half of Chapter 5 found its way into "The Making of the Stalin-Era Dacha," *Journal of Modern History* 74 (June 2002). (Conversely, the article contains detail on the 1930s that did not find a place in this book.) A few pages in Chapter 6 were used in

xii   "Soviet Exurbia: Dachas in the Postwar Era," in *Socialist Spaces in Eastern Europe and the Soviet Union, 1947–1991*, edited by Susan E. Reid and David Crowley (Oxford: Berg, 2002). I am grateful for permission to reuse all this material here, and I thank the editors—respectively, Diane Koenker, Sheila Fitzpatrick, and Susan Reid—for helping me to prepare the articles for publication.

Photographs are my own unless stated otherwise.

# Glossary

| | |
|---|---|
| *appanage lands* | (*udel'nye zemli*) land owned directly by members of the imperial family |
| *blat* | the informal exchange of favors as practiced in Soviet society |
| *chinsh* | a kind of hereditary lease |
| *dachniki* | users of dachas; "summerfolk" |
| *desiatina* | unit equivalent to 2.7 acres |
| *dom otdykha* | rest home |
| *DSK* | a dacha construction cooperative |
| *dvor* | a yard or a peasant household |
| *dvornik* | (pl. *dvorniki*) caretaker, yardsman |
| *exurbia* | an area beyond the city and the suburbs inhabited mainly by people who retain social, economic, and occupational ties to the city |
| *fligel'* | a residential building separate from the main house on an estate or plot of land |
| *guberniia* | (pl. gubernii) a province in tsarist Russia |
| *gulian'e* | a fête; popular festivities (usually associated with a public holiday) |
| *imenie* | a landed estate |
| *intelligent* | (pl. *intelligenty*) a member of the intelligentsia |
| *ispolkom* | an executive committee (part of the apparatus of the Soviet state) |
| *kottedzh* | in the nineteenth century, a cottage modeled most often on the English rustic house; in the late twentieth century, an exurban dwelling with the potential for year-round use |
| *KPSS* | the Communist Party of the Soviet Union |
| *meshchanin* | (pl. *meshchane*) nonnoble town dweller, petit bourgeois (sometimes pejorative) |
| *Mosgordachsoiuz* | the managing organization for dacha cooperatives in the Moscow region (1931–37) |
| *myza* | a farmstead or country estate (used mainly to refer to property near the Gulf of Finland, to the west of St. Petersburg) |
| *NEP* | New Economic Policy |
| *nepmen* | people who profited by buying and selling ("speculating") under NEP |
| *NKVD* | People's Commissarist for Internal Affairs |

| | | |
|---|---|---|
| xiv | *oblast* | an administrative region in Soviet Russia |
| | *obrok* | quitrent |
| | *ogorod* | allotment |
| | *ogorodnichestvo* | allotment cultivation |
| | *okrug* | Soviet territorial division |
| | Old Bolshevik | a person who had joined the Bolshevik Party before the coup of 1917 |
| | *OMKh* | department of local services |
| | *OSB* | Society of Old Bolsheviks |
| | *osobniak* | detached house, villa |
| | Petersburg Side | a cluster of islands directly north of the center of St. Petersburg (called the Petrograd Side since the First World War) |
| | *podsobnoe khoziaistvo* | subsidiary farm (agricultural land cultivated by a particular Soviet organization to guarantee a supply of produce) |
| | *pomeshchik* | landowner |
| | *pomest'e* | landed estate |
| | *poselianin* | (pl. *poseliane*) settler |
| | *poselok* | settlement |
| | *prigorod* | suburb |
| | *progulka* | promenade, stroll |
| | *pood* | unit equivalent to 16.38 kilograms |
| | *raion* | Soviet administrative unit approximating district |
| | *RSFSR* | Russian Soviet Federal Socialist Republic |
| | *sad* | garden |
| | *sadovod* | (pl. *sadovody*) a garden plot cultivator |
| | *sadovodstvo* | garden plot cultivation, or a garden plot settlement |
| | *sazhen* | unit equivalent to 2.13 meters |
| | *sluzhashchie* | employees, white-collar workers (in Soviet times) |
| | *Sovnarkom* | the Soviet government |
| | *tovarishchestvo* | association |
| | *uchastok* | plot of land |
| | *uezd* | tsarist administrative unit approximating county |
| | *uplotnenie* | "compression" (a Soviet practice of the 1920s and 1930s whereby new residents were forcibly moved into apartments and houses that were already occupied) |
| | *usad'ba* | (pl. *usad'by*) a country estate; a farmstead |
| | *USK* | building control committee |
| | *verst* | unit equivalent to 1.06 kilometers |
| | *volost* | the smallest administrative unit (typically, a few villages) |
| | *vremianka* | a temporary shelter built on a dacha plot |
| | Vyborg Side | the northernmost district of prerevolutionary St. Petersburg |
| | *zagorodnyi dom* | out-of-town house |
| | *zemstvo* | (pl. *zemstva*) elected rural assembly, local government (in the period 1864–1917) |

# Abbreviations

| | |
|---|---|
| AHR | *American Historical Review* |
| B&E | *Entsiklopedicheskii slovar' izd. Brokgauza i Efrona*, 41 vols. (St. Petersburg, 1890–1904) |
| BSE | *Bol'shaia sovetskaia entsiklopediia* |
| DSK | Dachno-stroitel'nyi kooperativ |
| JfGO | *Jahrbücher für Geschichte Osteuropas* |
| Kr | *Krokodil* |
| LG | *Literaturnaia gazeta* |
| LOGAV | Leningradskii oblastnoi gosudarstvennyi arkhiv v g. Vyborge |
| ML | *Moskovskii listok* |
| PG | *Peterburgskaia gazeta* |
| PL | *Peterburgskii listok* |
| PLL | *Pargolovskii letnii listok* |
| PSZ | *Polnoe sobranie zakonov Rossiiskoi Imperii*, 3 ser. (St. Petersburg, 1830–1911) |
| RGASPI | Rossiiskii gosudarstvennyi arkhiv sotsial'no-politicheskoi informatsii |
| RGIA | Rossiiskii gosudarstvennyi istoricheskii arkhiv |
| SEER | *Slavonic and East European Review* |
| SIu | *Sovetskaia iustitsiia* |
| SP | *Sotsialisticheskii prigorod* |
| SPb ved | *Sankt-Peterburgskie vedomosti* |
| SPP RSFSR | *Sobranie postanovlenii pravitel'stva RSFSR* |
| SPP SSSR | *Sobranie postanovlenii pravitel'stva SSSR* |
| SR | *Slavic Review* |
| SZ | *Sotsialisticheskaia zakonnost'* |
| TsGAMO | Tsentral'nyi gosudarstvennyi arkhiv Moskovskoi oblasti |
| TsGA SPb | Tsentral'nyi gosudarstvennyi arkhiv Sankt-Peterburga |
| TsGIA SPb | Tsentral'nyi gosudarstvennyi istoricheskii arkhiv Sankt-Peterburga |
| TsIAM | Tsentral'nyi istoricheskii arkhiv Moskvy |
| TsMAM | Tsentral'nyi munitsipal'nyi arkhiv Moskvy |
| VKG | *Vecherniaia krasnaia gazeta* |
| VM | *Vecherniaia Moskva* |
| ZhT-ZhS | *Zhilishchnoe tovarishchestvo—zhilishche i stroitel'stvo* |

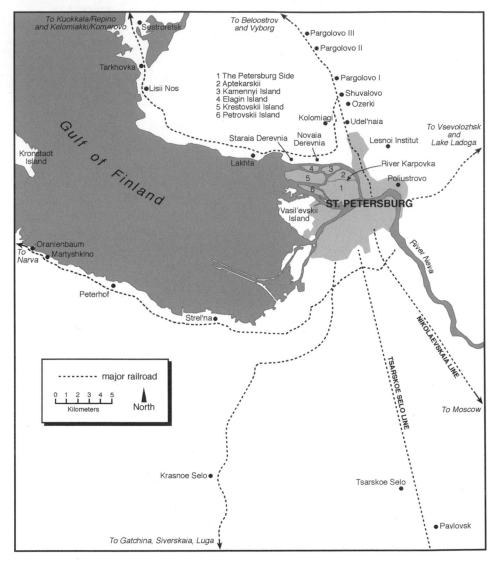

To Kuokkala/Repino and Kelomiakki/Komarovo

To Beloostrov and Vyborg

Sestroretsk

Pargolovo III

Pargolovo II

Tarkhovka

Pargolovo I

Lisii Nos

1 The Petersburg Side
2 Aptekarskii
3 Kamennyi Island
4 Elagin Island
5 Krestovskii Island
6 Petrovskii Island

Shuvalovo

Ozerki

Kolomiagi

Udel'naia

To Vsevolozhsk and Lake Ladoga

Kronstadt Island

Gulf of Finland

Staraia Derevnia

Novaia Derevnia

Lesnoi Institut

Lakhta

4 3
5 2
6 1

River Karpovka

Poliustrovo

ST. PETERSBURG

Vasil'evskii Island

River Neva

Oranienbaum

Martyshkino

To Narva

Peterhof

Strel'na

major railroad

0 1 2 3 4 5
Kilometers

North

NIKOLAEVSKAIA LINE

TSARSKOE SELO LINE

To Moscow

Krasnoe Selo

Tsarskoe Selo

Pavlovsk

To Gatchina, Siverskaia, Luga

Petersburg and surrounding area. This map includes many of the dacha places mentioned in the text. It is far from comprehensive, however. Dacha settlements can be found at almost every stop on the railway lines out of Petersburg as well as in many more remote parts of the region.

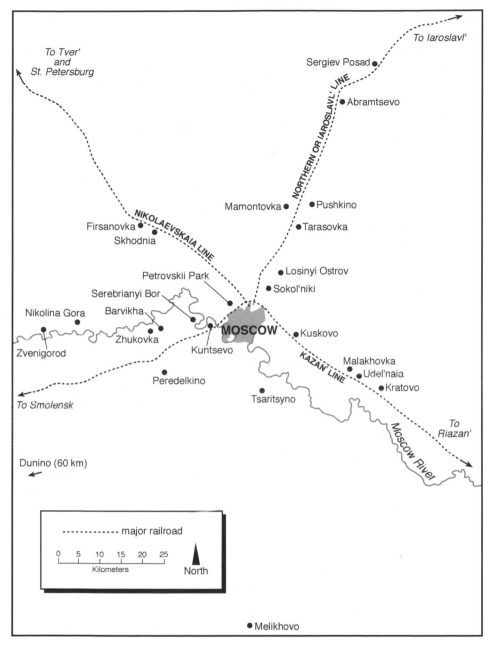

Moscow and surrounding area. This map includes the four railway lines that have been most influential in the history of the Moscow dacha. The other routes—northwest toward Riga, north toward Savelovo, southwest toward Kiev, east toward Nizhnii Novgorod, south toward Kursk and Volgograd—have also played their part, and are now densely overgrown with dacha and garden settlements. The first of these lines to be completed was the Nikolaevskaia in 1851; the latest—to Riga and to Savelovo—became operative in the early twentieth century.

Summerfolk

# Introduction

The subject of this book requires less introduction than many topics in European history, since "dacha" is that rare creature: a Russian term that has gained a firm foothold in the English language. Its impact has, moreover, gone well beyond lexicography. The word has left numerous traces in the imagination of the anglophone world. It may conjure up the summer houses of Chekhov's stories, or the out-of-town residences of the Soviet privileged classes, or even allotment shacks on the outskirts of post-Soviet cities. It is usually glossed in English dictionaries as "country house" or "cottage" and referred to as the Slavic equivalent of a vacation house or second home.

These notions have a lot of truth to them. A dacha is almost invariably a dwelling that is used intermittently, most often in the summer or on weekends. It stands on its own plot of land, is located out of town, but generally lies within reach of a large urban center (typically, no more than two or three hours' journey). Most heads of dacha households need to remain reasonably close to the city, as it is their main provider of employment and source of income. Unlike country estate proprietors, with whom they are sometimes confused, dacha folk do not seek to make money from their landholding. They treat their house in the country as a temporary refuge and a recreational amenity, spatially separate from the city yet usually still within commuting range. The dacha may therefore be regarded as occupying a space between town and country: at a significant remove from metropolitan civilization but distinct from the surrounding rural settlement by virtue of its urban clientele.

To this extent, the dacha may be considered a by-product of urbanization and thus analogous to forms of settlement elsewhere in the developed world: the suburban zones colonized by the North American and European bourgeoisie, or indeed the country retreats of the leisure class. As cities grow larger and wealthier and as their white-collar pop-

2  ulations expand, increasing numbers of people look to the nearby countryside for recuperation, domestic comfort, and enjoyment. Russia's *dachniki* (dacha folk) fit this pattern in many ways. Out-of-town dwellings offered them favorable conditions for family life, pleasures such as recreation and relaxed sociability, and above all the opportunity to escape the heat, dirt, and disease of the city in summer.

As a social and cultural institution, the dacha has a long history that runs roughly parallel to the course of Russia's urbanization. The story begins with the creation of St. Petersburg—Russia's first "modern," self-consciously Western city—in the early eighteenth century. Here, on the road that led from Petersburg to the palace settlement at Peterhof, courtiers built themselves out-of-town residences, thus marking out a space that lay beyond the city limits yet did not merge with the surrounding rural landscape. In the first stage of their history, dachas took their lead, both architecturally and in the way of life they fostered, from the aristocracy. Then, in the first third of the nineteenth century, the rental market for summer housing (mostly concentrated in the city's immediate environs) entered a period of expansion that lasted all the way through to the Revolution. Improved transport connections in the second half of the nineteenth century greatly increased the scope for suburban and exurban settlement. Economic and legal liberalization invigorated the market in land and property. Finally, during the last two prerevolutionary decades, in the face of ever more rapid urban and industrial development, dacha settlements began to converge with suburbs.[1]

This brief historical outline is useful as basic orientation but has its limitations. It does not, for example, do full justice to the dacha's local significance. Urbanization is a process whose outcomes depend heavily on how urban society is constituted in a specific time and place. The dacha's clientele has always been city-based, but it is far from being fixed or homogeneous. Over the past two centuries the word "dacha" has been used in various senses by many different members of Russian society. For an aristocrat in 1800, it would have meant what we would call a villa or even a mansion. Inhabitants of St. Petersburg in the 1850s might have rented their "dachas" from a noble landowner, a merchant, or even a peasant. For a wealthy urbanite in 1890 the word might have referred to a house in the Crimea or to a former manor house. For a medium- or low-ranking civil servant of the same period it very often denoted a modest cottage in St. Petersburg's or Moscow's summer equivalent of the commuter belt. Joseph Stalin used a "dacha" as his main residence for the last twenty years of his life. For any inhabitant of a major Russian city in 2000, a dacha is likely to be a glorified allotment.

As these examples may begin to suggest, dachas have enjoyed a widening social constituency over the last two centuries; not since the eighteenth century have they been re-

---

1. The few people who have written on this subject all agree, from their varying perspectives, on the broad outlines of this periodization: see O. I. Chernykh, "Dachnoe stroitel'stvo Peterburgskoi gubernii, XVIII–nachala XX vv." (dissertation, St. Petersburg, 1993); P. Deotto, "Peterburgskii dachnyi byt XIX v. kak fakt massovoi kul'tury," *Europa Orientalis* 16 (1997); Iu. M. Lotman, "Kamen' i trava," in *Lotmanovskii sbornik*, vol. 1 (Moscow, 1995); M. V. Nashchokina, "Dachnye poselki vtoroi poloviny XIX–nachala XX vv.," in *Sel'skie poseleniia Rossii: Istoricheskii i sotsiokul'turnyi analiz*, ed. O. G. Sevan (Moscow, 1995).

stricted to the elite. A crucial step toward diversification was taken in the first third of the nineteenth century, when the section of the Petersburg population that was not proletarian yet worked for a living increased noticeably. Members of the nobility (*dvorianstvo*) moved to the capital and began to pursue careers in the government bureaucracy, which many young men and their families now saw as a better route to material security and social status than military service. The number of nobles in the city more than tripled, from just over 13,000 in 1801 to almost 43,000 in 1831, while the overall population doubled in the same period, from just over 200,000 to well over 400,000. By the mid-1860s, the proportion of nobles in the Petersburg population was higher still: around 80,000 out of a total of nearly 540,000.[2]

Although they retained their formal membership in the *dvorianstvo,* many of the noblemen who took up residence in nineteenth-century St. Petersburg followed a professional career path and were at least partly dependent on the salaries and other benefits they received. If they owned landholdings in other parts of Russia, these properties did not always supply the means to support a decent standard of living in the big city. And even when Petersburg-based nobles could count on a substantial unearned income, their connection with the country estates that generated this income was weak: they were urbanites first, landowners second.

These noble but not necessarily wealthy Petersburgers proovided one element in a new, nonaristocratic, dacha-frequenting public that emerged in the early nineteenth century. They were joined by nonnoble contingents in the bureaucracy and other occupations, particularly by the *raznochintsy,* Russia's "men of various ranks," mostly sons of low-ranking army officers, civil servants, and priests, who provided the office workers of the Petersburg civil service and would acquire in the second half of the century a strong presence in professions such as journalism, law, and medicine. A third element in the dacha public was the merchant class, which, in the major cities at least, contained a reasonably affluent and socially aspirational upper stratum that was acquiring immovable property and adopting urban ways. In the 1830s these three sections of society (including dependents) together numbered in the tens of thousands, and by the mid-1860s they had reached a total well in excess of 100,000 (or nearly 25 percent of the overall population).[3]

The out-of-town public was recognized by contemporaries as a remarkable new phenomenon in the late 1830s and (especially) the 1840s. To many observers the dacha habit served notice of the changing character of urban life. Now Petersburg contained tens of thousands of people engaged in nonmanual occupations who lived in apartments rather than detached houses, called the city their home, and had no ancestral estate or other property to which to repair during the summer months. For tenants of this category, rented dachas had several advantages: they offered a safe haven from terrifying epidemics, they served as a recreational amenity, and they saved money, being cheaper to rent and maintain than apartments in the city center.

2. *B&E,* s.v. "Sankt-Peterburg," 28:307; *Sankt-Peterburg: Issledovaniia po istorii, topografii i statistike stolitsy,* vol. 3 (St. Petersburg, 1868), 46.

3. *Sankt-Peterburg,* 46–51.

4     The dachniki were a striking new group in Petersburg society not just for the fact of their summer migrations. Equally noteworthy was their intermediate cultural and social status: they occupied a middle ground between aristocratic sociability and popular culture. The bulk of the dachniki were not part of a beau monde constructed around dynastic association, patronage, and intensive ritual socializing, but they also kept their distance from the fairground, the tavern, and other sites of mass urban entertainment. Dachas formed part of an emerging leisure culture that had less to do with public spectacle, display, and revelry than with individual enjoyment and sociability in a relatively small circle of family, friends, and colleagues.

The dacha thus offers important insights into a section of Russian society that cannot easily be isolated or adequately conceptualized: the middling people of the big cities, that is to say, those who did not do physical labor or perform menial service yet were not grandees or landowning nobles. The amorphousness of Russia's urban middle only increased as the nineteenth century wore on: more nobles became déclassé, more merchants' sons intermarried with other groups and changed their occupation, and more petit bourgeois folk bedded down in the big city and began to acquire markedly urban tastes and habits. By 1900 the annual dacha exodus involved extremely diverse sections of society: from mandarins all the way to shopkeepers. All of these people, in their different ways, used the out-of-town experience to cultivate distinct lifestyles and articulate individual and group identities.

A middle class, however, is given unity and coherence not only by shared experiences but also by shared values and shared consciousness. Here the dacha can easily be found wanting. By the second half of the nineteenth century Moscow and Petersburg were large and fractious cities; their inhabitants often found it hard to agree on what constituted the authentic out-of-town experience, and the more vocal and articulate of them were usually ready to cast aspersions on the habits of their fellows. Mandarins, shopkeepers, literary intellectuals, and lowly bureaucrats may all have felt the exurban impulse, but it took them in different directions. The dacha thus became an institution that was ideologically charged and invested with various and often conflicting symbolic meanings.

From the 1840s on, dachniki were regularly lampooned and charged with all manner of vices: vulgarity, snobbery, stupidity, and many others. These problems of self-validation were partly a matter of unfortunate timing. The dacha came to prominence just as the noble country estate (*usad'ba*) was beginning to cast a long cultural shadow. As the heyday of the estate retreated into an increasingly remote Golden Age, the dacha came to be tainted by its association with a supposedly tawdry present. The difficulties it faced in positioning itself culturally were all the greater given the exceptionally polarized relationship of town and country in Russia: to transplant urban civilization beyond the city was to straddle not merely a divide but a chasm. But neglect and disparagement of the summerfolk (a word I will use interchangeably with "dachniki" to denote dacha users), both in scholarship and in other genres of writing, have several further causes. The dacha is a "second home," and second homes, being "inessential," draw the disapproval periodically accorded to all luxury items in the bourgeois age. This kind of critique was particularly powerful in Russia, given the widespread distaste (which extended, crucially, to elite intellectual circles) for "unproductive" use of the land, for physical idleness, and for private property. England, from the mid-nineteenth century, had well-defined and widely disseminated ideologies of individual ownership and private life, but Russians discussed these matters in very different ways. The etymology of the word "dacha" (from the root for "giving") aptly conveys its weak connection to property rights as understood in Western legal systems: originally, in the Middle Ages, a dacha was not acquired but received, and a gift of this kind implied duties and responsibilities as much as wealth and rights. In the nineteenth century, however, the dacha was largely freed of these associations and came to be regarded as an accessory of a comfortable lifestyle. The Soviet period then saw a reversion to the earlier model of state patronage: access to the most prestigious dacha sites was possible only with the approval, or at least the collusion, of the state authorities, and legal opportunities for homeownership were much more restricted than in the late imperial period. Although the basis of property rights was transformed after the Revolution, pre-1917 negative stereotypes of the dacha persisted to a large extent, and independent dachniki had to bear the brunt of periodic official sallies against private property.

So far the picture painted of publicly expressed Russian attitudes toward the dacha over the last two centuries has been a dismal one. This is an important part of the story but by no means all of it. Dachas have brought enormous improvements in the standard of living of Russian urbanites and been valued accordingly. They have been treated as a legitimate material aspiration, as a link to a deeply rooted rural way of life, and as the embodiment of a virtuous domesticity. Like other forms of habitation in other cultures, they have often been tied to notions of cultural authenticity and given a national coloring. North Americans, for example, have calmed their social anxieties —provoked mainly by the suspicion that they are threatened by urban disorder—by finding a reassuring small-town domesticity in the sprawling suburban zones around the major cities.[4] The dacha has similarly been invested with positive features of the Russian self-image: easygoing sociability, open-ended and vodka-soaked hospitality, rejection or ignorance of superficial niceties, appetite for physical toil, intuitive feeling for the natural world, and emotional freedom. Despite regular harassment from central and local authorities, dachas not only survived the Soviet period but—eventually—thrived. In the postwar era they came to be highly valued for the connection they created to a rural way of life that many Soviet urbanites or their parents had only recently relinquished; more prosaically, they gave people a way of supplementing the meager provisions available through the state distribution system. The final years of the Soviet era, though they were times of scarcity and anxiety for the urban population, were also the dacha's finest hour, as the out-of-town habit became truly a mass phenomenon. A survey of the early 1990s suggested that 60 percent of the inhabitants of major cities had access to plots (usually called "dachas") where they grew their own vegetables.[5]

The concept of a second home out of town is by no means unique to Russia, but

4. See John R. Stilgoe, *Borderland: Origins of the American Suburb, 1820–1939* (New Haven, 1988).

5. T. Nefedova, P. Polian, and A. Treivish, *Gorod i derevnia v Evropeiskoi Rossii: Sto let peremen* (Moscow, 2001), 384.

6    nowhere else has it been so deeply embedded in cultural memory and social practice. The dacha has been the Russian way of negotiating the stresses of urbanization and modernization, of creating a welcoming halfway house between metropolis and countryside. Elsewhere in Europe, to be sure, the stresses of modernization were hardly negligible, but in Russia they were extraordinarily acute, both before and (especially) after the Revolution. Although the laboring subordinate classes of Russia's major cities have been subjected to far more than their fair share of poor housing, unsanitary conditions, and punitive administrative attention, white-collar folk have not escaped these blights either. They have been strikingly unable to create the kind of "middle-class" suburban enclaves to which their Western European counterparts were retreating from the mid-nineteenth century onward. Under these circumstances, the dacha became a refuge from urban squalor and a bridgehead of domesticity. Although, as is often remarked, there is no word in Russian for "privacy," that does not mean that Russians have been uninterested in such a condition. Russian major cities in the nineteenth and twentieth centuries were full of people living in overcrowded and uncomfortable conditions, constantly mindful of surveillance by their landlord, their neighbors, the local housing committee, or the NKVD, and with little long-term control over their domestic environment. Yet, even in the formal absence of private property, twentieth-century Russians were able to feel that they "owned" their dachas. So the dacha, we might posit, has provided a substitute home: a house occupied by a single family, an island of enclosure in a sea of exposure.

Another great strength of the dacha has been its role in nurturing informal social interaction. Historians have often accorded Russian society in the last two centuries two complementary characteristics: first, the weakness of forms of grass-roots association that might form the bedrock of a "civil society"; second, the intensity of subpolitical forms of social interaction. The result has been a society in which the role of informal networks has been much greater than in the West. Here again the dacha may be seen to have played its part: by providing a setting for free-and-easy socializing across boundaries that in the city might prove rather less porous, and by contributing to the development of forms of intense informal intellectual association. It has served a similar purpose for Russia's many nonintellectuals, who have discovered in exurbia gentler forms of sociability, a more satisfying sense of community, and a less relentless rhythm of life than in the metropolis.

Though spatially detached from the urban hubs of political and economic activity, the dacha is not a marginal or esoteric topic for investigation. Far from being an obscure background phenomenon taken for granted by generations of Muscovites and Petersburgers, it has consistently engaged a wide range of beliefs, values, allegiances, and identities. It has formed complicated relationships—of convergence and divergence, antagonism and rapprochement—with several other models of settlement and modes of living: the small-town one-family home, the peasant izba, the suburban dwelling, the country estate, the villa, the allotment garden. It has evoked delight in and also hostility to leisure. It has been associated with estrangement from and rejection of agricultural labor and (more recently) with a "return to the soil." It has served as an emblem both of social rootlessness and of Russianness. It has been closely bound up with consumption, property, privilege, domesticity, and relations between the sexes. The fact that several of these aspects are contradictory does not necessarily make the dacha incoherent or radically discontinuous as a historical phenomenon. Rather, it suggests that a study of the dacha can help us to reconstruct, in all their complexity and interactivity, some of the major social and cultural processes at work in modern urban Russia.

# 1

## Prehistory

The dacha, now largely synonymous with life in a private sphere free from public surveillance, was in its medieval origins the result of a gift bestowed publicly. Derived from the verb "to give," the word "dacha" was present in Old Russian from the eleventh century, but by the seventeenth century it tended to denote specifically land given out to servitors by the state. It became a key concept in land surveys conducted from the time of Ivan the Terrible on; during the General Survey that was carried out from early in the reign of Catherine II right up to Emancipation, the dacha was the main legal and administrative form for the allocation of property rights.[1] This brief overview attests both to a long-term semantic transition and to a tension persistent in Russian history and rather significant for an analysis of the modern dacha; namely, the problematic relationship between the role of informal arrangements (the dacha received as a mark of grace and favor) and the public imperative to institute formalized legal relations (the dacha as a piece of property guaranteed by rights).

This tension was exacerbated—some would say created—by the Petrine era, a period that, among many other things, brought into being a new kind of dacha. Peter the Great,

---

1. This is the first meaning given for "dacha" in Vladimir Dal''s *Tolkovyi slovar' zhivogo velikorusskogo iazyka*, 2d ed., 4 vols. (Moscow, 1880–82). The Brockhaus and Efron Encyclopedia, similarly, discusses "dacha" in the context of the General Survey (*B&E*, 10:162–63). For extensive references to "dacha" as a legal concept, see the index to I. D. Mordukhai-Boltovskii, *Svod zakonov Rossiiskoi Imperii* (St. Petersburg, 1912). On the early history of the word, see *Slovar' russkogo iazyka XI–XVII vv.* (Moscow, 1975–). The *Slovar' akademii rossiiskoi* (St. Petersburg, 1806–22; this volume published in 1809) gives four meanings for "dacha": (1) "the giving of something"; (2) "a payment"; (3) "a particular area of land outside the town given by the Tsar or the government into someone's ownership, or acquired by purchase and built on"; (4) "lands belonging to an estate owner, or to state peasants."

like the rulers of the sixteenth and seventeenth centuries, had plenty of land available for distribution; but, unlike his predecessors, he was particularly eager to hand out dachas in order to accelerate the development of a modern urban space—St. Petersburg, his new city on the Gulf of Finland. Thus, for example, city-center plots between the Fontanka River and the tree-lined Sadovaia Street were doled out to the families of courtiers in the 1710s—but on strict condition that these families actually built on them and saw to their upkeep. As one historian has it:

> After you had received a plot of land for nothing, it was impossible just to offer your thanks and relax—Peter the Great might accidentally pay you a visit in his chariot to see how the recipient of his gift was getting on in his new place, and if the Emperor found that diligence had been lacking, justice and punishment were summary: Peter the Great was never parted from his cudgel.[2]

But Peter and his eighteenth-century successors were also able to offer land in locations that lay well outside the city's boundaries. Here dachas began to be developed as suburban residences designed primarily for leisure. The first such instance came in 1710, when Peter, as a response to his successful campaign against the Swedes, started to hand out plots of land on the route running between St. Petersburg and his new palace at Peterhof. Terraces were built, trees were planted, and the shore was banked up so as to give protection against flooding. The dimensions of the plots were regular—100 sazhens wide by 1,000 deep; they were thus laid out like the keys of a giant piano pressed up against the south shore of the Gulf of Finland.[3]

## The Dacha as Court Residence

Peter conceived of the Peterhof Road as a single architectural ensemble modeled on the route from Paris to Versailles. Residents were, for example, required to take good care of their property and strictly forbidden to chop down trees along the road: the more land owned and the wealthier the owner, the greater were Peter's architectural expectations of the residence erected on a dacha plot.[4] Subsequent eighteenth-century rulers took further measures to smarten the road up and improve its infrastructure. A decree of 23 August 1739 allocated funds for setting up milestones. In the mid-1750s paving of the road was undertaken, and in 1769 owners of dachas were made responsible for its maintenance (although in practice the money continued to be drawn from state revenues). In the early 1770s birch trees were planted along the road at public expense.[5] In 1777 came a proposal for rebuilding a substantial portion of the route. Throughout the eighteenth century, spe-

2. P. N. Stolpianskii, *Peterburg* (1918; St. Petersburg, 1995), 297.

3. For a survey of early maps of the Peterhof Road, see A. Korentsvit, "Dachi na Petergofskoi doroge," *Leningradskaia panorama*, no. 4 (1988), 35–37.

4. P. N. Stolpianskii, *Dachnye okrestnosti Petrograda* (Petrograd and Moscow, 1923), 5.

5. P. N. Stolpianskii, *Petergofskaia pershpektiva: Istoricheskii ocherk* (Petrograd, 1923), 16–17.

10   cial measures were taken to ensure that public order was maintained for the entire length of the road. In April 1748, for example, the chief of police received instructions to conduct a thorough inspection in advance of the imperial party so as to avoid "disorders"; taverns were to be removed from the roadside.[6]

The desired result of these measures was to create a row of imposing residences with elaborate and extensive gardens stretching all the way to the southern shore of the Gulf of Finland. As early as 1736, Peder von Haven, arriving in St. Petersburg as secretary and preacher for a Norwegian sailor, commented on the row of "extremely fine out-of-town households" that he saw as he was driven into the city along the Peterhof Road.[7] Eyewitness accounts of the Peterhof Road, like those of St. Petersburg itself, were not uniformly enthusiastic in its early days,[8] but by the mid-eighteenth century they were consistently rapturous. Particular attention was lavished on the gardens of the princes Naryshkin, which were left open to the public.[9] The positive assessments lasted well into the nineteenth century. A visitor of 1805 admired the view on heading out of Strel'na toward St. Petersburg: "As a parting gift my eyes were taken up by an unbroken chain of picturesque dachas—each one finer than the last—right up to the barrier at the entrance to St. Petersburg."[10] Fifteen years later, the author of an early guidebook found that the view from Strel'na had lost none of its charm: "From here a splendid mounded road leads to the magnificent dachas of the grandees and the wealthy."[11]

The prime function of these dachas was public sociability: their owners were able to receive a stream of visitors from foreign delegations, prominent noble families, and of course the imperial court. In July 1772, for example, Prince L. A. Naryshkin laid on a lavish set of entertainments at his dacha eleven versts along the Peterhof Road. The guests started assembling at three o'clock and were able to amuse themselves by wandering through the gardens with their intriguing patterns of streams and paths. At seven o'clock the empress arrived and a "Temple of Victory" (in honor of the recent victory over the Turks and Tatars) was spectacularly unveiled. The entertainment was completed with fireworks and a masked ball.[12] Five years later the Swiss scholar Jean Bernoulli called in at the Naryshkin dacha and commented especially on the tasteful English-style design of the gardens; he also noted with interest that the property was opened to the public twice a week.[13] Count Stroganov, similarly, liked to entertain in the grand style: his generous hos-

---

6. P. N. Petrov, *Istoriia Sankt-Peterburga s osnovaniia goroda, do vvedeniia v deistvie vybornogo gorodskogo upravleniia, 1703–1782* (St. Petersburg, 1884), 514.

7. Iu. N. Bespiatykh, *Peterburg Anny Ioannovny v inostrannykh opisaniiakh* (St. Petersburg, 1997), 309.

8. Foreign travelers' accounts of St. Petersburg under construction in the first half of the eighteenth century are analyzed in chap. 7 of J. Cracraft, *The Petrine Revolution in Russian Architecture* (Chicago, 1988).

9. See, e.g., M. I. Pyliaev, *Staryi Peterburg* (St. Petersburg, 1887), 409.

10. K. P. Shalikov, *Puteshestvie v Kronshtat 1805 goda* (Moscow, 1817), 53.

11. F. Shreder, *Noveishii putevoditel' po Sanktpeterburgu* (St. Petersburg, 1820), 9.

12. "Opisanie maskarada i drugikh uveselenii, byvshikh v Primorskoi L'va Aleksandrovicha Naryshkina dache, otstoiashchei ot Sankt-peterburga v 11 verstakh po Petergofskoi doroge, 29 iiulia 1772 godu," reprinted from *Sankt-Peterburgskie vedomosti* in *Sovremennik* 38 (1853), sec. 2, 96–102.

13. "Zapiski astronoma Ivana Bernulli o poezdke ego v Rossiiu v 1777 godu," *Russkii arkhiv*, no. 1 (1902), 11–12.

pitality cost him 500 rubles each Sunday as he threw open his dacha for music, dancing, and refreshments.[14]

The Naryshkin and Stroganov dachas in several ways conformed to the pattern of life often held to be characteristic of the elite country estate in the same period: display was valued over substance, short-term ostentatious hospitality over longer-term comfort. But this assessment needs to be qualified on two counts. First, the way of life on the Peterhof Road and at the country estate was not simply fixated on public spectacle. The Catherinian period was to a significant extent constructed by the new empress and her ideologues as a reaction against the artifice, luxury, and corruption of the reign of Elizabeth (1741–1762) and as a return to the austerity of Peter I's time. The turn away from showy festivity and toward the "English" virtues of practicality and emotional depth found expression in the taste for Romantic garden designs; it also led to a change of culture at the country estate, where *far niente* went out of fashion, the simple country life (or its appearance) came to be more highly valued, and greater emphasis was laid on purposeful and reflective pursuits—notably reading.[15] Life out of the city was, moreover, associated with a rejection of the status distinctions that underpinned social contacts in the city and at court. This relaxation of social rules prefigured an important and enduring cultural stereotype that would be articulated more forcefully in the nineteenth and twentieth centuries: exurbia was seen as a uniquely "democratic" site for social interaction. As the poet and state servant Gavriil Derzhavin observed of *parties de plaisir* he attended in the 1770s:

> Leaving behind in the city
> All that our minds does trouble,
> In simple cordial fresh air
> Do we spend our time.
>
> . . .
>
> We resolved among friends
> To preserve the laws of equality;
> To abandon the conceits
> Of wealth, power, and rank.

---

14. See E. Amburger, *Ingermanland: Eine junge Provinz Rußlands im Wirkungsbereich der Residenz und Weltstadt St. Petersburg–Leningrad*, 2 vols. (Cologne, 1980), 1:547–48. These entertainments ended in 1811, when Stroganov died.

15. See M. Floryan, *Gardens of the Tsars: A Study of the Aesthetics, Semantics, and Uses of Late Eighteenth-Century Russian Gardens* (Aarhus, 1996), 34 (on Catherine's taste for all things English) and 142–49 (on the new approach, dating from the 1770s, to horticulture as a practical hobby or even business). On anglophilia in garden design, see also A. Cross, *"By the Banks of the Neva": Chapters from the Lives and Careers of the British in Eighteenth-Century Russia* (Cambridge, 1997), 266–85, and P. Roosevelt, *Life on the Russian Country Estate: A Social and Cultural History* (New Haven, 1995), chap. 3. In the early nineteenth century, moreover, growing numbers of Russian noblemen were choosing to spend time on their estates and cultivating the lifestyle of the English gentry (Roosevelt 98). On changing models of estate life, see O. S. Evangulova, "Gorod i usad'ba vtoroi poloviny XVIII v. v soznanii sovremennikov," *Russkii gorod* 7 (1984): 172–88.

12

Оставя беспокойство в граде
И все, смущает что умы,
В простой приятельской прохладе
Свое проводим время мы.
[ ... ]
Мы положили меж друзьями
Законы равенства хранить;
Богатством, властью и чинами
Себя отнюдь не возносить.[16]

Second, the social and economic functions of the dacha in eighteenth-century Russia were quite distinct from those of the country estate. A residence on the Peterhof Road enabled people to have a break from the city without taking themselves too far afield. It allowed a lifestyle of short, habitual holidays instead of a single annual absence of several months at a far-flung country estate. The emergence of a modern (that is, post-Petrine) dacha depended on an administrative order that required regular and reasonably continuous attendance in the office or at the court by a class of state functionaries and noblemen. Its prime function was to enable prominent families to maintain contact with the grandees on whose favor their advancement depended, to safeguard their position in Petersburg's peculiarly patrimonial bureaucracy. This point was understood perfectly by F. F. Vigel', a memoirist unusually well placed to observe the overlapping worlds of aristocracy and elite civil service. In 1800 Vigel' was driven out to the residence of Count F. V. Rostopchin to request in person an appointment in the prestigious Board of Foreign Affairs. Not yet fourteen years of age, Vigel' was traveling along the Peterhof Road for the first time, and he marveled at the chain of splendid dachas that extended "almost uninterruptedly" on both sides for twenty-six versts. This was, he commented, the only place around Petersburg where "rich folk of all estates [vsekh soslovii]" could spend their summers; people of lesser means could not afford such a luxury. His remarks confirm the Peterhof Road as a place for the social elite; equally, however, they suggest that membership in this elite was determined not simply by aristocratic lineage but also by money and by position in state service. As an older man, Vigel' was less admiring of the dacha habits of St. Petersburg's mandarins, who, in his opinion, had abandoned the expansive ways of the country estate and opted instead for cramped and undignified suburban dwellings in their overriding anxiety to maintain proximity to the court. Their houses were, from this point of view, more reminiscent of servants' quarters than of truly aristocratic residences.[17]

This somewhat jaundiced view of the Petersburg dacha and the implied unfavorable comparison with the more autonomous estate culture of the Moscow aristocracy would become a mainstay of later social commentaries. Such typological distinctions between Russia's two major cities do, however, tend to obliterate historical nuances. Even in the

16. G. R. Derzhavin, "Pikniki" (1776), in his Stikhotvoreniia (Leningrad, 1957), 79.

17. F. F. Vigel', Zapiski, 2 vols. (Moscow, 1928), 1:98, 211.

eighteenth century, the social function and composition of the Peterhof Road was far from static. In the early days, its orientation toward the Peterhof palace was indeed at least as important as, if not more important than, its proximity to the city. But this initial stage of the modern dacha's history came to a symbolic end with the completion of the Winter Palace by Bartolomeo Rastrelli in 1768, after which the imperial household relocated to Petersburg. In actual settlement patterns, understandably enough, there was no such clear break; the palaces retained their social prominence and the more adjacent outskirts of the city were only gradually made fit for dacha colonization. Even so, one can observe a shift in elite residency toward the "East End" of the Peterhof Road in the second half of the eighteenth century.[18]

This spatial reorientation was accompanied by changes in social composition. In 1762 the first section of the road toward Peterhof—between the Fontanka and a substantial dacha named Krasnyi Kabachok—was subdivided into smaller plots and handed out to new owners. Krasnyi Kabachok had been given by Peter I to a translator named Semen Ivanov with full rights of inheritance (though without the right to sell the land), but when Ivanov died in 1748 his family was approached by the chief of police, Vasilii Saltykov, who had designs on this potentially profitable stretch of land. Under huge pressure, the family gave in to his demands and sold their estate for a mere 600 rubles. But Ivanov's sister appealed to Empress Elizabeth, who promptly canceled the contract of sale and allowed the Ivanovs to sell the property to whomever they pleased. Ivanov's sister soon took advantage of this ruling and cashed in her assets, and Krasnyi Kabachok changed hands several times over the following decades.[19]

The case of Krasnyi Kabachok is symptomatic of a liberalization of the property market on the Peterhof Road. As one observer noted in 1829, a change of ownership took place at the turn of the eighteenth century: "enormous seigneurial castles were replaced by the pleasant-looking cottages of the merchantry, or had entered the hands of this estate."[20] The diversification of the property market is reflected in the St. Petersburg court newspaper, *Sankt-Peterburgskie vedomosti*, which from the late 1760s ran advertisements for dachas along the Peterhof Road. In February 1769, for example, P. B. Sheremetev put up for sale several plots of land, including "a seafront property twelve versts from Petersburg, comprising a seigneurial residence [*gospodskie khoromy*] on a stone foundation, fully equipped and furnished, with two outbuildings, servants' quarters, kitchen and cellar, stable and farmyard, a planned garden, orangeries with trees and greenhouses, three ponds with fish of various kinds, among them a fair amount of carp; on the territory of the dacha [*v dachakh*] there is a good supply of wood and hay."[21]

18. See Amburger, *Ingermanland*, 1:473.

19. Stolpianskii, *Petergofskaia pershpektiva*, 21–22.

20. P. Svin'in, quoted in S. Gorbatenko, "Rastsvet Petergofskoi dorogi," *Leningradskaia panorama*, no. 7 (1989), 40.

21. *SPb ved*, 24 Feb. 1769, suppl., 3. The turnover of ownership on the Peterhof Road at a later period is reflected in a complaint of 1824 by a civil servant's widow, Elizaveta L'vova, regarding the use of water from the Ligovskii canal. L'vova noted that her plot had been left without an adequate water supply after the redrawing of dacha boundaries (her dacha was located between the larger landholdings of Baron Rall, who had accumulated

## The "Out-of-Town" House and the Environs of St. Petersburg

In the first half of Catherine's reign, the meaning of "dacha" as "plot of land" was clearly still primary. The word could, moreover, be used interchangeably with *myza* or (less frequently) *dvor*, both of which suggest more a farmstead than a primarily residential property. While these miniature estates would generally have a main house solidly built on a stone foundation, they also had space for extensive domestic agriculture (livestock, orchards, kitchen garden, even, in some cases, greenhouses). In the 1780s, although dachas were still thought of as plots of land rather than as homes, we begin to find evidence of a more rapid turnover of owners and a wider range of locations (including the Vyborg Side, the Neva islands, and the Tsarskoe Selo Road). In addition, there were signs of increased commercial exploitation of dacha plots as owners began to rent out smaller houses: "At the dacha of the privy councilor, senator, and knight Mikhailo Fedorovich Soimonov, near Ekaterinhof, two houses are available for rent complete with stables, outbuildings for carriages, and icehouses."[22] At the beginning of the nineteenth century a new concept begins to emerge: that of the out-of-town house (*zagorodnyi dom*) or house for summer entertainment (*dom dlia letnego uveseleniia*), both of which typically came with less land and fewer amenities. Just occasionally, individual rooms were made available for rent. For the first time, the house and associated lifestyle were becoming more important than the land on which the house stood.[23] It is in the last two decades of the eighteenth century that we can trace the origins of a new kind of entertainment culture: the focus was slightly less on lavish parties thrown for court society or on elaborate *fêtes champêtres* than on fluid and decentered forms of social interaction. This was, in other words, the beginning of a shift from the aristocratic *gulian'e* (fête) to the *progulka* (promenade) in a small group of family or friends, from the individually owned landscaped garden as a site for collective entertainment to the more public venues of park, embankment, and pleasure garden (*uveselitel'nyi sad*).[24]

A corresponding change can be observed in visual representations of the city and its outskirts. Early paintings of St. Petersburg offer "elemental" views, which typically exaggerate the width of the Neva, emphasize the river's importance by crowding it with

---

several plots, and Krasnyi Kabachok), and that she did not have the resources to have a pipe laid herself; she therefore appealed for Rall's water supply to be diverted to her plot (see RGIA, f. 206, op. 1, d. 562, l. 1). A comparison of lists of dacha residents on the Peterhof Road for 1779 and 1838 (presented in Amburger, *Ingermanland*, 2:924–31) makes clear the shift from primarily noble to more socially diverse patterns of residency.

22. *SPb ved*, 17 Mar. 1780, 272.

23. This shift in meaning is reflected in *Slovar' russkogo iazyka XVIII veka* (Leningrad, 1984–), which gives "recreational house out of town" as a new meaning for "dacha" that appeared at the end of the eighteenth century.

24. These developments are hinted at in I. G. Georgi, *Opisanie rossiisko-imperatorskogo stolichnogo goroda Sankt-Peterburga i dostopamiatnostei v okrestnostiakh onogo, s planom* (1794; St. Petersburg, 1996), 454–58. Georgi notes, for example, that outings in carriages and on horseback were not restricted to young men, but were also enjoyed by "ladies of the first classes and of the middle estate" (457).

ships, and provide a few grand facades on the embankments as the only evidence of    15
lasting human intervention in the landscape. Over time, as the city territory was more
densely settled and the natural elements were seen to have been tamed, came a shift to
representations that emphasized rather the city's more "civilized" aspect, its straight
lines, open spaces, and imposing grandeur. Later still, in the first part of the nineteenth
century, norms changed again as artists began to abandon the distant, all-encompass-
ing, admiring perspective on the city and instead to adopt a more intimate and "enclosed" viewpoint.[25] These long-term aesthetic trends had direct implications for the
way artists depicted the city's outskirts. A bleak view reminiscent of the earlier eighteenth century is the Swedish artist Benjamin Paterssen's *View of the Outskirts of Petersburg by the Porcelain Factory* (1793). Paterssen was a prolific painter of the city's central
areas, such as the Admiralty and Senate Square, but in this work he shows a flat and
empty rural scene with carriages heading both toward and away from the city and a
peasant woman and child wandering along the side of the roadway; the left side of the
painting is dominated by a river, here associated not with the granite grandeur of the
city but with the Finnish fishermen who are often counterposed to it in the Petersburg
myth.

But Paterssen himself was at the forefront of a new trend that emerged at the turn of
the century: suddenly artists were not so reluctant to present views of suburban life or to
draw such a sharp distinction between city and noncity scenes. The first examples of the
genre were paintings of aristocratic suburban residences such as the Stroganov dacha,
painted by Andrei Voronikhin in 1797 and by Paterssen in 1804. These paintings were,
however, in the same distanced style as the austere early representations of St. Petersburg's
central squares and embankments. More striking were depictions whose foregrounds
were filled with scenes of suburban life. Paterssen's *View of Novaia Derevnia* (1801), for example, has some people strolling along the embankment of Kamennyi Island in small
family groups. But, although this is a location detached from the city, formality has not
been abandoned. Families are dressed smartly, as for a stately promenade; although some
people are clearly in gentle motion, they are depicted as static, without individualizing
gestures that might hint at a narrative; and two uniformed figures on horseback hover at
the entrance to a neatly tree-lined avenue. Moreover, the location, though certainly not
urban, is hardly secluded and private: as these well-to-do families stroll, they are approached by peddlers, and on the opposite bank of the Neva they are faced by the densely
settled Novaia Derevnia, by all appearances a well-appointed suburb. By 1804, in his picture of the Kamennyi Island Palace from Aptekarskii Island, Paterssen was taking a significantly different approach. The palace is in this case merely a pretext: it is, admittedly, located in the center of the picture, but in the distance, almost on the horizon. The
foreground is dominated by a scene of domestic activity on the near shore. Here there are
four groups of figures and two distinct narratives. A woman greets or takes leave of a uniformed man at the steps to her family's residence; and a cabriolet sets off, pursued by a

25. For a much more elaborate treatment of these ideas, see G. Kaganov, *Images of Space: St. Petersburg in
the Visual and Verbal Arts* (Stanford, 1997).

B. Paterssen, *View of Novaia Derevnia from Kamennyi Island* (1801). Courtesy of State Russian Museum, St. Petersburg, and the Bodleian Library, Oxford (171 c.229).

B. Paterssen, *The Kamennyi Island Palace As Seen from Aptekarskii Island* (1804). Courtesy of State Russian Museum, St. Petersburg, and the Bodleian Library, Oxford (171 c.229).

dog and watched by a woman with three children. Both the woman and her children are dressed informally; and the unconstrained domesticity of the scene is emphasized by the uncluttered view of the opposite bank, by the sparse and unsculpted arboreal backdrop, and by the indistinct boundary between road and grass verge.[26]

The point of this excursus into the visual arts is not only to show how the outskirts of St. Petersburg were acquiring independent aesthetic and cultural value but also to suggest the increasing diversity and vitality of dacha life in this period. The dacha seems to have become a fixture on the social scene in the early part of the nineteenth century, when renting a summer house became a universal aspiration for well-to-do sections of Petersburg society. In 1802 F. F. Vigel' was struck by a transformation that had taken place since his first visit: arriving in September, he was surprised to find the city "empty," as people had not yet returned from their summer houses. During the two years he had been away from Petersburg, he surmised, the dacha habit had "already spread to all classes." Even if some allowances need to be made for Vigel''s youthful impressionability, his observation is strengthened by further details of the time. The early years of the reign of Alexander I brought a construction boom in Petersburg and its environs; land was drained, trees were felled, and dachas went up steadily.[27] In the early nineteenth century, moreover, dachas were advertised more widely and with greater attention paid to their commercial possibilities. Take the following notice from 1820, which is revealing of the contemporary craze for horticulture:

> An orangery 60 sazhens long with fruit trees, for example peaches, apricots, and plums . . . , next to it four sections with their own hothouse, which has vines, a barn for cherries of 20 sazhens, in it up to 150 trees in tubs, a kitchen garden 65 sazhens long, 12 sazhens wide, in it up to 20 rows of Spanish strawberries, red currant, black currant, white and pink currants, various kinds of gooseberry, and in addition, in various sections and the greenhouse, up to 200 pots of roses and up to 2,000 pots of other flowers, and also ten of the best kinds of hothouses for watermelons and melons.[28]

By the turn of the eighteenth century, the dacha market was not at all restricted to the routes linking the city and the palaces at Peterhof, Tsarskoe Selo, and the more recently built Pavlovsk. It now notably included the various islands in the Neva. In the first years of St. Petersburg's existence, these islands were handed out to Peter's relatives and favorites. Thereafter, during the eighteenth century, they changed hands quite frequently as their

26. See G. N. Komelova, G. A. Printseva, and I. G. Kotel'nikova, eds., *Peterburg v proizvedeniiakh Patersena* (Moscow, 1978). For works by other artists (for example, Semen and Sil'vestr Shchedrin) that continue the trends I have identified in Paterssen's oeuvre, see G. Grimm and L. Kashkarova, *Peterburg—Petrograd—Leningrad v proizvedeniiakh khudozhnikov* (Moscow, 1958), and A. M. Gordin, *Pushkinskii Peterburg* (Leningrad, 1974).

27. Vigel', *Zapiski*, 1:148, 180.

28. Quoted in V. N. Toporov, "Aptekarskii ostrov kak gorodskoe urochishche," in *Noosfera i khudozhestvennoe tvorchestvo* (Moscow, 1991), 248n.

18  owners were disgraced and dispossessed or decided to cash in the gift they had received. Prince Aleksandr Menshikov was the first owner of Krestovskii Island; after his disgrace, the island was given to Count Minikh by Empress Anna Ioannovna in 1731. Then, after Minikh's involvement in a palace plot of 1742, the island passed to the Razumovskii family. The Razumovskiis then became property entrepreneurs, renting out houses on the island to civil servants. In 1804 P.K. Razumovskii sold the island to Prince A.M. Belosel'skii-Belozerskii, who quickly took an even more entrepreneurial approach by increasing the number of plots.[29] An unflattering description of dacha life on the island was given by Iu. Arnol'd, who spent a summer there as an adolescent in 1827. To the east, he recalled, there were thirty-three peasant households, to the west no more than six or seven; amenities were limited to a tavern, an inn, and a small trader's stall; the island was cross-cut by only two roads. The peasant houses were rented out to "gentlemen":

> It was left to the tenants to concern themselves with making these dwellings more or less habitable and if possible comfortable. For this reason the "dachas" were usually rented for about five years. Our "dacha" . . . consisted of a house with six rooms, a mezzanine of three little rooms, and various outbuildings in a closed yard. At the front, facing the street, was a little patch of garden, and behind the yard an enormous expanse of communal meadow.[30]

The first references to dachas on Petrovskii Island came in the early 1790s. The island was given over to the Free Economic Society for agricultural purposes;[31] but these activities were abandoned after the disastrous flood of 1824. Instead, houses were built for rent, bringing in 3,950 rubles in the first year. After that, plots were let out for tenants to build their own houses; these buildings then became the property of the society. In 1841 the island was transferred to the future Alexander II. Dacha owners suffered a period of uncertainty as to whether their contracts with the society would remain in force, but after some discussion they were given assurances that they would retain rights to their houses. Aptekarskii Island, home of the first botanical garden in Russia, was kept under close imperial supervision until 1799, when private construction was first allowed there. When more intensive settlement did occur, it took place quite haphazardly, with winding streets and dead ends, and Aptekarskii gained a reputation as the most unplanned of the islands.[32]

The most splendid of the islands in the Neva delta was no doubt Kamennyi. Its early owners were G.I. Golovkin (the first Russian chancellor), his son A.G. Golovkin, and,

29. V.A. Vitiazeva, *Nevskie ostrova* (Leningrad, 1986). See also P.N. Stolpianskii, *Staryi Peterburg: Aptekarskii, Petrovskii, Krestovskii ostrova* (Petrograd, 1916), 47–52. Georgi (*Opisanie*, 455) wrote ten years earlier of the number of entertainments available on Krestovskii and noted that city dwellers sometimes rented houses for several weeks over the summer in the village on the island.

30. *Vospominaniia Iuriia Arnol'da*, 3 vols. (Moscow, 1892–93), 2:56–57.

31. The Free Economic Society (Vol'no-Ekonomicheskoe Obshchestvo) was a major scientific institution founded in 1765 with the aim of conducting research in agronomy.

32. Stolpianskii, *Staryi Peterburg*, 41–45, 1–24.

from 1746, A. I. Bestuzheva-Riumina, wife of the then chancellor. Her husband was arrested and disgraced in 1758; he was rehabilitated at the beginning of Catherine II's reign and in 1765 sold the island to the empress, who presented it as a gift to her son Paul, the future emperor. Dacha construction began in the late 1780s, and on a rather more secure basis than earlier in the island's history: Catherine's charter of 1785 had given nobles reason to hope that in future their property would not be subject to sudden confiscation. Paul allotted the first plots on Kamennyi to favored courtiers, thus establishing the island as the main site for official residences outside the suburban palaces. Here is a description of one of the early buildings, advertised for rent in 1789: "A rebuilt wooden manorial house, unfurnished, with two outbuildings, one of which has a bathhouse and large servants' quarters, the other has a kitchen, inside the yard there is a stable with six stalls, a cellar with an icebox and several storerooms, behind the yard [there is] forest and land tilled for a kitchen garden."[33] Residences and gardens on Kamennyi were, it seems, kept in impeccable condition, as befitted a place where members of the imperial family were liable to take strolls. In 1818 a visitor to the dacha of a senior civil servant observed that "everything about it was irreproachably clean and neat, every tree was nurtured like a rare tropical plant"; guests were forbidden to drive their carriages up to the entrance of the house for fear of disrupting this exemplary orderliness.[34]

By 1800, seventeen plots had been handed out on the eastern part of the island. Alexander I tried to keep strict control over new building: inns, shops, and coffeehouses were strictly forbidden, and the building of private dachas was kept to a minimum. But there was still considerable turnover of ownership, as in the Dolivo-Dobrovol'skii dacha, subsequently famous for the two summers that Aleksandr Pushkin spent there (in 1834 and 1836). The plot was originally given by Alexander I to a Naryshkin; it was then sold first to another old noble family, the Pleshcheevs, then (in 1816) to a petit bourgeois (*meshchanin*) named Kamenshchikov, from whom the plot was confiscated for debts in 1820. Then, in 1821, it passed briefly into the hands of a merchant before being sold to a woman named Dolivo-Dobrovol'skaia, wife of a high-ranking civil servant. The house where Pushkin lived was built between 1822 and 1830.[35] Contemporaries all agreed that it was not cheap; the writer's wife leased it after the money had arrived for the first issue of *Sovremennik* (The Contemporary), the journal that Pushkin hoped would rescue him from his straitened financial circumstances. The handful of memoirs that have come down to us paint a picture of domestic contentment and informality in his household. A summer on the island presented ample opportunities for socializing. Quite apart from the neighbors on the island, the opposite bank of the Neva (Novaia Derevnia) was well popu-

33. *SPb ved*, 17 Apr. 1789, 465.

34. D. N. Sverbeev, *Zapiski (1799–1826)*, 2 vols. (Moscow, 1899), 1:283. Alexander I was indeed apt to wander through the island: see the anecdote recalled in P. A. Viazemskii, *Staraia zapisnaia knizhka* (Leningrad, 1929), 204.

35. On the island's various dachas and their owners in the eighteenth and nineteenth centuries, see V. A. Vitiazeva, *Kamennyi ostrov* (Leningrad, 1991), 112–220.

20   lated; among its residents were the members of the Guards Regiment to which Pushkin's later antagonist, Georges d'Anthès, belonged.[36]

Pushkin, the best-known dacha resident of the period, was already a habitué of the islands. In the summer of 1830 he spent a lot of time with his friend Anton Del'vig, who had rented a dacha near Krestovskii Island. Del'vig's younger cousin (subsequently state inspector of private railways) recalled how the two of them went around Krestovskii noisily engaging the attention of passers-by in a way they had clearly done since their schooldays; for Pushkin, this was the last opportunity to enjoy the bachelor lifestyle.[37] Then and subsequently, Krestovskii had a reputation for strolling crowds, mildly unruly behavior, and a low level of actual residency. As a married man Pushkin spent a couple of summers at Chernaia Rechka (near the Stroganov gardens, on the north side of the island), later infamous as the location for his fatal duel. His landlord on both occasions was F.I. Miller, head butler under two tsars and one of the first dacha entrepreneurs. These were no mere vacation cottages: in a letter to her daughter in Warsaw, Pushkin's mother reported that her son's dacha had "over fifteen rooms."[38]

Pushkin left an insight into this socially exclusive dacha world in his fragment "The Guests Were Assembling at the Dacha" (1828). Here we discover that the dachas on the islands were so close to the city center that people could go there not just for a day or two but for part of a day, or even for part of an evening. In this unfinished story the guests have come straight from the theater and plunge immediately into drawing room conversation. The tone is free and easy, even facetious, but high society norms still obtain: the prolonged tête-à-tête of a married woman with an admirer on the balcony is noted by everyone and marked down against her. The dacha offers the opportunity for private communication in a very public setting—with all the risks it entails. In a word, this dacha is an exurban salon and the story is a society tale. If the setting may be said to give this highly conventional genre its own particular coloring, it is perhaps in a certain ease of narrative style. The fact that all the guests have come from a distance and crossed the urban/suburban divide divests them of their social biography; the dacha is a location where characters can be brought together and left to interact without too much scene-setting. It is significant that Pushkin's unfinished story is supposed precisely for this reason to have caught Lev Tolstoy's eye as he was mulling over his own tale of adultery, *Anna Karenina*, four decades later.[39]

36. S.L. Abramovich, *Pushkin: Poslednii god* (Moscow, 1991).

37. A.I. Del'vig, *Polveka russkoi zhizni: Vospominaniia A.I. Del'viga, 1820–1870* (Moscow and Leningrad, 1930), 148.

38. A.M. Gordin and M.A. Gordin, *Pushkinskii vek: Panorama stolichnoi zhizni* (St. Petersburg, 1995), 355–60. Nor was this exceptional by the standards of the time: a visitor from Riga left a description of a similarly spacious island residence, opposite Kamennyi on Aptekarskii, occupied by the director of the Postal Department, Konstantin Bulgakov. See V.V. Lents, "Prikliucheniia Lifliandtsa v Peterburge," *Russkii arkhiv*, no. 4 (1878), 451.

39. On the conventions of the 1820s, see N. Cornwell, ed., *The Society Tale in Russian Literature: From Odoevskii to Tolstoi* (Amsterdam, 1998). This volume follows much previous scholarship in linking the society tale to a new emphasis in Russian literature on observation and analysis (as opposed to imagination and invention).

The connection of these early suburban residences to the values of urban high society was emphasized by their design. Most owners took the Italian villa as their model.[40] The simple, heavy, "laconic" architectural style typical of the Alexandrine period was particularly prevalent on Kamennyi Island, as in the dacha of Prince Ol'denburg: "The round hall under the cupola is wonderfully fine: modest and solemn at the same time. This is precisely that 'wealthy simplicity' which was so well understood by artists of the first half of the nineteenth century; this is the ideal of a suburban house combining country-style coziness with refined luxury."[41]

And suburban was what these residences were becoming in the 1820s. Their closer relationship with the city was signposted by a law of 1833 that extended the jurisdiction of the St. Petersburg police to dacha areas from the Okhta to the Vyborg Side. But, although residents of such areas now had the assistance of the city authorities in maintaining "safety" and "decency," they retained a freedom in their use of space and architectural design that was denied to inhabitants of more densely settled parts of the city.[42]

As the mention of locations such as the Vyborg Side suggests, in the early nineteenth century there were other sites for dacha life besides court residences and island villas. To judge by advertisements of the time, several other areas had houses for sale and summer rental. Many of them were located in the northern part of the city, on the Petersburg Side or even farther afield. There was plenty of room for people to have spacious residences only a short carriage ride from the center; St. Petersburg still appeared bucolic to travelers who approached it in the 1800s.[43] Most dachas for rent came with outbuildings, kitchen garden, and furniture, and they commonly offered accommodation of ten rooms or so. Houses were made available for rental not only by grandees, prosperous merchants, or prominent civil servants but also by humbler folk. Peasants on Krestovskii Island, as we have seen, were letting out houses for the summer from the late eighteenth century, and villages on or near the Peterhof Road were similarly full of cheap rental opportunities for summering Petersburgers in the early nineteenth century.[44]

Among the earliest dacha landlords from a humble milieu were the German "colonists." German immigration to the St. Petersburg region dates back to the early years of the reign of Catherine II. Foreigners were attracted by a set of extremely favorable conditions, including freedom of confession, free lodging for six months on arrival, land grants, exemption from taxes, and start-up loans. The first German settlers duly arrived in

40. An influence attested by G. K. Lukomskii in his *Pamiatniki starinnoi arkhitektury Rossii* (Petrograd, 1916), 388.

41. "Posledniaia staraia dacha na Kamennom ostrove," *Starye gody,* July–September 1910, 182–85.

42. See *PSZ,* ser. 2, 8, no. 6660 (22 Dec. 1833). The first move in this direction had occurred in 1828, when police jurisdiction had been extended to the settlements (*slobody*) on the Okhta; an exception, however, had been made for dachas in this vicinity, as it was considered inequitable to subject dacha owners there to a property tax, given that, being rather thinly spread, they had relatively little need of the police, and also that dacha owners in other areas were not taxed (see *PSZ,* ser. 2, 3, no. 2054 [25 May 1828]).

43. J. Bater, *St. Petersburg: Industrialization and Change* (London, 1976), 34–35.

44. One such village is the setting for an episode in Faddei Bulgarin's engaging picaresque *Ivan Vyzhigin* (1828): see Bulgarin, *Sochineniia* (Moscow, 1990), 323–25.

22  St. Petersburg via Lübeck in 1762 and 1763; their first colony was named Novaia Saratovka and had an initial population of sixty families, each with thirty-five desiatinas of land. The next wave of settlement came in the 1800s, when a colony was established at Strel'na, on the south shore of the Gulf of Finland. In 1808 Alexander I made up to 20,000 desiatinas available for further German settlement in the region. In 1809, one hundred more German families moved from Poland to a new colony near Oranienbaum. This settlement was soon disbanded and the German peasants were resettled because the land proved unsuitable for agriculture, but the other colonies remained. The colonists at Strel'na, for example, paid quitrent (*obrok*) to the landowner; they did not have the right of private ownership, but neither were they constrained by the commune traditional in Russian peasant villages. They were able to make a living from the land under conditions much more favorable than those enjoyed by the majority of the population of the Russian Empire. And thanks to the surplus income they generated, the relative economic independence they enjoyed, and the favorable and expanding property market that obtained in the Petersburg region, many of them were able to build and rent out summer houses and to buy more land. The number of such settlements continued to increase in the second half of the century, and locations such as Strel'na and Novaia Derevnia had the reputation of being overwhelmingly German in their population.[45]

It is in the early nineteenth century also that we find the origins of another extremely enduring model of dacha life. In the 1810s, A. N. Olenin, president of the St. Petersburg Academy of the Arts and director of the public library, brought together many of the leading literary and artistic figures of his day at his residence, Priiutino, located seventeen versts from St. Petersburg, beyond the Okhta, in the direction of Lake Ladoga. Although in certain respects this property was a landed estate by virtue of its rural location and its relative detachment from the city and from other centers of social activity, visitors commonly referred to it as a dacha. Its function was not agricultural production but rather the encouragement of convivial and predominantly intellectual relations within a particular circle. Priiutino was the setting for a succession of prolonged house parties, and certain habitués—such as the poet and translator N. I. Gnedich and the celebrated poet and fable writer I. A. Krylov—were practically in permanent residence in the summer.[46] Olenin had built several smaller houses on the grounds of his own residence specifically in order to accommodate such long-term guests. And the guests kept on coming: one visitor recalled

45. See A. Fon-Gernet, *Nemetskaia koloniia Strel'na pod S.-Peterburgom, 1810–1910* (St. Petersburg, 1910); Amburger, *Ingermanland*, 1:271–81; and T. A. Shrader, "Pravovaia i kul'turnaia adaptatsiia nemetskikh kolonistov v peterburgskoi gubernii v poreformennoe vremia," in *Peterburg i guberniia: Istoriko-etnograficheskie issledovaniia*, ed. N. V. Iukhneva (Leningrad, 1989). For a clear summary of the early German immigrants' privileges, see R. P. Bartlett, *Human Capital: The Settlement of Foreigners in Russia, 1762–1804* (Cambridge, 1979), 47–48.

46. A short posthumous biography recounts how Krylov, renowned for prodigious feats of gluttony, uncharacteristically acted on the advice of his doctors and took to visiting dachas. Priiutino was farther from the city than most such places, but it was a "dacha" none the less. See M. E. Lobanov, "Zhizn' i sochineniia Ivana Andreevicha Krylova" (1847), in *I. A. Krylov v vospominaniiakh sovremennikov*, eds. A. M. Gordin and M. A. Gordin (Moscow, 1982) 73.

that even the seventeen cows at the dacha struggled to produce enough cream for all the 23
writers and artists summering at Priiutino. The social responsibilities of guests were strikingly limited: a bell summoned them several times a day to meals, but otherwise they were free to amuse themselves.[47]

Olenin's literary acquaintances were not slow to express their gratitude for this relaxed hospitality, especially given that Priiutino was easily accommodated within their early-Romantic worldview. In 1820, Gnedich dedicated to Olenin's wife a poem in which, playing lightly on the dacha's name (*priiut* means "shelter"), he spoke of the dacha as a blessed refuge from the noise and vanity of the city, as a place to flee life's "turbulence" and seek spiritual repose.[48] Konstantin Batiushkov, similarly, referred to Priiutino as a "refuge for kind souls" and a setting for "rustic festivities."[49] Olenin's country retreat may therefore be seen as setting up a powerful legitimizing model for dacha life: far from being a site for empty-headed entertainments, the dacha was a place for spiritual recuperation from the rigors of city life, informal and friendly social interaction, and intense intellectual and artistic creativity.[50]

## Moscow

So far the discussion has been focused on one city and its environs. It is true that Petersburg was in the vanguard of the early history of the dacha, because the urban/suburban divide opened up more suddenly and decisively there than elsewhere in Russia, and because of the concentration of imperial institutions and resulting opportunities for careers. The entertainment culture of the Moscow nobility was, moreover, structured rather differently from that of St. Petersburg. The city was ringed by aristocratic palaces, which were major social centers in their own right and for the time being obviated any need to create new entertainment-oriented suburban settlements.[51] A survey of advertisements for property in and around Moscow in the 1800s reveals that dachas, in the sense that is relevant here, are simply not mentioned. The nearest equivalent is the comfortable town house with spacious gardens but minimal landholdings (*khoziaistvo*).[52] Even in the 1830s the word "dacha" was used less often in Moscow than in Petersburg, and the distinction

47. *Dnevnik Anny Alekseevny Oleninoi (1828–1829)*, ed. O. N. Oom (Paris, 1936), xv–xvi.

48. N. I. Gnedich, "Priiutino," in his *Stikhotvoreniia* (Leningrad, 1956), 117–21. Gnedich was also the author of "Rybaki" (1821), a longer poem that on first publication was billed as "the first attempt at a Russian national [*narodnoi*] idyll" (ibid, 195–204). He takes a dachnik's viewpoint, conveying the idyllic quality of the national landscape by focusing on a pastoral space that derives its meaning above all from its proximity to the city. The spire above the Peter and Paul Fortress, for example, is contrasted to the empty and unspoiled banks of the Neva.

49. K. Batiushkov, "Poslanie k A. I. Turgenevu" (1817–18), in his *Polnoe sobranie stikhotvorenii* (Moscow and Leningrad, 1964), 235–36.

50. Moscow's bucolic environs could also inspire early-Romantic rapture, as in A. Raevskii, "Okrestnosti Moskvy," *Syn otechestva*, pt. 25, no. 40 (1815), 53–65.

51. On the exurban habits of the Moscow nobility in the early nineteenth century, see D. Blagovo, *Rasskazy babushki: Iz vospominanii piati pokolenii* (Leningrad, 1989), 158–63.

52. This conclusion is based on a general reading of *Moskovskie vedomosti* in the eighteenth and early nineteenth centuries.

24 between a dacha or *zagorodnyi dom* and a "town estate" or *gorodskaia usad'ba* was much less clear-cut. Take the following advertisement: "On the Serpukhov Road, at the fifth verst from Moscow, in the village of Verkhnie Koshly for summer rent: two houses together or separately with all amenities, with furniture or without, completely dry, built in a pleasant location from which the whole of Moscow can be seen; on the dacha itself [i.e., the plot of land] there is a small stream."[53]

In the early nineteenth century, however, Moscow gained ground on Petersburg. Turgenev's *First Love* (1860), for example, is set in 1833 in a dacha opposite Neskuchnoe at the Kaluga gates, at the same time Pushkin was occupying his fifteen rooms at Chernaia Rechka, yet it reveals a quite different model of dacha life. The colonnaded main house is occupied by the family of the narrator, Vladimir, who is sixteen at the time of the events described. It is flanked by two other buildings: one has been converted into a small wallpaper factory, while the other is rented out to summer guests. The tenant who arrives to spend the summer in this unprepossessing outbuilding is a pretentious "princess" whose first concern is to ask the narrator's parents to pull strings on her behalf to resolve a legal difficulty in which she has found herself entangled. Vladimir's mother is dismayed by the "vulgarity" of her neighbor, but she cannot avoid having something to do with her; Vladimir, by contrast, is much taken with the neighbor's daughter, Zina. What he fails to see is that his father is himself conducting an affair with Zina. *First Love* is of interest as a unique experiment in the dacha genre by a writer associated primarily with the country estate. The suburban setting seems to bring with it a change in psychological dynamics: the characters are thrown together more randomly than they would be at the country estate, and the revelation of the father's infidelity, though not surprising to the reader, is more shocking than anything in Turgenev's measured and evenly paced longer works. In a pattern quite characteristic of Russian literary representations in the later nineteenth century, the dacha is shown as a place that undermines traditional forms of social intercourse: first, by bringing together a larger and more socially diverse set of characters; second, by allowing this expanded cast greater freedom of action (notably, the freedom to transgress marital boundaries).[54]

Besides making a valuable contribution to the emerging poetics of the dacha, *First Love* indicates that the subdivision of estates into dachas for rent was under way in the Moscow region in the 1830s.[55] In this period the most significant new factor in dacha de-

53. *Moskovskie vedomosti*, 15 Mar. 1833, 1000.

54. *First Love* was apparently Turgenev's favorite of his own works because it was not "made up." On the autobiographical resonance of the story, see the notes in the standard Russian edition: I. S. Turgenev, *Pervaia liubov'*, in his *Polnoe sobranie sochinenii v tridtsati tomakh,* 2d ed. (Moscow, 1978–86), 6:479–80. The dacha location featured in Bulgarin's *Ivan Vyzhigin*, the village of Emel'ianovka on the Peterhof Road, is the venue for another scene of acute tension brought on by social misrecognition (an orphan girl from a noble family fallen on hard times is insultingly propositioned by a lecherous older man who, it turns out, was instrumental in ruining her mother): see Bulgarin, *Sochineniia*, 328–29.

55. The first signs of this practice can be dated even earlier. It seems that the Sheremetevs rented out buildings on their Ostankino estate as early as the 1810s, though the occupants at that time resembled more closely "paying guests" than impersonal "tenants"; the beginnings of a "dacha industry"—the construction of houses specifically as dachas on plots belonging to house serfs—would have to wait until the 1830s. See E. Springis,

velopment, and one common to Moscow and St. Petersburg, was the sale of substantial     25
areas of land just outside the city limits as dacha plots. In the St. Petersburg area, for instance, land belonging to the Forestry Institute (Lesnoi Institut) was initially sold off as
eighteen plots in 1832; the demand was so great that more were made available two years
later.[56] In Moscow the main example in this period was Petrovskii Park, an area totaling
seventeen desiatinas located between the city gates and the Petrovskii Palace, in the direction of Tver'. The first aristocratic dachas there dated back to the late eighteenth century,
but they were all destroyed during the Napoleonic invasion. Later, in the 1830s, the park
was revived as an up-market summer residential area: peasants were bought out from the
surrounding land and building plots were handed out to elite nobles. There were to be no
inns or similar watering holes, as the "purpose of building these dachas [was] respectability of aspect and conduct [*blagovidnost' i prilichie*]." Mikhail Zagoskin, director of the
Moscow theaters in the 1830s, had a dacha of the requisite decorous appearance. "The bal-
conies and squares were bedecked in flowers; wire gates, topped by a fragrant flowerpot
or convolvulus, were surrounded by small gardens."[57] Purchasers of plots in Petrovskii
Park were to have their house designs approved by the Building Commission, and if they
failed to build within three years, their plot would be resold at public auction. Against
those restrictions, they received ten years' relief from taxes and loans of up to 5,000 rubles
from the commission.[58] Observers were quick to sense that these developments had
brought about a change in the leisure habits of Moscow's social elite: in the opinion of the
memoirist M. A. Dmitriev (1796–1866), for example, the picnics and *parties de plaisir* favored by some aristocratic families became much less common in the 1830s, as Petrovskii
Park offered them a more permanent base for exurban recreation and invited new forms
of sociability.[59] In the 1840s the park remained a place for the summer residences of the
Moscow aristocracy and a venue for refined entertainments such as costume balls.[60]

BY THE mid-1830s we can see much of the dacha's subsequent nineteenth-century history in embryo. The period from 1780 to 1820 weakened the hold of the aristocracy and

---

"Moskovskie zhiteli v sele Ostankine: K istorii dachnoi zhizni stolitsy serediny—vtoroi poloviny XIX veka,"
*Russkaia usad'ba* 5/21(1999).

56. *PSZ*, ser. 2, 9, no. 7464 (16 Oct. 1834). An 1843 account of life in Lesnoi Institut is quoted extensively in
Amburger, *Ingermanland*, 1:563.

57. [S. Engel'gardt], "Iz vospominanii," *Russkii vestnik* 191 (1887): 703.

58. *PSZ*, ser. 2, 9, no. 6882 (5 Mar. 1834). A general history of the park can be found in S. Malafeeva,
"Poltora veka Petrovskogo parka," *Moskovskii arkhiv* 1 (Moscow, 1996): 107–17.

59. M. A. Dmitriev, *Glavy iz vospominanii moei zhizni* (Moscow, 1998), 278. The emergence of Petrovskii
Park as a dacha location was mentioned by one contemporary observer as an important step in the direction of
the Petersburg model of exurban development, although dachas were still considered to be a much less commonplace phenomenon in Moscow than in the imperial capital (see V. M-ch, "Peterburgskie i moskovskie
dachi," *Severnaia pchela*, 17 Aug. 1842, 723–24). The significance of the creation of Petrovskii Park and the role
played in it by the entrepreneurial A. A. Bashilov are noted in Blagovo, *Rasskazy babushki*, 1:160–62, and in S. M.
Zagoskin, "Vospominaniia," *Istoricheskii vestnik*, no. 1 (1900), 60–61.

60. P. Vistengof, *Ocherki moskovskoi zhizni* (Moscow, 1842), 90. Of the thirty-four dachas listed in one
guidebook of the late 1840s, twenty-six were in Petrovskii Park or "beyond the Tver' gates": see M. Rudol'f,
*Moskva s topograficheskim ukazaniem vsei ee mestnosti i okrestnostei* (Moscow, 1848), 31–34.

26 the court elite over the semirural retreats around St. Petersburg and brought Petersburg society closer to what might be called a "modern" leisure culture. That is, the arena for unofficial social interaction became polarized between, on the one hand, a small circle of family and intimates and, on the other, the anonymity of public spectacle. Attempts to combine the two spheres of public and private entertainment—as had occurred, for example, in the grand festivities at the Naryshkin dacha on the Peterhof Road—were made less frequently.

But this early stage in the dacha's history also has the virtue of illustrating the limitations of such ideal-typical accounts; it already points to a diversification not only of the social composition of the dacha public but also of the available models for dacha life. On the one hand, we have the dacha as an appurtenance of political influence, as a place where personal and official forms of social interaction are intertwined. The role of patronage in European political life of this period was doubtless enormous, yet Russia has often been seen as an extreme case: as representing an unattractive hybrid of indiscriminately applied forms of Western civility with none too deeply concealed systems of patrimonial power. This is what Martha Wilmot, a guest at numerous aristocratic dachas in the 1800s, was alluding to when she pointed to the "mixture of familiarity and pride" in the people she encountered; and her sister Catherine, somewhat older and a more penetrating observer, described Russia as "a superstructure from France—the Monkey rampant on the Bear's back" and as a "clumsy romping ignorant girl" with a "Parisian cap on her head."[61] The court dacha, as a place explicitly oriented toward informal socializing but at the same time embedded in networks of political and social influence, may seem to embody the contradictions identified by the Wilmots. The same point emerges, though in a much more positive light, from the memoirs of V. A. Sollogub. Famous as a conceited fop who almost fought a duel with Pushkin, Sollogub was born in 1813 into a family from the old Lithuanian nobility that had by the early nineteenth century bonded closely with the Russian aristocratic elite. His grandfather had married a Naryshkin, and in the 1820s he spent several summers in Pavlovsk in dachas rented from the Naryshkins and the Volkonskiis. Exhibiting a trait common to almost all dacha memoirists, Sollogub looked back on this time with immense fondness: "Life seemed to be a fragment of past times and past ways living out its days, a vanishing idyll of a patriarchal life that was disappearing forever."[62]

Despite the regretfully retrospective tone of Sollogub's description, the association of the dacha with "patriarchal" values would resurface later in the century, as would the idea of the dacha as a focus for superficial status consciousness. Yet even in the period he was writing about, as we have seen, several other models of dacha life were available. The

61. M. Wilmot and C. Wilmot, *The Russian Journals of Martha and Catherine Wilmot*, ed. The Marchioness of Londonderry and H. M. Hyde (London, 1934), 48, 195, 223.

62. V. A. Sollogub, *Vospominaniia* (Moscow and Leningrad, 1931), 213. Sollogub goes on to emphasize the point by recalling a trip to an estate his mother had just bought in Simbirsk province, where he learned that "besides the world of the court . . . there was another world too, a world with deep Russian roots, the world of the common people" (219).

Olenin estate at Priiutino can be seen as laying the foundations for an enduring intelligentsia tradition of conversation and creative work at the country retreat; the German colonists and other dacha owners and landlords of modest means were the pioneers of the low-rent summer vacation.

But what makes the phenomena of the eighteenth and early nineteenth centuries fundamentally different from what followed, what makes them part of the prehistory of the dacha as opposed to its main narrative, is the fact that they did not occasion the same self-consciousness as their later developments. The meaning of the word "dacha" had not settled down sufficiently; and it had not settled down because it was not yet important enough to people to distinguish between dachas and other forms of residence. To use or own a dacha did not yet make one a dachnik. All this would soon change radically, as we shall see, in line with the development of Russian urban society and culture in the 1830s and 1840s.

# 2

## Between City and Court
### The Middle Third of the Nineteenth Century

The year 1837 provides a convenient starting point for the next phase in the history of the dacha. The chronological marker is, for once, provided not by the death of Pushkin but rather by the completion of Russia's first railway line—from Petersburg to Tsarskoe Selo and Pavlovsk. This technological advance had immense practical and symbolic value. The formerly exclusive enclaves of the out-of-town imperial palaces and their adjoining settlements were now made accessible—at least in principle—to a much more broadly construed urban society. Not that the train was the only way to escape the metropolis. The development of the city outskirts as a recreational zone had already been encouraged by the creation of a public transport system. In 1832 came the first coach routes from the city to outlying areas (Krestovskii Island and Novaia Derevnia).[1] An eyewitness account of St. Petersburg in 1838 noted no fewer than twenty forms of horse-drawn transport.[2] In the late 1850s coaches with room for sixteen passengers were running to the factories on the outskirts of the city and to northerly outskirts such as Lesnoi Institut (the Forestry Institute), Kolomiagi, and Pargolovo; during the day they departed every thirty minutes or so on the more popular routes.[3] Moscow's first suburban railway line came in 1862 (the Northern line, to Sergiev Posad, built largely to profit

---

1. *Ot konki do tramvaia: Iz istorii peterburgskogo transporta* (St. Petersburg and Moscow, 1993), 10. The first intercity stagecoach (between St. Petersburg and Moscow) had started running in 1820; the first year-round omnibus routes in St. Petersburg were established in 1847.

2. V. Bur'ianov, *Progulka s det'mi po S. Peterburgu i ego okrestnostiam*, 3 vols. (St. Petersburg, 1838), 3:4.

3. *Spravochnaia knizhka dlia lits, poseshchaiushchikh peterburgskie dachi i zagorodnye uveselitel'nye mesta* (St. Petersburg, 1858). The routes given in a slightly earlier guidebook are oriented more toward the west (the Peterhof direction) than toward the north (although mention is already made of a regular coach to Pargolovo via Kushelevka): see A. Grech, *Ves' Peterburg v karmane* (St. Petersburg, 1851), 193–95.

from the traffic in pilgrims to the monastery located in that town). In the mid-nineteenth century the development of railways was still much slower in the Russian Empire than in Western Europe; as of 1866, there were only a handful of lines under one hundred kilometers in length. Yet these routes (from St. Petersburg to Tsarskoe Selo and Pavlovsk, Peterhof, Oranienbaum, and Krasnoe Selo, and from Moscow to Sergiev Posad) brought a range of out-of-town locations unprecedentedly close to city dwellers.[4]

In the middle third of the nineteenth century, then, the conditions were right for the dacha to expand its social constituency and to raise its public profile. The synchronized expeditions that occurred on public holidays or at the start of the "summer season" gave life in the city a different rhythm and held out to city dwellers the promise of relaxation, enjoyment, and increased physical and mental well-being. Out-of-town living captured the imagination of urban people, who found in the dacha an enticing middle ground between the unhygienic and increasingly disenchanting city and the high society of the suburban palaces and estates.

## The "House out of Town" Reconceived

In that same year of 1837, Faddei Bulgarin, a journalist sensitively attuned to changing Petersburg habits, noted the arrival of the dacha as a broad social phenomenon.[5] In his own youth, Bulgarin recalled, to have a dacha was to be rich: "There were people who acquired rank, who gained wealth, yet did not want to live at dachas so as not to arouse talk, slander, or envy." Now, however, shopkeepers, craftsmen, and tradesmen could all afford summer holidays out of the city. Bulgarin even felt justified in speaking of a "second city" that had come into being: "summertime Petersburg."[6]

Although Bulgarin may well have exaggerated slightly the extent of this new social trend (in order, as was his wont, to emphasize the advanced nature of Russian society under autocracy), his assessment of the situation is corroborated by other witnesses of the same period (as we shall see). But perhaps more interesting are the ways Bulgarin found to analyze and evaluate the dacha phenomenon. He noted particularly the emergence of the house out of town (*zagorodnyi dom*) as a positive cultural development inconceivable in a country ruled by brute force, where people had to shut themselves up in castles and fortresses for protection. Villas, he proclaimed, were a sign of cultural stability and prosperity; here he invoked the example of ancient Rome, a parallel that had enormous resonance for people of a generation that derived much of its inspiration from classical mod-

---

4. On the relatively neglected suburban railway lines, see J. N. Westwood, *A History of Russian Railways* (London, 1964), 45–50. Long-distance routes were of course prioritized because of their economic and military significance.

5. Bulgarin edited *Severnaia pchela,* the first privately owned newspaper in Russia and the first periodical to aim at a Russian "middle-class" audience. But he also "acquired notoriety as a police spy, a master of intrigue, and the progenitor of the Russian sensational press": N. Schleifman, "A Russian Daily Newspaper and Its New Readership: *Severnaia pchela*, 1825–1840," *Cahiers du monde russe et soviétique* 28 (1987), 127.

6. F. Bulgarin, "Dachi," *Severnaia pchela,* 9 Aug. 1837, 703.

30 els.[7] Dachas, moreover, had more immediate benefits: they improved the health of the population, they created extra space in the cities in the summer, and, by expanding the service industry, they helped to create jobs.

This broadly positive account did not, however, come without certain reservations. Although dachas were intended to improve the health of their residents, they were often damp and cramped. They might have strengthened the economy by improving employment prospects, but they had also stoked inflation, as tradesmen were driven to raise prices in order to fund their own forays out of town. Dachas could, moreover, be seen to undermine the economy by taking people away from their work for two months at the very least. Worse still, the lifestyle adopted by most people at the dacha—consisting mainly of sleeping and talking—was bound to engender lassitude.

Bulgarin was here setting a trend for subsequent decades: a survey of dacha life served as a springboard for far-reaching social commentary, and especially for speculation on the size and the nature of Russia's "middle class." Nor was his ambivalence anything remarkable: it was shared by many people writing both in his time and later. A like-minded view was expressed by Nestor Kukol'nik, a literary figure similarly tainted in the eyes of posterity by his easy acquiescence in political conservatism. In another article of 1837, Kukol'nik chose to see the dacha as evidence of the emergence of a middle class with the surplus wealth and leisure necessary to cultivate its own taste. Like Bulgarin, he cited classical models in support of the dacha, using "dacha" and "villa" as synonyms. Even so, the arrival of a middle class occasioned some regret for the decline of the grand suburban residences and spectacular entertainments of the great aristocratic families. "Simplicity is a pleasant thing, but there are places where it brings persistent tedium or melancholy upon the reflective spirit," Kukol'nik concluded.[8]

By the middle of the 1840s, however, such doubts were beginning to appear futile. To comment on the convoys of dachniki quitting the city each year at the beginning of June was fast becoming a commonplace, and the appeal of a summer in the country was held to be universally acknowledged.[9] The trend was sufficiently marked for an authoritative St. Petersburg guidebook to reflect in 1851 on an important shift in the meaning of the word "dacha": "Petersburg dachas have lost their original meaning of 'a place out of town given into ownership by the government or bought by a particular person,' and the name dacha is now frequently given to a peasant house rented by a city dweller for the summer months."[10] Rental opportunities of various kinds were widely publicized. Although newspapers continued, as in the 1820s, to contain advertisements for substantial dacha residences, typically with ten or twenty rooms (sometimes nearer thirty), several outbuild-

---

7. On the Russian cult of antiquity in this period, see the work of Iurii Lotman, notably "The Theater and Theatricality as Components of Early Nineteenth-Century Culture," trans. G. S. Smith, in Iu. M. Lotman and B. A. Uspenskii, *The Semiotics of Russian Culture*, ed. A. Shukman (Ann Arbor, 1984), esp. 143–44.

8. N. Kukol'nik, "Villa," *Khudozhestvennaia gazeta*, nos. 11–12 (1837), 185.

9. See, e.g., *Skol'ko let, skol'ko zim! ili Peterburgskie vremena* (St. Petersburg, 1849). The dacha fashion was given ample coverage in the early 1840s on the pages of *Severnaia pchela*, which is the best single guide to Petersburg commonplaces of the time.

10. Grech, *Ves' Peterburg*, 176–77.

ings, and ample stable space, they also offered more modest accommodations: a four-room peasant home, for example, or the top floor of a baker's house in a village a few versts north of St. Petersburg.[11]

Dachas were of interest to urban people not only as an amenity but also as a new type of dwelling that offered its owner space, freedom, and much richer possibilities for self-expression than a city residence could afford. Architectural pattern books offered advice on how to make full use of this potential. The out-of-town houses described in P. Furmann's *Encyclopedia of the Russian Owner-Architect in Town and Country* (1842) were solidly built and fully equipped for comfortable family life. They tended to have a study, a nursery, separate rooms for dining and entertaining, bedrooms, and further refinements such as boudoirs and "relaxation rooms." Servants might be accommodated in small rooms inside the main house or in outbuildings. Attention was expected to be paid to the house's external aspect; it was particularly important that there should be a clean and uncluttered approach for visiting carriages. This was sometimes called the "clean yard"; a grubbier one might be found to the rear of the house with perhaps an outhoused kitchen, a chicken coop, and a vegetable garden. The values of comfort and refinement were promoted in designs for wallpaper, furniture, gates, and railings. For the garden, neoclassical statues and faux-rustic garden furniture were recommended.[12]

Besides offering practical advice on design and issuing the common instruction not to build on low-lying, marshy ground, Furmann had interesting comments to make on style. On a trip around the provinces, he recalled, he had been shocked by the ugliness and tastelessness of many large houses that he encountered. He now sought to resist this trend by placing emphasis on simple, mainly classical architectural solutions. He also had kind words for the *style rustic:* a cottage-like dwelling was especially pleasing to the eye tucked away in parkland, and was highly suitable for putting up guests. The straightforwardness of its outward appearance did not, moreover, imply a spartan interior; the comforts concealed by the rustic exterior might "satisfy all a pampered sybarite's demands for refined luxury."[13]

Furmann's work was one of several publications of the time that gave coverage to a new kind of summer residence quite distinct from the manor house and the town house. This kind of dwelling, generally known as "dacha," "house out of town," or "country cottage" (*sel'skii domik,* to be distinguished from the less diminutive and more manorial *sel'skii dom*), came in two main types: the neoclassicism of solid, symmetrical, and often colonnaded residences and the countrified aspect of more modest and less symmetrical houses that often evoked the English cottage. Where it differed most strikingly from its architectural forebears was in the scope it offered for the whimsical and the exotic.

In this last respect, the dacha was in the aesthetic vanguard of its time. The 1830s were

11. These examples are taken from *SPb ved* in 1839.

12. P. Furmann, *Entsiklopediia russkogo gorodskogo i sel'skogo khoziaina-arkhitektora,* 3 vols. (St. Petersburg, 1842), vol. 1. Besides Furmann's extensive selection of designs, note K. Shreider, *Sobranie risunkov sadovykh i domovykh ukrashenii i vsiakikh prinadlezhnostei sego roda* (St. Petersburg, 1842).

13. Furmann, *Entsiklopediia,* ix, 34.

32

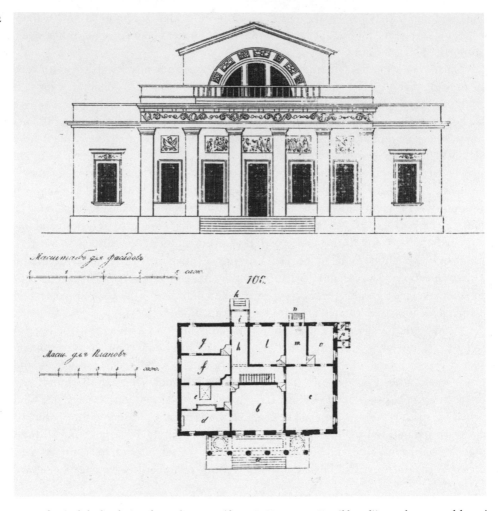

A neoclassical dacha design from the 1840s (from P. Furmann, *Entsiklopediia russkogo gorodskogo i sel'skogo khoziaina-arkhitektora* [St. Petersburg, 1842])

a decade when eclecticism, far from being a dirty word, was taken up enthusiastically by numerous commentators on architecture and the other arts. Civilization, it was widely believed, had entered a third, Romantic phase, following its "Eastern" and "Greek" eras. The normative boundaries of art were pushed back in several spheres, and the history of culture was raided for inspiration in creating novelty. Hence, for example, the "discovery" of the Middle Ages, the Gothic revival, and the commitment to stylistic experimentation. Romanticism was a disposition rather than a fixed style; or alternatively, it was, in the words of Wladimir Weidlé, "the loss of style."[14] Nowhere did architectural innovations achieve more striking results than in prime dacha territories such as Kamennyi Island,

14. Weidlé is quoted in E. A. Borisova, *Russkaia arkhitektura v epokhu romantizma* (St. Petersburg, 1997), 7.

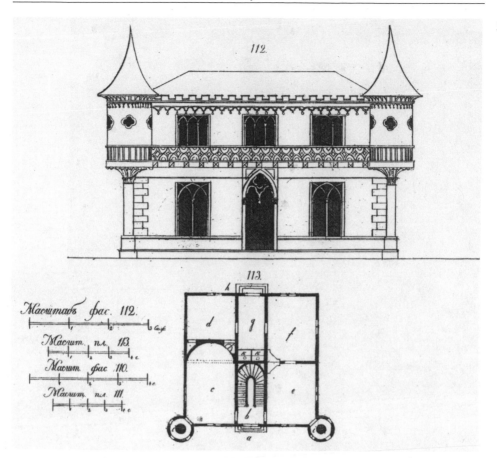

*112.*

*113.*

A dacha "in the Gothic style" (from P. Furmann, *Entsiklopediia russkogo gorodskogo i sel'skogo khoziaina-arkhitektora* [St. Petersburg, 1842])

where a whole range of new constructions went up in the late 1830s: Gothic mansions, white Dutch cottages with green shutters, Neapolitan glass galleries, Greek columns, Russian izbas, and Chinese pagodas.[15]

Perhaps the most remarkable characteristic of Russian Romanticism is not the range of its eclecticism or the ambition of its stylistic experimentation but rather the speed with which the styles it borrowed became dehistoricized and entered the mainstream. In large measure, as with Romanticism in other cultures, this process of cultural adoption and adaptation was bound up with the search for a national art; a search that was pursued with all the more urgency in Russia for that country's comparatively late arrival on the European cultural scene. Thus, for example, the Gothic style in architecture was quickly reappropriated as an emblem of Russian antiquity and its *nouveauté* accordingly forgotten. No less important, the new aesthetics of Romanticism had an impact in more every-

15. Bur'ianov, *Progulka s det'mi*, 1:142.

A dacha with a minaret "in the Mauritanian style" (from P. Furmann, *Entsiklopediia russkogo gorodskogo i sel'skogo khoziaina-arkhitektora* [St. Petersburg, 1842])

day areas of life too. House designs, both interior and exterior, bespoke a closer and more individual engagement with the home environment. In the 1830s and 1840s, for the first time, symmetry might be sacrificed in the interests of functionality, and the enfilade principle hitherto dominant weakened slightly in designs of country residences. In town houses it remained largely unchallenged, but the number of people who could afford to own and maintain such houses in the center of the city was shrinking. Here we find an important determinant of the dacha's social prominence in nineteenth-century Russia: as apartment living became the norm for more and more urban people of all social groups (and this change was felt especially acutely by the nobility), an out-of-town residence took on added significance as a center for the extended household and as a focus of domestic and proprietary instincts.[16]

The tone had been set by the imperial Kottedzh (Cottage), designed by Adam Menelaws for Nicholas I and built at Peterhof from 1826 to 1829. In its basic composition and in the early stages of its construction this residence was classically symmetrical, but in its finished form no two sides of the house were identical in facade, its aspect was lent visual interest by contrasts in tone and perspective, and its interior was rather reminiscent of a rich bourgeois Western European household. In its execution the Kottedzh had become acutely Gothicized. And the architectural ensemble of which it formed part contributed to a new domesticated mythology of power whereby the tsar was brought down to human dimensions and emphasis was placed on his family life.[17]

The values embodied by the Peterhof Kottedzh—domesticity, family life, home comfort, individuality—duly filtered down to less exalted dacha dwellers. As Furmann asserted, the Gothic style, with its invigorating "imprint of poetry," had come down to the modern age in a "pure" and "regular" form; the designs of well-known architects such as Aleksandr Briullov and Andrei Shtakenshneider had shown that it was fully compatible with the values of a civilized and no longer feudal culture.[18] Other residents of Peterhof shared these convictions and followed their tsar's lead—especially after 1832, when they gained full rights to the land on which houses stood (until then the land had been owned by the court, which retained the right to reclaim plots and remove buildings without compensation).[19] As early as 1837, Kukol'nik observed that the taste for grandiloquent archi-

---

16. On the building of detached houses in this period, both within and outside the city, see A. L. Punin, *Arkhitekturnye pamiatniki Peterburga: Vtoraia polovina XIX veka* (Leningrad, 1981), 162–86.

17. On the long and productive career of Adam Menelaws (for many years a stonemason working under the much better known Charles Cameron), see A. Cross, *"By the Banks of the Neva": Chapters from the Lives and Careers of the British in Eighteenth-Century Russia* (Cambridge, 1997), 297–305. On the architectural design of the Peterhof Kottedzh, see Borisova, *Russkaia arkhitektura*, 132–35. On its relation to the cultural myths of the period, see A. S. Loseva, "Obraz Petergofa epokhi romantizma" (dissertation, Moscow, 1997). On these cultural myths, see R. Wortman, *Scenarios of Power: Myth and Ceremony in Russian Monarchy*, vol. 1 (Princeton, 1995), chaps. 9, 10, and 11.

18. Furmann, *Entsiklopediia*, 1:35. A pattern book that speaks approvingly of the prevailing taste for "decorations" in house design is A. Kutepov, *Proekty dlia stroenii domov i drugikh raznogo roda postroek vo vnov' priniatom vkuse* (Moscow, 1852). On Briullov's designs and on other dachas of the period, see A. L. Punin, *Arkhitektura Peterburga serediny XIX veka* (Leningrad, 1990), 237–42.

19. See *Materialy o gorodakh pridvornogo vedomstva: Gorod Petergof* (St. Petersburg, 1882), 5, 24.

36   tectural gestures was passing, to be replaced by a tasteful eclecticism; in his opinion, Peterhof now equaled Versailles in beauty while avoiding its cultural pretensions.[20] Peterhof's domesticated Gothic was later recalled by one tenant of the 1860s, who remembered his father renting "a small cottage in the Gothic style with a high pointed roof and lancet windows; in front of the dacha there was a small patch of garden, in the middle of which stood an ancient maple tree whose branches stretched in through the windows of a rather high mezzanine."[21]

The style of dacha life cultivated in mid-century at Peterhof emerges in greater detail from the papers of one particularly well placed landlord, Aleksandr Pavlovich Kozhevnikov (1807–1875). In 1843, Kozhevnikov became the councilor of the Peterhof palace administration; his duties included supervision of Peterhof hereditary lands (*votchiny*) and of the town's affairs more generally. While in the job, he set about acquiring dachas of his own for rental, later complaining that his official salary was too low to cover his expenses. One of these houses, a stone residence facing the sea, with twenty-four rooms, brought in 1,200 rubles a year fully furnished. Kozhevnikov also owned two other stone houses of thirteen rooms and two wooden houses of nine and seven rooms. He catered to tenants with high expectations. In 1848, for example, one of his houses was rented by A. F. L'vov, director of the court choir. In a letter to his landlord, L'vov mentioned several pieces of furniture and other household items that he was having sent to supplement the furnishings provided (these included carpets and a bronze clock); he also requested that the gardener make fresh flowers available and hinted that Kozhevnikov should help to get the interior in order.[22] For L'vov, as for other residents of upmarket settlements such as Peterhof, the dacha, despite its distance from the metropolis, was synonymous with cultivated domesticity.

## The Dacha and the Natural World

The mid-century model of the dacha implied not only a new, more attentive and imaginative attitude to domestic space but also a different quality of engagement with the wider environment. The architectural recommendations were joined and amplified by public discussion of leisure and its relation to the natural world. Furmann's encyclopedia was in step with the times when it defined "dacha" as "a house out of town where city dwellers repair for the summer period in order to have a rest well away from the dust, noise, and bustle of the city and to enjoy the fresh delights of the fields and woods."[23] This was a rationale for the dacha that would be heard with ever greater frequency over the next few decades: human beings, born as part of the natural world, must not allow themselves to overexercise their rational, intellectual faculties, and must take time to enjoy—

---

20. N. Kukol'nik, "Novye postroiki v Petergofe," *Khudozhestvennaia gazeta*, nos. 11–12 (1837), 173–77.

21. *Sbornik v pamiat' P. I. Mel'nikova* (Nizhnii Novgorod, 1910), 37.

22. RGIA, f. 963, op. 1, d. 31, l. 1. Details of Kozhevnikov's activities as a landlord can be found ibid., d. 56.

23. Furmann, *Entsiklopediia*, 1:29.

even if only intermittently—the rural "good life." A dacha, then, not only made people cultivated and contentedly domestic, it also made them physically and morally robust.

The desirability of summer recreation out of the city was further emphasized by the prominence given to Russian sea resorts. Once again a precedent was set by Nicholas I, who was the first tsar to acquire a permanent residence in the Crimea, and whose public association with the Peterhof ensemble and consequent proximity to the sea fed the image of him as a Romantic individual as well as a good family man.[24] The tsar's efforts at self-fashioning were complemented and amplified by the first serious reports on Russian sea resorts. Spa towns—the aristocratic resorts of the Caucasus and the provincial mineral source in Lipetsk—first emerged in the early nineteenth century, at a time when "taking the waters" was becoming one of the most fashionable pastimes of the European aristocracy. The 1830s were associated with the rise of a more northern set of locations that catered more to an urban elite than to a landed gentry. Here again Faddei Bulgarin was a herald of social change. The sea baths at Helsingfors (Helsinki), he proudly declared, were "without any exaggeration one of the best institutions of their kind not only in Russia but in the whole of Europe."[25]

According to another contemporary, visitors were divided into three main categories: those taking the waters (both marine and mineral), those coming to Helsingfors out of curiosity, and younger people who were attracted by the social scene (especially the well-attended balls). At any one time more than 300 people would be taking cures, but the main building of the mineral waters complex was equipped for a rather broader public: it had a large hall (in which there was often dancing in the evenings), a billiards room, and a restaurant. For the summering Petersburger Helsingfors had the advantage of being clean, law-abiding, and cheap. New accommodation was created as the leisure industry grew, so that visitors no longer had to settle for a guesthouse: "The space separating the building of the [mineral] waters from the bathing booths is now beginning to fill up with dachas, and we can expect to see soon a continuous chain of pretty cottages that will replace the present view of the cliffs."[26] Certain resorts were by now so well established that their medical functions were taking second place to their social amenities. One Petersburg civil servant hoped to spend the summer of 1834 in Revel' (now Tallinn) recuperating with his wife, who had just given birth. What he found on arrival was a microcosm of well-to-do Petersburg society; as a result, he felt unable to shed urban formalities and to take full advantage of the setting, which he admitted was splendid.[27]

In general, however, medical and social attractions seem to have been considered not contradictory but complementary. The vacation habits of the Russian leisure class in this period fitted a pattern identified by Dominic Lieven in his study of the nineteenth-cen-

24. See Loseva, "Obraz Petergofa."

25. F. Bulgarin, *Letniaia progulka po Finliandii i Shvetsii v 1838 godu*, 2 vols. (St. Petersburg, 1839), 1:102. Similar praises are sung in I. Golovin, *Poezdka v Shvetsiiu v 1839 godu* (St. Petersburg, 1840), e.g., 17.

26. F. Dershau, *Finliandiia i finliandtsy* (St. Petersburg, 1842), 56–57.

27. V. I. Safonovich, "Vospominaniia," *Russkii arkhiv,* no. 3 (1903), 363–68.

38    tury European aristocracy: small-town spas came to be regarded as an agreeable hybrid of
the high society of the capitals and the quieter lifestyle of the country estate.[28] The rise of
the spa town brought with it an emphasis on a different range of pastimes: a vacation by
the sea was expected not merely to replicate the entertainments afforded by the salon and
the ball but also to provide opportunities for mental repose, healthy physical exertion,
and untroubled and "democratic" socializing. Bulgarin made a point of praising, besides
the health-giving properties of the local water, the hospitality of the Finns and the openness of Finnish high society. Another observer concurred, noting that "in Helsingfors all
ages and classes of people can find themselves the appropriate entertainments and spend
the summer as they please, without constraint, enjoying complete freedom in all places
and at all times."[29] Similar benefits—hygiene, public order, relaxed entertainment, and
healthy lifestyle—were promised in Revel'.[30] In July 1829 the young Nikolai Gogol, at the
end of his tether after a few months in St. Petersburg, took a trip to Lübeck, where he was
favorably impressed by the neat and well-appointed dacha hamlets outside the town: "The
cottages spread out beyond the town are planted and entwined with trees, bushes, and
flowers; they are delightful and very similar to Petersburg dachas."[31]

Gogol was doubtless extreme in the violence of his rejection of St. Petersburg, but he
was by no means exceptional in taking a dislike to the place. In the 1830s and 1840s attitudes toward the city became more self-conscious and, in general, more hostile; attention
was increasingly drawn to its "contradictions."[32] Petersburg became an unwholesome and
treacherous place, and trips to the dacha were regarded as an essential outlet. In other
words, the dacha gained definition as a space with a set of values not only different from
but also opposed to those of the city. In the summer Petersburg was left for unstable
dreamers such as the narrator of Fedor Dostoevsky's *White Nights* (1848), who spends
much of the opening pages of that work conveying his obsessive sense of abandonment as
his not even nodding acquaintances from Nevskii Prospekt all depart for their dachas;
with similar dismay he observes the long procession of carts piled high with furniture and
household items and the fleets of boats similarly loaded up crossing the river to Chernaia
Rechka or one or other of the Neva islands.

This annual exodus was motivated in part by very real health concerns. Petersburgers
in the middle of the nineteenth century lived in fear of periodic devastating outbreaks of
disease. The worst came in 1848, when the city lost over 12,000 people to cholera, and
memoirists recalled anxiously sitting out the summer and waiting for the epidemic to
abate. One man took refuge in a well-to-do location north of the city, but even here, he remembered, "terror reigned everywhere during the entire summer. There were almost no
deaths in the dachas near Lesnoy Korpus, but nevertheless, everyone was distraught and

28. See D. Lieven, *The Aristocracy in Europe, 1815–1914* (London, 1992), chap. 7, esp. 150–51.

29. Dershau, *Finliandiia*, i.

30. N. Reitlinger, *Putevoditel' po Reveliu i ego okrestnostiam* (St. Petersburg, 1839).

31. N.V. Gogol', *Polnoe sobranie sochinenii*, 14 vols. (Leningrad, 1937–52), 10:154.

32. See G. Kaganov, *Images of Space: St. Petersburg in the Visual and Verbal Arts* (Stanford, 1997), 103.

tense."[33] Even when the city in summer was not life-threatening, it was likely to be repellent. The combination of inadequate sanitation and hot weather brought a pervasive stench to the streets of St. Petersburg, and urbanites ran the further risk of being doused in paint and sand or struck down by falling wooden beams as they walked along: the summer months were the main time for construction and renovation work in residential buildings.[34]

Practical considerations of this kind soon received cultural elaboration and amplification. For those people with the time and money to spend prolonged periods out of the city, the dacha began to reinvent itself as a place not for idle and ostentatious entertainment but for healthful recreation, purposeful leisure, and virtuous family life. These were the main priorities emphasized in advice, liberally dispensed from the 1840s onward, on the conduct of life out of town. Dacha dwellers were urged not to try to haul all their belongings to the dacha, but rather to create a more straightforward lifestyle over the summer months, rising early and taking frequent invigorating walks, avoiding excessive mental activity, greasy and rich food, and mid-afternoon snoozes.[35] The most important considerations were "trees, a bit of water, and, above all, that you shouldn't have to put on airs, that you can leave the house in your smoking jacket, with a pipe in your mouth, without making yourself, or anyone else, blush."[36] The virtues of simplicity and practicality were similarly projected by architects' designs of the period, several of which take the English or the Swiss country cottage as their model.[37] Practice did not necessarily follow prescription, of course. It seems that advice to choose a not excessively damp site and an appropriate set of building materials was not always heeded. In any case, the design recommendations of the time left much room for misapprehensions. One man's tasteful Gothic was another's vulgarity; Peterhof-style eclecticism, if it fell into the wrong hands, was apt to seem impractical and pretentious. As one thoroughly typical retrospective account had it, many of the new Petersburg dachas were

> just houses of cards, not at all adapted to the climate, with Mauritanian and other adornments on the outer facade, but without the least conveniences inside, with verandas and belvederes but without stoves, with various means of defense against the sun, which so rarely shows its face in Petersburg, but without the slightest de-

33. A. Nikitenko, *The Diary of a Russian Censor,* ed. and trans. H. Jacobson (Amherst, 1975), 117. Another account can be found in "Vospominaniia D. A. Skalona," *Russkaia starina* 131, no. 9 (1907): 526 (the author [b. 1840] recalls being evacuated to the safe haven of Oranienbaum by a relative who also happened to be a doctor). A more quantitative account of this and the several other pandemics in nineteenth-century Russia is K. D. Patterson, "Cholera Diffusion in Russia, 1823–1923," *Social Science and Medicine* 38 (1994): 1171–91.

34. P. P. Sokolov, "Vospominaniia akademika P. P. Sokolova," *Istoricheskii vestnik* 122 (1910): 902.

35. See, e.g., *Dachniki, ili Kak dolzhno provodit'leto na dache* (St. Petersburg, 1849).

36. V. Mezhevich, "Zhurnal'naia vsiakaia vsiachina," *Severnaia pchela,* 24 June 1844, 565.

37. Furmann's *Entsiklopediia* contains a "Swiss" design. A fashion for Swiss chalets, cottages, and farmhouses was noticeable in Pavlovsk in mid-century: see F. M. Dostoevskii, *Polnoe sobranie sochinenii v tridtsati tomakh,* 30 vols. (Leningrad, 1972–90), 9:446 (notes to *The Idiot*).

fense against the cold, strong wind that blew right through all our dachas for the whole of our so-called summer.[38]

Even so, the morally fibrous qualities of the dacha did enter the public consciousness in mid-century. They find an unlikely literary beneficiary in Il'ia Il'ich Oblomov, the eponymous hero of Ivan Goncharov's novel (first published in 1858). Oblomov has gone down in Russian culture as the epitome of apathy. In part 1 of the novel he never quite manages to get out of bed; and then, at the beginning of Part 2, despite the vigorous pressure applied by his indefatigable German acquaintance Stolz, he shows no real signs of taking leave of his dream world and putting his affairs in order. A trip abroad, for which he makes the practical arrangements, is postponed indefinitely after he wakes up one morning with a swollen lip. But then, in one of the more astonishing spatial shifts in Russian literature, Oblomov does change both his location and his lifestyle:

> He gets up at seven, reads, takes books to a certain place. He does not look sleepy, tired, or bored. There is even a touch of color in his face and a sparkle in his eyes—something like courage, or at any rate self-confidence. He never wears his dressing-gown. . . .
>
> He reads a book or writes dressed in an ordinary coat, a light kerchief around his neck, his shirt collar shows over his tie and is white as snow. He goes out in an excellently made frock coat and an elegant hat. He looks cheerful. He hums to himself. What is the matter?
>
> Now he is sitting at the window of his dacha (he is staying at a dacha a few miles from the town), a bunch of flowers lying by him. He is quickly finishing writing something, glancing continually over the top of the bushes at the path, and again writing hurriedly.[39]

Goncharov here reverts to the style of present-tense reverie that he used earlier for Oblomov's dream of his ancestral estate, Oblomovka. And that points to an essential similarity between the two locations: the hero's move to the dacha is an attempt to abandon the bad habits of the city and create a rural idyll such as he remembers from his childhood (but without exposing himself to the unpleasant realities of grown-up life in the country). The difference is that the dacha is an open and uncluttered space, and one that receives remarkably little comment in its own right. The other three main locations in the novel (Oblomov's city-center flat on Gorokhovaia Street, Oblomovka, and the remote suburb of the Vyborg Side) are described in much greater detail and with much stronger value judgments.

This very lack of specificity in the account of Oblomov's summer outside Petersburg

38. V. R. Zotov, "Peterburg v sorokovykh godakh," *Istoricheskii vestnik* 39 (1890): 330.

39. I. Goncharov, *Oblomov*, in *Sobranie sochinenii v vos'mi tomakh* (Moscow, 1952–55), 4:195; English version (amended) from *Oblomov*, trans. D. Magarshack (London, 1954), 188.

suggests that the dacha had acquired its own way of life, its own ideology; that it had become a space more than a place. And this is undeniably an important stage in the development of any cultural space: the moment when it floats away from a set of physical coordinates and comes to be associated with its own set of practices and values. But these were by no means the only possible practices and values. Many people required more excitement and social stimulation than did Goncharov's placid hero, and in the middle of the nineteenth century institutions were appearing that could provide them.

## A New Entertainment Culture

The inhabitants of St. Petersburg and Moscow in the first half of the nineteenth century included a significant and increasing number of modestly prosperous people who lacked a substantial independent income, an illustrious family name, and the extensive social networks invariably associated with these benefits, but who had the time and education to feel deprived of them. They had no ready-made entrée into polite society, and their means and housing conditions did not allow them to entertain on any great scale and thereby project their own social profile. They could hardly be satisfied with an entertainment culture that until the 1830s remained polarized between two extremes: on the one hand, the privately organized and funded recreations of the elite nobility; on the other hand, the maximally inclusive urban popular festivities (*gulian'ia*). Aristocratic pastimes were inaccessible for want of both money and social prestige, while *gulian'ia* were unattractive, as they afforded little opportunity for the sustained and autonomous socializing craved by most "middle estates."[40]

In the space between these two extremes emerged a new urban entertainment culture, many of whose prime venues were to be found on the outskirts of the city and within easy reach of several dacha settlements. *Severnaia pchela* (The Northern Bee), an authoritative chronicler of the Petersburg social scene, reflected in 1850 on the recent arrival in Russia of a new concept: the "summer season." In the old days, it observed, people had mainly occupied themselves with "going on secluded family walks, receiving guests from town, or visiting dacha neighbors," and the only available public entertainment was the music on Krestovskii Island. Now, however, the immediate environs of St. Petersburg had become much livelier, and dacha locations were yielding many paying customers for the new amusements available.[41]

40. Many contemporary Russian sources cite *gulian'ia* as evidence that the Russian social order was, despite its autocratic political carapace, "democratic" in a way that could never be emulated by parliamentary nations: on festive occasions, it was claimed, people of all social classes came together, mixed freely, and forgot all distinctions and hierarchies. Foreign accounts suggest, however, that *gulian'ia* were conducted with no such carnivalesque abandon: commoners and nobles may have spent time in close proximity, but members of each group still knew their place. See, for example, the description of the Peterhof St. Peter's Day festivities in "Iz zapisok Ippolita Ozhe, 1814–1817," *Russkii arkhiv*, no. 1 (1877), 67–69, and the later, better known, and more hostile account of the Marquis de Custine in his *Letters from Russia*, trans. R. Buss (London, 1991), 101.

41. These points are made explicitly in surveys of the Petersburg social scene such as those to be found in the "Miscellany" section of *Severnaia pchela*: see, e.g., 12 June 1843, 513–14, and 24 June 1844, 565–66.

42     The best-known place of entertainment was the garden of the Artificial Mineral Waters, formerly part of the Stroganov lands at Novaia Derevnia. Far from simply performing a medical function, this institution soon became a major gathering place for well-heeled Petersburgers after it became independent and acquired charitable status in 1833.[42] Its character changed even more radically in 1848, when it was taken over by the energetic entrepreneur Johann Isler and turned into a commercial proposition. Taking advantage of the panic resulting from the cholera epidemic, Isler drew people in by stressing the health benefits of taking the waters, while at the same time laying on an impressive range of attractions: ample and high-quality refreshments, a choir of Moscow gypsies, military bands, fireworks, acrobatic displays, comedy actors, and themed balls.[43] Contemporary reports emphasized that the Artificial Mineral Waters required no elaborate dress or code of conduct—a significant departure from earlier upper-class amusements.[44] Isler's institution thus provided a model for a new kind of urban entertainment that was not directed at any one section of society but rather appealed to various cultural groups. It brought together the salon and the show booth and thus interwove elite and popular tastes.[45]

The gardens of the opulent dachas on the Neva—notably those belonging to the Stroganovs and the Kushelev-Bezborodkos—to some extent followed suit: as before, they were open to the public, but now they operated on a more commercial footing. In the early 1830s, for example, the Kushelev-Bezborodkos decided to develop a part of their Poliustrovo estate as a dacha zone: twenty plots were offered for sale in 1833, and in the 1840s four-room apartments were available for summer rental by those who wished to take advantage of the local mineral source.[46] Yet this was clearly not the only reason to spend the summer at one of the resorts north of the Neva: reports on these locations combined an emphasis on their health benefits with an account of the entertainments they offered (dancing, music, perambulations, open-air games).[47] As the memoirs of one resident, the artist P. P. Sokolov, make clear, Poliustrovo was valued by summer visitors for making available a range of refined and enjoyable pastimes: for bringing a mixed bunch of middling urbanites into civilized proximity with the world of the aristocracy without obliging them to conform to its habits and values.[48]

For several years in the 1830s and 1840s, places of public entertainment performed two rather ambiguously distinguished functions: they continued their traditions of entertainment for a homogeneous social group while at the same time opening themselves up to a broader public. Compare, for example, the above accounts of Isler's Mineral Waters with

42. On the decision to establish a public mineral source (for charitable, not commercial, purposes), see *PSZ*, ser. 2, 8, no. 6655 (19 June 1833).

43. L. Brant, "Gorodskoi vestnik," *Severnaia pchela*, 20 May 1850, 445–47.

44. See, e.g., *Severnaia pchela*, 18 Aug. 1842, 725.

45. This is the argument made in I. A. Steklova, "Fenomen uveselitel'nykh sadov v formirovanii kul'turnoi sredy Peterburga-Petrograda" (dissertation, Leningrad, 1991), 47–55.

46. G. G. Priamurskii, "*V Poliustrovo na vody i razvlecheniia* . . . " (St. Petersburg, 1996), 56, 65.

47. See, e.g., the report on the Kushelev-Bezborodko gardens in *Severnaia pchela*, 5 July 1847, 597.

48. Sokolov, "Vospominaniia," *Istoricheskii vestnik* 122 (1910): 902–8.

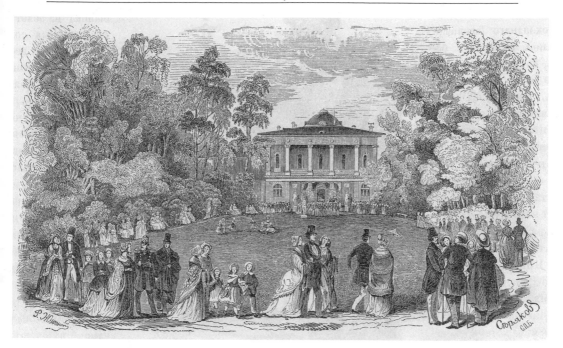

A *gulian'e* at the Stroganov gardens (from *Russkii illiustrirovannyi al'manakh* [St. Petersburg, 1858]). Courtesy of Helsinki Slavonic Library.

a roughly contemporaneous report that is more careful and staid in its description of the entertainments available:

> The events and balls that have for several years consecutively taken place at the mineral waters establishment near Novaia Derevnia have, according to the wishes of many persons, been arranged for this summer as well. They may be attended by nobles, military and state civil servants, honored citizens, merchants, scholars, and artists.[49]

As this quotation suggests, St. Petersburg's dacha locations and places of entertainment had their own social geography. Somewhat above the middle of the range was Isler's establishment, which, even after it became less explicitly exclusive, still had a socially restricted clientele, given the expense of a season ticket (15 silver rubles for a family in the late 1840s). As earlier in the century, an extremely broad section of urban society was encountered at popular festivities (*gulian'ia*) such as May Day at Ekaterinhof or the equivalent celebration at Sokol'niki in Moscow, which traditionally signaled the start of the summer season.[50]

49. "Letnie uveseleniia," *Severnaia pchela*, 24 June 1847, 561.
50. A. A. Pelikan, "Vo vtoroi polovine XIX veka," *Golos minuvshego*, no. 2 (1914), 137 (Pelikan is recalling St. Petersburg in the 1850s). Accounts of public celebrations at Peterhof in the first half of the nineteenth century are

44      Other venues were known to attract more specific sections of the urban population. Krestovskii Island, in the words of one memoirist, "was frequented above all by merchants, low-ranking civil servants, and all kinds of middling Petersburg people."[51] The son of a prosperous merchant family recalled his family taking regular after-dinner strolls there and drinking tea sold by an enterprising *meshchanin* who had set up a stall with a samovar. Marquees with music and dancing were set up at the end of the island, facing Elagin. A less well-off visitor to the islands was Nikolai Gogol, who during his brief career in the St. Petersburg civil service (1830–31) took frequent walks there in the late evening.[52] Moscow, too, was developing a suburban entertainment culture whose appeal extended far beyond the traditional social elite. For the son of a well-to-do merchant family in the 1840s, summer could be an endless round of visits, promenades, and balls:

> I'm dazed, I'm in the devil knows what kind of state of mind, my head is full of hot, burning kisses! The older folk want me to get down to serious matters!! . . . They don't understand what's happening to me! . . . Pokrovskoe keeps getting visited by musicians from Petrovskii Park, and not one band, but two.[53]

The impact of public entertainments on dacha life are most strikingly illustrated by the case of Pavlovsk, a location that epitomized upmarket hauteur in the early nineteenth century and to a large extent retained this aura until the early twentieth.[54] Built for the son of Catherine the Great who later became Paul I, the palace with its surrounding territory became the domain of Paul's widow, Mariia Fedorovna, after his assassination in 1801. The select clans who were permitted to live at Pavlovsk had the opportunity to walk freely in the palace gardens and to observe the imperial family's everyday habits at close quarters. Somewhat later, in the 1820s, many residents still had personal connections with the palace, and their households commonly adopted a style of open-house hospitality that implied membership in a close-knit community of social equals.[55] Even in the 1840s, little seemed to have changed:

---

quoted in E. Amburger, *Ingermanland: Eine junge Provinz Rußlands im Wirkungsbereich der Residenz und Weltstadt St. Petersburg–Leningrad,* 2 vols. (Cologne, 1980), 1:552–55. A useful early survey of entertainment culture in Moscow is P. Vistengof, *Ocherki moskovskoi zhizni* (Moscow, 1842), 83–94. One Moscow guidebook of the same period lists sixteen *gulian'ia*: see M. Rudol'f, *Moskva s topograficheskim ukazaniem vsei ee mestnosti i okrestnostei* (Moscow, 1848), pt. 1, 29–31.

51. G. T. Polilov-Severtsev, *Nashi dedy-kuptsy: Bytovye kartiny nachala XIX stoletiia* (St. Petersburg, 1907), 28.

52. Gogol', *Polnoe sobranie sochinenii,* 10:179–80.

53. N. Krestovnikov, *Semeinaia khronika Krestovnikovykh,* 2 vols. (Moscow, 1904), 2:10. The impact on another merchant's son of the less extravagant entertainments of 1830 are recorded in T. Polilov-Severtsev, "Iz dnevnika iunoshi 'tridtsatykh godov,'" *Vestnik Evropy,* no. 7 (1908), 104.

54. P. Shtorkh, *Putevoditel' po sadu i gorodu Pavlovsku* (St. Petersburg, 1843). An English guidebook of 1915 noted that "Pavlovsk calls the more fashionable section of society at holiday-time": see W. B. Steveni, *Petrograd Past and Present* (London), 300.

55. See Iu. Arnol'd, *Vospominaniia,* 1:13–15, for an account of the 1810s; the 1820s are covered in V. A. Sollogub, *Vospominaniia* (Moscow and Leningrad, 1931).

The Grand Prince, who owned Pavlovsk in those days, personally crossed off the names of dubious dacha ladies who wanted to move to Pavlovsk for the summer; every day he was handed a list of persons who wanted to rent a dacha in the spring. . . .

Not much of an audience came from the city on weekdays, so that all the regular attendees at concerts knew each other by face and by name.[56]

Old-style aristocratic sociability was, however, by now under threat in Pavlovsk. In 1837 the character of the settlement had begun to change with the opening of the Tsarskoe Selo railway. This new rapid transport link brought much closer together the "modern" city and the "Romantic" landscape of the palace ensembles; now these two contrasting worlds could no longer be conceived as being separate and sealed off from one another. In 1836 a competition was announced for designs for the station building, and the winning entry, that of A. I. Shtakenshneider, seemed to accentuate this meeting of two cultures: the station, a symbol of technological modernity, was in a thoroughly Gothic style.[57] *Pace* modernist cultural appreciations of the railway, this was not at all an anonymous point of arrival and departure but a major social center in its own right. The station complex included a large hall for dinners, balls, and concerts, two smaller halls, two winter gardens, and forty guest rooms. The railway authorities also laid on station concerts that were free of charge for the audience and soon began to draw a regular public.

Over the following few decades music at the station brought more and more people together as a stream of musical celebrities passed through Pavlovsk. In the early 1840s Franz Liszt and Robert and Clara Schumann visited, but the mainstays of concert life were German conductors brought over with their orchestras to provide the requisite mix of classics and crowd-pleasers (usually weighted in favor of the latter). In 1856 Johann Strauss the younger arrived for the first of many concert seasons. It was Strauss who turned Pavlovsk into a proper concert venue, insisting that music be played in a separate concert hall instead of in the dining room, where the musicians had to compete with loquacious diners and waiters. He also insisted on more Wagner and Beethoven in the repertoire, and in this programming policy we can see evidence of a standard "middle-class" stage in cultural history taking place in Russia: the invention of classical music.[58] Now people visited the Pavlovsk station not only for the sake of dinner and conversation in a social circle where everyone was at least a nodding acquaintance. The music was no

56. A. Ia. Panaeva, *Vospominaniia*, 4th ed. (Moscow and Leningrad, 1933), 144. A similar account was left by Count M. D. Buturlin, who recalled Pavlovsk dachniki being visited by the owner, Grand Prince Mikhail Pavlovich, in 1845: see "Zapiski Grafa Mikhaila Dmitrievicha Buturlina," *Russkii arkhiv*, no. 3 (1897), 521–23.

57. See Borisova, *Russkaia arkhitektura*, 247–48.

58. This process was taken further in the 1890s by the conductor N. V. Galkin, who consolidated the move toward "serious" music by performing numerous works by Russian composers (Glinka, Dargomyzhskii, Balakirev, Tchaikovsky). On the history of the Pavlovsk concerts, see A. S. Rozanov, *Muzykal'nyi Pavlovsk* (Leningrad, 1978). Galkin and the Pavlovsk concerts are mentioned by Osip Mandelstam as evoking the "sickly, doomed provincialism" of the 1890s: see the sketch "Muzyka v Pavlovske," part of Mandelstam's *Shum vremeni* (1925), in his *Sochineniia v dvukh tomakh* (Moscow, 1990), 2:6–8.

46   longer merely a pleasing diversion but rather an exciting cultural experience in its own right: a performance that took center stage, not a melodious background hum. Strauss became a huge celebrity—to the extent that he was held personally responsible for pushing up Pavlovsk rents.[59] Journalists and memoirists alike remarked on Strauss's celebrity, his extravagant style of performance, and his appeal to the opposite sex. In 1857, apparently, he "literally did not know where to hide from his female admirers," even if "on many people his affectations (his way of dancing along as he conducted) made an unpleasant impression."[60] The station concerts remained a commonplace topic for feuilletonists for several decades: in one story by the prolific sketch writer V. O. Mikhnevich, titled "Under the Bows of the Pavlovsk Violins," the hero falls in love with a married woman, who tests the strength of his affections by insisting he sit through Pavlovsk concerts all week. He fails the test, complaining bitterly of the monotonous repertoire.[61]

Despite the mild notoriety that attached itself to Strauss, Pavlovsk remained a respectable and decorous place in the second half of the nineteenth century. It had none of the unseemly behavior that was held to be characteristic of the immediate outskirts of the city, where urban popular culture regularly encroached on the sedate life of dacha settlements. The Pavlovsk concerts were certainly not mass entertainment. They were, however, a decidedly nonaristocratic phenomenon in a location that had from its earliest days been associated with the more enclosed and exclusive social rituals of the elite nobility. As such, they strengthened the dacha's real and symbolic association with new, more "middle-class" habits.

## Sociability: From Aristocratic Salon to Intelligentsia Enclave

Out-of-town recreations, formerly the prerogative of a high society that blended the mandarinic and the patrician, were now open to all those who could afford a ticket to the Pavlovsk station or the admission fee for the Petrovskii Park concerts. To be sure, court life followed its traditional course within and immediately around the imperial palaces, but these palaces no longer dominated the social scene or set the tone for urban people who sought convivial and culturally stimulating ways of spending their summers outside the city.[62] Dachas were no longer polite exurban drawing rooms where entry was by invitation only and the rules of behavior were understood by all. Now nonaristocratic urbanites were taking up temporary residence in exurbia and seeking to cultivate acquaintances

---

59. See Nikitenko, *Diary*, entry for 15 May 1869.

60. Pelikan, "Vo vtoroi polovine XIX veka," 166.

61. V. O. Mikhnevich, "Pod smychkami pavlovskikh skripok (tema dlia dachnogo fantasticheskogo romana)," in his *Vsego ponemnozhku: Fel'etonno-iumoristicheskie nabroski* (St. Petersburg, 1875).

62. A good source on aristocratic dacha sociability in the middle of the nineteenth century is M. A. Patkul', *Vospominaniia Marii Aleksandrovny Patkul' rozhdennoi Markizy de Traverse za tri chetverti XIX stoletiia* (St. Petersburg, 1903). A very stable, court-orientated way of life in mid century Tsarskoe Selo is recalled in A. P. Neelov, "Iz dal'nikh let," *Russkaia starina* 165 (1916): 111–17, 257–70. Elite dacha life in Peterhof was described as being little different from life in the city in its endless round of socializing: see M. G. Nazimova, "Babushka grafinia M G. Razumovskaia," *Istoricheskii vestnik* 75 (1899): 848.

and pursue activities that would bring them pleasure and excitement while remaining
harmonious and decorous.

This quest left its mark in literary accounts of the time, which, by rejecting the ambience and the poetics of the salon, may be said to have brought the dacha into the realist age. Ever since Mariia Zhukova received a favorable mention from the celebrated critic Vissarion Belinskii in the late 1830s (which, in typical style, he drastically revised a few years later), she has intermittently been regarded as a herald of the shift from Romanticism to realism; and her two best-known works are set at the dacha. In *Evenings by the Karpovka* (1837) she paints a picture of considerable social diversity on the Petersburg islands:

> Barouches, carriages, cabriolets swept along the roads, colorful crowds strolled in the gardens, balconies turned into living rooms, whole families with their samovars and their numerous children and nannies hurried over to Krestovskii or to the hospitable garden of Countess L., they spread out with their cold supper, ice cream, and tea on the slope of the hill or under the dense lime trees on the very shore. You saw there a German craftsman and his good family, and high-spirited groups of young civil servants, and a Russian merchant with his wife and children of all ages, and two young artists discussing a forthcoming exhibition, and the chic mantilla of a high society beauty, and a servant girl's pretty kanzu.[63]

The main focus of the story, however, is not the day trippers on Krestovskii but the dacha of an elderly lady, Natal'ia Dmitrievna Shemilova, in the Karpovka district—a mere stone's throw from the dachas inhabited and fictionalized by Pushkin. Shemilova's dacha serves as a framing device for the stories that make up the body of *Evenings*: she receives a handful of regular visitors from various walks of life, who over the course of several evenings spin yarns to entertain the others. The dacha is a domestic world of everyday concerns and routine informal socializing. It is in pronounced contrast to the exurban salon of Pushkin's experience, which is a more public and convention-ridden arena for conversation. It also differs from the salon in its cultural detachment from the city. Shemilova's house and the stories told by her guests have no place for the conflict between urban artifice and natural virtue that tends to provide the emotional dynamic of the society tale.[64]

The conventions of the society tale are less gently probed in Zhukova's *Dacha on the Peterhof Road* (1845). This story, in its bare outlines, is structured by a set of Romantic tropes. A prince (Evgenii) chases after an eligible young woman (Mary) but is undone at the last moment because his past catches up with him: he has raised and dashed the hopes

---

63. M. S. Zhukova, *Vechera na Karpovke* (Moscow, 1986), 5–6.

64. On the basis of his study of Zhukova's works and other society tales of the time, Joe Andrew has given the dacha some credit for the victory of the realist chronotope in Russian literature: note the assessment of *The Dacha on the Peterhof Road* as a "generic melting pot" for sentimentalism and realism in his *Narrative and Desire in Russian Literature, 1822–49: The Feminine and the Masculine* (Basingstoke, 1993), 168.

48 of (that is, seduced) another girl, Zoia, whose consequently shredded nerves have not stopped her from becoming Mary's close companion, and who raises a scandal when she recognizes Evgenii. But this straightforward story line is undercut in several ways. For one thing, Evgenii is lazy and vapid and has to be pushed in Mary's direction by his forceful aunt, who sees that a match of this kind is essential to rescue the family finances. Romantic and realist worldviews clash openly in a discussion between Zoia and Mary on the meaning of true love. Moreover, the dacha setting serves to play off sentimentalist motifs against a realist authorial sensibility. On the one hand, the two girls are trying to create an arcadia in the manner of a pair of late eighteenth-century noble shepherdesses. The garden has a carefully landscaped section, but at the back it opens up toward the sea; here the girls can seek perfect solitude and commune with nature. The stylized interior of the house makes it a shrine to Russian-style reverie (*mechtatel'nost'*). Other things about this dacha, however, make it an unlikely backdrop for a pastoral idyll. Although it is one of the finest dachas on the Peterhof Road, it has changed hands since it was first owned by an "aristocratic gentleman" and now belongs to an owner "whose name seemed surprised to see itself on the plaque attached to a gate that once opened hospitably for counts and princes and their expensive carriages." The grounds of the dacha are no longer as splendid as they were in its aristocratic heyday: they contain a number of crumbling little houses, once used to accommodate the many guests who arrived at the dacha, but now rented out very cheaply. And the dacha certainly cannot be regarded as a secluded rural retreat: the Peterhof Road is a "real small town in its own right, a colony where people come together from all over Petersburg, where they get to know one another, even if not immediately, but where they still try to find out who everyone is, where they've come from, whom they receive, how they live."[65]

The pattern of life fictionalized by Zhukova is confirmed (and sometimes bemoaned) by other sources. As a leading guidebook of the time observed, the dacha plots on the Peterhof Road had long since been sold by their original owners, and most of them now contained several subsidiary houses for rent to separate tenants. Peasant villages adjacent to the road also served as dacha locations.[66] One former resident recalled at the end of the century that "by the 1850s the once fashionable Peterhof Road had become completely empty [empty, that is, of the beau monde], although by comparison with what it is now it might seem full of life."[67]

Other observers were less wistful as they noted the weakening presence of high society in dacha areas. Much of Karolina Pavlova's *Double Life* (1844–47), a late-Romantic society tale, takes place at a dacha in Moscow's Petrovskii Park, a location that is depicted as being antipathetic to meaningful human relations:

> Several days had passed since Vera Vladimirovna had moved into one of those nice pseudo-Gothic-Chinese buildings that Petrovsky Park is strewn with. Here

65. V. V. Uchenova, ed., "*Dacha na Petergofskoi doroge*": *Proza russkikh pisatel'nits pervoi poloviny XIX veka* (Moscow, 1986), 259, 268.

66. Grech, *Ves' Peterburg* (1851), 177, 191–92.

67. S. Sheremet'ev, *Vospominaniia, 1853–1861* (St. Petersburg, 1898), 15.

too everything corresponded to the demands and conditions of society. Surrounding the luxurious cottage was a luxurious garden, its greenery always an excellent, a choice, one might say an aristocratic greenery. Nowhere a faded leaf, a dry twig, a superfluous blade of grass; banished was everything in God's creation that is coarse, vulgar, plebeian. The very shrubbery around the house flaunted a kind of Parisian haughtiness, the very flowers planted in every available space took on a certain semblance of good form, nature made herself unnatural. In a word, everything was as it should be.[68]

Pavlova's critique of the undue formality, false friendliness, and servile cordiality of Russian high society may be seen as continuing a venerable tradition started by foreign observers such as the Wilmot sisters. A similar view was taken by A. F. Tiutcheva, lady in waiting for two empresses, in her diary: in Tiutcheva's view, the empty daily rituals of life in Peterhof and Tsarskoe Selo served to entrench a strict hierarchical order that precluded warm and genuine relations between individual members of the palace entourage.[69] Even the reforming Alexander II (ruled 1855–81) brought no perceptible change to court mores. When Alexander went out to stroll in the Tsarskoe Selo grounds in the late 1850s, aristocratic hangers-on would make a point of being there too. As one witness commented, "everyone tried to come before the eyes of the emperor. [They all wanted to see] whom he would speak to, and who would only receive a bow."[70]

Such unflattering impressions of official society had as their corollary an alternative tradition that, by presenting the dacha as a way of avoiding the contamination of public life, sought a more authentically rustic experience. V. Bykova, born in 1820 and a graduate of the Smolny Institute for Noble Young Ladies, issued an *exalté* farewell to her dacha (rented on the Peterhof Road) in a diary entry of August 1841: "Farewell, pleasant strolls, farewell bright days and moonlit nights!" Although Bykova was susceptible to the entertainments available at Isler's Mineral Waters, she continued (as an older woman, by now a teacher at the institute, in the 1850s) to steer clear of the more densely populated dacha locations. In 1854, for example, she went to Kolpino with her sister and another family, the two groups renting adjacent cottages. The view from her window was "simple, quite rural. No constraints at all, life was free, quiet, and peaceful." Two years later she found the social scene at the Pavlovsk station concerts much less to her taste: the program was monotonous, consisting exclusively of waltzes and polkas; the conductor, Strauss, was too high and mighty, even getting a servant to turn the pages for him; and there was too much audience chatter in foreign languages.[71]

Similarly, N. E. Komarovskii, having spent time at dachas on the Peterhof Road and on Kamennyi Island, reflected that he had been happiest in his childhood at an altogether more

68. K. Pavlova, *Polnoe sobranie stikhotvorenii* (Moscow and Leningrad, 1964),252; in English, *A Double Life*, trans. B. Heldt, 2d ed. (Oakland, Calif., 1986), 31.

69. A. F. Tiutcheva, *Pri dvore dvukh imperatorov: Vospominaniia, dnevnik, 1853–1882* (1928–29; Cambridge, 1975).

70. Neelov, "Iz dal'nikh let," *Russkaia starina* 165 (1916): 264.

71. V. Bykova, *Zapiski staroi smolianki*, 2 vols. (St. Petersburg, 1898), 1:124, 286, 373.

50 modest location on the river Okhta, to the southeast of St. Petersburg, in the 1850s.[72] And the same nostalgia for the simple exurban lifestyle can be found in the memoirs of the Moscow-based M. A. Dmitriev, who in the 1840s celebrated his promotion to chief prosecutor and concomitant pay raise by fulfilling his long-standing ambition to rent a dacha for the summer. The house he chose was modest—"almost a peasant izba, but with large windows and Dutch tiled stoves; it was new, clean, and neat"—and it was located in the village of Zykovo, just beyond the Tver' gates to the north of the city. Although the Dmitrievs' dacha was only a short walk from Petrovskii Park, it gave them a much-valued feeling of rural seclusion.[73]

This commitment to the simple dacha lifestyle and hostility to the social vanities was shared by prominent members of the first generation of the Russian intelligentsia. It is ironic, given Karolina Pavlova's disapproval of the Petrovskii Park haute bourgeoisie in her *Double Life,* that Ivan Panaev, when he visited Pavlova and her husband at Sokolovo (a little more than fifteen miles outside Moscow, in the Petersburg direction) in the early 1850s, criticized their dacha on rather similar grounds: for its "artificiality" and "dandified primness."[74] For several years in the 1850s Panaev wrote regular articles in the socially engaged journal *Sovremennik* (The Contemporary), where he offered a survey of Petersburg society and its recreations, and this venue afforded him ample opportunity to pass further scornful comment on the bourgeois dacha public.[75]

But Panaev and his fellow representatives of the intelligentsia had their own "authentic" dacha model, one that was created in the 1840s as Russian intellectual life became increasingly metropolitan.[76] In 1845, for example, the historian T. N. Granovskii, the translator N. Kh. Ketcher, and Aleksandr Herzen moved with their families to the village of Sokolovo, where Pavlova spent her summers a little later:

> The village belonged to the landowner Divov, who retained the large mansion there for himself for any trips he might take to his family estate but leased to tenants the two wings of the mansion and a cottage behind it plus a magnificent linden and birch grove that ran from the house down a hill to the river. On the other side of the river and hill, in keeping with the common character of Russian landscapes, a solid line of peasant huts was strung out. The Herzen and Granovsky families occupied the wings and Ketcher the rear cottage.[77]

72. N. E. Komarovskii, *Zapiski* (Moscow, 1912).

73. M. A. Dmitriev, *Glavy iz vospominanii moei zhizni* (Moscow, 1998), 460–62.

74. I. I. Panaev, *Literaturnye vospominaniia* (Moscow, 1950), 178.

75. The series of articles was called "Petersburg Life: The Observations of a New Poet" ("Peterburgskaia zhizn: Zametki novogo poeta"); it can serve as an encyclopedia of contemporary journalistic commonplaces regarding St. Petersburg.

76. The importance of the dacha as a place for writers, artists, and people of other "free" professions is noted in V. M-ch's useful article "Peterburgskie i moskovskie dachi," *Severnaia pchela,* 18 Aug. 1842, 727.

77. P. V. Annenkov, *The Extraordinary Decade: Literary Memoirs,* trans. Irwin R. Titunik (Ann Arbor, 1968), 129. Before renting out the houses at Sokolovo as dachas, Divov had moved most of the local peasants to neighboring villages; all that remained was a minimal service personnel of six people. See *Severo-zapadnyi okrug Moskvy* (Moscow, 1997), 347.

Herzen also mentioned this summer at Sokolovo in his memoirs, *My Past and Thoughts*. With his characteristic ironic detachment, he observed the peculiarities of the landscape on the two sides of the park: "On one side our Great Russian sea of wheat unfurled itself, on the other opened out a spacious view into the distance, and for this reason the owner did not pass up the opportunity to call the pavilion placed there 'Belle-vue.'"[78] Herzen commented further that the aristocrats of the eighteenth century, "for all their failings," had at least had a certain "breadth of taste," their own sense of style.

This last comment reveals that in the eyes of a sophisticated member of the literary intelligentsia in the 1840s, the culture of the country estate had lost its cultural vitality: at best, it was a living monument to an enlightened earlier generation of the aristocracy, at worst a reminder of enduring social ills. Even if they rented their summer houses on "traditional" country estates, members of Moscow intellectual circles were at pains to distinguish their values and pattern of life from those of their landlords.

The tensions that might exist between aristocrats and their tenants are well illustrated in Ivan Panaev's memoirs. In the summer of 1851 Granovskii and his friend N. G. Frolov, a publisher and translator, rented a small house on the Iusupov estate of Arkhangel'skoe. Panaev and V. P. Botkin arrived to visit, and were soon invited by the young prince Iusupov to visit him in the main family residence on the estate. (Panaev, a nobleman, was already well acquainted with the Iusupov family.) In due course, Iusupov extended the invitation to Zagoskin too, but at this point Frolov took huge offense on Zagoskin's behalf, supposing that Panaev and Botkin had instigated the invitation and arguing that an eminent and independent man such as Zagoskin was not to be patronized by such marks of aristocratic favor.[79]

The intelligentsia's countermodel of country life was exemplified by the Sokolovo group in the mid-1840s. Herzen and his friends entertained guests on a grand scale, went for regular walks together, and above all engaged in prolonged and passionate discussions (it was here, for example, that an important fissure within the intelligentsia—between the Westernizers and the proto-populists—opened up).

> only one thing was not allowed at Sokolovo—to be a limited person. Not that one was peremptorily required to be an effective speaker and display flashes of brilliant capabilities in general; quite the contrary, people wholly engrossed by their own specialties exclusively were held in very high esteem there. What was required were a certain intellectual level and a certain dignity of character. All the discourse of the circle was devoted to refining people's intellect and character, no matter what the talk was about.[80]

78. A. I. Gertsen, *Sobranie sochinenii v tridtsati tomakh* (Moscow, 1954–66), 9:207. Herzen also refers to the summer at Sokolovo as a *villeggiatura* (ibid., 208), which is dutifully glossed in the standard Soviet edition as "dacha life."

79. Panaev, *Literaturnye vospominaniia*, 223. Zagoskin himself did not, apparently, share Frolov's doubts, and handled the squabble with dignity and delicacy.

80. Annenkov, *Extraordinary Decade*, 137.

52    But the Moscow circle's model of dacha life, centered on the country estate and valuing comfort and open-ended sociability, was not shared by the Petersburg-based radicals, with whom it parted intellectual company in the 1840s. In an extremely influential essay first published in 1844, Vissarion Belinskii contrasted the warm, open, contented, family-oriented Moscow with the cold, official, but high-achieving St. Petersburg. To Moscow Belinskii went so far as to ascribe the value of *komfort,* which in this period was widely held to be uniquely an attribute of the English.[81] Belinskii, however, was condemned to spend his summers in a succession of drafty huts on the outskirts of St. Petersburg. In 1845 he rented a dacha near Lesnoi Institut; but, according to Avdot'ia Panaeva, a well-connected member of progressive circles and subsequently the common-law wife of Nikolai Nekrasov, it can have done his fragile health little good:

> What kind of a dacha was this! An izba with an internal partition that did not reach all the way to the ceiling, in which there was a kitchen on one side and on the other his room, a kind of lumber room, where he worked and slept. On hot days you could suffocate at this dacha, and when it was wet, you'd shiver to the marrow of your bones from the dampness and the wind that blew through the cracks in the floor and walls.[82]

This austere lifestyle (not, let it be said, adopted by choice) became one of the emblems of the radical tradition of which Belinskii was the founding father.

## Suburbia Prefigured

Belinskii's dacha experiences reflect a wider trend whereby dachas in St. Petersburg's closer environs underwent a radical change in their function and character. Take the Koltovskaia district on the Petersburg Side, whose boundaries were the Karpovka to the north, the Zhdanovka to the southwest, and Bol'shoi Prospekt to the southeast. Briefly, in the 1820s the Koltovskaia was among the smartest dacha locations (note that it contained the dacha of Mariia Aleksandrovna Naryshkina, mistress of Alexander I). By the 1840s, however, it was mainly the preserve of middling and hard-up civil servants, whose poor living conditions and difficult rental arrangements formed commonplaces of popular journalistic accounts of the time.[83] The Petersburg Side as a whole had plunged down-

81. V. G. Belinskii, "Peterburg i Moskva," in his *Polnoe sobranie sochinenii,* 13 vols. (Moscow, 1953–59), vol. 8. Panaev quotes Ketcher making a similar distinction somewhat earlier, in 1839: "Well, do you have anything of the kind in Petersburg? Your dachas are wretched houses of cards on mud and marshland, but just look at the splendor here!" (*Literaturnye vospominaniia,* 167).

82. Panaeva, *Vospominaniia,* 164.

83. See, e.g., P. A. Karatygin's "Dom na peterburgskoi storone" (1838), where a "barn" (*sarai*) is described by a landlord on the Petersburg Side as "accommodation fit for a lord" (*barskii pokoi*); the landlord also draws attention to the property's dual function as main residence and dacha. See N. Shantarenkov, ed., *Russkii vodevil* (Moscow, 1970), esp. 147. Drafty low-rent Petersburg dachas were a favorite subject for the actor and stage hack Karatygin: note also the ditty extracted from his comedy *Peterburgskie dachi* (1848) in *Peterburg-Petrograd-Leningrad v russkoi poezii* (Leningrad, 1975), 118–19.

market since its early days, when Peter I built himself a palace there. In a contribution to
Nikolai Nekrasov's seminal almanac *The Physiology of Petersburg* (1845), E. P. Grebenka,
commenting on the "dacha mania" of the time, wrote:

> The richer people [get] farther away [from the city], but the poor folk head for the
> Petersburg Side; they say it's just the same as the country, the air there is clean, the
> houses are made of wood on the whole, there are plenty of gardens, it's close to
> the islands, and, above all, it's not far from the city. . . .
>
> Because of these considerations, all the houses and cottages, all the mezza-
> nines and attics are occupied by dacha folk; shopkeepers lay in three times more
> supplies than usual; on Klavikordnaia Street, which leads to the Krestovskii ferry,
> carts thunder along and countless traders and manufacturers take up residence;
> every evening the streets and alleys come alive with people out for a stroll, with
> crowds of colorfully dressed ladies and their gentlemen.

And a little later in his article Grebenka has this to say about the houses on the Petersburg
Side inhabited by dachniki and permanent residents alike: "Everywhere [you see] identical or almost identical little houses with or without mezzanines, front gardens with two
lilac bushes, or a yellow acacia."[84]

Several things catch the eye in this account: the opening up of the dacha to a less well
heeled public, the existence of such a low-grade dacha location so close to the elite areas of
Kamennyi Island and the Karpovka, and its amazing proximity to the city center. Another
noteworthy development is the intermeshing of the dacha with suburbia, both physically
(in the sense that the Petersburg Side was both a dacha settlement and a low-rent suburb,
and a single street could belong to both) and culturally (in the sense that these dachas,
with their front gardens, lilac bushes, and dark-green wallpaper with scenes from ancient
mythology, conform so closely to Western stereotypes of lower-middle-class life). In the
culminating passage of Grebenka's article, the petit bourgeois domestic impulse is taken
to an unsightly extreme: one resident of the Petersburg Side, determined to beautify his
front garden, diverts the contents of his drainpipes into a large barrel in order to create a
fountain—which spouts green water.[85]

Until the 1860s the Petersburg Side remained remarkably underdeveloped; its ad hoc
arrangement of streets was in striking contrast to the ordered planning of the city center,
on the other side of the river.[86] In 1864 the Koltovskaia district was finally paved, and the
roads became more or less passable. But the area had already acquired a quasi-bucolic
image that it could not properly shake off. In his epic of the 1860s, *Petersburg Slums*,
Vsevolod Krestovskii takes a break from his main themes (illegitimate children, fallen
women, night life in Petersburg dives) in order to show us the charming old Povetin
couple, who have lived in Koltovskaia forever, have their own kitchen garden and chick-

---

84. E. P. Grebenka, "Peterburgskaia storona," in *Fiziologiia Peterburga* (Moscow, 1991), 77, 80.
85. Ibid., 90.
86. For more detail, see V. N. Toporov, "Aptekarskii ostrov kak gorodskoe urochishche," in *Noosfera i khudozhestvennoe tvorchestvo* (Moscow, 1991).

54 ens, and lead a life of untroubled domesticity (quite an achievement in the nineteenth-century novel, especially in the Russian tradition). Koltovskaia has become gently run-down since the days when it was a luxury dacha location: it is now teeming with "numer-ous breeds of civil servant, from collegiate registrator to court counselor inclusive," who are divided into those rushing about their official business and those "resting in the bosom of their families after the end of their official career." The houses reflect the con-servative values of the population:

> little cottages, with three or five windows, with a mezzanine, with green shutters, the obligatory patch of garden and the dog chained up in the yard. In the windows with their prim curtains you'll see pots with a geranium, a cactus, and a Chinese rose, some kind of canary or siskin in a cage, in a word, wherever you turn, what-ever you look at, everything makes you think of a kingdom of peaceful, quiet, mod-est, family-based, patriarchal life.[87]

The image of dacha folk projected in the press overlapped to a significant extent with Krestovskii's depiction of the Petersburg Side. In newspapers of the 1850s the dachnik emerged as a cultural personage in his own right, characterized, in the more approving accounts, by modest, restrained tastes, by a sense of responsibility for his property, and by a concern for his family's well-being. Dacha dwellers did not require "salon-style com-fort"; all they needed was a small patch of land with a rowan tree. As usual, the Teutonic population was held up as the ideal of modest, well-ordered domesticity: a stroll through the German section of Krestovskii Island presented the visitor with "images of family tranquility, of peaceful home life, just like the cover illustration of *Gartenlaube*, which is the favorite publication of these dachniki."[88] In 1850, similarly, in the "Miscellany" section of *Sovremennik*, a journalist described wandering into Novaia Derevnia and finding a "huge row of miniature cottages with microscopic patches of garden."[89] His impression was corroborated by other writers of the time, for whom this location was the embodi-ment of a not altogether admirable neatness and orderliness.

A correspondent of the prominent newspaper *Sankt-Peterburgskie vedomosti* was in 1850 already able to say that the dacha was a tired theme for the feuilleton.[90] Another jour-nalist commented eleven years later that the humbler dachas should not be denigrated, as they brought much joy to the "laboring class of the Petersburg population."[91] Neither of these opinions was much heeded by the bulk of their colleagues in the city's newspapers and journals. By the early 1860s, dachas had received an extraordinary amount of verbal

---

87. V. Krestovskii, *Peterburgskie trushchoby: Kniga o sytykh i golodnykh* (St. Petersburg, 1867), 1:326–28.

88. I. Domosedov (pseud.), "Peterburg zarechnyi," in *Russkii illiustrirovannyi al'manakh* (St. Petersburg, 1858), 140, 151.

89. "Santimental'noe puteshestvie Ivana Chernoknizhnikova po peterburgskim dacham," *Sovremennik* 22 (1850), sec. 6, 60.

90. "Peterburgskaia letopis'," *SPb ved*, 6 June 1850, 501.

91. I. Chernoknizhnikov, "Novye zametki peterburgskogo turista," *Vek*, no. 24 (1861), 765.

punishment in the press; derogatory names attached to them included "houses of cards," "toothache resorts," "reservoirs of rheumatism," "undertakers' delight," and "sideshows of vanity."[92] These jocular designations were complemented by more serious apprehensions concerning the changing character of dacha settlements close to the city. As the censor Aleksandr Nikitenko noted in his diary for 1854: "I've grown awfully sick of Lesnoy Korpus. Everything has changed—the woods have been destroyed, the fields taken up with kitchen gardens, the population has grown, taverns have multiplied—in a word, it has turned into a wretched little town."[93] The outskirts of St. Petersburg were in the 1850s and 1860s becoming much more intensively developed for leisure purposes, and Isler's pleasure garden was fast being overtaken by a wide range of other entertainments, which included, for the lowbrow audience, Italian organ grinders, drunken bears, monkeys, and mouth organs.[94] If dacha locations were not derided for their conservative and bourgeois profile, they might be disdained as hotbeds of proletarian rowdiness.[95]

As the dacha became regularly the object of disparagement in the Petersburg press of the 1850s, so the dachnik tended to be treated as a figure of fun. Some of the stock characters created by the out-of-town feuilletonists were fanatical believers in the health-giving properties of water, air, and dew. Others were pretentious dacha owners who ruined the appearance of their homes by topping them with hideous cupolas and bedecking them with exotic fruits and flowers. Still others were ludicrous snobs whose aspirations to rusticity were allied to an obsessive concern with marks of social status.[96] In a vaudeville of 1850, a not overly wealthy civil servant is begged by his wife and three daughters to rent a place for the summer. A dacha, they argue, is essential to uphold the family's social prestige. But an inserted ditty puts their ambitions in an unflattering light:

> For a rich man or aristocrat
> It's no sin to live at the dacha,
> But for the likes of us
> It's quite strange and ridiculous.
> Look at the next man renting a shack
> Or some kind of barn
> And shouting self-importantly to his friend:
> Come and visit us *at the dacha!*

92. Ibid., 761.

93. Nikitenko, *Diary*, entry of 15 May 1854.

94. On street entertainments, see A. F. Koni, *Peterburg: Vospominaniia starozhila* (Petrograd, 1922), 76–77.

95. This was especially true of places just north of center with a high density of lower-class population. One such area was the much-derided Novaia Derevnia: see Domosedov, "Peterburg zarechnyi,"152. Gogol left a dismayed description of one of these *gulian'ia* in a letter home to his mother (*Polnoe sobranie sochinenii*, 10:140).

96. Representative examples can be found in "Santimental'noe puteshestvie," *Sovremennik* 22 (1850), sec. 6, 177–257; Kniaz' Kugushev, "Stseny na chistom vozdukhe: Fotograficheskii snimok s natury," and A. Iaroslavtsev, "Na dache i na bale, eskiz iz pisem molodogo cheloveka," both in *Sbornik literaturnykh statei, posviashchennykh russkimi pisateliami pamiati pokoinogo knigoprodavtsa-izdatelia Aleksandra Filipovicha Smirdina* (St. Petersburg, 1859), 5:147–218 and 219–49, respectively.

Богачу, аристократу,
Жить на даче не грешно,
А уж нашему-то брату,
Как-то дико и смешно.
Вон, иной наймет лачугу,
Иль какой-нибудь сарай,
И кричит преважно другу,
К нам *на дачу* приезжай![97]

Far from providing the necessary restorative for overwrought urbanites, dachas were often little better than shanties for the Petersburg office proletariat. Instead of providing a genuine alternative to urban existence, they were inhabited largely by people who could never hope to escape the physical and moral pollution of the city. For the first time, but by no means the last, the dacha was finding itself compromised by the discrepancy between its apparent aspirations to healthful exurban gentility and the less than genteel realities of life on the fringes of the city.

THE INCREASED importance of the out-of-town house in the middle of the nineteenth century received its most telling recognition in the appearance of a new cultural stereotype: the dachnik. At best vaguely delineated in the urban imagination of the previous generation, dachas and their inhabitants now gained sharper definition. The first satirical depictions of dacha folk appeared in the 1840s and 1850s, but they were good-natured and lighthearted in comparison with the more serious disapprobation that would be dispensed by the intelligentsia in the later nineteenth century. If dachniki found themselves in drafty, unhygienic houses at no significant remove from the city, that did not make them morally culpable—just unfortunate, foolish, or misguided.

The negative stereotypes of out-of-town life that were projected in the Petersburg feuilletons should not, moreover, be allowed to obscure the many things the dacha had in its favor. It offered health benefits to the inhabitants of crowded and unsanitary cities and provided a much appreciated amenity for an urban population that was moving decisively in the direction of apartment living. It also stood in gratifying opposition to the values of order, formality, and hierarchy that were embodied in the Russian imagination by St. Petersburg. The dacha, by contrast with the capital city, presented a site for untroubled family life, for open-ended interaction within small social groups, and for genteel (but markedly nonaristocratic) pleasures. In this respect, it can be seen as analogous to various sites in the United States and Western Europe of the same period where bourgeois habits and identities were constructed and consolidated: spa towns, vacation resorts, affluent suburbs.

These parallels should not be taken too far, however. Russia differed from Western

---

97. D. Andreevskii, *Dachemaniia ili Razve my khuzhe drugikh?* held at St. Petersburg State Theater Library, Department of Manuscripts and Rare Books, I.38.2.33 (this quote on 6–7). Later in the play, the wife swoons stagily in order to have her way.

"bourgeois" societies (and the Western societies, let it also be said, differed from one another) in two important respects. First, in the pattern of its urban and exurban development. As Russia's major cities frayed at the edges, the dacha could no longer always be located safely on the far side of a sharp boundary between town and country. Other societies—notably the United States and England—were much more successful in creating and shoring up middle-class enclaves within a framework of high-speed urban expansion. Second, Russia differed in its social structures and ideologies. The middling urbanites who formed the dacha's largest constituency were a motley group whose most vocal spokesmen (often known as the intelligentsia) were becoming increasingly fractious and suspicious of any bourgeoisie that might coalesce under the watchful eye of an oppressive and autocratic state. The middle of the century may be regarded as a transitional period when the dacha gained by distancing itself from the upper-class entertainments of a slightly earlier age and thus positioning itself comfortably between the pompous court and the grimy city. By the 1870s this advantageous intermediate status was coming to seem extremely problematic, and by the end of the century it would be untenable, largely because it left the summerfolk unconnected to the vast rural world outside the court and the city. The history of the dacha was about to become a lot more complicated, contentious, and diverse.

# 3

## The Late Imperial Dacha Boom

In the 1850s, dachas were still an exciting symptom of the recent emergence in Russia of a nonaristocratic urban public. By the end of the century, this public was widely considered to have all but taken over the major cities; confirmation of the waning powers of the aristocratic elite was no longer required. Commentators on the dacha phenomenon happily abandoned all restraint. Like later historians of the Western European bourgeoisie, they spoke of inexorable expansion fueled largely by recruitment from lower social classes. One apparently overworked architect reflected in 1894:

> Who isn't looking to go to the dacha these days? From the petty shopkeeper, salesman, and member of a work cooperative right up to the rich banker, office director, and man of leisure inclusive—all of them, as soon as the first days of spring are upon them, dream of nothing but how to spend the summer outside the "dusty" city, at the dacha, in the "fresh air."[1]

So deserted were the central areas of St. Petersburg after the annual mass departure for the dacha that the police had to take special measures in the early 1880s to safeguard the property of absent residents. Local superintendents were required to compile a list of all the apartments where property had been left under the supervision of servants or caretakers (*dvorniki*); police officers were then expected to keep an eye on these addresses and caretakers to conduct inspections to check that locks to outside doors were intact.[2] Mstislav

---

1. K. Ia. Poluianskii, *Dachi: Temnye storony naemnykh dach i vygoda stroit' sobstvennye dachi* (St. Petersburg, 1894), 1.

2. *Alfavitnyi sbornik rasporiazhenii po S.-Peterburgskomu Gradonachal'stvu i Politsii, izvlechennykh iz prikazov za 1866–1885 gg.* (St. Petersburg, 1886), 110–11. These regulations went into force between 1879 and 1885.

Dobuzhinskii recalled of his childhood in the 1880s: "Petersburg was empty in summer, the 'gentlefolk' had all headed off to their dachas or to various foreign countries, and cooks, janitors, and maids became the masters of the city."[3]

The dacha boom of the last third of the nineteenth century was linked to several economic and demographic factors, not least the further development of the railways. The travel season reached its peak with the heavy dacha traffic in June and July, and the late nineteenth century saw a significant rise in the proportion of short trips (in 1894, 58 percent of passenger trips in the Russian Empire were of less than fifty versts).[4] Steam trains were supplemented by other forms of transport: Russia's first horse-drawn railway (in St. Petersburg) started operations in 1863, and its network was steadily extended during the 1860s and 1870s. The first experiments in using steam-driven trams took place in 1880, and in 1886 routes for regular traffic were opened.[5]

But if transport had an impact on the suburban and exurban development of the Moscow and Petersburg regions, it did so rather differently than in Western Europe. Russia still lagged behind in transport provision (the first electric trams in St. Petersburg, for example, did not start running until the late 1900s), and movement both within the city and from the city center to the outskirts was less easy than in Paris or London. Russian workers—both in offices and in less genteel employment—were tied to their workplaces to a much greater extent than their counterparts in Britain or France. These limitations of urban infrastructure, however, did much to stimulate the development of dacha settlements; that is, to make the city's inhabitants disposed to summer migration rather than to year-round residence in suburbia. Daily commuting was for the most part unfeasible, for reasons both of cost and of time, and as a result the city center became hugely overcrowded; the acceleration of population growth brought no corresponding expansion of the city's territory. Epidemics were rife, especially in the summer. In the second half of the nineteenth century, St. Petersburg was notorious as the least healthy yet most expensive capital in Europe.[6]

## What Was a Dacha?

If the social and geographical factors underlying the dacha boom seem clear enough, much less obvious is how we should begin to analyze the phenomenon; whether, indeed, it is possible to provide an elegant categorization of all the forms of dwelling that were called "dacha." The only existing book-length work on the subject advances a sensible typology of summerfolk settlement in this period.[7] First comes the "dacha suburb" (*dachnyi prigorod*), consisting of dachas that were built as part of an overall framework of

3. M. Dobuzhinskii, *Vospominaniia*, vol. 1 (New York, 1976), 31.

4. J. N. Westwood, *A History of Russian Railways* (London, 1964), 79.

5. See *Ot konki do tramvaia: Iz istorii peterburgskogo transporta* (St. Petersburg and Moscow, 1993).

6. An excellent account of St. Petersburg in the nineteenth century is J. Bater, St. *Petersburg: Industrialization and Change* (London, 1976), which discusses all these points in exhaustive detail.

7. See O. I. Chernykh, "Dachnoe stroitel'stvo Peterburgskoi gubernii XVIII–nachala XX vv." (dissertation, St. Petersburg, 1993), 1:38–43.

60 urban planning (such as St. Petersburg's Neva islands or towns within its orbit, such as Gatchina, Luga, and Sestroretsk) or that sprang up on a major estate or palace settlement within easy reach of the city (Peterhof, Oranienbaum, Pavlovsk, Tsarskoe Selo). This is the oldest form of dacha settlement: depending on how exactly the dacha is defined, it can be said to date from the 1710s or 1720s, but it had certainly made its appearance by the middle of the reign of Catherine II. Second, the "dacha village" (*dachnaia derevnia*) includes, quite simply, those villages where peasants and other property holders rented out their houses to city dwellers. Peasants in the St. Petersburg region were earning nonagricultural income of this kind from the beginning of the nineteenth century, if not before. The third category is the "dacha location" (*dachnaia mestnost'*). This is a form of settlement that has a strong dacha orientation (where many or even most houses were used as dachas) but that was not created with this function in view. Dacha locations were typically former villages (Beloostrov, Krasnoe Selo, Pargolovo, Toksovo) or estates (Dudergof, Kushelevka, Poliustrovo, Shuvalovo) or a combination of the two (Kuokkala, Raivola, Terioki). Finally, we have the "dacha settlement" (*dachnyi poselok*), designed specifically for recreational dacha use (Alesksandrovka, Vladimirovka, Vyritsa, Ol'gino, Siverskaia, Udel'naia, and many others): this phenomenon grew in significance toward the end of the nineteenth century, and it came into its own at the start of the twentieth.

Even a set of definitions as broad as this does not include everything that went under the name of "dacha" in the last third of the nineteenth century. It is fitted specifically to the dacha patterns of St. Petersburg guberniia and so does not even claim to reflect the trend for locations much farther from the city. People with the freedom and the inclination to absent themselves for the whole of the summer might rent a house in the country several hours away in remote corners of neighboring regions. In the early 1870s dachas might be located fifty versts or more from the nearest railway station. This new model of the dacha as a full-fledged summer retreat rather than as a temporary vacation cottage within easy reach of Moscow or St. Petersburg was exemplified by the habits of Fedor Dostoevsky. Recently returned from a lengthy period abroad, the writer spent the summer of 1872 in Staraia Russa, a medium-sized provincial town in Novgorod guberniia. In a letter to his sister he explained all the advantages of his decision: "It's cheap, it's quick and easy to move here, and finally, the house comes with furniture, even with crockery, the station has newspapers and journals, and so on." The Dostoevskys rented this house from a local priest; the following summer they chose a dacha owned by a retired lieutenant colonel that subsequently—in 1876—they bought outright. As Dostoevsky's wife reported, it was "not a town house, but rather took the form of a country estate, with a large shady garden, a vegetable garden, outbuildings, and cellar."[8]

After Dostoevsky's time, the spread of locations continued to expand and prices to come down. In the 1880s, for example, it was nothing out of the ordinary for Petersburg dachniki to venture far into Finnish territory, renting often rather modest houses in a long string of settlements that extended all the way to Vyborg. Muscovites were even more adventurous in their summer habits: for them the dacha concept had become broad enough to include houses near provincial towns such as Tver' and Rybinsk, or in distant

8. L. M. Reinus, *Dostoevskii v Staroi Russe* (Leningrad, 1969), 8, 36–37.

regions such as Ukraine. By the 1900s, moreover, newspapers carried a healthy sprinkling of advertisements for "dachas" in the Crimea, a location that was no longer by any means the preserve of pleasure-seeking high society.[9]

As well as expanding enormously, the dacha market became much more differentiated in the last third of the nineteenth century. Rented summer accommodations were sought by everyone from craftsmen to aristocrats; accordingly, dachas varied enormously in size, level of amenities, and cost. The humblest dachniki would have an annual income of just a few hundred rubles; solid "middle-class" salaries in the major cities began at around 1,000 rubles, while certain categories of professionals (university professors, the upper ranks of the civil service) might easily bring in more than 2,000 rubles, as well as enjoying additional perks such as free or subsidized apartments. Dacha prices for the season reflected this spread of incomes. They could be as low as 40 rubles for a peasant izba; they were typically in the range of 150 to 200 rubles for something a middling civil servant might consider respectable; the grander summer residences might cost 1,000 rubles or more.[10] By the 1880s, advertisements were found for modest dachas of as little as two rooms, some of them intended "for a solitary person"; at the top end of the market were spacious villas of twenty rooms or more; while a typical medium-sized family dacha might consist of six or eight rooms with modest servants' quarters and a couple of outbuildings. This many-layered stratification was reflected in new, more elaborate terminology adopted in many newspaper advertisements of the time. Rather than referring simply to a "dacha," they employed a range of compound nouns. Near the bottom of the range was a "dacha apartment" (*kvartira-dacha*), which in most cases comprised a few rooms rented in someone's house. A more private and spacious option was a "dacha house" (*dom-dacha*) or a "detached dacha" (*dacha-osobniak*). Tenants who wanted accommodations for use outside the summer months could rent a "winter dacha" (*zimniaia dacha*). Customers with more refined tastes might require a "lordly dacha" (*barskaia dacha*), while those with manorial aspirations could look for a "dacha estate" (*dachnoe imenie* or, less grandly, *usad'ba-dacha*).

The increasingly differentiated requirements of the dacha market are reflected in the articles and books on dacha design and construction that proliferated in the 1890s. Architects, like advertisers, began to employ subtle distinctions among the "dacha," the "house," the "dacha house," the "detached house," and even the "detached dacha house," with variations in price to match.[11] They also showed increasing awareness of the material constraints and other practical difficulties likely to be facing their customers, who by and

---

9. Generalizations in this and following paragraphs are based on a study of advertisements in *Peterburgskii listok, Vestnik Sankt-Peterburgskoi gorodskoi politsii, Moskovskii listok,* and *Russkoe slovo.*

10. On middling civil servants, see S. F. Svetlov, *Peterburgskaia zhizn' v kontse XIX stoletiia (v 1892 godu)* (St. Petersburg, 1998), 21–22. Indications of the price range for rented dachas can be found in guidebooks; e.g., N. Fedotov, *Opisanie i podrobnye plany dachnykh mestnostei po finliandskoi zheleznoi doroge* (St. Petersburg, 1886) (this is an especially valuable source, as the author apparently did not rely on newspaper advertisements but made inquiries directly of dacha owners and caretakers); and L. A. Feigin, *Sputnik dachnika po okrestnostiam Moskvy* (Moscow, 1888).

11. See, e.g., G. M. Sudeikin, *"Al'bom proektov" dach, osobniakov, dokhodnykh domov, sluzhb i t.p.* (Moscow, 1912), 7–9.

62    large represented an identifiably new type of dachniki: "working people who don't pos-
sess large financial resources and who therefore aim to build themselves a dacha or a
house as economically as possible."[12] Many such volumes of the 1900s contained detailed
advice on building materials and instructions on how to draw up agreements with contractors. The dacha neophyte would also be advised on interior and exterior decoration.
Indoors, wallpaper might be hung or patterns stenciled on the walls; for the outside, yellow was the recommended color.[13] Instructions were also given on the design of gates,
benches, pavilions, terraces, and verandas.[14]

From the early 1870s many traders addressed themselves specifically to the dacha consumer. The market in consumer goods included garden furniture, clothing, cutlery, and
bathroom appliances (with water closets, perhaps unsurprisingly, represented most
prominently). By the 1890s a much greater spread of goods was being offered, and emphasis was increasingly placed on modern convenience and functionality. General advertisements for furniture and baths were replaced by specifics: fold-away storage cup-
boards, electric bells, steel cutlery, nails, hammocks, bidets, "American trays," spades, and
coat hangers. Among the less functional goods offered were terra-cotta vases, ladies'
pelerines, and candleholders. The dacha gourmet might be tempted by hampers stuffed
full of delicacies such as olive oil from Provence and Scots porridge oats.

Life at the dacha was not, however, a consumer goods paradise; it entailed significant
practical difficulties. First among them was the ordeal of searching for a place to rent. By 1880
St. Petersburg had an agency dealing with dachas, but most people chose less formal channels: they simply went to a village or settlement where they wanted to spend the summer and
negotiated directly with potential landlords. The dacha search could, by all accounts, be a
time-consuming and frustrating business, but often it was unavoidable. Urbanites needed to
make a good choice, as in many cases the dacha would become a family's main or only residence over the summer months. To retain an expensive city apartment during the dacha season was a luxury that relatively few could afford. The tendency was, it seems, for cash-
strapped dachniki to spend longer and longer time in the country each summer so as to delay
their return to the urban rental market with its inflated prices.[15] But this practice made finding a new apartment, given the housing shortage in the major cities, even more problematic.
An editorial of 1912, for example, contrasted the "torment" of looking for an apartment in St.
Petersburg in the autumn with the ease of finding accommodations in a town in Ohio that
was much smaller but had an efficiently functioning real estate office.[16]

The difficulties did not end even after city dwellers had found a dacha to rent. They
then had to move their furniture and other possessions to their summer house. Departing
dachniki might hire movers—although, to judge by most accounts, they had few guaran-

---

12. V. Stori, *Dachnaia arkhitektura*, vol. 1, *12' proektov i smet deshevykh postroek* (St. Petersburg, 1907), 3.

13. A. I. Tilinskii, *Deshevye postroiki: 100 proektov, v razlichnykh stiliakh, dachnykh i usadebnykh domov,
sadovykh besedok, ograd, palisadnikov, kupalen, sadovoi mebeli* (St. Petersburg, 1913), 55–56. Similar is A.
Dal'berg, *Prakticheskie sovety pri postroike dach* (St. Petersburg, 1902).

14. P. Griundling, *Motivy sadovoi arkhitektury* (St. Petersburg, 1903).

15. See, e.g., K. Barantsevich, "Poslednii dachnik," in his *Kartinki zhizni* (St. Petersburg, 1902).

16. *Dachnitsa*, 15 June 1912, 1–2.

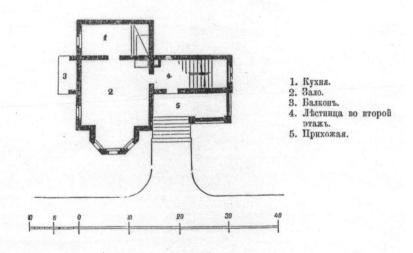

1. Кухня.
2. Зало.
3. Балконъ.
4. Лѣстница во второй этажъ.
5. Прихожая.

A modest design of the 1870s (from *"Arkhitekturnyi sbornik" sel'skikh postroek i modnoi mebeli* [Moscow, 1873])

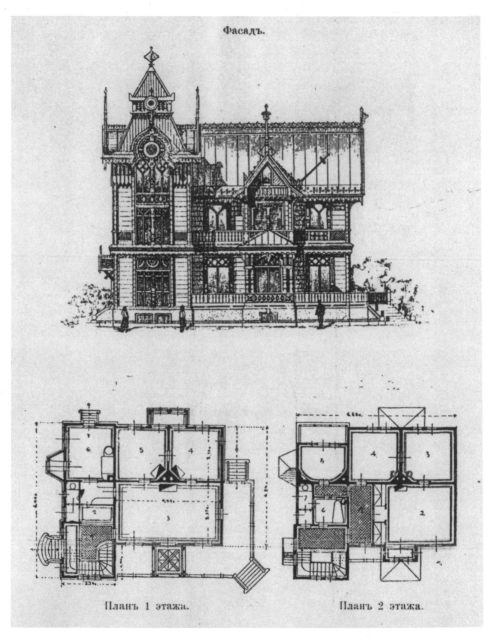

Фасадъ.

Планъ 1 этажа.　　　　　Планъ 2 этажа.

A more elaborate dacha of the late imperial era (from A. I. Tilinskii, *Deshevye postroiki* [St. Petersburg, 1913])

tees that their furniture would arrive intact. Journalists delighted in making puns on the term *lomovoi izvozchik* (which means moving carter, although "lom-" is the root of *lomat'*, "break").[17] To judge by newspaper reports and the advice dispensed in the press, dachniki did themselves no favors by piling their carts too high.[18] It was only the wealthier dachniki who could afford to leave much of their furniture behind in the city. A typical bourgeois or petit bourgeois family might rent unfurnished dachas in several locations over the years; only if their material situation became more secure did the spring ritual of moving out of town become less onerous.[19]

And then there was the problem of keeping the household running through the summer in the absence of an urban range of shops and services. To a large extent summer visitors were at the mercy of the local population, who were able to ask high prices for basic foodstuffs and services. Take the following description of a dacha landlord in the mid-1870s: "When renting the place out she promised everything you like—a laundry, a barn, an icehouse—but once she'd got the deposit and the money in advance, she didn't even begin to think that her tenants wouldn't find any of these things at her dacha."[20] In view of such cases, one household magazine urged dachniki to discuss the provision of basic services (laundry, firewood) in advance, and under no circumstances to rely on caretakers or watchmen. Summer visitors were also advised to check the details of their accommodations before arrival, as landlords—like landlords the world over—were liable to pass over in silence inconvenient details. Dacha owners liked to create more rooms for rent, and so more windows were installed and insulation deteriorated; the best safeguard against dank rooms was to heat the dacha through and give it an airing in advance of arrival.[21]

## The Growth of Dacha Settlements, 1860s–1890s

The main casualty of the dacha boom is often assumed to be the country estate. From well before Emancipation observers bemoaned the decline of the landowner lifestyle and its replacement, under economic pressure, by more densely populated forms of settlement. Regrets of this kind gathered force over time. When Anton Chekhov's Lopakhin purchased Ranevskaia's estate, complete with its cherry orchard, he was setting the terms

17. See, e.g., A. Miliukov, *Rasskazy iz obydennogo byta*, 2d ed. (St. Petersburg, 1875), 49–54.

18. See "Podgotovitel'nye rasporiazheniia pered pereezdom na dachu," *Domostroi*, no. 1 (1892), 2–3. An alternative was to put furniture in storage, a practice described in E. Mandel'shtam, "Vospominaniia," *Novyi mir*, no. 10 (1995), 126.

19. The financial advantages of moving from an expensive city apartment to a cheap dacha in a village outside Moscow are emphasized in M. Tikhomirov, "Detskie gody: Moskva i podmoskov'e," *Moskovskii arkhiv* 1 (Moscow, 1996): esp. 482–83. Tikhomirov, later a well-known historian, was born in 1893 into a petit bourgeois family: his father worked all his life for the Morozovs, a prominent late imperial family of entrepreneurs.

20. "Peterburgskie otgoloski," *PG*, 15 May 1875, 1.

21. "Podgotovitel'nye raporiazheniia." Well-to-do families would send an advance party of servants so as to give the house a thorough spring cleaning: see V.N. Kharuzina, *Proshloe: Vospominaniia detskikh i otrocheskikh let* (Moscow, 1999), 268. Kharuzina (born in 1866 into a prosperous merchant family) is here recalling the 1870s.

66  for much subsequent discussion of the "decline" of the Russian nobility in the second half of the nineteenth century. Opinions differ on the nature of this decline—it is unclear, for example, whether the sale of estates by noble families should be seen as a symptom of socioeconomic crisis or as a rational response to changing economic conditions after 1861— but its role in furthering dacha entrepreneurship is undeniable.[22]

On occasion the development of new dacha settlements did conform to the *Cherry Orchard* model. One example was Koz'ma Soldatenkov (nicknamed Koz'ma Medici), who bought the Naryshkin estate at Kuntsevo in 1865 and promptly started renting out plots of land to wealthy merchant families.[23] But other scripts were also possible. Most merchants were nowhere near as wealthy as Lopakhin or Soldatenkov, and bought themselves quite small plots of land that met only the needs of their own extended family. And well-to-do urban families might lease land directly from a village in order to build themselves country retreats. One example was the merchant and Old Believer Sergei Karlovich Rakhmanov, who in 1870 built a dacha for his son in Dunino, a village in a scenic spot at the western end of Moscow guberniia. The son subsequently married the manager of the Rakhmanov dachas in the village. The house of Rakhmanov *fils* had around ten spacious rooms; it also had a room for a live-in servant and came with several outbuildings. Sergei Karlovich's own dacha next door was even grander: in Soviet times it served as several discrete family dwellings. By the 1900s the village existed primarily to service the dachniki, who had taken the most picturesque sites overlooking the river.[24]

Noble families, too, could show themselves to be alert to the commercial possibilities of their holdings. In the 1850s and 1860s, for example, landowners along the Nikolaevskaia railway line (between Moscow and St. Petersburg) were so keen to clear their land for sale that they met peasant resistance.[25] The Nikolaevskaia line was subject to particularly intensive development, as land tended to be cheaper there than in traditional dacha locations.[26] Another major focus for development was the Northern line from Moscow to Sergiev Posad, which opened in 1861. Pushkino, for example, became a thriving dacha colony in little more than a couple of years. Muscovites with spare cash were encouraged to build by the opportunity to obtain land on a ninety-five-year lease for 24 rubles per year per desiatina (a separate but lower charge was made for the forested land that dachniki were entitled to use).[27]

Dacha entrepreneurship, on various scales, was also encountered in more heavily de-

22. For two well-researched but, in the conclusions they draw, radically opposed studies of the post-Emancipation nobility, see R. Manning, *The Crisis of the Old Order in Russia* (Princeton, 1982), and S. Becker, *Nobility and Privilege in Late Imperial Russia* (De Kalb, Ill., 1985).

23. M. Gavlin, *Rossiiskie Medichi: Portrety predprinimatelei* (Moscow, 1996), 75. A similar example was Liublino, an estate that was bought by a merchant in mid-century and developed as a dacha settlement: see K. A. Aver'ianov, "Liublino," in *Istoriia sel i dereven' podmoskov'ia XIV–XX vv.*, vol. 2 (Moscow, 1993), 69.

24. Details in this paragraph are drawn from conversations with the present inhabitants of these dachas, who are for the most part descendants of the original owners.

25. G. V. Il'in, "Zelenograd (vozniknovenie i razvitie)," *Russkii gorod* 5 (1982): 40.

26. G. Znakomyi, *Dachi i okrestnosti Peterburga* (St. Petersburg, 1891), 44.

27. S. Smirnov, *Putevoditel' ot Moskvy do Troitskoi Sergievoi Lavry* (Moscow, 1882), 10–11.

The dacha of Rakhmanov *fils*

veloped locations nearer the city. In 1877, 1878, and 1882 the family of the young Alexandre Benois (subsequently a renowned artist of the fin de siècle) was at the Kushelev-Bezborodko dacha, formerly one of St. Petersburg's elite suburban residences, which had just recently been sold off in lots; the previous owners had built a few villas in the grounds "partly for their own house guests and partly to let." The dacha dwellers had as their immediate neighbors an English cotton factory, a paper factory, a brewery, and a rope factory (which had been started up by Benois's uncle); the largest dacha on the site was rented as a community center for foreign workers at the rope factory. So Benois had as the aural backdrop to his summer vacation "a single, not unpleasant, blur of sound that resembled the noise of a waterfall."[28]

Owners of medium-sized and large estates in the Petersburg area found a wide variety of ways to generate income. Besides selling agricultural produce, they might earn money by providing a range of services and by renting out all manner of buildings: inns, mills, factories, and of course dachas. It was a rare estate that did not have at least a handful of houses for rent during the summer. Thus in 1886 Count Stenbok-Fermor used his estate of 4,148 desiatinas at Lakhta as follows: a total of twenty dachas were rented out; four houses were leased as inns for 760 rubles annually; one other house was rented as two shop premises; a bowling alley generated 750 rubles; sand was sold for 142 rubles; rights to fish and to collect fruit and mushrooms were also sold; finally, smithies and a raft for laundresses brought in 80 and 50 rubles respectively. The 385 desiatinas owned by Count-

28. A. Benois, *Memoirs,* vol. 1 (London, 1988), chap. 11.

68 ess Orlova-Denisova at Kolomiagi had, albeit on a more modest scale, a similar range of commercial functions that included nine dachas rented out for a total of 1,735 rubles each summer.[29]

Changes in nineteenth-century dacha life on private estate lands are well illustrated by the case of Pargolovo, part of the Shuvalov estates to the north of St. Petersburg. Pargolovo became known as a faintly bohemian place in the 1830s, when students from St. Petersburg University would go there for noisy parties in the woods. Dacha life proper began around the same time, when the area began to attract significant numbers of summer visitors. Entertainments—boating, riding, fishing—were laid on by the owners of the estate, while food and accommodations were provided by the local peasants: "Not much tilling of the soil goes on here, and peasants mostly make a living by selling firewood and coal, as cab drivers, and by renting out their homes, as numerous inhabitants of Petersburg move here for the summer and all houses without exception get taken."[30] Then and afterward, although its clientele became extremely varied, Pargolovo had a reputation as a place for intellectuals of modest means. In 1845, for example, Vissarion Belinskii lived there; from 1878 to 1906 the renowned arts critic Vladimir Stasov rented each summer the same peasant-owned house in a village half an hour's walk from Pargolovo; and the composer Nikolai Rimsky-Korsakov was married in a church in the Shuvalov park. The population in 1882 was described as "tens of thousands of protean, variegated, but at any rate intelligentsia people."[31]

The construction of the Finland railway line, completed in 1870, marked a new stage in the history of Pargolovo. Hitherto land in the prime dacha territory around the lakes had been rented out by the Shuvalov family on thirty-year leases.[32] Now, however, it became potentially much more profitable and amenable to larger development. In 1877 it was decided to sell the land not as individual plots but in one chunk of over fifteen desiatinas. A company of seventy shareholders bought up this territory for 350,000 rubles. Other parts of the estate were given over to commercial development and rapidly subdivided for sale. The result was a series of densely populated summer settlements (including also Shuvalovo and Ozerki; Pargolovo itself was divided into three settlements—Pargolovo I, II, and III) made up of "several hundred dachas of varying size, from enormous, three-story buildings of the most fanciful rather than splendid architecture to hovels

---

29. *Materialy po statistike narodnogo khoziaistva*, vol. 16, *Chastnovladel'cheskoe khoziaistvo v S.-Peterburgskom uezde* (St. Petersburg, 1891), 26–31.

30. V. Bur'ianov, *Progulka s det'mi po S. Peterburgu i ego okrestnostiam* (St. Petersburg, 1838), 3:196. A similar but less informative account is I. Pushkarev, *Putevoditel' po Sanktpeterburgu i okrestnostiam ego* (St. Petersburg, 1843), 465–66.

31. "Chto ob nas govoriat i pishut?" *PLL*, 6 June 1882, 2–3. The population of Shuvalovo (the lakes and Pargolovo I) was in 1881 estimated to be 30,000; in Pargolovo II there were 277 male property owners and in Pargolovo III 141. See *Peterburgskie dachnye mestnosti v otnoshenii ikh zdorovosti* (St. Petersburg, 1881), 21–22.

32. The terms of leases varied significantly from one location to another: for lands in private ownership a typical period was twenty-five or thirty years, but further conditions could be imposed. Dacha plots at the estate of Levashevo (north of St. Petersburg) had to be not less than half of one desiatina in area, and on this land only one dwelling could be built; for this reason, the take-up rate in the 1880s was much lower than in Pargolovo or Shuvalovo (see Fedotov, *Opisanie*, 54–57).

thrown together quickly from barge timber."[33] The pace of development in the northern suburbs of St. Petersburg is shown by the profitability of the Finland railway: the part of the line that ran through Russian territory (as far as Beloostrov) had receipts of 93,000 rubles per verst in 1897, while the more remote Finnish section was bringing in just 7,967 per verst.[34] Petersburgers were attracted to buy plots here by the good transport links to the city, by the promise of unspoiled landscapes (Pargolovo was billed as "the Russian Switzerland"), and by perks such as street lighting and watchmen paid for by the company.[35] The Petersburg press reported in 1880 that Samson'evskii Prospekt, leading north toward Pargolovo through the Vyborg Side, was crammed full of cartloads of furniture heading for the dacha. Land prices were going up accordingly, from 2.25 rubles per square sazhen to as much as 6 in Ozerki. The company formed to manage the Shuvalov dacha territories decided to raise the price of unsold land further, to pay a dividend of 10 percent to shareholders, and to provide electric lighting in Ozerki.[36]

The plots at Shuvalovo varied in area from around 400 square sazhens to well over 1,000. Several buildings were usually found on them: a main residence, a laundry, a stable, a cellar, a woodshed, and a kitchen. Usually there was room for more than one residential building.[37] Servants might be accommodated in a small room in the main house or in a separate building. The social profile of applicants for planning permission was quite varied. For the most part, they were located in Russian society's amorphous middle (civil servants, general majors, honored citizens), but there were peasants too.[38]

The social breadth of Pargolovo and its adjoining settlements became a stereotype of the time. It is stressed in D. N. Mamin-Sibiriak's *Features from the Life of Pepko*, a novel recounting the adventures of two students (the narrator, Popov, and his friend Pepko) who are trying to make careers as writers in the early 1870s. Popov has been confined to St. Petersburg for the last two summers, and this year he still does not have the money to go home and visit his family. But, inspired by Pepko's can-do attitude, he joins his friend in taking a suburban train out north to Pargolovo III, the remotest and cheapest of the three Pargolovo settlements. Their means are so limited as to make them extremely implausible dachniki: their Petersburg landlady bursts into convulsive laughter when she is told their plans for the summer. On the way to Pargolovo they pass through a number of unglamorous dacha settlements (among them Udel'naia), but Popov finds even these uplifting:

33. V. N. Sveshnikova, "Liniia Rikhimiaki–Sankt-Peterburg Finliandskoi zheleznoi dorogi (ot Sankt-Peterburga do Beloostrova)," in *Pamiatniki istorii i kul'tury Sankt-Peterburga: Sbornik nauchnykh statei*, ed. A. V. Kornilova (St. Petersburg, 1994), 39–40. The statutes of the dacha company (*tovarishchestvo*) were published in *PSZ*, ser. 2, 52, no. 57577 (16 July 1877); the founders were high-ranking civil servants and members of the military and of the first and second merchants' guilds.

34. Sveshnikova, "Liniia," 35.

35. Znakomyi, *Dachi*, 53–54.

36. "Nachinaiushchaiasia dachnaia zhizn'," *PL*, 12 Apr. 1880, 2–3.

37. This fact will receive confirmation in the later account of the 1920s, when Soviet authorities found most residents of suburban settlements to own multiple dachas and confiscated their surplus property.

38. RGIA, f. 1424, op. 2, d. 241 (Plany zemel'nykh uchastkov i stroenii raznykh lits v myze Shuvalovo, 1880–1910).

70 "So here were the first dachas with their run-down quaintness, their puny little gardens, and their modest desire to create the appearance of an untroubled refuge for simple dacha happiness. But I like these dachas that are cobbled together out of barge timber and remind you of birdhouses."[39] Arriving at Pargolovo III, the two friends discover that it is much more a village than a dacha settlement (by 1894, the time the novel was completed, it had been much more intensively developed as a summer destination). Popov and Pepko rent a no-frills izba for the fantastically low price of 10 rubles for the season. Their experiences tally with the (admittedly far from neutral) journalistic accounts of the time, which described Pargolovo as a dreary backwater whose few attractions—horseback riding, rowing, country walks, fresh milk—were quickly exhausted.[40]

Privately owned estate lands were not, however, the only source of dacha plots. From the middle of the nineteenth century land owned by the state and directly by the imperial family (the latter known as *udel'nye zemli,* or appanage lands) were increasingly made available for such purposes. A law of 1850 specified the procedures whereby state land could be transferred into individual ownership; that is, by a kind of hereditary lease called *chinsh.*[41] Ten years later the availability of *chinsh* land was extended to the Moscow dacha areas of Sokol'niki (twenty-seven plots) and Shiriaevo Pole (seventeen). Regulations were fairly strict: residents were not allowed to engage in commercial activities and were forbidden to build high fences around their houses, which, it was emphasized, should have a "decent appearance." But they were also given twenty years' exemption from property taxes and from responsibility for upkeep of the road, and the right to roam freely on the surrounding lands as long as they caused no damage.[42]

The effects of an increasingly dynamic property market fed by various sources—private estates, state land, palace land, appanage land—soon made themselves felt. By the mid-1860s, patterns of ownership were looking somewhat fragmented. An 1865 survey of St. Petersburg uezd listed 455 dacha owners, classified mainly as merchants and civil servants, most of them with relatively small landholdings (under ten desiatinas). These plots of land tended to have not one building but several (typically, between five and ten), many

39. D. N. Mamin-Sibiriak, *Cherty iz zhizni Pepko,* in his *Sobranie sochinenii,* 10 vols. (Moscow, 1958), 8:306. The barge timber detail shows the derivative nature of the description.

40. For a small selection, see *Putevoditel' po S.-Peterburgu, okrestnostiam i dachnym mestnostiam s planom stolitsy, imperatorskikh teatrov i tsirka* (St. Petersburg, 1895), 135; N. A. Leikin, *Neunyvaiushchie Rossiiane* (St. Petersburg, 1912), 181–91, and *PG,* 22 May 1875, 3.

41. *PSZ,* ser. 2, 25, no. 24207 (5 June 1850). *Chinsh* was formerly an equivalent of quitrent for the Polish-Lithuanian nobility that allowed for a much more legally defined and guaranteed set of property rights than did the Russian *obrok.* It can be seen as analogous to legal arrangements made in Western Europe (e.g., the German *Erbzinsrecht*) to institute a nonfeudal system of property: by allowing nonnobles access to landownership it was possible to settle vacant lands and to revitalize economies that had become disastrously inefficient under serfdom (see the entry in *B&E,* vol. 38). A classification of the various types of ownership possible under late imperial law is to be found in I. D. Mordukhai-Boltovskii, *Svod zakonov Rossiiskoi Imperii* (St. Petersburg, 1912), vol. 10, bk. 2, arts. 406–15.

42. *PSZ,* ser. 2, 35, no. 35415 (5 Feb. 1860). Similar restrictions were enforced for residents of Kamennyi Island, which was under the direct authority of the imperial court: see ibid, 34, no. 34446 (2 May 1859). For more on the development of Sokol'niki as a dacha location in the nineteenth century, see A. V. Bugrov, "Sokol'niki," *Istoriia sel i dereven' podmoskov'ia XIV–XX vv.,* vol. 10 (1995), esp. 20–21.

of which were presumably rented out as summer houses.[43] The number of minor dacha owners increased rapidly in the 1880s and 1890s as the leasing of state lands for private cultivation and property development continued with greater intensity. Large territories within reach of the city might be divided up into dozens or hundreds of plots, typically of 500 or 600 square sazhens. Tenants would sign a lease, often for twenty-five years, and make an annual payment of 20 or 30 rubles for rental of the land. The bulk of such tenants were categorized in the official records as civil servants, merchants, and military men, but there were also tradespeople, artisans, and peasants. The sizes of individual holdings varied significantly, from one plot to several bunched together. Very often a single plot contained more than one building fit for habitation—surely an indication that many of these dachas were built to be rented out. The most common description was "single-story wooden dacha," usually priced for taxation purposes between 1,500 and 2,500 rubles.[44]

A detailed survey conducted in the late 1880s revealed a great increase in the number of minor property owners since the 1860s. In St. Petersburg uezd, for example, the number of private landowners had risen from 419 in 1864 to 1,385 in 1877–78 to 3,391 in 1889, while the amount of land in private ownership had not grown correspondingly; rather, it had decreased since the 1870s as the city expanded. The class structure of ownership remained largely intact: the major landholdings were still overwhelmingly in the hands of the nobility (which, in 1889, owned 86 percent of private land, as compared to 96 percent in 1865). But the market for smaller plots was lively, fueled by the sale of parcels of land from large noble estates. Most landowners had small holdings (less than ten desiatinas), and very many such people had a few dachas for rent. These dwellings would remain as the staple of the summer housing market even after the turn of the century, when large-scale dacha entrepreneurship really took off.[45]

## Peasants and the Dacha Industry

As transport links improved and more and more villages and settlements in the Moscow and St. Petersburg regions were colonized by dachniki, these outlying areas came increasingly to be oriented toward the capitals and their annually migrating population. The dacha market was, as ever, greatly expanded by the contribution of peasants, who readily made their izbas available for rent to summering city folk; for rural people who lived within reach both of St. Petersburg and the sea, the dacha industry was commonly their most important source of income.[46] The wealthier peasants would plow their surplus money into dacha construction, and even the poorer families in the Moscow and Petersburg regions could accommodate paying guests by clearing out of their izbas and living in a barn for the summer months. Usu-

43. P. Neigardt, ed., *Spisok zemel'nykh vladenii S.-Peterburgskogo uezda* (St. Petersburg, 1865), 38–91.

44. Details of one case, the territory of the appanage farm (*udel'naia ferma*) outside St. Petersburg, can be found at TsGIA SPb, f. 1205, op. 12, dd. 369, 370.

45. *Materialy po statistike narodnogo khoziaistva*, esp. 97–99.

46. E. Amburger, *Ingermanland: Eine junge Provinz Rußlands im Wirkungsbereich der Residenz und Weltstadt St. Petersburg–Leningrad* (Cologne, 1980), 1:564. This volume has the best available account of St. Petersburg's dacha life from the point of view of a social and economic rather than cultural or architectural historian (see esp. 562–73).

72  ally city folk did not have to look too hard for rental opportunities of this kind, as a horde of dacha hawkers would descend on the first cart or train arriving with prospective summer visitors. Haggling was obligatory, and was often conducted not with the owners themselves but with truculent caretakers.[47] According to one memoir account, the dacha-renting procedure ran as follows: at Shrovetide dachniki would arrive at the local station, where peasants would be waiting to offer them a ride into the settlement. During the cab ride the peasant would try to sell his own izba or that of a family member; if the passenger asked to stop and look at other dachas, the peasant would do everything to prevent him from doing so, saying, "It's no good here: the landlady is a nag and it's full of bugs." Eventually the two parties would negotiate a price and get to know each other better over tea and vodka.[48]

The more active involvement of some peasants in the dacha industry was in large part a result of the greater economic independence they enjoyed after the Emancipation of 1861. By the mid-1860s, many peasants enjoyed formal legal ownership of a plot of land, and on this land, especially in the more densely populated regions, they might well decide to build new dwellings.[49] While these houses were anything but places of leisure, they served to change peasants' outlook in ways that have significance for the subsequent history of the dacha: for a section of the village population the izba became not simply a building that enabled them to exercise their age-old right to work the land but a piece of property implying new rights and status.[50]

Changes in legal status were not, moreover, the only factor in fostering new proprietary instincts in villages within the orbit of the major cities. Emancipation had also brought an increase in labor mobility and a slight weakening of the traditional communal way of life. New attitudes toward housing were particularly evident in villages with a large proportion of migrant urban wage earners (*otkhodniki*), where the multigenerational patriarchal household was coming under strain and members of the younger generation were more likely to peel off and build their own homes. These villages were, in general, closer to the city and hence better able to take advantage of nonagricultural economic opportunities. For those peasants who had made good in the city and returned to the village in middle age to take on their patriarchal responsibilities, urban styles and standards of housing were highly desirable. Windows and metal roofs were added; the izba interior was partitioned to create new rooms.[51]

---

47. See V. O. Mikhnevich, *Peterburgskoe leto* (St. Petersburg, 1887), 22–25.

48. D. A. Zasosov and V. I. Pyzin, *Iz zhizni Peterburga 1890–1910-kh godov: Zapiski ochevidtsev* (Leningrad, 1991), 181.

49. The extent of peasant ownership of houses in the St. Petersburg region is suggested in Neigardt, *Spisok zemel'nykh vladenii.*

50. The new trend is reflected in a pattern book of 1853 that includes designs for "prosperous" and "rich" peasants: see *Atlas proektov i chertezhei sel'skikh postroek* (St. Petersburg), figs. 18 and 28. The importance of the new peasant householder is reflected in later do-it-yourself building books: F. N. Korolev's *Rukovodstvo k vozvedeniiu v selakh ognestoikikh zdanii* (St. Petersburg, 1880), which proved popular enough to have sold out by the publication of the same author's *Sel'skoe stroitel'noe iskusstvo* (St. Petersburg, 1887).

51. See J. Burds, *Peasant Dreams and Market Politics: Labor Migration and the Russian Village, 1861–1905* (Pittsburgh, 1998), 160–63.

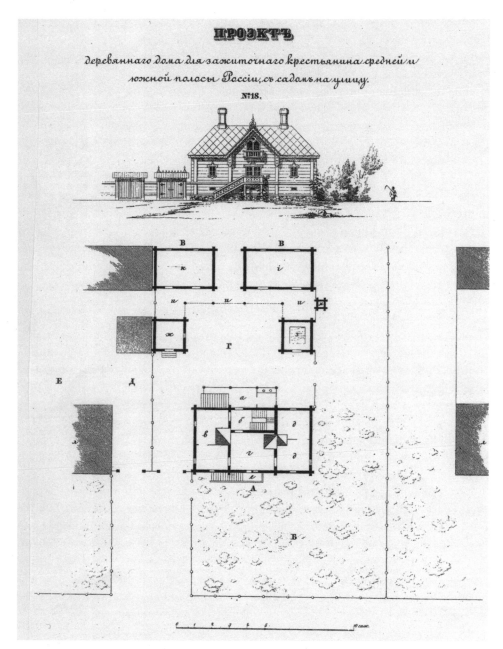

A house for a "prosperous peasant" in the central and southern regions of Russia (from *Atlas proektov i chertezhei sel'skikh postroek* [St. Petersburg, 1853])

74    This view of the home as a new economic unit, not exclusively agricultural, led peasants to service the expanding dacha market by making their houses available to city folk. Along the Northern line out of Moscow, for example, rural communities catered explicitly to summerfolk by raising the level of comfort in their dwellings, planting flowers and trees, leveling the path from the station to the settlement, offering their services as cab drivers, and opening boating stations.[52] By the 1880s and 1890s, "suburban" peasants were observed to be building dachas "very actively, as far as their means allow."[53] In 1887, 1,560 peasants in the Petersburg region were estimated to be renting out their property, around 400 in Pargolovo volost and over 600 in the Staraia Derevnia district.[54] The high representation of these areas points both to their undoubted importance in the summer residency patterns of the St. Petersburg population but also, perhaps, to the failure of the researchers to look in proper detail at less well-established locations (for example, those south of the city). It should also be assumed that many of the subjects in this survey were "peasants" in name only, and that they were actually earning wages in the city. Nonetheless, these statistics do begin to hint at the scale of "simple" families' involvement in the dacha economy.

## Urban Encroachment

The result of peasant involvement in the dacha market was not necessarily a ruralization of dacha life; "peasants" were by no means guaranteed to be laborers in agricultural communities. Increasingly common on the outskirts of Moscow and Petersburg were "dacha" settlements that contained artisans and tradespeople as well as summer visitors. A survey of Moscow guberniia at the turn of the nineteenth century commented: "There are rather a lot of population centers of this kind, which are not peasant settlements but which cannot be considered urban either, which are composed of a group of households connected by many common interests, both economic and social, but which have no form of public administration, no organization to oversee them."[55]

The extension of urban settlement affected the character not only of peasant communities. Back in the 1840s, writers of the "physiological" school were observing that the northern districts of St. Petersburg (the Petersburg and Vyborg Sides) were turning into low-rent suburbs. From the 1860s on this state of affairs became even more pronounced. The shortage of cheap housing in the city center ensured that many of the wooden dacha-type houses on the islands and the Vyborg Side were occupied year-round.[56] Former green-belt areas had in effect become slums. According to one sketch of the 1870s, the previously well-to-do Karpovka was now "the poorest part of the city," inhabited "primarily by low-ranking civil servants." During the winter these unfortunates huddled to-

---

52. See V. N. Arseev, N. S. Lepeshkin, and A. S. Livshits, "Mamontovka," *Istoriia sel i dereven' podmoskov'ia XIV–XX vv.*, vol. 3 (Moscow, 1993), 119.

53. Poluianskii, *Dachi*, 6.

54. Amburger, *Ingermanland*, 569–70.

55. *Moskovskaia guberniia po mestnomu obsledovaniiu, 1898–1900 gg.*, vol. 1 (1903), x.

56. See Bater, *St. Petersburg*, 156–57.

gether in dachas, paying little or no rent for the privilege, as owners were only too glad to have someone to keep an eye on their property. Often bachelors moved in with a married friend and split the costs of the household; at times they were reduced to fishing bits of wood out of the river or to filching it from neighbors' fences in order to keep warm. In the dacha season these young men gave way to the dachas' owners, relocating to attics, barns, and empty stables. Sometimes they even slept out on the bank of the Karpovka.[57] The Petersburg Side in the 1860s and 1870s was recalled as being a place where people would live all year round in wooden houses and where the absence of domestic comforts was only partially compensated by the cleaner air.[58]

Dacha areas on the city's immediate outskirts had become decidedly seedy. Novaia Derevnia, not much favored by journalists at the best of times, was reckoned to be the preserve of hard-up civil servants and loose-living young people. The requirements of its population were reflected in the range of entertainments offered: operetta had forced out theater, inns had supplanted libraries, and *cafés chantants* had displaced the "delights of *ins Grüne*."[59] Isler's Mineral Waters, the institution to which Novaia Derevnia owed much of its original popularity, seemed tame by comparison with the forms of entertainment fashionable in the 1880s. The nearby Chernaia Rechka was fast becoming an insalubrious suburb for low-paid office workers. Houses were packed close together, brick dwellings were very few (although many residents spent the whole year there), and hygiene was dreadful (there was no proper sewage system and canals often smelled foul).[60] Nor were the smarter Neva islands invulnerable to change; the common perception was that they had been colonized by merchant families.[61] Even Kamennyi had "long since been democratized and just about the majority of its dachas have come into the possession of prosperous market traders."[62]

Other suburban districts were even less fortunate, being taken over by factories and overcrowded worker settlements. The example most frequently cited was the route leading along the south side of the Gulf of Finland—the Peterhof Road, where the modern dacha phenomenon had originated. The old-style dacha on the Peterhof Road was still alive in the 1870s, when advertisements for fifteen-room furnished residences with stables could still be found. The family of Alexandre Benois lived there for a couple of summers when Benois's father was a court architect. And Felix Krzesinski, successful dancer at the Aleksandrinskii Theater and the nineteenth century's most celebrated exponent of the mazurka, rented a dacha at Ligovo in the early 1870s.[63] By the 1880s, however, it was a

57. I. Kushchevskii, "Drabanty," in his *Malen'kie rasskazy* (St. Petersburg, 1875).

58. K. E. Kil'shtet, *Vospominaniia starogo Petrogradtsa* (Petrograd, 1916), 23–24.

59. Znakomyi, *Dachi*, 9–15. For more on Petersburg places of entertainment, see *Arlekin na dache: Letnii iumoristicheskii kalendar'* (St. Petersburg, 1888), and (also on the 1880s) A. Pleshcheev, *Pod sen'iu kulis* (Paris, 1936), 113–20.

60. *Peterburgskie dachnye mestnosti v otnoshenii ikh zdorovosti*.

61. P. K. Mart'ianov, "Nasha dachnaia idilliia," in *Lopari i samoedy stolichnykh nashikh tundr* (St. Petersburg, 1891).

62. Mikhnevich, *Peterburgskoe leto*, 74.

63. See M. Kshesinskaia, *Vospominaniia* (Smolensk, 1998), 14.

76  commonplace to associate the first section of the Peterhof Road—at least to the settlement of Avtovo—with urban squalor. The next section, leading to Krasnyi Kabachok, was
taken up with garden plots; it was only beyond Ligovo that uninterrupted woodland was
to be found—and even here almost all villages were densely populated by summerfolk.[64]
Ekaterinhof, although it retained in its restaurant traces of a more upmarket past, was
taken over on holidays by disorderly workers from the nearby factories, who formed a
"garish crowd with the cheapest pretensions to entertainments"; the air and the river
smelled foul, and a temporary hospital for infectious diseases was set up.[65] Settlements in
the Peterhof direction such as Volynkina were becoming little more than shanty sprawl
with inadequate sanitation and educational provision.[66]

The urbanization of traditional dacha locations from the 1860s on was also well attested in Moscow. Petrovskii Park, full of upper-class villas in the 1840s, was in the 1860s
becoming a "summer town" with direct connections to the city along the horse-drawn
tram lines; houses there were increasingly being used for year-round residence.[67] Kuskovo
had turned into "some kind of summer open-air inn"; and Ostankino was grubby and
overcrowded. Of Sokol'niki it was remarked in 1860 that "the transition from city to
noncity is imperceptible." The city's environs were poorly geared to the needs of families
of modest means, but they were amply provided with entertainments—firework displays,
orchestras, theaters.[68] The 1904 Moscow census was the first to include "suburbs" (*prigorody*) as a separate category; the population of these places was found to be over 82,000
(of whom more than 66,000 were categorized as peasants).[69]

## Exurban Property Development and Entrepreneurship, 1890s–1910s

Toward the end of the nineteenth century, the dacha industry reached a new level of
intensity as it began to receive organized state encouragement. In May 1896 the State
Council passed a law encouraging the long-term leasing of unoccupied state lands for the
construction of dachas. The land was to be rented out by auction, typically for a period of
ninety-nine years. Apart from paying rent and taxes, leaseholders were obliged to erect all
buildings stipulated in their original application within three years. Every twelve years the
amount of rent paid could be reviewed, but any increase was not to exceed 5 percent. This

64. See, e.g., "Potolkuemte, chitatel'," *PL*, 27 Apr. 1880, 1.

65. "Iz dachnykh mest," *PL*, 22 May 1880, 3, and 29 June 1880, 3.

66. "Iz dachnykh mest," *PL*, 19 July 1880, 3. A gloomy assessment of the health risks of dacha areas (including industrial pollution) is *Peterburgskie dachnye mestnosti v otnoshenii ikh zdorovosti*.

67. See S. M. Liubetskii, *Moskovskie okrestnosti, blizhnie i dal'nie, za vsemi zastavami, v istoricheskom otnoshenii i v sovremennom ikh vide, dlia vybora dach i gulian'ia* (Moscow, 1877), 17–18.

68. For examples of contemporary journalism, see "Gorodskaia khronika," *Razvlechenie*, no. 25 (1860);
"Moskovskii nabliudatel'," *Razvlechenie*, no. 23 (1866); N. Skavronskii, "Nashi dachi," *Razvlechenie*, no. 28
(1866). Overviews of prerevolutionary dacha settlements around Moscow can be found in *Vsia Moskva na ladoni*
(Moscow, 1875); Liubetskii, *Moskovskie okrestnosti; Vseobshchii putevoditel' i spravochnik po Moskve i okrestnostiam*, 4th ed. (Moscow, 1911).

69. *Perepis' Moskvy 1902 goda*, pt. 1 (Moscow, 1904). St. Petersburg's "suburbs" had been included in census
figures somewhat earlier, in 1881.

initiative led to quick results in several gubernii besides Moscow and St. Petersburg: Voronezh, Kiev, Tula, Tomsk, and others.

The policy had obvious advantages for the public purse, as it was a highly profitable use of state lands (the average annual rent was 196 rubles per desiatina), but it was a success with dachniki too. By the middle of 1900, 963 dacha plots had already been created as a result of the May 1896 law, and many more applications had been received.[70] By 1903, dacha plots had been created in fifty-two locations in eighteen gubernii; in total they were bringing in 75,000 rubles annually.[71] As usual, however, the provision of basic services was lagging behind the pace of dacha development, which in some locations led to a sharp decline in demand for land.[72] In 1901 the Forestry Department raised the problem with the State Council, arguing that, although the state would still have to meet certain basic expenses (such as surveying and the drainage of land), residents of a settlement should be required to contribute to the costs of providing basic infrastructure. The money thus received should be specially earmarked for the needs of the settlement: it should not just disappear into the state budget. This condition was accordingly written into the statutes of many dacha settlements. Even so, the State Department of Economics decided by 1903 that the state had to make a greater contribution.[73]

The high speed of sale and distribution of land for construction marked out the 1900s as a qualitatively new stage in the dacha's history. Dachas were now becoming part of a large-scale "industry" that operated cheap resorts at a conveniently short distance from the city. A case in point was the Sestroretsk settlement on the Gulf on Finland, which was enlarged by land made available by the Ministry of Agriculture and State Property in 1898.[74] In 1900 the new territory had around one hundred dacha plots regularly laid out as well as several larger dachas (effectively summer camps) for children. On neighboring lands were agricultural plots belonging to locals.[75] As of 1903, Sestroretsk had 350 dachas and a total of 1,200 rooms, with the standard two-room accommodation costing between 60 and 80 rubles per month. Orchestras performed every day during the season, and the other entertainments included a casino.[76]

Nor was the state by any means the only initiator of dacha entrepreneurship. The intensive development by private owners of estate lands located on the outskirts of the major cities continued into the twentieth century. In 1899, A. D. Sheremetev owned 322

70. RGIA, f. 1152, op. 13, d. 108.

71. Ibid., d. 298, l. 2.

72. This had been a problem earlier when appanage lands had been leased: see TsGIA SPb, f. 1205, op. 12, d. 1401.

73. RGIA, f. 1152, op. 13, dd. 108 and 298, l. 5.

74. S. A. Simkina, "Dachi moderna na severnom poberezh'e Finskogo zaliva," in *Pamiatniki istorii i kul'tury Sankt-Peterburga: Issledovaniia i materialy*, vol. 4, ed. A. V. Kornilova (St. Petersburg, 1997), 341–42.

75. TsGIA SPb, f. 387, op. 11, d. 53368, l. 5. Contemporary reports suggest that local peasants resented the construction of dachas on land they considered should be theirs for pasture: see *Dachnik,* 20 May 1909, 2.

76. *Putevoditel' po dachnym okrestnostiam g. S.-Peterburga na 1903 god* (St. Petersburg, 1903), 41; G. Moskvich, *Prakticheskii putevoditel' po S.-Peterburgu i ego okrestnostiam* (Odessa, 1903), 285–88; O. Keller, *St. Petersburg and Its Environs, Finland, Moscow, Kiev, Odessa* (London, 1914), 98–99.

78  plots (typically of 600 square sazhens) in Mar'ina Roshcha that brought in a total of 26,000 rubles in rent over the year; his 262 plots in Ostankino were slightly less profitable, as the land was cheaper. Rent levels were fixed by custom (under the terms of *chinsh*), and so not commercially driven. In 1912, Sheremetev showed impatience with this state of affairs by submitting a petition claiming the right to demolish small rented dachas and replace them with income-generating large apartment buildings (*dokhodnye doma*).[77] A less acrimonious venture was undertaken in 1912 on the estate of Count Stenbok-Fermor at Lakhta, to the north of St. Petersburg. With the approval of the Ministry of Trade and Industry, 2,750 desiatinas of land at Lakhta was bought by a group of shareholders for 1.9 million rubles.[78] The company grew quickly, by all appearances: its balance sheet as of 31 December 1914 showed total assets of nearly 9 million rubles.[79]

The Lakhta company stated in its constitution that it would build in St. Petersburg guberniia "dacha settlements with the aim of making accommodations cheaper in combination with improvements in their variety and quality."[80] This provision points to an important aspect of property development in late imperial "dacha" locations: the summer hordes of dachniki were joined by increasing numbers of permanent residents.[81] To take just one example, Tsarskoe Selo was in 1886 only a very small town with just over 500 taxable properties (most of them with extensive outbuildings and gardens).[82] In 1895 the town was still of modest size: it numbered some 2,000 inhabitants.[83] By 1910, however, it had a permanent population of just over 30,000 (swelled by 7,000 in summer by the influx of dacha folk and summer workers).[84]

## Russia's Out-of-Town "Settlers"

Tsarskoe Selo provides a convenient illustration of a much broader trend. As early as 1891, it was estimated that 5,000 "dacha husbands" were commuting daily to work along the Finland line alone.[85] In the early 1900s appeared the first guidebooks that wrote about the dacha suburbs not from the point of view of native Petersburgers but from that of new arrivals to the city looking for a cheap and convenient place to live for the summer.[86] This depopulation of the central parts of Moscow and St. Petersburg was not caused by a yearning for fresh air; escalating housing costs in the city were driving people into new

---

77.  A.M. Anfimov, *Krupnoe pomeshchich'e khoziaistvo evropeiskoi Rossii (Konets XIX–nachalo XX veka)* (Moscow, 1969), 275.

78.  RGIA, f. 23, op. 12, d. 1722. Stenbok-Fermor retained his palace and surrounding land of sixty-one desiatinas.

79.  Ibid., op. 28, d. 1194, l. 7. The basic capital was 60,000 shares at 100 rubles each, released in two issues.

80.  Ibid., op. 12, d. 1722, l. 5.

81.  A further indication of winterization is the appearance of advice issued to "dachniki" on kitchen gardening (*ogorodnichestvo*): see M. R-ov, "Dachnye ogorody," *Dachnyi vestnik*, no. 1 (1899), 7–8.

82.  TsGIA SPb, f. 722, op. 1, d. 5.

83.  See *Putevoditel' po S.-Peterburgu* (1895), 122–25.

84.  S.N. Vil'chkovskii, *Tsarskoe selo* (St. Petersburg, 1911).

85.  Znakomyi, *Dachi*, 49.

86.  See F. Raevskii, *Peterburg s okrestnostiami* (St. Petersburg, 1902).

settlements. Old dacha places on the outskirts of these cities were becoming thoroughly suburbanized; such, for example, was the fate of Novaia Derevnia and Chernaia Rechka in the 1900s. Comments on crowding in Moscow locations such as Petrovskii Park were likewise frequently heard.

So prospective suburbanites looked to develop new territories. At Moscow's Losinoostrovskaia, a new station on the Iaroslavl' line was opened in 1898. The neighboring forest land (owned by the appanage administration) was chopped into plots (averaging one desiatina) that were leased out for thirty-six years. In the first few years of the settlement's existence almost all the plots were allocated and built on; houses for year-round habitation predominated. Residents thus solved two problems at once, acquiring an apartment and a dacha rolled into one and enjoying the opportunity to "live on quite large plots in the manner of a small landowner, with their own vegetable garden and orchard."[87] A society for the improvement of local services was formed in 1905, and new amenities quickly followed: street lamps, watchmen, squares, a summer theater, tennis courts, a telephone network, a local newspaper, a school, a postal service, a library, and a pharmacy.

New settlements such as Losinoostrovskaia aimed to avoid the urban blight that had infected Novaia Derevnia and other city outskirts adjacent to the center. In part they took their inspiration from the garden city movement, which had a growing public profile in Russia.[88] Confronted with ever worsening overcrowding in Moscow and St. Petersburg, some observers looked to Letchworth and Hampstead Garden Suburb for inspiration. As one journalist wrote, fresh from a trip to Britain, "it's not just for fresh air and greenery that people want to move to garden cities. They want more: a more integrated, friendly, straightforward life, less conflict, more institutions for the common good, new legal and economic forms."[89] The optimal size for a garden city was held to be 2,400 desiatinas, of which 400 desiatinas were to be built up and the remaining 2,000 were to provide a surrounding agricultural belt. Adopting a line of argument characteristic of Russian thinking in many fields, the first book-length treatment of Ebenezer Howard's ideas argued that Russia, by virtue of its late entry into modernity, could take advantage of the accumulated experience of urban planning in the West and integrate this experience into its own traditions of settlement.[90] Russia's characteristic small town (*malyi gorod*) made it especially suitable for the garden city: the prerevolutionary period abounded in planning proposals for pleasant green suburbs around major cities of the Russian Empire.[91] The small town, which for most of the nineteenth century had been a powerful symbol of backwardness, came to be regarded, improbably, as the cutting edge of urban development. The recep-

87. *"Losinoostrovskaia" i ee okrestnosti: Putevoditel' i spravochnaia kniga* (Moscow, 1913), 9.

88. Ebenezer Howard's *Garden Cities of To-morrow* was translated into Russian in 1904, and in 1913 a Russian garden city society was formed (it re-formed after the Civil War, in 1922).

89. D. Protopopov, "Goroda budushchego," *Gorodskoe delo*, no. 17 (1909), 855–56.

90. V. Semenov, *Blagoustroistvo gorodov* (Moscow, 1912).

91. See V. L. Ruzhzhe, "Goroda-sady," *Stroitel'stvo i arkhitektura Leningrada*, no. 2 (1961), 34–36. One of the first such projects was drawn up for the Stroganov lands just north of the Neva: see "Pervyi gorod-sad v Rossii," *Gorodskoe delo*, nos. 15–16 (1911), 1183–84.

80 tion and implementation of exurbanizing ideas varied from city to city in the Russian Empire. Of Nizhnii Novgorod, for example, it was written that "only very wealthy people go to the dacha. Run-of-the-mill folk are quite happy with the city parks."[92] But exurbia was by no means restricted to the Moscow and St. Petersburg regions: several other densely populated cities—Warsaw, Odessa, Kiev, for example—shared an interest in using out-of-town areas for summer habitation.[93]

The interest in exurbanizing projects brought with it a cult of English simplicity and practicality in house design. The new ideal of the pared-down *kottedzh* drew explicitly on foreign, mainly Anglo-Saxon, models. The Russians, it was commonly claimed, tended to overreach, to opt for surface grandeur rather than comfort, to give up domestic space for public entertaining, and to underequip the family's private quarters. They did not mold the domestic environment so as to meet the requirements of convenience and efficiency; they failed, for example, to understand that entrance halls, instead of presenting a formal and forbidding front to visitors, could be used as living spaces. The Russian striving for showy effect over habitability was thought to be reflected in the taste for elaborate dacha design. A simply furnished, solidly built cottage with a plot of land was much preferable to the "Hellenic" and "Gothic" excesses of the time. Often, it was felt, foreign architectural models were transplanted unthinkingly to Russian soil with little account taken of the differences in climate. An ostentatious fountain in the front garden was to be avoided; the Russians should emulate the English commitment to comfort and ease of living. Thus, for example, the kitchen should be at the front of the house, while living quarters should look out onto a quiet back garden.[94] The garden should itself be light, airy, and well maintained; paths laid out geometrically in the French style would not work without open perspectives from which to view the arrangement, and tall trees, if too densely planted, would only make the garden cold and damp.[95] As one commentator admiringly noted: "An Englishman lives at home, in the family, and for this very reason the pride of English architecture is a residential house, a cottage. Not beauty, but practicality and utility—that is the top priority for the English!"[96] The *kottedzh* was the ideal, the culmination of progress and civilization in domestic design. And not the least important of its features was the compact garden that gave the home a touch of "poetry" as well as making a gesture toward cozy self-sufficiency.[97]

---

92. *Dachnitsa*, no. 5 (1912), 2. However, advertisements from *Nizhegorodskii listok* in the 1900s suggest that the range of dachas available there was rather similar to those of Moscow and St. Petersburg, even if the absolute numbers were much smaller.

93. On the need for greater infrastructural provision in dacha settlements outside Warsaw, see *Dachnyi listok*, 24 July 1909. The dacha habits of middle-class Odessans are described briefly in P. Herlihy, *Odessa: A History, 1794–1914* (Cambridge, Mass., 1986), 277.

94. A. Saladin, *Putevoditel' po prigorodnym i dachnym mestnostiam do stantsii Ramenskoe Moskovsko-Kazanskoi zheleznoi dorogi* (Moscow, 1914), 21.

95. P. N. Shteinberg, *Dekorativnyi dachnyi i usadebnyi sad*, 3d ed. (Petrograd, 1916), and P. I. Kamenogradskii, *Dachnyi sad: Razbivka i obsadka nebol'shikh sadov i parkov derev'iami, kustami i tsvetami*, 3d ed. (Petrograd, 1918).

96. Semenov, *Blagoustroistvo gorodov*, 1.

97. See, e.g., V. Portugalov, "Sanitarnoe znachenie zhilishcha," *Nashe zhilishche*, no. 1 (1894), 2–5.

The influence of these ideas is felt in the growing self-assertiveness evinced by the residents of new settlements. As an editorial of 1909 proudly noted: "The life of these settlements is extremely original and absolutely does not fit within the limits of the concept of 'dacha' life in the narrow sense of this word."[98] Three years later, the leading dacha organ was more specific in identifying the change that had taken place: "Dacha life has ceased to be a whim and a luxury for rich people who used to leave the hurly-burly of the city for two or three months in order to relax in the open air, and at the present time it would be more accurate to describe dacha settlements in the Moscow region as suburban settlements."[99]

These settlements, of which there were estimated to be several hundred in the Moscow region alone in the early 1910s, set themselves a number of practical goals in the early years of their existence: to improve rail links; to establish a regular police presence and a fire-fighting force; to provide medical care and schools; to improve sanitation; to plan and administer the territory of the settlement effectively; and, on the political front, to establish a productive working relationship with local councils (*zemstva*) and city authorities.[100] In the 1900s and early 1910s dozens of settlements applied for registration to the Moscow guberniia administration. Almost all of them had their own societies for improving services and infrastructure (*obshchestva blagoustroistva*).

"Settlers" (*poseliane*) sought to develop their own way of life and a set of values clearly distinct from those of the city; their efforts to cultivate a new cultural identity were only fueled by the superficial and dismissive treatment they continued to receive from city journalists.[101] Promotional brochures presented exurban settlements as the salvation of a "middle class" that was currently at the mercy of rapacious landlords in the big cities; as more and more people joined up and the level of infrastructure and services improved, a dacha suburb would become a cheap, healthy, and pleasant alternative to life in a cramped urban apartment.[102] One prominent architectural guidebook of the time recommended the "detached house" (*dom-osobniak*) as the optimal form of dwelling for the "middle class of people":

> Here a person can spend his private life in peace, satisfying his personal requirements and inclinations, without troubling himself or others. Everything takes on the imprint of his individuality, everything acquires the more enclosed, intimate character that is so valuable for concentrated and productive work, for the devel-

98. *Dachnyi vestnik*, no. 1 (1909), 4.

99. *Dachnik*, no. 1 (1912), 2.

100. All these problems were discussed at length in 1909 at the first St. Petersburg congress of local societies from dacha and suburban settlements. See the reports published in *Trudy pervogo S.-Peterburgskogo s"ezda predstavitelei podstolichnykh poselkov, 28–31 avgusta 1909 goda* (St. Petersburg, 1910).

101. One response to the prevailing stereotypes of life in dacha settlements is "Chto ob nas govoriat i pechataiut?" *PLL*, 13 June 1882, 2.

102. See, e.g., *"Novye Sokol'niki:" Dachnye uchastki: Imenie Anny Nikolaevny Kovalevoi* (Moscow, 1911), and *Opisanie Edinstvennogo v Rossii Blagoustroennogo Podmoskovnogo Poselka "Novogireevo" pri sobstvennoi platforme* (Moscow, 1906).

82 opment of independence, self-awareness, and the cultural strength that follows from these.[103]

But the value of the exurban settlement was not conceived of only in individualistic terms. Efforts were made to construct a new kind of collective spirit based on an informed commitment to community life. Periodicals representing the settlements complained of the unruly behavior of city dwellers who frequented the local theater and turned it into a "cabaret" and "seedy bar," and discussed the problem—one of acute public concern in late imperial society—of thieves and "hooligans"; it also registered the difficulty of harmonizing the interests of settlement dwellers (*posel'chane*) with those of dachniki proper (the latter were unwilling to pay taxes and generally to pull their weight in maintaining the settlement's infrastructure). *Posel'chane* were urged to develop their own communal self-help ethos.[104]

## Constraints on Exurbanization

Through little fault of their own, the settlements achieved only limited success. The practical obstacles they faced were enormous. Public transport systems developed so slowly and sporadically that the possibilities of decentralization were limited.[105] Adna Weber, an influential pioneer of comparative urban geography, in 1899 identified four principal means of avoiding unacceptably high levels of urban concentration: a shorter workday, ownership associations for workers, cheap transit, rapid transit.[106] As of 1917, Russia had achieved none of them.

The difficulties faced by the settlements were not, moreover, simply a matter of infrastructure. They were caught in a no-man's-land between *zemstvo* and city, and hence received financial support from neither.[107] The neighborhood spirit necessary to overcome this disadvantage never really developed, given the absence of appropriate institutions (such as town councils).[108] The 600 or so dacha settlements in the Moscow region by the time of World War I had come into being without any planning on the part of the municipal or regional authorities. Their emergence had been commercially driven, so there was little opportunity to coordinate the provision of basic services; many of them

103. E. Iu. Kupffer, *Zhiloi dom: Rukovodstvo dlia proektirovaniia i vozvedeniia sovremennykh zhilishch* (St. Petersburg and Moscow, 1914), 197.

104. Note the strictures of the anonymous columnist "Old Resident" ("Staryi posel'chanin") in *Poselkovyi golos* (St. Petersburg, 1909–10). A similar range of concerns are reflected in *Losinoostrovskii vestnik* (1909–17) and *Vestnik poselka Lianozovo* (1908, 1913).

105. Electric trams, for example, were not running in St. Petersburg until 1907. For comparison, Kiev had an electric system in the early 1890s; London had extensive suburban railways in the 1860s and a whole underground system in 1910.

106. A. Weber, *The Growth of Cities in the Nineteenth Century: A Study in Statistics* (1899; Ithaca, N.Y., 1963).

107. For a contemporary diagnosis of the problems, see K. Raush, "Prigorody bol'shikh gorodov i ikh puti soobshcheniia," *Gorodskoe delo*, no. 16 (1909), 802–10.

108. T. Colton, *Moscow: Governing the Socialist Metropolis* (Cambridge, Mass., 1995), 60–63.

were too large and crowded to offer their inhabitants a reasonable exurban standard of living. Crucially, settlements did not have the authority to levy taxes, so they had no way to force residents to contribute to the costs of improving infrastructure.[109] Most of the local newspapers of the time complain of underprovision of basic services and of inadequate building standards caused by the pressure to exploit the land commercially; it was estimated, for example, that only 10 percent of buildings in Shuvalovo/Ozerki would meet fire safety regulations. Many dachniki felt short-changed by the shareholders' companies, which were ostensibly responsible for the management of the settlement but in reality shifted the burden of basic maintenance to residents. Losinyi Ostrov, a settlement formed in 1899 that had over 2,000 permanent residents (as well as many more seasonal visitors) by the end of the 1900s, was typical in the problems it experienced:

> Houses are multiplying endlessly. One fence adjoins another, forming long straight lines. On one side of the fences there is culture: one can see neat paths covered with sand, flowers, and fountains. But on the other side there is something vaguely reminiscent of a pavement, which, along with the roads, is layered with impassable mud in rainy weather, is a dustbowl when it's dry, and is buried in snowdrifts in winter.[110]

It was almost impossible, the same editorial complained, to make residents show more concern for the settlement's public spaces: "Shut away on our plots of land, we live aloof from one another."

Dacha communities felt particularly acutely the lack of strong institutional backing in the face of the growing problem of maintaining public order. The settlement of Starbeevo, just outside Moscow, for example, in 1904 proposed to solve its security problem by imposing two hours of compulsory watch duty for each plot with a house.[111] Other settlements might petition the police to send extra constables their way. The Sheremetev estate at Kuskovo was by 1904 attracting up to 3,000 dachniki in the summer (spread over 600 desiatinas) as well as thousands of day trippers on public holidays. The local constable wrote in desperation to the police chief of Moscow uezd that disturbances were becoming ever more common for two main reasons: first, the imposition of a state liquor monopoly, which meant that drunken crowds tended to congregate at particular retail outlets instead of dispersing around the many watering holes that used to exist; second, the spread of popular theater and other entertainments, which acted as magnets for the rowdy lower social strata. A further problem was the watchmen, who, paid a mere 15 rubles per month,

---

109. P. N. Durilin, "Moskovskie prigorody i dachnye poselki v sviazi s razvitiem gorodskoi zhizni," *Arkhiv gorodskoi gigieny i tekhniki,* no. 1–2 (1918), 63–101.

110. Editorial, *Losinoostrovskii vestnik,* no. 1 (1909), 1–2.

111. TsIAM, f. 483, op. 3, d. 344, l. 8. Starbeevo was spread over 200 desiatinas and had 778 plots owned by 367 people. Each year it attracted "up to 300 dachniki."

84  were less than vigilant. On average, between fifteen and twenty dachas were burglarized each season.[112]

The issue of public order in Petersburg dacha locations was publicly recognized in 1871, when a "suburban" police force was set up to look after settlements whose status fell in between city and village; in the late 1870s it was expanded to take in Shuvalovo, Sestroretsk, Ligovo, Lakhta, and others.[113] Yet problems remained. Particularly vulnerable were those dacha locations that adjoined worker settlements. One such place was Sestroretsk, a center for the arms industry but also a vacation resort, whose population of 5,000 in the mid-1880s was policed by a mere three constables.[114] Some dacha communities made their grievances known to the higher authorities. In 1901 the police department of the Ministry of Internal Affairs reported that the Pargolovo society for local services had petitioned the guberniia authorities to have two state-owned liquor shops closed to eliminate regular drunken disturbances in the area. At the same time, the police put in a bid to the Ministry of Finances for extra personnel, noting that in summer only eleven constables were employed to maintain law and order in settlements whose combined population swelled to 25,000. Village constables could not be sent in, as Shuvalovo-Ozerki did not fall under their jurisdiction.[115]

Unrest increased with the events of 1905, when suburbs and exurbs were widely perceived to be caught up in the same revolutionary disturbances as the cities. One owner of an estate near Kuntsevo, to the west of Moscow, wrote to her bank in 1908 asking for a deferment of her mortgage payments, given the collapse of the dacha market after 1905. Workers' protests had spilled over beyond the factory limits; agitational meetings had been held in parks and forests that were privately owned and adjacent to dacha areas. In the end, Cossacks had been called in to disperse the undesirable elements, but even so, dacha life had been "destroyed":

All this so scared and repelled dachniki that over the last two years (1906 and 1907) Muscovites have not only failed to rent any dachas at Troekurovo [the estate in question] but they haven't even come to view them, despite a mass of publications in all the newspapers. But in point of fact over the ten years preceding 1905 Troekurovo dachas were always occupied by rich Moscow merchants, who were happy to pay more than 2,000 rubles annually.[116]

112. Ibid., d. 367, ll. 1–2.

113. See *PSZ*, ser. 2, 46, no. 49718 (8 June 1871), and "Ustroistvo peterburgskoi prigorodnoi politsii," *PL*, 11 May 1880, 2. Property in the suburban district was taxed at the rate of 0.5% of value in order to fund the police: see Mordukhai-Boltovskii, *Svod zakonov*, vol. 5, *Ustav o priamykh nalogakh*, arts. 116–18. The debates on public order that culminated in the creation of the suburban police force are well summarized in R. Zelnik, *Labor and Society in Tsarist Russia: The Factory Workers of St. Petersburg, 1855–1870* (Stanford, 1971), 255–68.

114. "Iz dachnykh mest," *PL*, 24 May 1885, 2.

115. RGIA, f. 1152, op. 13, d. 300, ll. 2–3. The police were granted their wish: Witte personally authorized the appointment of six more constables to cover the area.

116. TsIAM, f. 483, op. 3, d. 1513.

The local police constable wrote to the bank in support of this appeal, citing in particular 85 the danger of "expropriations" (i.e., burglaries) for "owners of wealthy, remote dachas." Never before had the position of dachniki, as unprotected representatives of urban society in an alien nonurban environment, seemed so vulnerable.

LIKE SO many other aspects of late imperial socioeconomic history, the fate of the pre-revolutionary summerfolk seems grimly overdetermined. Dacha settlements, with their inadequate economic and institutional backing and their unsure administrative status, were vulnerable to all the malaises of Russia's high-speed but volatile and squalid urbanization. One historian of St. Petersburg concludes that "deficient municipal services and retarded technology in public transport hindered the creation of bucolic suburban enclaves for the elites and the emerging middle classes, thus limiting use of the defensive strategy against perceived urban ills commonly employed by elites in cities throughout Europe and America."[117]

Yet it is important to avoid taking too teleological an approach to the history of the dacha by tying its significance too closely to the fate of Russian society in general, or by asserting that its historical trajectory was leading inexorably from the eighteenth-century aristocratic villa to the late imperial suburbs. The dacha was a much richer phenomenon than either of those interpretations would allow. The enormous expansion of the out-of-town public was not a symptom of social decline or dilution but rather a remarkable opportunity for diverse urban groups and individuals to explore and reflect on a new range of experiences. The problems thrown up by urbanization did not prevent thousands of dachniki from spending tranquil, enjoyable, and culturally productive summers in the last few prerevolutionary decades; if anything, quite the opposite. For this reason, the next chapter will swap teleology for plurality, take a step away from socioeconomic history, and examine the many meanings attached to the dacha, both publicly and privately, in the late imperial period.

117. J. Bater, "Between Old and New: St. Petersburg in the Late Imperial Era," in *The City in Late Imperial Russia*, ed. M. Hamm (Bloomington, 1986), 73.

# Between Arcadia and Suburbia

## The Dacha as a Cultural Space, 1860–1917

The dacha was not just a place but a way of life. Of this the many observers of out-of-town society in the mid-nineteenth century were in no doubt: the dacha brought with it a certain range of social rituals, forms of sociability, patterns of behavior, and cultural values. But the second half of the nineteenth century outdid earlier periods in the number of models of exurban life in circulation and in the intensity with which they were articulated. The word "dacha" meant many more things than it had previously and it engaged the interest of a society increasingly committed to self-contemplation. The last decades of the nineteenth century were the dacha's golden age not only for the socioeconomic reasons outlined in Chapter 3 but also for the cultural prominence it attained.

Dachas put tens of thousands of urban Russians at a safe distance from the world of work, giving them unprecedented opportunities to enjoy more leisure and to use it more freely, to seek new pastimes, and to adopt a new lifestyle independent of occupation or lineage. Out-of-town settlements quickly developed their own subcultures. Collective entertainments were organized, local newspapers were published, self-help societies were formed, and the exurbanite emerged as a new type. These dachniki were remarkable creatures: urban Russians who took their identity not from their legal or professional status or from their relation to the means of production but from their nonwork activities. They were not guests on a country estate or summer visitors to a rural community but—increasingly and unashamedly—vacationers: that is, people who exercised choice in how they spent their money and their time, and whose choices had implications for the kind of persons they were or wanted to become.

This is by no means to say, however, that the dachniki were a homogeneous and like-minded group. Summer houses in the late imperial era took many forms and bespoke various and sometimes incompatible values and cultural allegiances. Many meanings were attached to and generated by the summerfolk in the last few prerevolutionary decades. A particularly prestigious and influential idea was of the dacha as a rural retreat, a scaled-down country estate. A less culturally prestigious but more commonplace response was to associate exurbia with a distinctive lifestyle, centered on leisure, entertainment, and domesticity. Another approach was to judge dachas by the people who used them, and to construct an often unprepossessing general image of the summerfolk. Yet another move was to accord the dachniki a place in discussions of Russian society and its prospects. The dacha, for all its apparent marginality, held some prominence in the late imperial imagination. As an exposed and precarious outpost of urban civilization in an overwhelmingly rural and undercivilized country, it served as a focal point for the anxieties of an educated society that was extremely complex, rather unsure how to describe itself, and in general darkly apprehensive of what the future might hold.

## The Dacha as Country Retreat

In the last third of the nineteenth century, summerfolk were no longer recent and insecure arrivals in exurbia. Their presence had been felt for several decades, and they represented sections of the urban population whose social prominence and economic clout were rapidly increasing. Now dachniki might try to shed once and for all their parvenu status by swapping their vacation cottage for a full-fledged country retreat, and thereby laying claim to the authentically rural, even arcadian, spirit associated with the country estate (*usad'ba*).

Opportunities to meet aspirations of this kind were offered most obviously by architecture. The late imperial era entertained a widening eclecticism that allowed everyone from the urban dachnik to the rural landowner to choose styles ranging from the English cottage to Mauritanian Gothic. But this eclecticism had rather different priorities from those of Kukol'nik and Furmann in the 1830s and 1840s. It formed part of a national revival whereby details of izba architecture might be appropriated by wealthy estate owners (as, for example, in the various outbuildings at Savva Mamontov's Abramtsevo) or by exurbanites less well endowed with land and money. By the 1870s, although neoclassical symmetries still retained some prominence in dacha designs, they no longer enjoyed supremacy. The emphasis had firmly shifted to wood instead of brick as the building material of preference and to vernacular styles instead of the Palladianism that had still been current in the 1840s. Pattern books of the 1870s suggest strongly that the boundary between the "rural house" (*sel'skii dom*) and the dacha had become blurred. Dachas, in other words, were not mere villas or "out-of-town" houses, whose main function was to provide a brief respite from the rigors of the city; rather, they were properly embedded in the rural landscape and represented a more substantial commitment by city dwellers to an alternative lifestyle.[1] By the 1880s, in the words of one scholar, "cottage life became es-

---

1. Pattern books that illustrate this trend are *"Arkhitekturnyi sbornik" sel'skikh postroek i modnoi mebeli* (Moscow, 1873); and N. Zheltukhin, *Prakticheskaia arkhitektura gorodskikh, zagorodnykh i sel'skikh zdanii* (St. Pe-

88  tate life writ small."[2] Thanks at least in part to an emerging arts and crafts movement, rusticity gained further ground in house design and interior decoration in the last part of the nineteenth century; by the early twentieth, it found a home on the pages of so Westernized a publication as the lavishly illustrated lifestyle magazine *Stolitsa i Usad'ba,* which in general projected itself as an arbiter of taste for the anglophile moneyed classes. In between advertisements for cigars and automobiles could be found recommendations to patronize the vernacular culture: "any remotely cultured family that does not want to 'fall behind the times,'" the magazine informed its readers, should without fail acquire at least a few pieces of antique Russian furniture.[3]

But, as one recent historian of the *usad'ba* is at pains to point out, even if the architectural forms of the dacha sometimes bore a resemblance to those of the country estate, its "culture" was still of a rather different order:

> It is important to emphasize that, when touching on the theme of the gradual increase of typical dacha features in wooden buildings on country estates, we need to be clear that this kind of architecture by no means always served to facilitate the operation in its environment of the superficial, unreflective, banal everyday life characteristic of the dacha.[4]

Of course, the line between banality and originality is not always easy to draw (particularly in an era of eclecticism), so it is little wonder that some property owners self-consciously took on the role of landowner (*pomeshchik*) in preference to that of dachnik. The property of Shakhmatovo, acquired by Aleksandr Blok's maternal grandfather, A. A. Beketov, in 1875, was deemed by its owners to be a landed estate (*pomest'e*), although its architecture and landholdings easily qualified it to be categorized as a dacha. In the words of Blok's cousin: "It was always emphasized that we live 'in the country' and not 'at a dacha.' The dacha way of life was a synonym for vulgarity."[5]

---

tersburg and Moscow, 1875). Whereas the pattern books of the 1830s and 1840s (discussed in Chapter 2) commonly speak of the "country cottage" (*sel'skii domik*) for dacha-type constructions, in the 1870s the diminutive is removed and the *sel'skii dom* becomes the focus of attention. From this change we might infer that in the earlier period rusticity had been a form of stylization, whereas later on it was treated with less cultural detachment.

2. J. Randolph, "The Old Mansion: Revisiting the History of the Russian Country Estate," *Kritika* 1 (2000): 744.

3. I. Lazarevskii, "Kollektsionerstvo i poddelka," *Stolitsa i Usad'ba,* no. 7 (1914), 24.

4. T. P. Kazhdan, *Khudozhestvennyi mir russkoi usad'by* (Moscow, 1997), 181. Some of the ungainliness of the original has been preserved in the translation.

5. Quoted in A. Pyman, *The Life of Aleksandr Blok,* vol. 1, *The Distant Thunder, 1880–1908* (Oxford, 1979), 38. Even where a family's summer residence was unhesitatingly called a "dacha," in intelligentsia circles emphasis tended to be placed on its remoteness from urban civilization and its rustic simplicity. One example was the house in Tarusa (Kaluga guberniia) where Marina Tsvetaeva and her sister Anastasiia spent much of their childhood. Anastasiia (no doubt self-deludedly) recalled the summers they spent there as a time of untroubled simplicity: see her *Vospominaniia* (Moscow, 1971), 52–60. Marina's memories were also extremely upbeat, but she presented Tarusa more assertively as emblematic of her family's heroic spirit and as radically opposed to the cluttered and pretentious interior she found at the "dachlet" of an acquaintance who lived nearby: see "Zhenikh" (1933), in her *Sochineniia v dvukh tomakh,* 2 vols. (Moscow, 1988), 2:16.

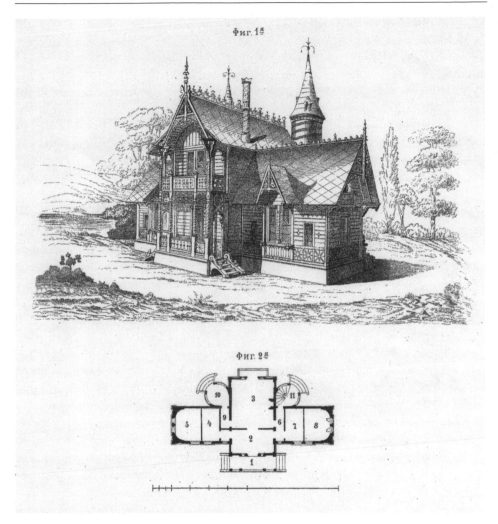

A floridly rustic dacha of the 1870s (from N. Zheltukhin, *Prakticheskaia arkhitektura gorodskikh, zagorodnykh i sel'skikh zdanii* [St. Petersburg and Moscow, 1875])

The Beketovs were a well-established noble family who had fallen on slightly hard times after 1861; by the 1870s their social and cultural allegiances made them members of the "old" intelligentsia rather than of the nobility. Their preference for the estate over the dacha was shared, if for rather different reasons, by Anton Chekhov, very much a member of the "new" intelligentsia. Driven by the need to conserve his health and to save money (the cost of maintaining an extended household in Moscow was stretching his means to the limit), but also by a long-standing aspiration to own and maintain an independent rural landholding, Chekhov bought in 1892 the estate of Melikhovo, located in Serpukhov uezd, at the southern end of the Moscow region. But even before that, in the 1880s, the "dachas" that Chekhov rented had tended to resemble *usad'by*: most of them were buildings rented from estate owners and were remote enough to require an arduous journey.

90   The Pasternaks, who in many ways resembled the Chekhovs (their family too was headed by a brilliantly successful self-made artist from the periphery of Russia), were similarly able to experience the splendid isolation of estate life while holding the formal status of dachniki: from 1903 on they rented a house on a near-deserted and agriculturally inactive *usad'ba* located one hundred versts southwest of Moscow and owned by one of the princes Obolenskii.[6] For those summerfolk willing to make a more long-term commitment to country life, the ideal was to buy up a neglected manorial estate trimmed of its serf landholdings, to repair as necessary its crumbling main residence, and to restore its social and economic vitality.[7]

  A dacha was defined less by the size or design of a house or by the layout of its grounds than by the way its occupants used it. The Melikhovo estate, for example, had become more like a dacha after the residence of its previous owner, the stage designer N. P. Sorokhtin, who had installed an overelaborate carved porch and neglected the landholdings. The Chekhov family directed Melikhovo back toward its function of *usad'ba* by planting trees, carrying out noncosmetic repairs, and taking very seriously their role as owner-managers. But even so, their lifestyle retained something of the dacha in that they received a steady stream of visitors from Moscow, and Melikhovo became a focus for the informal sociability with which the dacha even then had become synonymous.[8]

  Despite this point of resemblance, the Chekhovs were keen to dissociate themselves from the dacha. In the words of Chekhov's sister, "Our country life on our own estate, surrounded by forests and fields, was better than any 'dacha' life that we had experienced previously."[9] This attitude was hardly untypical: the culture of the time regularly presented the dacha as a meretricious, low-grade alternative to the country estate, as at best a stepping-stone to the *usad'ba*. In one of the situation comedies that were a staple of pre-revolutionary theater, a disenchanted dacha resident reflects regretfully on his decision to sell his ancestral estate so as to move to Moscow. Now he is renting a drafty and overpriced dacha and enduring an unpleasant daily commute. His wife, by contrast, adores the new arrangement, as she has entertainments at hand and the opportunity to amuse herself by speculating in stocks and shares.[10] The uneasy relationship between the world of the traditional landed nobility and that of the dachnik is captured more subtly in Vladimir Nabokov's *Pnin*, where the unsympathetic narrator recalls how, as the adolescent son of the lord of the manor, he haughtily turned down his hero's awkwardly delivered invitation to take part in amateur theatricals.[11]

---

6. A. L. Pasternak, *Vospominaniia* (Munich, 1983), 95–97.

7. See, e.g., A. Ianishevskii, *Dacha na Volge* (Kazan', 1900).

8. An account of Chekhov's experiences can be found in Kazhdan, *Khudozhestvennyi mir,* 291–303. Kazhdan identifies Melikhovo as an "intermediate" form between estate and dacha; she sees it as a "Chekhovian" model of the estate, quite distinct from the "Turgenev" model (301–2).

9. Chekhova, *Iz dalekogo proshlogo,* 116.

10. N. L. Persiianinova, *Bol'shie i malen'kie* (Moscow, 1912). Eventually, of course, the wife sustains huge losses on her dealings and offers to teach evening classes to make up the money.

11. V. Nabokov, *Pnin* (London, 1997), 148–50. Note also Nabokov's *Speak, Memory,* where the author's first love, Tamara, comes from the culturally remote dacha (thereby, perhaps, gaining added fascination in his eyes).

But tensions of this kind had emerged only recently. Formerly, roughly up to the
1860s, the distinction between the dacha and the country estate had been relatively clear-
cut and nonemotive. The dacha was oriented toward the city and represented temporary
occupancy and brief periods of leisure unencumbered by the management of extensive
lands and agricultural concerns; the estate, by contrast, was embedded in a rural environment, involved some sort of agricultural commitment, and had a markedly "traditional"
way of life and set of values based on seasonal and domestic routines and on lasting relationships with neighbors and the local community. What happened in mid-century, in
the words of one art historian, was that the country estate moved from being the "subject"
of culture to being its "object."[12] Or, more bluntly: it acquired a cultural prominence out
of proportion to its social significance. By this time life at the estate had diversified to such
an extent that its social profile was complex and not conducive to easy generalizations.
Economic factors, moreover, were reducing the scale and the number of country estates.
But here a compensating cultural mechanism played its role: the *usad'ba* became an emblem of a golden age of social harmony, high (especially literary) culture, and rural authenticity. The dacha, by contrast, began to connote "the vulgarity and prosaic aspects of
reality and its unattractive, distorted features. This kind of dacha world, in which people
lost touch with themselves, could not become the subject of culture."[13] The strength of
this stereotype is shown by its power to shape scholarly perceptions even in the 1990s, as
the passage quoted above on "the banal everyday life characteristic of the dacha" amply illustrates.

There were, of course, ways of avoiding the charge of banality. As we have already
seen from the example of Chekhov, dacha folk from the cultural elite were able to construct their own model of cultured exurban existence, drawing where necessary on the
traditions of the *usad'ba*. Some of the most creative efforts in this vein came from the
merchantry, a section of society that had always struggled to find an authoritative public
voice but now was growing in cultural activity and assertiveness. This occupational group
was large and heterogeneous, like any of imperial Russia's social "estates" (*sosloviia*).
Membership in a guild had been the main route of social advancement for generations of
peasants; most of them remained modest tradespeople rather than prosperous entrepreneurs. As time wore on and their socioeconomic position stabilized, many ordinary merchant families were abandoning their former cultural isolationism, becoming assimilated
to urban civilization, and taking up the dacha habit that had emerged as an essential part
of this civilization. The journalist N. A. Leikin, a self-made authority on Russia's Grub
Street, was in no doubt of the softening of merchant ways that took place on acquisition
of a dacha by the Karpovka: tattered shoes were exchanged for elegant pumps, a printed
cotton smock gave way to a linen shirt, and the newly exurban tradesman even stopped
eating Lenten dishes on Wednesdays and Fridays.[14]

12. G. Iu. Sternin, "Abramtsevo: Ot 'usad'by' k 'dache,'" in his *Russkaia khudozhestvennaia kul'tura vtoroi
poloviny XIX–nachala XX veka* (Moscow, 1984), 186.

13. Ibid., 199.

14. N. A. Leikin, *Neunyvaiushchie Rossiiane* (St. Petersburg, 1912), 227.

The top end of the merchantry made an even more striking contribution to dacha culture. A small number of wealthy entrepreneurial families had intermarried with the nobility and the intelligentsia, and came to play a prominent part in the cultural life of the fin de siècle. For these select clans, the dacha was not an entrée into urban "respectable" society but rather a social center in its own right, a minor country estate connected not so much to the local community as to independent, often literary and artistic social networks. For this reason, they looked farther afield for their summer residences than Pavlovsk, Peterhof, or the Karpovka. A. A. Bakhrushin, head of a family that had made its money in the leather trade and founder of the Theater Museum in Moscow, first rented a dacha when he already had a family, in the late 1890s. After a first summer in Izmailovo, he took a house on the estate of Gireevo for the next few years. His son recalled that these were "not even dachas, but little wooden houses built on someone's whim and subsequently abandoned." The dwellings were widely spaced out on the estate lands; a couple were occupied by the owners, the Terletskii family. The oldest Terletskii, who owed his fortune to the vodka trade, was a man of an "antediluvian" stamp. His son, however, by now over fifty, although he had the main estate residence at his disposal, preferred to build himself an "anglified little dacha" with all conceivable comforts (full plumbing, electricity, even a phonograph). The main house was used only for lavish entertaining on the younger master's name day.[15]

If the Terletskiis combined the country estate traditions of generous hospitality with a more up-to-date commitment to home comforts, the Bakhrushins valued Gireevo for the opportunity it gave them to rest from the rigors of city and commercial life. A. A. Bakhrushin enjoyed fishing and reading in the open air, while his wife took a more practical interest in planting flowers and tending the garden. Very unusually for people of their social position, in the early 1900s they departed for Gireevo as early as mid-March and returned to Moscow only in mid-September. By 1907, however, they were driven to look for another vacation spot, as the Terletskiis had begun to develop the estate for construction of smaller dachas and the place was quickly losing its secluded and unspoiled feel. They soon accepted an offer from the writer N. D. Teleshov of a spacious dacha on the Malakhovka estate with ten desiatinas of bordered land. This move marked a distinct shift toward a landowner way of life.[16]

The Bakhrushins were not alone among major merchant families in moving from a relatively modest rented dacha to something grander. P. M. Tret'iakov and his wife spent their first three summers together in a rented dacha off the Smolensk highway. They then spent ten years in Kuntsevo, about ten versts to the west of Moscow, in a two-story log house rented from the landowner Solodovnikova. The settlement was not wholly secluded, but the total number of dachas was small: eight owned by Solodovnikova, fifteen by the merchant Soldatenkov, and a few by another local landowning family, the Shelaputins. Kuntsevo was effectively an enclave for Moscow's merchant elite, as is evinced by

15. Iu. A. Bakhrushin, *Vospominaniia* (Moscow, 1994), 101–7.
16. On Malakhovka, see ibid., 290–95.

its rich cultural life and its level of amenities (most families, for example, had their own bathing tents moored to the bank of the Moscow River). The tempo and style of life were modeled more on the country estate than the dacha settlement. In the 1870s, for example, there were no permanent trading points: the baker staggered over regularly from a neighboring village, the butcher and the greengrocer came by cart from Moscow twice a week, and all other foodstuffs were bought from the local peasants. Yet Kuntsevo was close enough to Moscow for a merchant paterfamilias to commute to work daily throughout the summer.[17] When the time came for a move, Tret'iakov was extremely resistant to his wife's idea of buying a property "of the Turgenev type." In his daughter's words, he "did not recognize the right to own land of people who did not work the land with their own toil." The compromise eventually reached was the long-term rental of a middling estate, Kurakino, on the Iaroslavl' railway line. This move transformed the social life of the Tret'iakov family—not least because it brought them closer to the Mamontov clan, who owned an estate nearby.[18]

Savva Mamontov's Abramtsevo is perhaps the most famous case of intervention by new money in the cultural life of late imperial Russia. Mamontov bought the estate from the descendants of I. S. Aksakov in 1870; his subsequent development of the property neatly illustrates the transition from the old world of the country estate to something more culturally dynamic. Mamontov sought to invest the forms and some of the traditions of life on the estate with a radical new content: guests were invited not for their allegiance to a clan but rather for the contribution they could make to the life of the community. Once again, whether we should describe Abramtsevo as a dacha depends on whose perspective we adopt. Mamontov himself, as the owner of the property and manager of its affairs, certainly regarded it as an estate; but his visitors perhaps thought of it more casually as a dacha, where they had no household responsibilities and were in residence only temporarily. In the opinion of Il'ia Repin, Abramtsevo was "the best dacha in the world."[19]

At the dacha, better than anywhere else, we can find evidence of the coming together of merchant bourgeoisie and intelligentsia—of the creation of a cultivated "middle-class" lifestyle. The self-sufficiency and cultural hermeticism of even elite members of the merchant estate around 1840 contrasted strikingly with the Westernized self-confidence of the Tret'iakovs and Bakhrushins in the 1900s. Merchant families of this third generation were able to see themselves as a leisured class and were quite prepared to think of themselves

---

17. The ease of commuting is evident in P. A. Shchukin, "Iz vospominanii Petra Ivanovicha Shchukina," *Russkii arkhiv,* no. 12 (1911), 546–57. Similar were the experiences of the Kharuzin family (another merchant dynasty, whose money came from the textile trade), who rented a dacha at the Iusupov estate of Arkhangel'skoe every summer from 1870 to 1879. At that time, only seven houses were let out as dachas, so tenants enjoyed a high degree of privacy (the Kharuzins, e.g., had very little to do with their neighbors and spent their time in an extended family group): see V. N. Kharuzina, *Proshloe: Vospominaniia detskikh i otrocheskikh let* (Moscow, 1999), 265–336 passim.

18. V. P. Ziloti, *V dome Tret'iakova* (New York, 1954), esp. 189.

19. Quoted in Kazhdan, *Khudozhestvennyi mir,* 212.

94    outside their social and occupational contexts.[20] An exuberant contribution to this new leisure culture was made by the Alekseev merchant dynasty, one branch of which bought the estate of Liubimovka (at Tarasovka, on the Iaroslavl' railway line) in 1869: fifty desiatinas remaining from the formerly enormous landholdings of the Trubetskois and Belosel'skiis in this area. Liubimovka soon became the venue for numerous amateur performances, initially in a decrepit outbuilding but then (from 1877) in a purpose-built theater. Among the most enthusiastic participants was the young Konstantin Alekseev (better known by the name he later assumed, Stanislavsky). As a grown man, Stanislavsky, as much as anyone, sought to develop a socially and culturally mature intelligentsia by overcoming the boundaries separating commercial and cultural elites. And in his experience, no setting did more to erode those boundaries than exurbia.[21]

The dacha, then, gained some respectability from its partial cultural convergence with the country estate; but it was also lent legitimacy by perceptions of its unmediated relation to the natural world and to the rural "good life." Ivan Shishkin may be seen as having initiated this change in sensibility when in 1856, as a promising student at the St. Petersburg Academy, he spent the summer working on landscapes at Lisii Nos, subsequently a dacha location highly valued precisely for its scenery and fine views over the Gulf of Finland.[22] In his later career Shishkin painted dozens of forest scenes that became canonical as representations of an authentically Russian landscape.

The following generation of the intelligentsia may be said to have followed Shishkin's lead by conceiving of the dacha as a secluded retreat entirely removed from the city. Nikolai Rimsky-Korsakov spent the summer of 1880 on the Stelevo estate, thirty versts the other side of Luga, on which he remarked: "For the first time in my life I've had the chance to spend the summer in the genuine Russian countryside . . . everything was in special harmony with my pantheistic mood at that time." One of Rimsky's fellow composers went even farther afield, to a dacha in Tula guberniia: "the dacha consisted of a spacious peasant izba. They [the Borodins] didn't take many things with them. There was no kitchen range, they prepared food in a Russian stove. Life was clearly extremely uncomfortable, crowded and with all kinds of privations."[23]

The values of simple lifestyle and natural beauty are often ascribed to the dacha in

20. See, e.g., Christine Ruane, "Caftan to Business Suit: The Semiotics of Russian Merchant Dress," in *Merchant Moscow: Images of Russia's Vanished Bourgeoisie,* ed. J. West and Iu. Petrov (Princeton, 1998).

21. On Stanislavsky and Liubimovka, see N. Shestakova, *Pervyi teatr Stanislavskogo* (Moscow, 1998). Stanislavsky's views on the social and cultural potential of his generation of the merchantry come across strongly in chap. 2 of his memoir *My Life in Art,* trans J. J. Robbins (Boston, 1924). In chap. 29 he recalls how a barn on a friend's estate a few versts from Liubimovka provided the venue for early rehearsals of a troupe that would soon become the Moscow Art Theatre.

22. *Ivan Ivanovich Shishkin: Perepiska. Dnevnik. Sovremenniki o khudozhnike,* ed. I. N. Shuvalova, 2d ed. (Leningrad, 1984), 38–39. The migration of landscape artists to the north is recognized as an established phenomenon in "Peterburgskoe obozrenie," *Severnaia pchela,* 7 May 1860, 416; it received increased institutional backing in 1884 with the establishment of a retreat (later named the "academy dacha") in Tver' guberniia where students of the St. Petersburg Academy of the Arts could refine their skills each summer. See I. Romanycheva, *Akademicheskaia dacha* (Leningrad, 1975).

23. N. Rimskii-Korsakov, *Letopis' moei muzykal'noi zhizni (1844–1906),* 3d ed. (Moscow, 1926), 237, 224.

émigré writings, which are so often informed by the idées fixes of the prerevolutionary intelligentsia. Zinaida Zhemchuzhnaia, by her upbringing very much a creature of the country estate, came to recognize the appeal of the dacha lifestyle in emigration in north China, where she saw thick forest that reminded her of home and breathed air "like in Switzerland."[24] And the writer Boris Zaitsev, visiting Kelomiakki (now Komarovo, a dacha location famous in Soviet times as a center for the Leningrad intelligentsia) in 1935, found it a vivid reminder of the Russia he valued. "How much there is of Russia here! . . . The smells are quite Russian: a sharply sour one of marsh, pine, and birch. . . . And the whole cast of life here is Russian, like before the war."[25]

Zaitsev here echoes numerous prerevolutionary voices: at the turn of the century the North came to be seen as the main geographical repository for Russianness. Proximity to the coast only heightened the effect of resorts such as Kelomiakki by drawing attention to a location's detachment from civilization (to face the sea every morning was, for a Russian, truly to feel that one had reached the end of the world). Seaside retreats, preferably built in the fashionable pseudo-Russian style, gained great cultural prestige through the 1890s and 1900s. The family of Viktor Shklovskii had aspirations to build themselves a vacation home on the Baltic coast, but their money ran out and they had to sell the property.[26] More successful was the writer Leonid Andreev, who in 1908 moved into a fifteen-room dacha modeled on an "ancient Norwegian castle" with a turret and splendid views over the Gulf of Finland. The family retained a flat in St. Petersburg, but Andreev increasingly gravitated toward his country residence, which he called a "house," not a "dacha."[27] As the most spectacularly successful Russian writer of this period, Andreev was able to live on the grand scale: several of the rooms were (given the severe winters) impractically enormous, guests arrived frequently, and a large staff of servants was in constant attendance. With its Gothic fittings and dark-oak interior, moreover, the house served as a fitting arena for the writer's increasingly fraught and self-dramatizing behavior.[28]

But Andreev's house, which reflected so well that writer's extravagant and obsessive personality, was far from typical. In the 1900s, other representatives of the artistic intelligentsia were busy reinventing the dacha as a place for intense and purposeful sociability, creative work, and self-sufficiency. This dacha ethos was exemplified by Kornei Chukovskii, the self-made critic, scholar, and writer, who by the time he moved to a house

24. Z. Zhemchuzhnaia, *Puti izgnaniia: Ural, Kuban', Moskva, Kharbin, Tian'tszin* (Tenafly, N.J., 1987), 203. The comparison with Switzerland is a commonplace of prerevolutionary descriptions of the dacha.

25. Boris Zaitsev to Ivan Bunin, 1 Sept. 1935, quoted in A. Liubomudrov, "Monastyrskie palomnichestva Borisa Zaitseva," *Russkaia literatura*, no. 1 (1995), 154.

26. V. Shklovskii, *Tret'ia fabrika* (Leningrad, 1926), 21, 24. Fellow enthusiasts of the dacha on the coast were the Bertenson family, headed by a well-known prerevolutionary physician, who in 1907 built themselves a spacious two-story house overlooking the sea at Terioki after several years of renting dachas in this village: see S. Bertenson, *Vokrug iskusstva* (Hollywood, 1957), 99. The popularity of Finnish dachas among middle-class Petersburgers is discussed in N. Bascmakoff and M. Leinonen, *Iz istorii i byta russkih v Finliandii*, vol. 1 (Helsinki, 1990).

27. Vera Andreeva, *Dom na chernoi rechke* (Moscow, 1980).

28. This comes across very strongly in Leonid Andreyev, *Photographs by a Russian Writer*, ed. R. Davies (London, 1989). For a discussion of Andreev's house, see esp. 50–56.

A dacha in the style of "northern modernism," located at Aleksandrovka (north of St. Petersburg). This dacha served as the summer residence of a professional family before the Revolution. In Soviet times it was split into four apartments.

A dacha at Siverskaia. According to its present owners (who bought the property in 1946), this is the oldest surviving house in the settlement. It was built in the 1890s.

A dacha at Aleksandrovka, another typical prerevolutionary design.

in the Finnish seaside village Kuokkala in 1906 was already one of the more prominent figures on the Petersburg intellectual scene. Kuokkala was the perfect place for him to indulge his puritanical habits and overdeveloped work ethic. From his daughter Lidiia's memoirs we learn that he could not stand idleness—in his own family or in others. Nor could he understand the purpose of purely social visits (here, of course, he differed from most of the nineteenth-century dacha-frequenting intelligentsia). If he dropped in to see one of his near neighbors at Kuokkala (now Repino)—notably Il'ia Repin himself—it was to engage immediately in intense intellectual discussion. He did not shirk physical work, carrying out all home repairs himself. And there was plenty of physical work to be done, as life at Kuokkala was far from luxurious. Water, for example, had to be fetched from Repin's Penaty; and Chukovskii particularly relished painting fences and other odd jobs. The Chukovskii family stayed at Kuokkala for portions of the autumn and winter, and for this reason saw themselves as authentic "locals," unlike dachniki, who "scuttled back to Petersburg as soon as autumn, rain, and storms began."[29] The household shared by Repin with his companion, Nataliia Nordman, had a similar commitment to purposeful activity, physical exertion, and straightforwardness of conduct, though it bore the rather specific imprint of Nordman's vegetarianism and democratism: servants were given a detailed and, by the standards of the time, generous work contract, and visitors were informed on arrival, by a notice placed on a gong stand, that a regime of "SELF HELP" ex-

29. L. Chukovskaia, *Pamiati detstva* (New York, 1983), 27.

98  isted at Penaty; guests should not expect a servant's help in transferring their outdoor clothing to the hat stand.[30]

## Exurban Recreations

The dachniki I have discussed so far were by and large members of the "free" professions. For them, time unencumbered by work commitments was nothing remarkable: they were well practiced in making what they considered to be gainful use of periods of recreation. But most of the dachniki who "scuttled back" to St. Petersburg or Moscow in the autumn did not have the option of staying longer: they might not own their own house in the country, and in any case their regular presence was required in the city. For summerfolk who were not writers or artists, exurbia brought with it an enticing novelty: a relative abundance of leisure time. The dacha represented a radical break with urban routine, and hence an opportunity to adopt a different, more open-ended pattern of life.

The projection of an exurban lifestyle and the legitimation of *far niente* can be traced through the proliferating magazines with illustrations (some of them even in color), many of which made tea on the garden terrace a regular tableau and accorded dignity to such activities as promenades, mushroom picking, and even postprandial snoozes. It was no longer shameful to do nothing or simply to want to enjoy oneself. As one columnist opined, after apologizing for what was already a commonplace, "we [Russians] don't remotely know how to have fun and experience the 'joys of life.'"[31] Various forms of commercialized leisure in Russian cities at the turn of the nineteenth century—shopping, dining, cinema, light music, and so on—were in the business of instilling the requisite decorous joie de vivre and helping Russians to abandon the undesirable extremes of boorishness and undue earnestness that were conventionally ascribed to them. The dacha stood apart from these urban recreations yet in a sense surpassed them, as its whole environment predisposed city folk to relaxation, diversion, and domestic consumption. Such values were, for example, projected steadily in the local dacha periodicals that mushroomed in the 1890s and 1900s. Home decoration and home improvement were regular topics; advice was given on matters such as egg painting and the correct organization of a game of croquet; gossipy reports on local happenings were published in abundance; beauty tips were dispensed to women; and readers of both sexes were invited to savor the fictionalized exploits of dacha "Don Juans" and "Romeos."[32]

The association of the dacha with leisure and consumption was strengthened by its detachment from the masculine workplace and its real and symbolic role in family life. Throughout its history the dacha has been above all a place for women and children, as

30. C. Kelly, *Refining Russia: Advice Literature, Polite Culture, and Gender from Catherine to Yeltsin* (Oxford, 2001), 184–86.

31. *Khudozhnik*, no. 1 (1891).

32. Note the following examples: *Dachnaia zhizn'* (a supplement to the middlebrow magazine *Raduga*, published in Moscow in 1885 and 1886); *Dachnyi kur'er* (a St. Petersburg newspaper published in 1908); *Dachnaia gazeta* (published in St. Petersburg in 1908); *Dachnaia biblioteka*, St. Petersburg, 1911; *Dachnitsa* (a weekly newspaper published in St. Petersburg in 1912); *Dachnik* (Moscow, published in 1912).

men have generally continued to commute to work throughout the summer months (compare this situation with the parallel, but on the whole much more positively construed, "feminization" of American suburbia from the 1820s on).[33] Comforting domesticity was, accordingly, a prime value for summerfolk. A proper family dacha might be of modest size, but it was to be kept clean and well appointed; everything in it should "breathe contentment."[34]

Perceived to be a female dominion, dachas gave rise to stereotypes and humorous narratives concerning relations between the sexes. As early as the 1870s the put-upon *dachnyi muzh* was becoming a cliché of writings on the dacha. In 1899 the term was glossed in a dictionary of catchphrases as "a husband who leaves for work from the dacha and is given various errands by his wife, sisters-in-law, mother-in-law, and neighbors."[35] In a Chekhov story, "Superfluous Men" (1886), a dacha husband arrives home tired from work only to find that his wife is out rehearsing for amateur theatricals; when she finally comes back, it is in the company of her fellow actors, and they proceed to conduct a further noisy rehearsal into the small hours.[36] Other accounts went further still, suggesting that married women, in the prolonged absences of their commuting husbands, were able to establish suspiciously free-and-easy social relations with other men. The most famous novel of adultery in Russian literature contains a pivotal scene at Peterhof that enables Anna Karenina and Vronskii to have an uninterrupted and crucial tête-à-tête. Perhaps we should not accord too overriding a role in Anna's affair to the dacha, as her infidelity is so thoroughly overdetermined (quite apart from being constrained by Tolstoy's chain of symbolic connections, she is pregnant by this stage); but the fact remains that the dacha offered women more latitude than many writers professed to be good for the sanctity of marriage.[37]

As well as placing a premium on feminized domesticity, the dacha brought a release from the strict standards of urban decorum. Instead of going to the expense of taking with them all the furniture from their city apartments, summerfolk were urged to fill sacks with hay and use them as armchairs. Immobile intellectual pursuits were to be avoided; much better were tennis, croquet, boating, and bathing—and even "loud and lively conversation" could do much to aid the digestion.[38] The three key elements in con-

33. On America, see K. Jackson, *Crabgrass Frontier: The Suburbanization of the United States* (New York, 1985), esp. chap. 3.

34. *Leto v Tsarskom Sele: Rasskazy dlia detei* (St. Petersburg, 1880), 16. Note also *Dachnyi poezd* (Moscow, 1917), another children's book, plushly illustrated in full color, with the cherubic children clothed in prim anglophile attire.

35. M. I. Mikhel'son, *Russkaia mysl' i rech': Opyt russkoi frazeologii* (St. Petersburg, 1899), 227.

36. A. P. Chekhov, "Lishnie liudi," in his *Polnoe sobranie sochinenii i pisem v tridtsati tomakh* (Moscow, 1974–83), 5:198–204.

37. Thus in several Chekhov stories women are confronted with the tedium of married life and driven, usually against their better judgment, into extramarital liaisons ("Ot nechego delat'," "Neschast'e," both 1886).

38. M. V-v, *Kak provodit' leto na dache (Dachnaia dietetika)* (St. Petersburg, 1909). Similar in its insistence on simple furnishings and the rational use of domestic space is *Khoziaika doma (domoustroistvo)* (St. Petersburg, 1895). The virtues of physical activity and exposure to the natural environment are also extolled in *"Dachnik": Dachnye mestnosti vblizi g. Kieva* (Kiev, 1909). A parody of good intentions for the summer is Sasha Chernyi's fourth "epistle" (of 1908) from the Baltics, in his *Sobranie sochinenii v piati tomakh* (Moscow, 1996), 1:135–36.

100    duct at the dacha were "simplicity," "hospitality," and "modesty." Casual visitors should
be given a light snack (the servants should unobtrusively be asked to bring something in).
Hosts should not treat longer-term house guests with urban formality. And guests should
reciprocate by treating servants and animals in a friendly manner.[39] To set store by urban
hierarchies was to invite ridicule. In a sketch of the 1890s, a civil servant named Maksim
Nikolaevich walks past a garden in his dacha settlement where the residents are playing
cards. He himself is itching for a game, but is reluctant to invite his neighbors to visit because he considers them his social inferiors: one is a cook, the other a barber. To engage
them in conversation, he contrives a pretext for stopping outside their fence: "I like your
association. The fact that you've associated with one another and formed at least a small
entertainment society. You know, this has a real European flavor."[40] The dacha, as presented in advice literature and illustrated magazines, was tied in with the search for new,
more "civilized" forms of social intercourse, such as small talk, that allowed free, non-
hierarchical, nonsexualized relations between men and women. As in so many other areas
of late imperial middle-class culture, England was the preferred model for emulation.

Social mixing of this relatively unstructured kind did, of course, leave considerable
scope for embarrassment, as people of high social station—especially women—often had
to enter relationships with their inferiors. There was no harm in such unequal acquaintances, one etiquette guide suggested, as long as both sides maintained "tact" and "delicacy"; but they also held potential for unpleasantness if one or another of the parties took
liberties. If relations did become strained, the return to the city at the end of the season
was an "extremely convenient" occasion to break them off. A social hierarchy was clearly
implied in the ways visits were conducted. Those of higher social status could clearly expect to receive more visits than they paid. But with equals it was recommended that one
take the initiative by paying visits to neighbors on arrival (just sending a card would not
do, although a card *pour prendre congé* at the end of the season was permissible).[41] The notion that the informality of dacha life made residents vulnerable to impromptu and prolonged visits from friends and relatives became a commonplace in journalism and fiction
alike. One humorous "encyclopedia" of dacha life had a special entry for "Guests": "they
'descend' the day before holidays and on the holidays themselves. They wreak complete
havoc at the dacha, drinking and devouring everything that is available."[42]

The unpredictability of dacha life is evoked more artfully in Dostoevsky's *The Idiot*.
Dostoevsky is above all a novelist of urban enclosure (both in Petersburg and in the small
towns of *Devils* and *The Brothers Karamazov*), and the early sections of *The Idiot* contain
some of his most claustrophobic writing, corresponding to the Gothic gloom of the interiors and to Myshkin's heightened perceptions of his urban environment as, dimly aware

39. *Zhizn' v svete, doma i pri dvore* (St. Petersburg, 1890).

40. N. A. Leikin, "Vinter," in his *Na dachnom proziabanii*, 4th ed. (St. Petersburg, 1912), 56.

41. *Zhizn' v svete*, 108–10.

42. *Dachnik*, no. 5 (1912), 12. Similar is Chekhov's story "Dachniki" (1885), where newlyweds enjoying their
privacy at the dacha unwisely take a stroll to the railway station and meet the husband's uncle and his large family, who have come to visit. Unwelcome dacha guests are also the subject of Sasha Chernyi's "Mukhi" (1910): see
his *Sobranie sochinenii*, 1:65–66.

of being pursued by Rogozhin, he approaches an epileptic state. In Part 2 of the novel Myshkin manages to extricate himself from the city and, convalescent after his fit in the stairwell, takes up residence in a dacha sublet to him, surprisingly, by the reptilian Lebedev, who occupies one of the wings with his family. But the dacha does not provide the restful environment that Myshkin was expecting: life continues at an urban pace with a near-identical (in fact expanded) cast of characters. In some ways, the pace of life actually intensifies, as the dacha, unlike a city flat, is open to the street: one door gets you into the main room. And the shorter distances and more relaxed etiquette of the dacha serve to facilitate the unexpected visits so common in Dostoevsky. The dacha terrace is a boundary space more highly charged even than the threshold, whose significance in Dostoevsky's poetics was noted in Mikhail Bakhtin's celebrated study. In *The Idiot* the openness of the dacha to all comers is emphasized by the fact that this is a space where Myshkin is the host; so social rules are nonexistent and conversation becomes a free-for-all. The Epanchins, by contrast, have an imposing dacha of their own just 300 yards away; but its presence is largely symbolic, and the Lebedev dacha remains the focus of the novel's frenetic goings-on.

The main consequence of dacha informality, judging by the numerous short stories and feuilletons on this subject, was that it provided ample opportunity for summer romances (conventionally conducted in pavilions and avenues). The miniature love story set at the dacha, sentimental and facetious by turns, became a staple of light magazine fiction. The garden at the country estate had been established for several decades as a location for trysts, but the park at the dacha settlement had the advantage of being a semi-public space offering a certain anonymity while at the same time guaranteeing the observance on the male side of certain conventions of decorous restraint (a parody of these conventions is to be found in Prince Myshkin's early-morning meeting with Aglaia Epanchina in *The Idiot*). The dacha park in nineteenth-century culture seems to be a more productive location for the romantic rendezvous than the garden at the country estate, whose atmosphere, soaked as it is in sentiment, tends to be overlaid with oppressive poignancy.[43] Most accounts suggest that at the dacha life proceeded without such constraints; formal social rules were, if not entirely disregarded, then at least coyly subverted. As point 1 of Chekhov's "Dacha Rules" has it: "The following people are forbidden to live at the dacha: lunatics, the insane, carriers of infectious diseases, the elderly, juveniles, and the lower ranks of the army, as nowhere is there a greater danger of contracting matrimony than in the open air."[44] So common was the association between dacha parks and nonpublic interaction between the sexes that respectable "young girls" were advised not to go walking in remote avenues where it might be suspected that they had arranged a meeting with an admirer.[45]

43. See D. Rayfield, "Orchards and Gardens in Chekhov," *SEER* 67 (1989): 530–45.

44. Chekhov, "Dachnye pravila," in *Polnoe sobranie sochinenii*, 3:21. There is a strong parallel here with bourgeois beach culture in Western Europe, which presented the seaside as an ideal location for acquaintances to be made and matches to be expedited.

45. *Zhizn' v svete*, 109.

102        Socializing of a less intimate but still extremely informal nature was made possible by
a wide range of other settings and activities. The local railway stop provided an important
focus for social activity and offered opportunities, relished especially by the younger generation, to make unplanned acquaintances. Dachniki in search of diversion would wait
there looking for conversation, amusement, and, if we are to believe the magazines, husbands. Once acquaintances had been made, they could be pursued in other gatherings. In
the smaller settlements, the atmosphere often approached that of a large house party, as
the dacha tenants would go on walks in large groups and arrange musical evenings; young
people had opportunities to meet in the grounds or on the tennis court.[46] Outdoor games
and other physical activities figured large: besides tennis, croquet, river bathing, and hik-
ing were among the favored pastimes. Locations near the coast offered the still more invigorating exercise of sea bathing, an activity that was claimed to yield benefits both physical and moral. Not only did it make the human organism generally more robust,
conscientious parents could also safeguard their children against the "English sickness" of
masturbation by immersing them, morning and night, in the cold salt water.[47] The largely
sedentary people who made up the dachnik population were urged to use the summer
months to restore some of the bodily vigor that the cramped city had sapped. Urban culture at the turn of the century was acquiring an "obsession with fresh air and exercise"
that could be generously indulged in exurbia.[48]

        Dachas also gave summerfolk scope to explore the new technologies of leisure. Cy-
cling had caught on, first in St. Petersburg and then in Moscow, in the early 1880s; by the
early 1890s there were twenty cycling societies in Russia and numerous smaller associations.[49] This new means of locomotion was extremely well suited to life out of town.
Whereas cycling was permitted only in specific places in the city, it did not fall foul of any
regulations out of town. More positively, it brought settlements closer together and was
valued especially by young people for providing them with an exciting new form of exercise and for greatly expanding their freedom of movement. Dacha periodicals regularly
passed comment on the cycling phenomenon: some articles assessed its health benefits,
while others referred to the nuisance value of two-wheel speed demons on narrow rural
roads. Cyclists, according to one observer, were "afraid of nothing and no one," and at
critical moments thought nothing of maiming themselves or others; in some settlements
ditches had been dug to hinder the progress of these "pioneers of bicyclical civilization."[50]

        The impact of the phonograph came slightly later but was even more marked. The
first Russian recordings date from the late 1890s, but it was not until around 1910 that the
phonograph became a commonly owned piece of equipment rather than a technical in-

        46. One memoir account is V. D. Tsvetaev, *Dubrovitsy: Iz dachnykh vpechatlenii* (Moscow, 1907). Descrip-
tions of such entertainments are abundant in late imperial dacha periodicals.
        47. N. Fedotov, *Putevoditel' po dachnym mestnostiam* (St. Petersburg, 1889), 200, 215.
        48. L. McReynolds and C. Popkin, "The Objective Eye and the Common Good," in *Constructing Russian
Culture in the Age of Revolution: 1881–1940,* ed. C. Kelly and D. Shepherd (Oxford, 1998), 77.
        49. Iu. Blok, *Velosiped: Ego znachenie dlia zdorov'ia, prakticheskoe primenenie, ukhod za mashinoiu i pr.*
(Moscow, 1892), 25–26.
        50. A. K. Sobolev, *Podmoskovnye dachi (Ocherki, nabliudeniia i zametki)* (Moscow, 1901), 27.

Ст. Клязьма.
Les environs de Moscou.

Postcard view of Kliaz'ma station. Courtesy of Helsinki Slavonic Library.

novation to be marveled at. In dacha settlements it provided a novel aural backdrop to all manner of domestic activities and gave new life to social gatherings: now people could have music to bring a festive spirit to social occasions at all times of day and night.[51] The main cultural effect of sound reproduction, as of other innovations such as bicycles, improved rail links, telephones, and street lighting, was to give people a new sense of control over their own time.

Theater was another important form of collective entertainment for dachniki. Many of the larger settlements had theaters where performances were held regularly throughout the summer season. Besides forming the audience for visiting professional companies, dacha folk might also be involved in their own amateur productions. In the latter case, participation went far beyond merely bestriding the stage: a theatrical production was an enterprise that required coordinating the forces and resources of an entire dacha community. The standard practice, often remarked on in memoirs and fiction, was for a few enthusiasts to take the initiative and ask members of the community to contribute their time or money.[52] For both amateurs and professionals, the staple repertoire consisted of comedies, vaudevilles, and one-act plays, many of them insubstantial farces set at the dacha,

51. For an interesting brief history of early Russian sound reproduction, see L. I. Tikhvinskaia, "Fragmenty odnoi sud'by na fone fragmentov odnoi kul'tury," in *Razvlekatel'naia kul'tura Rossii XVIII–XIX vv.: Ocherki istorii i teorii,* ed. E. V. Dukov (St. Petersburg, 2000). An ironic comment on the dacha gramophone craze is S. Marshak, "Dacha" (1911), in his *Sobranie sochinenii v vos'mi tomakh* (Moscow, 1968–72), 5:475–76.

52. Door-to-door collection is described in the story "Ob"dinenie," in N.A. Leikin, *Na dachnom proziabanii,* 4th ed. (St. Petersburg, 1912).

104  with stock situations and characters.[53] Plays were often put on by close-knit groups of acquaintances (such was the case with the gatherings at Abramtsevo and Liubimovka), but performances might also be arranged for a broader section of the local population. Unsurprisingly, amateur theater met a hostile response from many of the theater journals, which took it upon themselves to defend the high art of the professionals. But the amateur performances, as far as we can judge, were generally well attended and well received. They were, it seems, a rather different kind of cultural institution from the "serious" theaters, deriving much of their appeal from easy audience identification with the events acted out onstage.[54] Dacha theaters, allied to the many other summerfolk recreations, testified to a cultural independence and assertiveness that was unwelcome to some observers.

## Discourses on the Dachnik

As will perhaps be apparent by now, social observation in late imperial accounts of the dacha was often overlaid with stereotype and prejudice. The dacha, despite—or rather because of—its ever increasing accessibility to urban Russians, had an increasingly serious image problem from the 1870s on. More precisely, the dacha had become too broad a phenomenon to condemn out of hand, and so distaste for the petit bourgeois philistinism (*meshchanstvo*) that it seemed to harbor was displaced onto the dachnik. Run-of-the-mill comfortable middle-class pleasure seekers were anathema both to wealthy conservatives and to the Russian intelligentsia, being seen by the former as vulgar upstarts and by the latter as unbearably complacent and materialistic. A lot of the objections raised were familiar from earlier generations of exurban commentary. The dacha boom was seen to be driven by fashion, by a "herd instinct of imitation."[55] A soulless love of luxury was replacing the stylistic restraint of earlier decades; ostentatious dachas were subject to disapproval as being parasitical.[56] Where owners had to choose between superficial flourishes and basic building standards, they opted for the former. Just as earlier in its history, Krestovskii Island was cited as an overcrowded enclave for "cardboard houses imitating Gothic castles and Greek villas."[57] Fears of declining taste, commonly expressed from the 1840s on, only intensified in the early twentieth century. "The main decorative element in our dachas is provided by innumerable carved decorations, which give the buildings a

---

53. The Department of Manuscripts and Rare Books of the St. Petersburg State Theater Library (the repository for manuscripts of all plays approved for performance in prerevolutionary Russia) contains more than thirty plays with some direct reference to the dacha in the title; the number set at the dacha must be significantly greater. On the generally acknowledged need for a lighter repertoire in the summer theaters, see S. Krechetov, "Letnii teatral'nyi stil' i Malakhovskii teatr," *Rampa i zhizn'*, no. 32 (1912), 10–11.

54. See M. V. Iunisov, "'Lishnii' teatr: O liubiteliakh i ikh 'gubiteliakh,'" in Dukov, *Razvlekatel'naia kul'-tura Rossii*.

55. V. O. Mikhnevich, *Peterburgskoe leto* (St. Petersburg, 1887), 14.

56. S. Cherikover, *Peterburg* (Moscow, 1909), 206.

57. Al'fa, "Arkhitekturnye zametki," *Domovladelets* (St. Petersburg), no. 4 (1906), 6.

vulgar and unsettled look that absolutely does not harmonize with the natural environment."[58]

Although the Russian intelligentsia's much-fabled oppositional unity was coming
under severe strain as early as the 1880s, some of their cultural hierarchies have remained
intact to the present day. And the dachnik has often been located near the bottom of such
hierarchies, on a par with the *meshchanin*. It is worth pondering why. The reason appears
to be that, in the eyes of the opinion-forming intelligentsia, dachniki, unlike *meshchane*,
ought to know better. They have education and—by definition—leisure, and have an
obligation to do more with these advantages. Take the following soapbox pronouncement
made by a character in Gorky's sub-Chekhovian *Dachniki* (part of a trilogy of plays that
Gorky, with his customary light touch, envisaged as a critique of the "bourgeois-material-
istic intelligentsia"): "The intelligentsia—that's not us! We're something else . . . we are
dachniki in our own country . . . some kind of foreign visitors. We rush about, try to find
ourselves comfortable niches in life . . . we do nothing and talk a disgusting amount."[59]
The opposition between talking and doing is a standard contribution to a cultural tradition: several generations of literary heroes (Chatskii, Onegin, Rudin) had shown talk to be
cheap and ineffectual. But dacha folk were doubly vulnerable to criticism because they
both liked talking and—unlike Rudin and Gorky's character—were unconcerned by their
failure to "do" things. Dachniki were strangers in their own land: not tortured "superfluous" people but something akin to the self-satisfied German tourist, the butt of much unkind comment in our own time. This notion is picked up in a sketch by Nadezhda Teffi,
one of the leading contributors to the humor magazine *Satirikon*: "The first dachnik arrived from the West. He stopped near the village of Ukko-Kukka, had a look around, ut-
tered the words 'Bier trinken,' and sat down. And around him a croquet lawn, a card
table, and a red-hemmed canvas parasol instantly materialized."[60]

The quotations from Teffi and Gorky also convey the shameless self-interest assumed
to be characteristic of dacha folk. In typical accounts, dachniki are neglectful of other
people's property and of the environment; they are, moreover, unreceptive to anything
that does not contribute to their material gain or short-term amusement. Thus in Ivan
Bunin's "Na dache" (1895) an architect's son is sent for carpentry lessons to a Tolstoyan,
Kamenskii, who lives at a nearby mill. In due course Kamenskii is invited to dinner by the
dachniki, who want only the opportunity to poke idle fun at him.[61] The dacha was commonly associated with a suspect detachment from the burning social and political issues
of the day. In A. I. Gomolitskii's "Na dache" (1911), descriptions of the view out of a dacha
window are humorously and incongruously interposed with reflections on contemporary

---

58. V. S. Karpovich, ed., *Motivy dereviannoi arkhitektury* (St. Petersburg, 1903), preface.

59. M. Gor'kii, *Polnoe sobranie sochinenii*, 25 vols. (Moscow, 1968–76), 7:276.

60. N. Teffi, "Dacha" (1910), in her *Iumoristicheskie rasskazy* (Moscow, 1990), 113. Note the dacha locations
that Teffi is specifically targeting in her satirical portrait: Ozerki, Lakhta, Lesnoe, Udel'naia, and all three Par-
golovos.

61. See I. A. Bunin, *Sobranie sochinenii v deviati tomakh* (Moscow, 1965–67), 2:114–51. The story is none too
subtle: it was rejected by *Novoe slovo* as being too "journalistic" (*fel'etonno*).

106   politics.[62] The fourth of Sasha Chernyi's "epistles" from a Baltic resort in 1908 observes the peaceful and harmless pursuits of other dachniki who in their working lives—as admiral, chief of police, teacher, and bureaucrat—are rather less inoffensive.[63]

Despite the prevalence of these unsympathetic portraits, however, it would be a serious oversimplification to divide dacha commentators into two opposing camps: a killjoy intelligentsia and a fun-loving proto-bourgeoisie. For one thing, representatives of the self-appointed cultural elite could not stand apart from the dacha phenomenon in the same neat way they could distance themselves from many manifestations of urban entertainment culture (taverns, *cafés chantants,* dance halls, and so on). Quite simply, they needed the dacha for their own purposes, a fact that was never wholly obscured by their attempts to draw a distinction between authentic and inauthentic models of exurban life. The same Gorky who railed against the dachniki in his play of the same name was a regular summer vacationer; he was even observed to shed tears at a melodrama playing at the local cinema in Kuokkala.[64]

Even more important, dachniki outside the elite cultural intelligentsia were not all fancy-free pleasure seekers. Unalloyed hedonism was not a viable option in an urban culture that, though it accorded increasing prominence to entertainment and consumerism, also clearly projected values such as self-sufficiency, prudence, restraint, hospitality, gentility, refinement, respectability, and cleanliness.[65] Mainstream summerfolk were, in other words, not at all impervious to intelligentsia values. They too were likely to want hygiene, public order, and a civilized but not ostentatious lifestyle; they might even aspire to emulate aspects of the *usad'ba.* Many of the negative stereotypes and stories of dacha life circulated in periodicals that were read largely by dachniki. These stock narratives should therefore be regarded not as attempted suppression of the vacationing impulse but rather as implying a code of out-of-town values and behavior. They seem in significant ways analogous to Western urban legends. As Americans tell stories about cement-filled Cadillacs, ax-wielding maniacs, microwaved dogs, and deep-fried rats, so late imperial dacha narratives regularly returned to henpecked husbands, unruly youngsters, and cunning or drunken peasants. Although these stories seemed on the surface to show the dacha in an unfavorable light, their deeper function was to provide a safe outlet for common anxieties, to trigger shared emotional responses (laughter, diversion, schadenfreude), and to give expression to consensual notions of what dacha life should properly entail.

Besides the obvious topoi of conflict with peasant landlords, public indecency, and accidents (especially fires), dacha stories regularly returned to various kinds of antisocial behavior within the summerfolk population. Disagreements between neighbors, conducted over the garden fence, were a particular favorite. In one episode of 1875, a squabble between dacha wives rapidly escalated when the young son of one of the women threw a

62.  See I. S. Eventov, ed., *Russkaia stikhotvornaia satira, 1908–1917 godov* (Leningrad, 1974), 135.

63.  Chernyi, *Sobranie sochinenii,* 1:134–35.

64.  Iu. Annenkov, *Dnevnik moikh vstrech: Tsikl tragedii,* 2 vols. (New York, 1966), 1:28.

65.  These attributes are extracted from S. Smith and C. Kelly, "Commercial Culture and Consumerism," in Kelly and Shepherd, *Constructing Russian Culture,* 112.

brick over the fence as the other's husband returned home.[66] One dacha owner of the early
1900s showed awareness of the long-standing stereotype when he wrote to his neighbor to
clear up a dispute arising from the repair of a fence dividing their two properties: "I think
that such a trifling quarrel is like the Gogol story 'How Ivan Ivanovich Quarreled with
Ivan Nikiforovich.' . . . So let's not argue and let's be good neighbors, especially as we've
known each other since January 1876—in other words, we're old acquaintances."[67]

Although at its best the dacha could be emblematic of harmonious family life, it was
also regularly presented as unbalancing relations between the sexes. Throughout the summer months, the "dacha husband" of the feuilletons was subjected to constant indignities
as he trudged back and forth between home and office. In the more extreme depictions,
married women came across either as green-belt strumpets or as harridans. Newspapers
published with relish scenes of domestic conflict such as the following: "A crowd of curious onlookers gathered outside the dacha to watch the wife of the decorator G. M. beating
her husband and then drawing blood by scratching the face of the lad who worked in her
husband's business. Blood flowed freely and the shouts could be heard all over Pargolovo."[68] The reporting of such incidents upheld the moral code of the implied dachnik
audience while at the same time conveying a certain discomfort. For, although the dacha
gave a wide range of urban folk unparalleled opportunities to develop a cultured,
leisured, and enjoyable lifestyle, it also took them out of their natural habitat, leaving
them as an isolated bridgehead of urban civilization in a rural world that did not share
their commitment to fine living.

## The Dacha and Late Imperial Social Diagnostics

There are few more eloquent commentators on post-Emancipation social anxieties
than the unpredictable narrator of Dostoevsky's *The Idiot*. Take the following description
of Nastas'ia Fillipovna and her entourage as they prepare to descend the three steps to the
Pavlovsk bandstand, thus provoking one of the novel's several climactic *skandaly*:

> Many of them, it might well have been thought, were drunk, though some of
> them were wearing smart and elegant clothes; but among them were also men
> who looked very peculiar, in peculiar clothes and with peculiarly flushed faces;
> some of them were army officers and some were far from young; there were also
> among them men who were comfortably dressed in wide and well-cut suits, wear-
> ing diamond rings and cufflinks, and magnificent pitch-black wigs and side
> whiskers, with an imposing though somewhat fastidious expression on their
> faces, who in society are, as a rule, avoided like the plague. In our holiday resorts

66. "Kolomiagskie dachnitsy," *PG*, 12 July 1875, 2.
67. TsIAM, f. 483, op. 3, d. 245, l. 4. Of course, the reason this document is stored in Moscow's Central Historical Archive is that the plaintiff, unable to resolve the dispute on his own, turned to the local police for assistance.
68. *PG*, 17 July 1875, 2.

[*zagorodnye sobraniia*] there are, of course, people who are remarkable for their quite extraordinary respectability and who enjoy a particularly good reputation, but even the most circumspect person cannot always be expected to protect himself against a brick dropping from the house next door. Such a brick was about to drop now on the highly respectable public who had gathered to listen to the music of the band.[69]

Dostoevsky was not the only observer to notice a distinct change in the composition of concert audiences at Pavlovsk. Newspapers of the 1870s readily passed comment on the "mixed public," which included "workmen with unpleasant faces," "salesmen and minor civil servants and their families"; Pavlovsk, it was alleged, had become "the haunt of all ranks and all social estates."[70] In 1891 a feuilletonist commented that the moneyed bourgeoisie had largely elbowed aside the titled aristocracy; even worse, "physiognomies of the Jewish type" and "ladies of 'that' kind" had made their appearance. All in all, a public holiday in Pavlovsk had become indistinguishable from those in open spaces in the center of the city.[71] Rents were considered to have been kept too high in view of competition from places such as Shuvalovo and Ozerki.[72] By the early twentieth century, Pavlovsk was even starting to look neglected.[73]

The report on vacation places with built-in social commentary became an established minor genre of journalistic prose in the second half of the nineteenth century. Take the following description, contemporaneous with Myshkin's Pavlovsk misadventures, of a public holiday in the sleepy spa town of Lipetsk:

The public walk around the paths in twos and threes, with dignity, maintaining a deep silence, with long faces and placid expressions, as if forming some kind of procession. . . . There's no liveliness or gaiety, no originality in dress, no variety in people's behavior; everyone looks at everyone else, worried that they might stand out from the others in some way. This is obviously a provincial public who expend all their energy on not compromising themselves in the eyes of visitors from the capital by undue familiarity or anything unusual.[74]

69. F. M. Dostoevskii, *Polnoe sobranie sochinenii v tridtsati tomakh* (Leningrad, 1972–90), 8:288; English version from *The Idiot*, trans. D. Magarshack (London, 1955), 361.

70. A. S. Rozanov, *Muzykal'nyi Pavlovsk* (Leningrad, 1978), 66.

71. G. Znakomyi, *Dachi i okrestnosti Peterburga* (St. Petersburg, 1891), 3–8. Similar in its perception of social decline at Pavlovsk and in its anti-Semitism is N. A. Leikin, *Neunyvaiushchie Rossiiane* (St. Petersburg, 1912), esp. 240. Another account of the "democratization" of Pavlovsk in the 1880s can be found in the memoirs of the theater critic A. A. Pleshcheev, *Pod sen'iu kulis* (Paris, 1936), 108–13. A less alarmist account that pertains to the 1890s is Osip Mandel'shtam's sketch "Muzyka v Pavlovske," in *Shum vremeni* (1923), in his *Sochineniia v dvukh tomakh* (Moscow, 1990), 2:6–8.

72. See, e.g., *PL*, 8 June 1880, 3.

73. L. Afanas'ev, "Padenie Pavlovsk," *Dachnitsa*, no. 3 (1912), 2.

74. "Lipetsk 3 iiunia," *Lipetskii letnii listok*, 7 June 1870, 1.

Here the emphasis was on provincial backwardness, but reports on dacha places near the
two major cities were most often presented specifically as evidence of the nobility's weakening social position, which might be construed as social degeneration or as a more
healthy social development, according to the author's preference. The latter view was
taken by one Moscow journalist in 1860:

> These days Sokol'niki is more the home of merchants, foreign traders, in fact all
> foreigners, who spend more on their lifestyle and are more expert in doing so
> than the enlightened Russian nobility. But whining patricians to this day don't
> like rubbing shoulders with the middle estate, they don't even like observing them
> at close quarters. I don't know what has caused this: whether it's simply an inher-
> ited Asiatic caste prejudice or vanity gnawing away inside or, finally, an unex-
> pressed awareness that real advantages these days do not at all correspond to es-
> tate privileges.[75]

By the 1870s and 1880s, the Petersburg and Moscow sensationalist press, while it had
no particular love for "whining patricians," tended to view overcrowded and heterogeneous dacha settlements as following a trajectory of inexorable social decline.[76] Commentators noted a decline in linguistic propriety: "Instead of the tender murmurs and war-
blings of young resonant voices you hear flat, cynical quips, coarse jokes, and obscene
conversations," noted one Petersburg journalist of Novaia Derevnia.[77] Leonid Andreev
wrote that the population of Moscow's night shelters each summer relocated to dacha settlements, where they slept outdoors and engaged in petty thievery.[78] Andreev's piece,
alarmist though it is, does demonstrate that dacha settlements were particularly vulnerable to perceptions of social malaise, because they were filled with people of no instantly
definable occupation; scroungers and spongers became stock dacha characters in the
feuilletons of the time.[79]

Newspapers reported with particular relish violent and otherwise socially disruptive
incidents in formerly prestigious settlements such as the Peterhof Road, Tsarskoe Selo,
Krasnoe Selo, Peterhof, and Lesnoi Korpus. Thus in the summer of 1880 it came to public
attention that a dacha governess had been trying to seduce a boy in her charge, that ladies
had been harassed on the station platform at Krasnoe Selo, and that Peterhof had been afflicted by swindlers and falling prices.[80] After a watchman told a cab driver in the Par-

75. "Gorodskaia khronika," *Razvlechenie*, no. 25 (1860), 304.

76. The ways in which the "new" phenomena of urban crime and public unruliness were treated in the
press are analyzed in detail by Joan Neuberger in her *Hooliganism: Crime, Culture, and Power in St. Petersburg,
1900–1914* (Berkeley, 1993).

77. Znakomyi, *Dachi*, 11.

78. L. Andreev, "Moskovskoe leto nastupaet," in his *Sobranie sochinenii*, 1:144–47.

79. See, e.g., V.M. Garshin, "Peterburgskie pis'ma" (1882), in his *Sochineniia* (Moscow and Leningrad,
1951).

80. *PL*, 26 June and 2, 8, and 23 July 1880.

"Dacha delights," a satirist's view of the strains of dacha life (from *Razvlechenie,* no. 25 [1885])

golovo area to slow down, the passenger leaped out, shouted insults, and then physically assaulted him.[81] Thirty years later, the tenor of newspaper reporting had changed little. In a dacha settlement outside Warsaw the bloodied body of a "respectably dressed girl" was found at the edge of a wood. A youth, "an educated man [*intelligent*] by appearance," was seen running away from the scene of the crime. The girl, it transpired, was the daughter of

81. *PLL,* 1 Aug. 1882, 2.

a merchant, and the young man had been pressing for her hand in marriage.[82] In the village of Martyshkino, a bathing dacha lady came across a drowned worker.[83] On reporting a suicide in the second-class carriage of a train heading for Peterhof, one local newspaper alleged that the victim was about to "commit some sort of terrorist act."[84]

Reports of suicides tied in neatly with the dubious reputation of many dacha settlements, especially those on the way to becoming suburbanized. Modern civilization, with its soulless cult of luxury and of the individual self, was held responsible for the suicide "epidemic," as was the migration of hundreds of thousands of peasants to the city, which confronted them with moral dangers that they were ill equipped to resist. Almost invariably, the principle that suicide directly reflected social pathology was taken as axiomatic.[85] And so reports of suicides in dacha areas, themselves characterized in the journalistic imagination by social and cultural marginality, were doubly resonant. Here journalists had the discursive support of some of Russia's leading literary lights. Aleksandr Blok's "Neznakomka," for example, a genuine sensation on its first appearance in 1906, evoked the suburban seediness of Ozerki as the setting for the "unknown woman" of the title, who is a louche version of the Lady Beautiful so prominent elsewhere in Blok's poetry.[86]

Journalists' accounts were frequently peppered with observations that dacha locations contained a disproportionate number of foreigners. As usual, Germans were the butt of much unkind comment. Thus, for example, the son of a merchant family recalled rowdy toasts to the Kaiser at the neighboring dacha: "Notwithstanding the fact that the majority of them were German only in name and had been born and bred in Russia, the force of gravitation drew them to the land of their origin with such attraction as to make them avowed traitors to the country of their birth."[87] Germans attained more public prominence than was seemly at their annual Kullerberg celebrations on the eve of St. John's Day (23 June).[88] They were commonly alleged to be ubiquitous all through the summer in dacha settlements. As Vsevolod Krestovskii commented in the mid-1860s: "From May on dacha humanity can be sorted as follows: Pavlovsk is reserved for the beau monde; Novaia Derevnia equals Germans; Krestovskii equals Germans; Petrovskii—Germans again; Poliustrovo—civil servants and—alas!—Germans yet again!"[89] An account of 1867 divided the Novaia Derevnia settlement into three parts: the trading area (with its inns, booths, and peddlers), the German district, and the "Jewish quarter" (a name that had taken hold, but in fact this district was not notably more Jewish than others). The

---

82. "Romanicheskoe ubiistvo," *Dachnyi listok,* 21 June 1909, 3.

83. *Dachnitsa,* no. 3 (1912), 3.

84. *Oranienbaumskii dachnyi listok,* 30 May 1907, 3.

85. As Susan Morrissey observes in a useful discussion, "suicide was transformed into a phenomenon in which the individual was almost absent": "Suicide and Civilization in Late Imperial Russia," *JfGO* 43 (1995): 211. For more on the origins of the suicide epidemic and meanings ascribed to it, see I. Paperno, *Suicide as a Cultural Institution in Dostoevsky's Russia* (Ithaca, N.Y., 1997), esp. chaps. 2 and 3.

86. On the reception and immediate context of "Neznakomka," see Pyman, *Life of Aleksandr Blok,* 1:240–44.

87. V. Polunin, *Three Generations: Family Life in Russia, 1845–1902* (London, 1957), 181.

88. See I. Gensler, *Kullerberg, ili Kak guliali peterburgskie nemtsy na Ivanov den'* (St. Petersburg, 1909).

89. V. Krestovskii, *Peterburgskie zolotopromyshlenniki: Ocherki* (St. Petersburg, 1865), 39–40.

112    staid atmosphere of the German district was in sharp contrast to the lively atmosphere of the Russian area. These differences in temperament had led to violent confrontations between the national groups.[90]

As the last example suggests, Jews were at least the equal of Germans as objects of disparagement. Of the lake district to the north of St. Petersburg it was observed that "these days Jews are aristocrats too . . . anyone who has money must be an aristocrat."[91] N. A. Leikin, speaking specifically of Pavlovsk, commented on the preponderance of "Jews, Jews, Jews, beginning with stockbrokers and contractors right up to concessionaires— polished Jews who try as hard as they can to cover their garlicky odor with eau de cologne."[92]

Finnish peasants were also harshly treated on occasion, though attitudes toward them were on the whole less pointed and more affectionate. The worst that could be said about them was that they were surly and not overly concerned with hygiene; in particular, they took a long time to bury their dead and left manure and human excrement in open pits that fouled the atmosphere.[93] The northern side of the Gulf of Finland had the reputation of being expensive (especially given the need to pay customs duties) and not unfailingly welcoming to Russians.[94] But Finnish settlements had the compensating advantage of being quiet and safe (Terioki, for example, had none of the public disorder that characterized Russian locations).[95]

The greatest source of angst for late imperial dacha commentators, as for educated Russian society in general, was the native Russian peasant. As early as the summer of 1860, a Moscow columnist sent in a report from Kuntsevo, where he was staying at one of the dachas belonging to the Naryshkin family. The journalist assumed the position of one of the Naryshkins' house guests, admiring the views, the hospitality, and the picturesque local peasants. But the latter refused to keep a respectful distance: "Peasant kids of both sexes run around the gardens trying to get tangled up under your feet and offering you bundles of lilacs or other flowers from the fields or the forest, depending on the season."[96] Although this incident presented only a very mild inconvenience and would hardly have registered with journalists two or three decades later, it anticipates yet another argument mobilized in late imperial Russia against the dacha: the summer vacation industry was held responsible for diverting peasants from their fitting agricultural or artisanal occupations. Peasants who had not left to take menial jobs in the city occupied themselves with

---

90. *Peterburgskie dachi i dachniki* (St. Petersburg, 1867). On the rise of anti-German stereotypes in the first half of the nineteenth century, see A. V. Zhukovskaia, N. N. Mazur, and A. M. Peskov, "Nemetskie tipazhi russkoi belletristiki (konets 1820-kh–nachalo 1840-kh gg.)," *Novoe literaturnoe obozrenie* 34 (1998): 37–54.

91. P. K. Mart'ianov, "Nasha dachnaia idilliia," in *Lopari i samoedy stolichnykh nashikh tundr* (St. Petersburg, 1891), 249.

92. Leikin, *Neunyvaiushchie Rossiiane*, 240.

93. *Peterburgskie dachnye mestnosti v otnoshenii ikh zdorovosti* (St. Petersburg, 1881), 3.

94. *Putevoditel' po S.-Peterburgu, okrestnostiam i dachnym mestnostiam s planom stolitsy, imperatorskikh teatrov i tsira* (St. Petersburg, 1895), 135.

95. Fedotov, *Putevoditel'*, 7.

96. "Gorodskaia khronika," *Razvlechenie*, no. 23 (1860), 288.

small-scale kitchen gardening, woodcutting, fishing, and petty trade—all with the dachnik consumer in view.[97] Some villages had given up agriculture and handicrafts and moved over entirely to the dacha economy; such cases were inevitably treated with severe disapproval, as they were seen as contributing to the moral erosion of the countryside.[98] The incursion of a money economy into the villages was supposedly cutting peasants loose from feudalism and pushing them in the direction of an unwholesome modernity.

The prolific feuilletonist V. O. Mikhnevich was reluctant to use the neutral *krest'ianin* in reference to the dacha peasantry; instead he wrote of "dacha *paysans*," of "suburban peasants" (*prigorodnye muzhichki*), or of *posadskie* (suburban tradespeople), a term that, although archaic by the time he was writing (the 1880s), Mikhnevich felt captured the dislocated status of this group. For evidence to support his disapproving attitude Mikhnevich turned to the population of Pargolovo, a location beloved of journalists ever since the 1840s. Pargolovo peasants, he found, did not share the kindly nature of their patriarchal counterparts. They had ambitions above their station, but refused to work to realize them by honest labor. Instead, they looked to make large profits from supplying the local dacha population with goods and services (laundry, gardening, wood chopping) and to bend their backs as little as possible. Such peasants were commonly described disapprovingly as "prosperous." It was very hard to define the occupation of these small-time traders; they had certainly lost all interest in working the land. Very often they leased out land for richer folk to build themselves dachas. On paper, these agreements were advantageous to the peasants, often stipulating that when the lease expired, the land with all buildings on it would revert to the original owners. In practice, however, peasants so desperately needed rent payments in ready cash that the leasing agreement continued indefinitely. The money thus obtained (in the region of 50 to 100 rubles per season even for the humblest of izbas) relieved them of the need for the land that traditionally guaranteed their subsistence.[99]

But it was not only intellectuals of a populist persuasion such as Mikhnevich who bemoaned the changing character of village life within the dachnik catchment area of the major cities. The freeing of peasants from their agricultural pursuits stoked fears of social tensions and even unrest. The village of Tosno, for example, had been greatly affected by the opening of the Nikolaevskaia railway line (between St. Petersburg and Moscow). Agriculture was in decline, and now peasants could not even derive supplementary income from ferrying dachniki about, as the railway provided a regular and efficient transit service. Local peasants mostly earned money by piecework in the city; but they were left little time for kitchen gardening and animal husbandry, and ended up buying a lot of their food at inflated prices from traders. The tourist orientation of the village was confirmed when the manager of Tosno station—to the dismay of local peasants—invited gypsy musicians to perform so as to attract visitors.[100] According to many press reports of the 1880s

97. See S. Cherikover, *Peterburg* (Moscow, 1909), 203–4.

98. N. Skavronskii, "Nashi dachi," *Razvlechenie*, no. 25 (1866), 395–97.

99. V. O. Mikhnevich, *Peterburgskoe leto* (St. Petersburg, 1887), 33–51.

100. *PL*, 9 and 23 July 1880.

114 and 1890s, peasant responses to social and economic dislocation often went a lot further than mere dismay. Here again Pargolovo was a popular example:

> The St. Peter's Day holiday was celebrated by Pargolovo aboriginals for three whole days. On the first day everything was fine and proper: peasant girls, women, and lads went around the village in groups singing and playing the harmonica; but by the evening there was a complete change of ambience: decorum was replaced by impertinence and unruliness, and all of a sudden the dachniki were under siege.[101]

The report went on to describe how an elderly gentleman had had his hat knocked off by a peasant lad, how two ladies had been harassed by drunken and foul-mouthed locals, and how three men had been prevented from entering a local restaurant by a group of drunken peasants who were urinating by the entrance. All the while the local police were nowhere in evidence. Reports on peasant violence in dacha settlements were as old as the Petersburg boulevard press itself, and they continued to the end of the imperial period.[102] In Pargolovo in 1880 a peasant boy hanged himself after he had taken the family's plow out without asking permission and his horse fell at the first furrow, breaking the shaft.[103] In 1909 a journalist reported that in Pargolovo III there were "four pubs, two wine stores, a wineshop, and other similar institutions" within a stretch of only 100 sazhens. "This once peaceful dacha resort now resounds every evening with drunken singing and the swearing of local hooligans."[104]

The local newspaper for Pargolovo volost, although it often disputed the sensationalized reports found in the boulevard press, shared its perception of social tensions. In 1882 it contended that the "upper layers of the dacha population"—with the exceptions of "minor cases of bullying that have brought dachniki to the local police cell and of suggestions of dramas and romances that are supposed to have taken place during the present season"—should not bear responsibility for the general decline in standards of public behavior. Rather, blame should be attached to servants and to various kinds of migrants (in winter, spring, and autumn, these were laborers; in summer, peddlers, organ grinders, and beggars). In summer the population swelled from around 2,000 to 10,000 registered residents (the real number was significantly greater). The six village constables currently employed could not cope with the resulting waves of drunkenness and burglaries, and dachniki were unwilling to hire yardmen to keep an eye on their property.[105]

Mutual suspicion and incomprehension between dachnik and peasant had also become a common theme of fiction set in dacha settlements. Literary representations of the

---

101. *PL*, 3 July 1880, 2.

102. See, e.g., *PL*, 21 July 1871, which marks out Pargolovo peasants for their drunkenness, mendicity, and neglect of the land. The same year's issues contain numerous reports of assaults perpetrated by and on peasants in Pargolovo and other dacha locations. For a later, equally discouraging account of Pargolovo, see *Dachnik*, 10 May 1909, 2.

103. "Iz dachnykh mest," *PL*, 7 M~v 1880, 3.

104. *Dachnik*, 10 May 1909, 2.

105. "Na skol'ko my nravstvenny?" *PLL*, 25 July 1882, 3.

peasantry had by the 1880s a sizable history. In the sentimentalist age, representatives of the common people were human props in dramas of sensibility; in the mid-nineteenth century they emerged as full-fledged human beings with the potential to be dramatic heroes; but in the 1870s disappointment with the peasantry set in, and it only deepened thereafter. Poverty, hunger, adultery, and crime (without repentance) became dominant themes.[106]

In Gleb Uspenskii's *Quick Sketches* (1881), the narrator, an educated commoner named Lissabonskii, has come back in despair from an expedition to spread enlightenment to the Russian village. His burning desire to communicate with the common people has given way to a powerful urge to lie face down in the damp grass and blank out all thoughts. The location he chooses for this summer of recuperation is a village some 150 versts from St. Petersburg. Here, however, he runs into the same problems he had encountered in his more socially engaged recent past. Take the following exchange with a "village proletarian":

> "Excuse my asking, but what kind of title might you have?"
> "Why do you need to know that?"
> "Just so's I know, sir. You know, where are you from, how did you get here? These days, as you know yourself, you get all sorts of charlatans turning up."
> "I've come to spend the summer at the dacha," I replied categorically. "I need to spend time in the country for my health."
> "So that's what it is. You mean, you've come to us from Petersburg for your health in actual fact?"
> "In actual fact for my health. Don't you feel what the air is like here! Well, I want to fill my lungs with it."
> "With the air, sir?"
> "Yes, with the air."
> "But isn't there any air in Petersburg?"
> "There is, but it's awful."
> "Well, I never! So you mean it's just for the air?"
> "Yes!"
> "Aha. You came here by machine [i.e., by train] actually because of the air?"
> Silence.
> "Nice to have you here."
> He fell silent and looked at me goggle-eyed, as they say.[107]

Peasants' unreceptive attitude toward the dacha impulse is the subject, albeit from a different perspective, of a sketch by N. A. Leikin: a servant of peasant origin leaves her masters' employment when she discovers they have rented a dacha near Oranienbaum,

106. See A. Donskov, *The Changing Image of the Peasant in Nineteenth-Century Russian Drama* (Helsinki, 1972), and D. Fanger, "The Peasant in Literature," in *The Peasant in Nineteenth-Century Russia*, ed. W. Vucinich (Stanford, 1968).

107. G. I. Uspenskii, *Beglye nabroski*, in his *Polnoe sobranie sochinenii*, 10 vols. (Moscow, 1940–54), 7:243.

116   which she considers a "backwater": "We purposely left the village to come to Piter [Petersburg], and here you are dragging us back to the village. What kind of dacha is that—in a village!"[108]

Perhaps the most famous account of failed communication between dachnik and peasant is Chekhov's "New Dacha" (1898). In this story an engineer and his family take up residence in a dacha and make every effort to build bridges with the peasants of the neighboring village. (In fact, the engineer has quite literally built a bridge in their village.) But here again the peasants have difficulty understanding the dacha concept as it is explained to them: "In the new estate . . . they won't be sloughing or sowing, they'll just be living for their own pleasure, just so as to breathe the fresh air."[109] The peasants soon reach the conclusion that these dachniki are no more than landowners in disguise ("They're landowners just the same") and treat them accordingly: they shamelessly steal from them and encroach on their property, and at the same time expect their appointed feudal lord to keep an eye on them and resolve their problems.

THE PEASANTS in the stories by Uspenskii and Chekhov are bewildered by the designation "dachnik" until they impose their own very partial interpretation of it. Yet for all their ignorance, they were not so very unusual for their time in finding difficulties in understanding and using the language of social description. Discussion of imperial Russian society was based largely on the ostensibly fixed categories of "estates," which, especially by the 1890s and 1900s, concealed a huge amount of social fluidity. The word "peasant," for example, covered a multitude of occupations and social identities, many of them—especially in the Moscow and St. Petersburg areas—distinctly and increasingly urban in orientation.

Dachas, of course, did not provide a marker for a distinct social estate, but they became a useful shortcut for identifying people living in the major cities who were not peasants. The dacha came to be seen as one of the defining attributes of a late imperial "middle class." All urban people, from members of the high political establishment down to shopkeepers, might own or rent a country house for the summer months. For all the changes in the dacha and its social constituency in the nineteenth century, one thing remained more or less constant: dachas were almost always used intermittently by people whose main place of work and residence was the city. They were a form of settlement spatially separate from the city but in every other way—socially, culturally, economically—contiguous with it. Summerfolk, unlike the noble families of Russian cultural iconography who repaired to their country estates, did not take up residence out of town so as to relinquish their ties to the urban environment. Take the following rapturous musings by a re-

---

108. Leikin, "Pered dachei," in his *Na dachnom proziabanii*, 6. The idea that servants, as a "relic of serfdom," had become less deferential and less diligent gained such wide public currency in late imperial Russia that extensive debates took place on the extent and the nature of the police controls to which they should be subjected. The image of the deracinated peasant servant taken over by urban and materialistic values also found its way into the fiction of the time. See A. Rustemeyer, *Dienstboten in Petersburg und Moskau, 1861–1917: Hintergrund, Alltag, Soziale Rolle* (Stuttgart, 1996), 179–83, 216–19.

109. Chekhov, "Novaia dacha," in his *Polnoe sobranie sochinenii*, 10:116.

cent bride strolling up and down a dacha platform with her husband in Chekhov's "Dachniki" (1885): "How wonderful it is, Sasha, how wonderful! . . . You really might think that all this is a dream. Just see how cozy and affectionate the trees look. How lovely these solid, silent telegraph poles are! They . . . liven up the landscape and tell us that over there, somewhere, there are people and—civilization."[110] The dachnik was by definition a marginal figure in the rural landscape: a heavy-footed intruder breathing tuberculosis and the Neva onto the ruddy-faced village population, an Adam munching his own urban apple in an (admittedly far from paradisiacal) Russian Eden.[111]

This is not to suggest that the summerfolk were a monolithic bunch. Of course, the dacha differentiated as much as it united. Members of the State Council took their summer vacations in surroundings rather unlike those experienced by a tradesman. Quite apart from such obvious differences in scale and splendor, dacha users varied strikingly in the ways they thought of their summer houses; and such variation was socially and culturally marked. The conflicts and convergences between engagé intelligentsia and commercial elite, between noble and nonnoble, between visual and verbal culture were modeled by attitudes toward the dacha and—especially—the dachnik.

In an account of the dacha it is thus easy to rehearse familiar truths about the failure of the late imperial middle to cohere into a self-conscious, civically active bourgeoisie. What seems more noteworthy, however, is the extent to which the dacha engaged the attention and the cultural energies of Russian urban society. On a personal level, most members of this society had a stake in the out-of-town experience. Dachas were valued subjectively as a relaxing and pleasurable amenity, as a way of testing a lifestyle prophesy made in the first issue of Russia's equivalent of *Country Life:* "Fine living is not accessible to everyone, but it does nonetheless exist, it creates special values that someday will be possessed by all."[112] Yet, if we examine the cultural meanings circulating more widely in urban society, the lot of summerfolk sometimes appears to have been an unhappy one. As in England one can consider oneself a member of the middle class and yet use the term "middle-class" as a pejorative, so in late imperial Russia it was quite possible to love one's dacha yet poke fun at the dachniki. Dachas were able to elicit multiple and ambivalent responses because they stood apart from the city while remaining entirely the prerogative of urbanites; because they brought together people who, although they inhabited the same city, might otherwise belong to different worlds; and because, as isolated pockets of middle-class culture in a polarized society, they provided an opportunity for that middle class to contemplate itself. Paradoxically enough, if we wish to study the urban civilizations of Moscow and St. Petersburg in the late nineteenth century, there is no better place to start than outside the city.

110. Chekhov, *Polnoe sobranie sochinenii*, 4:16.

111. Here I paraphrase Vladislav Khodasevich's fine poem on the subject, "Bel'skoe ust'e" (1921), in his *Stikhotvoreniia* (Leningrad, 1989), 142.

112. Editorial, *Stolitsa i Usad'ba*, no. 1 (1914), 4.

# 5

## The Making of the Soviet Dacha, 1917–1941

I t is a startling fact that dachas, which had enjoyed such a high profile before the Revolution, had by the 1930s gained a secure niche in a new order that existed under very different social and economic conditions and espoused an ideology radically hostile to cultural remnants of the old regime. But is this continuity real or illusory? Can one really see any meaningful connection between the dachas depicted in Chekhov's stories and those of the Soviet elite in the 1930s? Are not these two sets of phenomena separated by a violent rupture that makes continuity hard to conceptualize in any satisfactory way?

Improbable as it might seem, points of connection can be found. The survival of the dacha calls into question the notion of the Revolution as a clean break in the social and cultural history of the major cities. The dacha is hardly the only thing that survived, of course: ostensibly improbable continuities have been traced in other areas of early Soviet life ever since Nicholas S. Timasheff, in a pioneering work of 1946, coined the term "Great Retreat" for the partial abandonment of radical social policies and values by the elite of the 1930s.[1] In the light of the cogent arguments made by Timasheff and others, the dacha might well be seen as just one of several prerevolutionary cultural status symbols that were appropriated by a new Soviet "middle class."

Even if we find signs of the past in Stalin-era culture, however, we are still left with

---

1. See Nicholas S. Timasheff, *The Great Retreat: The Growth and Decline of Communism in Russia* (New York, 1946). Timasheff's sociological approach has an important cultural-historical analogue in Vladimir Papernyi's *Kul'tura "dva"* (1985; Moscow, 1996), which, to state crudely a rich argument, reveals a shift from a dynamic, decentered, avant-garde "Culture One" (which pervaded the public discourse of the 1920s) to a static, monumentalist "Culture Two" (which increasingly took over in the 1930s and 1940s).

important questions unanswered. For example: What were the causes of the Great Retreat—social or political expediency, the self-interest of an elite, or some more complex
set of historical factors? How did it fit in with other aspects of Soviet life that, far from
suggesting a retreat from revolutionary aspirations, remained aggressively radical and
transformative? There is a need, in other words, to test the Timasheff paradigm against
detailed social history: to show how the interaction of continuity and change took place in
practice, how it informed social practice and affected people's lives.

These tasks can usefully be related to an enduring historical debate that investigates
the balance between "traditional" and "modernizing" principles in the working of the
emerging Soviet system: the Great Retreat, so one argument runs, took place in a society
that was very self-consciously entering a form of modernity, and it is this assertively modern orientation of Soviet society, not its traditional or conservative aspects, that needs to
be emphasized.[2] Another approach directs attention elsewhere: to the ways in which
modernizing structures, policies, and intentions led to "neotraditional" results.[3] One example is the Soviet bureaucracy, which, though designed to strengthen the centralized
state and inculcate impersonal standardized practice, may actually have forced people
into greater reliance on more "traditional" forms of behavior, ranging from unofficial
networking to the cultivation of allotments for subsistence.

To seek out traditional and modern elements in Soviet society, then, is a worthwhile
project but on its own it is inadequate. The next step is to examine their interaction over
time, and we can best do so microcosmically—by fixing our attention on limited objects
of study, such as the dacha. As well as bringing us face to face with the charged issue of periodization in Soviet history, the dacha can thus also provide insights into the workings of
early Soviet urban society.

## Exurbia in Revolution and Civil War

The revolutions of 1917 brought a rapid depopulation of the dacha areas surrounding
the major cities. Just as in 1905, when popular unrest in the outlying areas of Moscow and
St. Petersburg had scared away some dachniki for years, people were unwilling to expose
themselves to the risk of revolutionary violence and in many cases simply left their property behind. Other dachas fell vacant not because they had been abandoned but because
their owners had been called away—to the front, to the city, on business, or to relatives in
other regions.

Housing in the major cities was liable to be suddenly and violently appropriated by
the new regime. In Petrograd, for example, where revolutionary vengefulness was intense,

---

2. For more on this kind of argument, see D. Hoffmann and Y. Kotsonis, eds., *Russian Modernity: Politics,
Knowledge, Practices* (Basingstoke, 2000).

3. See K. Jowitt, "Soviet Neotraditionalism: The Political Corruption of a Leninist Regime," *Soviet Studies*
35 (1983), and T. Martin, "Modernization or Neo-Traditionalism? Ascribed Nationality and Soviet Primordial-
ism," in *Stalinism: New Directions,* ed. S. Fitzpatrick (London, 2000). For a thought-provoking comparative case,
see A. G. Walder, *Communist Neo-Traditionalism: Work and Authority in Chinese Industry* (Berkeley, 1986).

120   "bourgeois" families had good reason to fear instant eviction from their homes.[4] The situation in exurban locations was less clear and more variable. Although in some places privately owned houses were municipalized almost instantly, the authorities had neither the time nor the inclination to take full control of the dacha stock. The action taken in a particular village or settlement depended on the vigilance and activism of the local soviet—and, not least, on the behavior of the local population. Isaiah Berlin (b. 1909) and his mother escaped "the increasing tension and violence in the city" by moving to Staraia Russa for the summer of 1917. And, at least in the eyes of a young boy, life proceeded much as normal: "There were fancy-dress parties, tombolas, and afternoons in the park listening to an Italian orchestra playing at a bandstand." The Berlins spent the next two summers in Pavlovsk, though here the Revolution did catch up with them, as they were subjected to a humiliating search by the Cheka in 1919.[5]

In general, dachniki seem to have been considerably less vulnerable than estate owners to revolutionary violence: many of them rented their houses, and even those who were owners of private property could not be seen by peasants as egregiously laying claim to large tracts of land they did not use or need. A case in point was Iurii Vladimirovich Got'e, professor of history and associate director of the Rumiantsev Museum in Moscow, who by September 1918 had resigned himself to losing the modest estate in Tver' guberniia where he and his family had passed their summers before the Revolution. Instead, for the following few years Got'e spent time in various villages and dacha locations in the Moscow region; most often he sought refuge in Pestovo (forty kilometers north of Moscow), a settlement that during the Civil War was reached by a twelve-verst trek from the nearest railway station. Pestovo had few comforts but offered compensating advantages—it offered a more reliable supply of basic foodstuffs than did the city, and it was largely ignored by the Soviet authorities; by engaging in hard physical activities, moreover, Got'e achieved brief periods of oblivion from the underlying despair he felt at Russia's catastrophic social and political situation.[6]

The dacha zones most at risk were those that had been all but swallowed up by the city. In Moscow's Sokol'niki, any dachas left unattended were liable to be looted, and wooden constructions were sometimes completely dismantled for firewood.[7] In Petrograd, one of the first victims of the breakdown of political authority after the February Revolution was the Durnovo dacha on the Neva, seized by anarchists and converted into

---

4. See H. F. Jahn, "The Housing Revolution in Petrograd, 1917–1920," *JfGOE* 38 (1990), and N. B. Lebina, *Povsednevnaia zhizn' sovetskogo goroda: Normy i anomalii, 1920–1930 gody* (St. Petersburg, 1999), 178–84.

5. M. Ignatieff, *Isaiah Berlin: A Life* (London, 1998), 25 and 28. Another young witness recalled that the Revolution had brought Udel'naia (a dacha location significantly closer to Petrograd) only relatively slight changes: policemen were no longer in evidence and passers-by wore red ribbons. See L. I. Petrusheva, ed., *Deti russkoi emigratsii* (Moscow, 1997), 484.

6. Iu. V. Got'e, *Time of Troubles: The Diary of Iurii Vladimirovich Got'e*, trans. and ed. T. Emmons (Princeton, 1988). Similarly, old residents of Moscow's Udel'naia recalled that this dacha settlement had provided a refuge for members of the city's intelligentsia in the years after 1917 (in the mid-1920s, however, it was dealt a heavy blow by the campaign against "former people"). See N. Chetverikova, "Byt' li muzeiu dachnoi kul'tury," *Russkaia mysl'*, no. 4321, 8–14 June 2000, 19.

7. TsMAM, f. 2311, op. 1, d. 28, l. 520b.

a "house of rest" for workers. After a lengthy standoff between the anarchists and the Ministry of Justice, the unlawful occupants were evicted by force. But to keep the dacha in private ownership was still unrealistic; even Durnovo's own staff, on being informed by the anarchists that the dacha was now the "property of the people," had readily believed this to be the case. In September 1917, Durnovo offered to hand over the dacha as a hospital for tuberculosis patients.[8]

The Durnovo dacha was a very public and obvious target in view of its central location (by the early twentieth century it was a dacha in name only) and of the fact that P. P. Durnovo had a lengthy record of state service (he had been governor general of Moscow during the 1905 Revolution). Dachas farther from the public eye, however, might also fall victim to revolutionary violence. Aleksandr Blok was one dismayed observer of the devastation of resorts outside Petrograd that had been among his favorite haunts before the Revolution.[9] The damage inflicted by looters would often stretch to several thousand rubles' worth in a single property as houses were laid waste, their fittings stolen, and their interiors vandalized.[10]

Many dacha owners had already fled, but not everyone was so lucky: some were forced to look on as their property was raided or requisitioned. A woman named Efremova, resident at a dacha in the Moscow region, had in the summer of 1919 been away in the town of Kolomna, where her husband, employed in the financial department of the local soviet, had just died of typhus. On her return, she discovered that neighbors had lured her infirm mother over to their house by promising her regular meals and had taken the opportunity to steal numerous pieces of furniture and other household items. They had plundered property not only from the living quarters but also from the two outbuildings, the keys to which they had confiscated. And they had let out one of the buildings, taking all the rent money for themselves.

Efremova was a typical minor dacha owner of the period. She, her husband, and her father-in-law had bought a plot of 1,209 square sazhens in 1911 and on this land had built three dachas (only one of which was equipped for year-round habitation) with the aim, in Efremova's words, of "securing the old age" of their parents (in all probability, she intended to rent out the two surplus houses each summer for a modest unearned income). Efremova's father-in-law, who worked as a typesetter in Moscow, had died in 1915, and since then she and her husband had lived at their dacha continuously.[11] People such as the Efremovs, although two of the three "dachas" on their plot were little more than outbuildings, were soon to be classified as multiple property owners and the surplus housing made subject to appropriation by the municipal authorities.

During the Civil War and the first half of the 1920s a huge free-for-all took place in

8. See the Durnovo correspondence published in " 'Zakhvatchiki, imenuiushchie sebia "narod" . . .': Neskol'ko dokumentov iz fonda P. P. Durnovo (1917–1919)," *Zvezda*, no. 11 (1994), 156–68, and the general account in P. Avrich, *The Russian Anarchists* (Princeton, 1967), 130–32.

9. Blok's account of Lakhta in a diary entry of 11 June 1919 is in his *Sobranie sochinenii v vos'mi tomakh* (Leningrad, 1960–63), 7:365–67.

10. See, e.g., the report by a local housing committee in TsGA SPb, f. 78 (Primorsko-Sestroretskii raiispolkom), op. 1, d. 158, l. 63.

11. TsGAMO, f. 2591 (Moskovskii uezdnyi otdel kommunal'nogo khoziaistva), op. 3, d. 1, ll. 27–29, 33.

122 areas lying just outside the city limits. Peasants and other locals were able to occupy houses that had been left vacant. Owners occasionally wrote anxiously to the authorities asking for a protection order on their property, but in most cases were powerless to do anything. The scholar, critic, and children's writer Kornei Chukovskii was one such victim of theft. When he returned to his dacha in Kuokkala (now on the other side of the Soviet-Finnish border) in January 1925 after an absence of several years, Chukovskii found that his furniture and a large part of his library had been sold by an unscrupulous acquaintance whom he had unsuspectingly allowed to sit out the Civil War there.[12] In 1923 the people's courts were still being swamped with appeals concerning what was often euphemistically called the "unauthorized seizure of property" in exurban locations; it was decided that such cases should have top priority, as any delay meant that the dacha season might come to an end before a verdict was passed.[13]

Burglaries and acts of random violence against property were, however, by no means the only concern of dacha owners. They also had the new regime and its representatives to reckon with. Municipalization of the housing stock began immediately in Moscow and Petrograd, in adjacent towns, and in high-profile dacha locations with a large number of wealthy householders. In Moscow, all such areas located within the railway ring (Petrovskii Park, Petrovsko-Razumovskoe, Ostankino, Sokol'niki, Serebrianyi Bor, and a few others) were subject to automatic municipalization in 1919.[14] A total of 543 country palaces and dachas were used as vacation resorts for workers between 1918 and 1924.[15] Thirteen dachas on Petrograd's Kamennyi Island, formerly reserved for high-ranking state personnel, were turned over to a children's labor colony (named after the first minister of enlightenment, A. V. Lunacharskii) at the beginning of 1919. One dacha owner, Klara Eduardovna Shvarts, was informed abruptly (in person) on 26 December 1918 that her house and its contents were to be appropriated by the Commissariat of Education. This decision was carried out unceremoniously: the house was broken into continuously, and furniture and other items were removed without written authorization.[16] The vulnerability felt by prerevolutionary property owners was captured by Got'e in a diary entry of 3 May 1918: "A strange feeling. It is as if everything were as before, but the fact is that the gorillas can come and drive out the legal owners on 'legal' grounds."[17]

The dacha's vulnerability to the depredations of the new regime was exacerbated by its suspect ideological standing. Many representatives of Soviet power in the early 1920s considered summer houses to be among the least acceptable manifestations of private

---

12. K. Chukovskii, *Dnevnik, 1901–1929* (Moscow, 1997), 312–17. For a typical appeal to the authorities from a dacha owner whose property had been plundered, see TsGA SPb, f. 78, op. 1, d. 158, ll. 236–37.

13. TsGAMO, f. 2591, op. 3, d. 1, l. 3450b.

14. TsMAM, f. 2311, op. 1, d. 28, l. 47.

15. M. Bliznakov, "Soviet Housing during the Experimental Years, 1918 to 1933," in *Russian Housing in the Modern Age: Design and Social History*, ed. W. C. Brumfield and B. Ruble (Cambridge, 1993), 85–86.

16. A short memoir by a resident of the children's colony and a letter of complaint by Klara Shvarts to her local commissar for education are to be found in V. Vitiazeva, *Kamennyi ostrov* (Leningrad, 1986), 244–58.

17. Got'e, *Time of Troubles,* 140. "Gorillas" is the term Got'e uses throughout his diary to refer to the Bolsheviks.

property. In 1924, for example, Foreign Minister Boris Chicherin and the head of state, Mikhail Kalinin, had to enter into correspondence with the Leningrad regional executive committee to force this organization to assist Soviet citizens who were reasserting their rights to dachas that were now on the other side of the Finnish border. The committee had refused to support the establishment of a "Society of Dacha Owners in Finland," claiming that the existing provisions in the Civil Code were quite sufficient and that to encourage such an organization would contradict the "rigorously implemented" policy of municipalizing privately owned houses in Leningrad.[18]

Policies on dacha ownership during the Civil War were correspondingly severe. A three-month absence was sufficient for a dacha to be classified as ownerless, and failure to register one's property was also grounds for confiscation. Owners of more than one dacha in a single settlement would typically be left with only one house. Yet evictions by local soviets in dacha areas tended to have only a shaky legal foundation. Strictly speaking, the early Soviet decree on the abolition of private property related only to cities, not to settlements; here, as later in the Soviet period, exurban locations represented an area of uncertainty for Soviet legal procedure.[19] In any case, the law, such as it was, seems to have been only haphazardly interpreted and implemented in the early 1920s; influential contacts were the most reliable guarantee of preserving property, though determination and sheer good luck also helped.[20]

As the new regime sought to extend its control over the capitals and their outlying areas, the newly formed basic territorial units of Soviet power—the district executive committees, or raiispolkoms—were entrusted with supervising the dacha stock. The Primorsko-Sestroretskii raiispolkom, for example—based in one of the most popular St. Petersburg dacha locations of the years before 1917—was kept frantically busy in 1919 and 1920 as it tried to keep some measure of control over the properties that had suddenly fallen under its jurisdiction. In February 1920 its department of local services (Otdel mestnogo khoziaistva, or OMKh) was warned by the regional authorities that it should stop handing out furniture and other household goods to private citizens until it had carried out an inventory of all abandoned and requisitioned property. Even so, the local ispolkom continued to be inundated with requests from individuals for household items, articles of furniture, and entire houses. The range of confiscated items was considerable, from bed linen to clothes brushes, from pots and pans to wallpaper.[21]

---

18. RGASPI, f. 78, op. 7, d. 32.

19. An appeal to the letter of the law is made by an evicted dacha owner in TsGAMO, f. 2591, op. 3, d. 32, l. 288 (though it did not lead to his reinstatement).

20. One example: a woman who had married a wealthy Moscow merchant's son before the Revolution managed to hold on to the family's spacious dacha in the village of Dunino, thanks to her personal acquaintance with the revolutionary Vera Figner (interview with the woman's granddaughter, September 1999). The two other families I spoke to in Dunino were also the direct descendants of the well-to-do prerevolutionary owners of their dachas; one household had retained the property by gathering the large extended family in it and arguing that they were occupying no more than their normal housing entitlement, the other simply by going through the necessary bureaucratic procedures to register the dacha in their name with the Soviet authorities.

21. TsGA SPb, f. 78, op. 1, d. 158, l. 216.

124      In the early 1920s the pressure on housing was enormous as people flocked to the major cities. As a result, the prerevolutionary dacha stock had been almost entirely redistributed by 1922. In September of that year, the department of local services in Petrograd uezd wrote to the Pargolovo ispolkom inquiring about dachas that could be made available for rest homes, sanatoria, children's summer camps, and summer vacation homes for people working in regional state institutions. The answer was that all dachas suitable for these uses had already been allocated to new owners and tenants; none had been, or would be, handed out to organizations.[22]

An impulse to impose some measure of order on the chaotic dacha stock had been provided by a Soviet government decree of 24 May 1922 that called on ispolkoms to compile within two months a precise list of all municipalized dachas (that is, all dachas that were under the control of the soviets). This decree did not signal the start of dacha municipalization (which, as we have seen, was under way in some locations as early as 1918); rather it launched a period of stocktaking.[23] During the Civil War, houses had often been municipalized on local initiative, not according to any coherent overall policy; the absence of such a policy had also permitted many dachas ripe for municipalization to stay in private hands. In the way of Soviet decrees, the 1922 decree was promptly translated into an NKVD *instruktsiia* (that is, a set of guidelines as to how the decree was to be implemented in practice). The latter document called for restraint in redistribution of dacha properties: given the huge demand, only "well-founded applications" should be given consideration; and the transfer of whole dacha settlements to a single institution was strictly forbidden. The communal dacha stock was to be made up, first, of dachas whose owners were absent; second, of "lordly" (*barskie*) dachas (defined as dachas with at least one of the following attributes: running water, bathroom, electricity, heating; outbuildings; extensive gardens and parks; and fancy fittings); and third, of dachas whose owners had other such property in the same area (in such cases, the owners were to be left with one dacha only). The NKVD suggested a further criterion for those areas (and we must assume they were the majority) where the dacha pool obtained by the above methods was insufficient: on plots where there were several residential buildings, the owners were to be left with one building only.[24]

In June 1923 the Communal Department of the Moscow uezd soviet reported on its implementation of the municipalization policy.[25] It estimated that "up to 35 percent" of all dachas in its territory had now been municipalized. A breakdown by district revealed that the traditionally "bourgeois" settlements located on the Kazan' and Northern (Iaroslavl') railway lines had borne the brunt of reappropriation. In all, well over 5,000 dachas had been municipalized: nearly half (49.2 percent) of them had been deemed

22. Ibid., f. 469, op. 2, d. 5, ll. 35, 42. The OMKh did not desist, however: it subsequently issued several requests to investigate the social background of residents at particular addresses.

23. There was some confusion at the time on this point: see the clarification offered in S. Kisin, "Dachi i desiatiprotsentnaia norma," *ZhT-ZhS*, no. 24 (1927), 10–12.

24. P. A. Portugalov and V. A. Dlugach, eds., *Dachi i okrestnosti Moskvy: Spravochnik-putevoditel'* (Moscow, 1935), 176–77.

25. TsGAMO, f. 2591, op. 3, d. 1, ll. 329–57.

"unfit" (*beskhoziaistvennye*); 46.6 percent had been appropriated on the grounds that their owners had other dachas; and 4.1 percent were classified as "lordly" (though it may safely be assumed that many of the "unfit" dachas would have fallen into this category had their owners stuck around to find out).

In order to avoid municipalization, dacha owners had to register their property with the local soviet. By the time of the report, 5,001 private dachas had been registered and a further 2,918 applications were being considered. The understaffed department was struggling to keep pace, especially as applications required proper investigation (apparently many families registered several dachas in the names of various members).

What, though, did the Moscow regional administration do with the 6,000 dachas that were under its control as of summer 1923? The first task it defined was to "review the social composition of those renting municipalized dachas and to take them away from non-laboring elements [*netrudovye elementy*] if their number exceeds the regulation maximum." Municipalized dachas, in other words, were to be subjected to the dreaded "compression" (*uplotnenie*). No less than 90 percent of the communal dacha stock was to be allocated to the "laboring masses" and to institutions. Rents were set prohibitively high for those outside legitimate employment: from 1 October 1922 to 1 May 1923, nonlaboring elements occupied 75 municipalized dachas and paid 119,341 rubles in rent; workers and employees (*sluzhashchie*) were allocated 2,223 dachas and charged only 37,516 for the privilege.

Yet the same report contains ample evidence that there were ways around these punitive policies. For one thing, employees generally outnumbered workers, especially in dachas that were rented out to institutions. The category of *sluzhashchie* was elastic enough to include almost anyone in a nonmanual occupation. The Communal Department clearly distrusted certain tenant organizations, which it suspected were doing little to institute the desired affirmative action policy. In some cases, it was alleged, they simply reinstated the former owners. Such abuses were especially galling given the continuing shortage of accommodations for institutions: in summer 1923 more than 600 institutional applications for dacha space had not been satisfied. Above all, however, dacha owners were putting up resistance to the expropriation of their property. As the report concluded: "In effect a civil war is being played out around the municipalization and demunicipalization of dachas."[26]

## NEP and Its Liquidation

In due course, however, this civil war showed signs of abating. Citizens were able to appeal for the reregistration of a property in their name as legal regulations and bureaucratic procedures became slightly more stable. Norms for property registration were not so restrictive as they became later in the Soviet period: plots might vary wildly in size, from under 1,000 square meters to over 10,000; in general, however, the area was in the

26. Ibid., l. 349.

126   range of 1,500–2,000.[27] The demunicipalization policy introduced in 1921 for housing in
general began to increase the opportunities for dacha ownership. Glosses on demunicipalization emphasized that its main purpose was to ensure that the housing stock was better maintained. To this end, the criteria for dacha municipalization were to be interpreted
more loosely: the mere fact of a Dutch stove was no longer grounds for removing a dacha
from private possession. Rather, only "a combination of comfortable appliances and con-
veniences" gave local authorities the right to put a dacha in the "lordly" category.[28]

Despite the draconian policies of the preceding period, housing legislation of the
1920s seems laissez-faire compared to that of much of the later Soviet era. The desperately
underresourced Soviet state was willing to sanction various kinds of local and private initiative in order to reduce the burden on the center. Until the first five-year plan, national-
ized housing played a relatively insignificant role: in 1926, local soviets controlled nearly
60 percent of the overall state sector, and this state sector itself accounted for only around
20 percent of total housing.[29] Private and cooperative building were encouraged as a temporary solution to the housing crisis.

But this overview of NEP housing policy is misleading, for two main reasons. First,
cooperative housing—which, in the major cities especially, tended to predominate—was
by no means independent of Party and state authorities (as the sudden elimination of
most urban housing cooperatives in 1937 would subsequently demonstrate). Second,
there was great variation from one city to another. The housing crisis was always particularly acute in the major urban centers, and demunicipalization was extremely uncommon
there. It was by and large only in provincial towns that urban single-family houses remained in private possession.[30]

Dachas had an intermediate status. In many ways they were analogous to single-family dwellings in small towns or villages, but they also fell within the catchment area of the
major cities where housing policy was most interventionist. In Moscow and Leningrad especially, municipal authorities strove increasingly to establish administrative control not
only over the urban housing stock but also over the traditional administrative blind spot
of suburban settlements. By 1929, the "trust" now responsible for municipal dacha administration in the Moscow region had taken over 3,100 dachas in around forty settlements.[31] In Leningrad, similarly, a separate "communal trust" was formed to supervise
and administer the dacha sector. As of July 1926 it reckoned to have control over more
than 3,500 dachas.

The intention was to use these new administrative structures to push through centrally directed measures more effectively. By the beginning of 1926, the Moscow soviet had

27. See, e.g., TsGA SPb, f. 469, op. 2, d. 784.

28. D. I. Sheinis, *Zhilishchnoe zakonodatel'stvo*, 3d ed. (Moscow, 1926), 150.

29. G. D. Andrusz, *Housing and Urban Development in the USSR* (Albany, 1984), chap. 2.

30. See S. Fitzpatrick, *Everyday Stalinism: Ordinary Life in Extraordinary Times* (New York, 1999), 46, esp.
n. 22.

31. TsGAMO, f. 182, op. 1, d. 13, l. 12. At the beginning of 1930, Moscow's municipal dacha stock was distributed as follows: 4,000 under the trust; 7,300 under local ispolkoms; 1,000 under the oblast department of education (*BSE*, 1st ed.).

formulated a set of rules for the drawing up of contracts and the renting out of municipalized dachas to institutions and individuals. The rent varied according to the occupation of the tenants: for people working in state, Party, trade union, and cooperative organizations the annual payment was to fall between 5 and 10 percent of the cost of the
dacha; factory and office workers and artisans were to pay 3–10 percent; but the "nonlaboring element" was expected to pay not less than 15 percent.[32]

These new regulations were, however, at best only partially successful in putting
dacha ownership and rental on a sound legal footing. Dacha municipalization was never
conducted with the thoroughness suggested by policy statements on the subject. There
were three main reasons for this failure. First, the huge housing crisis, which, once the
Civil War had ended, turned former dacha areas around Moscow and St. Petersburg into
shanty settlements inhabited by daily commuters (and so a house, even if classified as a
dacha, was likely to be appropriated for year-round habitation). Second, the weakness
and disorganization of the local authorities, which often were not able to keep pace with
new instructions from the center. Third, the openness of the instructions to variable interpretation (a "lordly" dacha, for example, was very much in the eye of the beholder, and
a timely and well-directed bribe would presumably have swayed the judgment of many
inspectors from the local housing department).

In the 1920s, Muscovites were so desperate for living space that they were not put off
by the disastrous state of most suburban housing. The municipalized stock in 1923 contained 725 dachas (12.8 percent) that were "dilapidated," 1,771 (31.1 percent) that were
"semidilapidated," and 2,531 (31.1 percent) that required "minor repairs."[33] Yet reports
suggest that dachas were almost never left vacant; a very high proportion, moreover, were
occupied by commuting year-round residents. As one journalist reported of a village outside Moscow: "Most of the dachniki here are dachniki against their will, they live here all
year round because it's closer to the city where they can't find an apartment."[34] Special
concessions were made to encourage residents to rebuild the housing stock: if a dacha required "major repairs," tenants were exempted from rent for the first five years they lived
there.[35] The regional and local authorities received numerous requests for permission to
demolish existing buildings and start afresh. Given the acute shortage of housing in the
postrevolutionary era, it is little wonder that many people tried to take over or build
themselves houses outside the city. The building control committee (*Upravlenie
stroitel'nogo kontrolia,* or USK) of each okrug tried to keep up with this wave of individual
construction. Many people, having obtained a plot of land, went ahead and built with or

---

32. Portugalov and Dlugach, *Dachi,* 166.

33. TsGAMO, f. 2591, op. 3, d. 1, l. 339.

34. K.N., "Po dacham," *VM,* 7 May 1925, 2. Moscow's municipalized stock was reported to comprise 3,000
dachas in 1927, but more than half of them were occupied by permanent residents: see M. K., "Dachi," *ZhT-ZhS,*
no. 16 (1927), 12–13. Leningrad was similar: as many as 40% of houses in its satellite towns (such as Detskoe Selo,
Slutsk, and Ligovo) were taken up by commuters: see Mikhail [*sic*], "O derevne, prigorodakh i okrainakh,"
*Zhilishchnoe delo,* no. 13 (1925), 8.

35. TsGAMO, f. 2591, op. 3, l. 346. The encouragement of private reconstruction in dacha areas is signaled
in A. Sheinis, "Stroit' li zanovo ili dostraivat' i vosstanavlivat'?" *Zhilishchnoe stroitel'stvo,* no. 4 (1922), 15.

128   without the necessary permission; others turned former dachas into houses for year-round habitation by installing a heating system; still others converted outbuildings into dachas or shacks for permanent habitation.[36] The result of these make-do solutions was a spread of shanty settlements with very low standards of maintenance. One observant British visitor recalled coming across "what appeared from the outside to be a ten-roomed villa or *datcha* of wood" on a trip into Leningrad's northern dacha zone in 1937. This house, despite its impressive scale, "was surrounded by a potato-patch and looked so neglected that I thought it must be empty, but I was assured that anything from fifty to eighty people slept there."[37]

It is little wonder, then, that the dacha trusts had enormous difficulty persuading local ispolkoms to admit to free dacha space. When the Leningrad okrug administration tried to gauge the extent of the dacha stock in the summer of 1927, very few local ispolkoms volunteered information, mainly because most former dachas had been converted to year-round residences. The one that did provide dacha statistics was the Rozhdestveno volost (taking in Siverskaia and several other settlements to the southwest of Leningrad), which gave a total of over 500 municipalized dachas spread over thirteen settlements. Of these, 152 were being rented out to individuals, 110 were being used by the local ispolkom, 197 were controlled by the education sector, and the rest were empty or unfit for habitation.[38]

Given that available dacha space was so scarce, the trusts had almost no accommodations to offer the many applicants for a rented summer house. On their own, they had no way of alleviating the shortage, and so more publicity was given to alternative approaches. Some land was offered to individual dacha builders on long-term leases.[39] A more striking new development was the coverage given to the cooperative movement. House-building cooperatives had been sanctioned from the beginning of NEP as a means of making good the inadequacies of municipal housing provision. The one-family house of one or two stories was regularly proposed as a solution to the problems facing Soviet urban planning; the prerevolutionary vogue for Ebenezer Howard's garden cities had not yet run its course.[40] The showcase development of this kind was the Sokol settlement in the suburbs of Moscow, where construction began in 1923. This settlement consisted mainly of one-family houses of varied design: from the pseudo-Karelian log house to wood-paneled and even brick houses. The design of the houses emphasized their individual character, while the layout of the settlement—with its small tree-lined streets, some of them curving to

36. LOGAV, f. R-3736, op. 1, d. 16; f. R-3758, op. 1, d. 117.

37. U. Pope-Hennessy, *Leningrad: The Closed and Forbidden City* (London, 1938), 40.

38. LOGAV, f. R-2907, op. 1, d. 47, l. 2. It seems, however, that the municipalized housing stock was not always managed with great efficiency: the OMKh produced a list of seventy-two unused municipalized buildings in Slutsk (formerly Gatchina) as of 1 Oct. 1928 (ibid., ll. 71–72).

39. "Rasshirenie dachnogo stroitel'stva," *VM*, 27 Apr. 1925, 2. It is unlikely, however, that many of the dachas built on this scheme were used as summer houses (as opposed to year-round residences).

40. Reports on English garden cities and on other Western European models of deurbanization appeared quite regularly in the press: see, e.g., "Goroda-sady," *Zhilishchnoe tovarishchestvo*, no. 6 (1922), 29; V. Flerov, "Tipy rabochikh poselkov," *Zhilishchnoe delo*, no. 4 (1924), 18–21; S. Chaplygin, "Poselok-sad," *ZhT-ZhS*, no. 1 (1927), 9; S. Lebedev, "Letnii otdykh v Germanii," *ZhT-ZhS*, no. 22 (1927), 16–17.

A house at Sokol

form an arc—contrasted with the rectilinear, aggressively modernizing patterns of much early Soviet urban planning.[41]

The houses at Sokol were not dachas but were designed for permanent residence. In the mid-1920s, however, the idea of dacha cooperatives received fresh encouragement, the idea being that they would generate the resources to restore dilapidated dacha stock and to build new settlements.[42] Cooperative building projects were further supported by the publication of standard designs for prefabricated dachas that could be assembled in a day without knocking in a single nail and with the help of just a few casual workers.[43]

Dacha cooperatives established in the second half of the 1920s were suitably modest in their objectives. Most houses built under their auspices were small and made of plywood. Even so, the practical difficulties proved to be immense. Cooperatives required considerable startup capital at a time when bank loans and other kinds of institutional funding were not easy to come by, and individual members did not generally have the personal

41. A good short account of the Sokol settlement is M. V. Nashchokina, "Poselok 'Sokol'—gorod-sad 1920-kh godov," *Arkhitektura i stroitel'stvo Rossii*, no. 12 (1994), 2–7. Sokol was a high-prestige project that espoused the "modern" values of comfort and convenience rather than any socialist collectivism. By January 1924 the cooperative already had 250 members, drawn mainly from the intelligentsia.

42. In 1928 there was even a move to transfer part of the Leningrad dacha trust's holdings to cooperatives (LOGAV, f. R-2907, op. 1, d. 47, l. 49).

43. See "Perenosnaia dacha," *VM*, 5 May 1925, 2, and "Razbornye dachi," *VM*, 10 May 1927, 2.

130    means to make up the shortfall.[44] At the start of the next decade construction projects became more ambitious. In 1932, cooperatives were entrusted with building 1,300 new
dachas in the Moscow region (each to a standard design with two apartments, each of
three rooms). But here too the press reported severe practical difficulties in obtaining the
necessary credits and in coordinating the activities of the cooperative's various branches.[45]
In due course, attempts would be made to resolve these problems by tying the activities of
a cooperative ever more closely to its sponsor organization; as we shall see, the "departmental" principle in dacha management triumphed comprehensively in 1937, when the
cooperative movement was dealt a severe blow. Despite the negative press coverage, however, it seems that cooperatives functioned as efficiently as could reasonably have been expected, given the bottlenecked state of the Soviet economy. They also had a deserved reputation for apportioning space more liberally than did municipal settlements. In 1928–29
a dacha cooperative in the Leningrad area, for example, built new settlements at Toksovo
and Tarkhovka. By later Soviet standards, these dachas stood on extremely spacious plots.
The Toksovo settlement had forty-two plots that averaged 250 square meters, and the proportion of area given up to roads was unusually high; typically, only three or four plots
stood in a row.[46]

   But most Muscovites and Leningraders looking for a dacha in the 1920s did not have
access to the municipalized stock and were not able to join a cooperative. Instead, they
rented rooms or a whole dacha from locals. In April 1926, a representative of the Moscow
dacha trust publicly admitted that his organization could not realistically compete with
the private dacha market.[47] A guidebook to the environs of Moscow, published in 1928, es-
timates a total of around 300 settlements populated in summer by vacationing Muscovites (these included both dacha settlements proper and peasant villages where houses
were rented to city dwellers).[48] Dachas were differentiated according to location and
amenities. Prices could range from a few dozen rubles for the summer to around 300.[49]
The dacha's social constituency was by and large urban, educated people for whom the
annual migration into the countryside was both a deeply ingrained habit and a cheap and
relatively well provisioned alternative to maintaining an urban apartment through the
summer months. Memoir accounts suggest that members of the intelligentsia perceived
the dacha as a haven for prerevolutionary traditions, a place where they could take their

   44. V. S. Plotnikov, *Deshevoe dachnoe stroitel'stvo* (Moscow, 1930), chap. 2. The 1920s press, similarly, reported that dacha cooperatives were slow to develop: see Andr., "O dache, pochkakh i kooperatsii," *VM*, 15 May
1926, 2.
   45. *VM*, 31 Mar. 1932, 2.
   46. LOGAV, f. R-3758, op. 1, d. 132.
   47. See "Appetity dachevladel'tsev," *VM*, 2 Apr. 1926, 2.
   48. The distinction between "dacha settlements" and "rural settlements" had real administrative significance: inhabitants of dacha settlements were automatically granted Moscow registration (*propiska*), while in
rural settlements this right was extended only to temporary residents (i.e., dachniki). See the resolution of the
Moscow uezd ispolkom of 23 Apr. 1928, published in *Zhilishchnoe zakonodatel'stvo: Spravochnik postanovlenii i
rasporiazhenii tsentral'noi i mestnoi vlasti s prilozheniem sudebnoi praktiki za 1928 god* (Moscow, 1929), 388–89.
   49. *Dachi i okrestnosti Moskvy: Putevoditel'* (Moscow, 1928).

family (and in many cases servants too) and reestablish domestic patterns that were under severe threat in the early Soviet city.[50] Even so, there was no concealing the fact that most people's exurban living conditions had taken a substantial turn for the worse. One memoirist, born in 1915 into a noble family resident in Petrograd, recalled being taken to the dacha each year in the 1920s. In 1927, for example, his mother and aunt rented two rooms in the village of Gorelovo in a "large izba" where everyone slept on hay mattresses; Gorelovo was known at the time to be one of the cheapest dacha locations and was renowned for the quality of its potatoes (a detail that conveys the low expectations of 1920s dachniki).[51]

Newspapers of the period show the dacha concept being employed in broad and variegated ways. In advertisements of the 1920s and 1930s, the word "dacha" very often expands to mean, approximately, "any single-occupancy house out of town but not in the country."[52] As one would expect for a period of unceasing housing shortage, there were frequent references to "winter dachas" (that is, houses for year-round habitation). Dachas' size and level of comfort varied enormously, from a dozen rooms to two or three, from full heating, electricity, and running water to zero amenities. Location was another significant variable: for the most part advertisements concentrated on places familiar to the prerevolutionary dachnik, yet other locations were several hours' journey away. Boris Pasternak, for example, spent the summer of 1930 with his wife at a winterized dacha "of a substantial size" near Kiev.[53] The wife of the prominent Soviet writer Vsevolod Ivanov recalled frantically consulting the advertisements in *Vecherniaia Moskva* in 1929 when she was searching for summer accommodations for herself and her children; in the end she had to settle for a modest izba-style dwelling.[54]

For certain categories of the population such assiduity was not required. The more comfortable dachas in prime locations in the Moscow and Leningrad regions were soon made available to the families of highly placed Party workers. Dachas in Serebrianyi Bor were seized immediately and the first rest home (*dom otdykha*) there was set up in August 1921 by decree of Lenin. By 1924 this location contained three children's homes and one

---

50. For an account that argues that prerevolutionary habits were preserved "in a truncated form" in 1920s Leningrad, see " ' . . . I kazhdyi vecher za shlagbaumami . . . ,' " interview with E. E. Friken by Tat'iana Vol'skaia, *Nevskoe vremia*, 10 Aug. 1996. Similar is V. Pozdniakov, "Petrograd glazami rebenka," *Neva*, no. 2 (1994), 285, 288. This view of the social composition of the dacha public of the 1920s is also shared by N. B. Lebina in her *Povsednevnaia zhizn' sovetskogo goroda*, 251–52 (Lebina cites several other memoir sources).

51. V. Shefner, "Barkhatnyi put': Letopis' vpechatlenii," *Zvezda*, no. 4 (1995), 26.

52. Thus a 1935 collection of "dacha" designs included only houses that were equipped for year-round habitation: see G. Liudvig, ed., *Rekomendovannye proekty: Al'bom dach* (Moscow, 1935). Note also G. M. Sudeikin, *Al'bom proektov zimnikh dach . . .* (Moscow, 1928). Here the author acknowledges the difficulty of establishing a precise classification of types of dwelling: "The designs do not give the buildings names such as izba, worker's house, dacha, and so on . . . because several names apply to a single design, and this can cause confusion for the nonspecialist reader" (v). A handbook of the following decade divides dachas into four categories: *zimnii, poluzimnii, letnii,* and *palatochnyi* ("winter," "semiwinter," "summer," and "camping"): see G. M. Bobov, *Arkhitektura i stroitel'stvo dach* (Moscow, 1939).

53. E. Pasternak, *Boris Pasternak: The Tragic Years, 1930–60* (London, 1990), 25–26.

54. T. Ivanova, *Moi sovremenniki, kakimi ia ikh znala: Ocherki* (Moscow, 1984), 30.

132 sanatorium, and also accommodated 648 permanent residents in ninety-one buildings. During the 1920s and 1930s many Old Bolsheviks and other prominent figures spent their summers there.[55] A dacha settlement named after Mikhail Kalinin was set up by taking over wealthy dachas on the Moscow–Kazan' railway line; the dacha complex comprised twenty-four houses, many of them spacious prerevolutionary bourgeois residences with parquet floors and charmingly colored Dutch stoves.[56] In January 1928 the secretary of the Society of Old Bolsheviks (OSB) wrote to the Central Communal Bank asking for credits toward the construction of twenty two-story dachas, each with accommodations for four families, in Serebrianyi Bor or Kratovo. The letter of application mentioned that some dachas were already in use by the society, but that they were limited to a "select" few. After the bank expressed reluctance to oblige, maintaining that its credit limit for the year had been exhausted and authorization was required to eat into its reserves, a further appeal was made, directly to the Soviet government, and treated more favorably. The main settlement run by the OSB became the one at Kratovo, where the prerevolutionary dacha stock was substantially taken over by the new regime.[57]

Other favored citizens might spend their vacations in attractive resorts that did not have an exclusively organizational profile. Elena Bonner (b. 1923), daughter of an Old Bolshevik summoned in 1926 to Leningrad after a period of exile in Chita, recalled a carefree summer in Sestroretsk in 1928. Here she was left with her brother and their grandmother and nanny; their parents spent their vacation at a southern resort and made only brief appearances. Life was comfortable and untroubled. The children were indulged with ice cream sandwiches and frequently taken on outings and picnics; the local station had a restaurant with live music and even a *kursaal*; and the dacha itself was in a wonderfully unspoiled location—in pine forest, not fenced in on any side.[58]

Yet even for Party families dacha life was not always so idyllic. The following year Bonner was again sent to Sestroretsk for the summer, but this time the dacha fitted a very different model: not unblemished wooded expanses but cramped suburbia. The family did not even have use of the vegetable garden to the rear of the house, and the restaurant had closed down. The year after that (1930) conditions became still less comfortable: Bonner spent the summer in what was effectively a "dacha commune"—a large two-story house, reserved for Party workers occupying "positions of responsibility," which accommodated three or four families on each floor. Each family had a room of its own (sometimes two). Again her parents were absent for practically the whole summer.[59]

55. A. S. Livshits and K. V. Avilova, "Serebrianyi bor," in *Severo-zapadnyi okrug Moskvy* (Moscow, 1997), 233–34. It was in Serebrianyi Bor that the sixteen-year-old Anna Larina was courted by Nikolai Bukharin in 1930: see Larina, *This I Cannot Forget* (London, 1993). Larina was the stepdaughter of Iurii Larin, a leading Bolshevik intellectual close to Lenin's inner circle.

56. See the inventory in TsGAMO, f. 182, op. 1, d. 8, ll. 238–42.

57. Details of correspondence with the Communal Bank and Sovnarkom are drawn from RGASPI, f. 124, op. 3, d. 368.

58. E. Bonner, *Dochki-materi* (Moscow, 1994), 50–54.

59. Ibid., 60–63, 80–81. Memoir material suggests that Bonner's experiences were quite typical of the Old Bolshevik milieu. Nina Kosterina (b. 1921), daughter of two members of a Civil War partisan unit, spent much of her childhood in government institutions and Young Pioneer camps; in the summer of 1937 she was farmed

The leading Bolsheviks' personal willingness to enjoy "bourgeois" leisure facilities was not, of course, reflected in publicly expressed attitudes toward the dacha. Newspaper reports of the late 1920s concentrated on the outrageous prices asked for summer rental of even a tiny izba. As early as February, people were looking for somewhere to spend the summer months, but most of them were disappointed: dachas at affordable rents were simply not available. The beneficiaries of this situation were, predictably, alleged to be the nepmen, the nouveaux riches of the 1920s: "Only the wives of nepmen in their sealskin and astrakhan coats go around with radiant smiles on their faces. The best dachas in the thousand [rubles] bracket are theirs."[60] As the summer season approached, however, landlords began to lose their nerve if their property had still not been booked, and it was possible to snap up a dacha for less than half the original asking price. Potential tenants still had to be firm in their dealings with the "dacha brokers" who hung around all suburban stations: "they hike up the prices dreadfully, so you simply have to bargain with them. So for a small three-room house with the inevitable veranda they'll first name you a price of 60 tenners (so as not to scare off the clientele with figures in the hundreds, everything comes in tenners), then they reduce it to 50, and in the end they come down to 400 rubles."[61]

The existence of a dacha market was tolerated for most of the 1920s, but it was still treated with deep suspicion. The authorities were especially keen to follow up accusations of profiteering on the dacha market. In 1927 the engineer for Luga okrug (in the Leningrad region) wrote to the presidium of the Luga city soviet to report on alleged serial "speculation": a current applicant for a building plot by the name of Semenov-Pushkin had several times in recent years registered himself as the owner of empty plots or semidilapidated dachas, only to sell his right to build (*pravo zastroiki*) without even starting (re)construction work.[62] Dachas were further tainted by their association with corrupt practices: in a decade of desperate shortage, it was commonly alleged that the only way to obtain decent summer accommodations, if one was not a bourgeois, was to abuse one's official position.[63]

To remark on the unwholesomeness of the dacha became a commonplace of the time. A detailed guidebook of 1926 treated with frank approval any dacha settlement located in the vicinity of an industrial enterprise, but was unremittingly scornful of locations that had apparently preserved their "traditional" clientele and way of life. The following ac-

---

out to relatives in a village near Tuchkovo, on the Moscow River. See *The Diary of Nina Kosterina,* trans. M. Ginsburg (London, 1972). The diary was first published, to great acclaim, in *Novyi mir* in December 1962. Kosterina was killed in action in December 1941. The most famous absent parents of the 1920s were Joseph Stalin and Nadezhda Allilueva, who would commonly spend the summer in Sochi while their children lived at their dacha, mostly in Zubalovo, an estate formerly owned by prominent industrialists (the Zubalovs) that was turned into an enclave for the Party elite in 1919. See S. Allilueva, *Dvadtsat' pisem k drugu* (London, 1967).

60. "Ugroza dachnomu sezonu," *VM,* 8 Feb. 1927, 2.

61. "Tseny na dachi upali," *VM,* 14 May 1927, 2.

62. LOGAV, f. R-3736, op. 1, d. 16, ll. 67–68.

63. See, e.g., the cartoon "Dachi i protektsionizm" (*VM,* 20 May 1927, 2), which has as its caption the following dialogue: Peasant: "Do you need a big place?" Fat dachnik in checked jacket: "No, not that big, just for the general section of our organization: my mother-in-law, my wife, and the kids."

134 count of a settlement on the Kazan' railway line was clearly based on prerevolutionary stereotypes (with, to be sure, a generous admixture of anti-NEP ideology):

> The train pulls into a noisy, bustling platform—it's Malakhovka. Various people clamber out of the carriages: "dacha husbands" loaded up with more packages than they can carry; "ladies" with dazzling toilettes; flighty Soviet dames with square "valises" and people in "positions of responsibility" with respectable briefcases that are probably full of old newspapers and journals. . . .
>
> Visitors from Moscow stretch out in a long line along the streets of Malakhovka living in luxurious dachas that are for the most part occupied by moneyed Moscow—by the nepmen.[64]

The general distaste for the dacha on ideological grounds was mirrored by the attitudes of the artistic and literary avant-garde, for whom the dacha was synonymous with the social and cultural arrière. Note, for example, the metaphors chosen by Sergei Tret'iakov, a prominent figure in the revolutionary arts organization LEF, in this 1923 rallying cry:

> [Representatives of the Party] always remember that they are in the trenches and that the enemy's muzzles are in front of them. Even when they grow potatoes around this trench and stretch out their cots beneath the ramparts, they never allow themselves the illusion that the trench is not a trench but a dacha . . . or that their enemies are simply the neighbors in the dacha next door.[65]

A journalistic piece of 1922 by Isaac Babel' describing the conversion of a dacha settlement in Georgia into a resort for working people mixes class hatred with a distaste for everyday life and material comfort typical of Russian modernism: "You petty bourgeois who built yourselves these 'dachlets,' who are mediocre and useless as a tradesman's paunch, if only you saw how we are enjoying our rest here. . . . If only you saw how faces chewed up by the steel jaws of machinery are being refreshed."[66]

This unease in publicly expressed attitudes toward the dacha was exacerbated by the uncertain legal status of ownership. Land disputes were rife in former dacha areas in the 1920s. The review of dacha municipalization after the decree of May 1922 had, it turned out, been far from comprehensive, rigorous, and consistent. On inspection (for example, after the death of the owner), a house might turn out to be on neither the municipal nor the nonmunicipal list, which left the local ispolkom unsure how to act. Neighbors might appeal to the local authorities for land bordering their plots. And, especially toward the end of the decade, people's property rights might be undermined by investigation of their

---

64. *Illiustrirovannyi putevoditel' po okrestnostiam Moskvy* (Moscow, 1926), 57. This example could be supplemented by innumerable newspaper reports of predatory dacha landlords and nouveau riche tenants.

65. S. Tret'iakov, "LEF i NEP," *LEF*, no. 2 (1923), 72, quoted in E. Naiman, *Sex in Public: The Incarnation of Early Soviet Ideology* (Princeton, 1997), 11.

66. I. Babel', "V dome otdykha," in *Zabytyi Babel'* (Ann Arbor, 1979), 130.

social origins. In 1928, for example, the Workers' and Peasants' Inspectorate (Rabkrin) insisted that a local ispolkom investigate the social origins of the family of a former "hereditary honored citizen" (that is, a former merchant) and then dispossess them. The property in question, a spacious two-story "lordly" dacha (total area: 233 square meters), had anomalously not been municipalized in 1922. The ispolkom concluded after its investigation that the house should indeed have been municipalized, but that it was now impossible to change the situation because the latest government circular forbade any further action of this kind.[67] Many local sovicts did not have such scruples, inspecting dachas that earlier slipped through the net of municipalization for signs of "lordliness."[68]

Official controls on exurban communities may have been relaxed somewhat in the mid-1920s, but they were reapplied with greater zeal and violence in 1928 and (especially) 1929, when a crackdown on unregistered and misregistered dacha owners formed part of the campaign against "former people" (that is, people of "bourgeois" social origins). Demuncipalization was in many cases reversed without due legal process; registration of private property was canceled on the grounds that administrative errors had occurred.

Not that administrative errors were too hard to find, given the haziness of legal arrangements in the 1920s. Take the following case cited as exemplary in a guide to dacha legislation published in 1935. In 1923, in the settlement Novogireevo (Moscow region), a dacha belonging to one Shchedrin was classified by representatives of the NKVD as being of the "lordly" type and hence municipalized; but Shchedrin had sold it by private agreement to a woman named Ivanova, who in 1922 had gone to court to have herself recognized as the de facto owner. Armed with this judgment, she was then able (in 1923) to register the property in her name. In 1927 she sold it to a new owner, Dobrov. In 1931, in the course of verifying property registration, the local ispolkom uncovered these legal irregularities (that is, the fact that a building originally municipalized was now registered as someone's private property) and went to court to have Dobrov evicted. The court concluded that Dobrov should indeed be forced to vacate the property, but only after he and his family had been allocated equivalent living space elsewhere.[69]

So the municipalization decree continued to cause dacha folk enormous trouble even several years after it had supposedly been implemented—but it might also be ignored or manipulated to their advantage until the housing authorities decided to examine the situation more closely. Legal processes, it seems, tended to reflect the specific relationship between individual dacha residents and the representatives of state or municipal power whom they encountered. The class warfare of the late 1920s, however, tipped the balance of power comprehensively in favor of the local ispolkoms and against dachniki. The brutal design of this campaign is clear from an NKVD circular of 1930 that explicitly extended the war against "former people" to dacha locations. The earlier municipalization measures were deemed to have been insufficiently thorough; now the aim was to check the

67. Details in this paragraph are from LOGAV, f. R-2907 (Leningradskii okruzhnoi otdel mestnogo khoziaistva), op. 1, d. 167.

68. See, e.g., TsGAMO, f. 182, op. 1, d. 8, ll. 252–53.

69. Portugalov and Dlugach, *Dachi,* 173–74.

136 whole of the private dacha stock and to eliminate "profiteering." Absolutely no more de-municipalization was to be permitted. Even before this, however, the regional department of local services had instructed the dacha trust to check the social composition of tenants throughout the uezd, paying particular attention to "locations that formerly served as vacation places for the bourgeoisie and now for nepmen and people of free professions."[70]

The hard-line policies of the late 1920s had the predictable effect of encouraging localized and personal abuses in the war against social undesirables. Local soviets were aided in their work by a wave of denunciations,[71] though it seems they scarcely needed this assistance, as in many cases they were already itching to take control of dachas occupied by "former people." In 1927–28 a resident of Kuntsevo named Perevezentsev, who had lived with his wife in the same dacha for seventeen years, had had to suffer the forced occupation of several rooms by the secretary of the local soviet. The justification for this action was that he and his wife, having owned seven dachas in Kuntsevo before the Revolution, had retained one dacha each; the local soviet argued that they should move together into one. To add to the pressure, the secretary of the Party cell of the soviet and secretary of the local police committee moved in and began to terrorize the owners, storming into the house drunk at night and threatening them with a revolver. For this behavior the people's court gave him a derisory fine of 10 rubles for "arbitrariness" (samoupravstvo); the dacha's owners were evicted all the same.[72]

The 1920s thus culminated in an assault on exurban settlements whose aim was to eliminate the prerevolutionary dacha owner. Yet far from spelling the end of the dacha, the offensive prepared the way for its further development in the Stalin era.

## Dachas in Stalin's Time

In the 1920s leisure was not a well-established concept for Soviet society. Public discussion of the off-work behavior of Soviet citizens clustered around two opposing poles. On the one hand, mention was made of private activities such as drinking, dancing, and dacha rental; these were usually treated in an ambivalent, not to say hostile, manner. On the other hand, more approving accounts were given of collective and politicized recreational institutions such as rest homes (doma otdykha) and children's colonies. Thus Serebrianyi Bor, formerly the "favorite residence for prominent Moscow merchants," now became a leisure complex consisting of thirteen collective dachas, each accommodating between fifty and seventy people. One report explained: "There aren't any sick people here. The people here just need a rest." The daily timetable was strictly laid out: early rising was followed by calisthenics, swimming, walking, and sunbathing; drinking was strictly forbidden, and smoking was permitted only outside the buildings.[73]

All this changed in the early 1930s. Soviet society started to acquire a new ideology of

70. TsGAMO, f. 182, op. 1, d. 5a, ll. 66, 76–79; d. 20, l. 90. The locations named were Malakhovka, Kliaz'ma, Mamontovka, Tarasovka, Tomilino, and Kraskovo.

71. For examples, see ibid., d. 8, l. 390, and d. 20, l. 8.

72. Ibid., d. 20, l. 135.

73. M. A., "Otdykh v Serebrianom boru," VM, 7 June 1927, 2.

leisure not just as a means of weaving citizens into a seamless collective or as a brief inter-
lude between bouts of shock labor and social combat on the factory floor but rather as a
cultural experience that could make an important contribution to the new Soviet way of
life and the formation of a new Soviet citizen. It is around this time that the Soviet discourse on leisure—as something quite distinct from work—begins in earnest. As one slo-
gan of the time ran: "Working in the new way means relaxing in the new way too." In part,
the new attitude toward leisure was reflected in practical measures. Existing facilities were
to be expanded and improved.[74] Parks, such as those surrounding the palaces in the
Leningrad region, were to have extra facilities provided. In Detskoe (formerly Tsarskoe)
Selo, accordingly, the number of visitors was expected to increase from 500,000 in 1933 to
945,000 in 1934.[75] Quantitative improvements were matched by qualitative changes, as
leisure institutions took account of the cultural advances proclaimed on behalf of Soviet
society. New rest homes retained their function of collective, organized recreation, but the
pattern of life they imposed was not so militarized as in the 1920s. As one article explained, things had moved on greatly from earlier vacation camps, where the only cultural
work that went on was folk dancing, the only way of combating drunkenness was to de-
stroy all alcoholic drinks on the premises, and the staff were dismayed by the uncivilized
behavior of the "masses."[76]

In a booklet of 1933 Soviet functionaries and their families were offered advice on how
"correctly to organize their recreation, [how] most rationally to make use of their day
off." Such people were urged to take advantage of leisure and to take part in mass events
in such prime greenbelt locations as Gorki, Arkhangel'skoe, Zvenigorod, and Kolomen-
skoe; in moments free from physical activities they might indulge in a bit of local history
in a museum.[77] In 1934, about 800 institutions were offering summer leisure activities in
the Moscow region; the total number of beds was 90,000. Each summer weekend, approximately 500,000 Muscovites set off into the greenbelt.[78] In 1936 *Vecherniaia Moskva*
(the Moscow evening newspaper) proudly reported that from one station alone 250,000
Muscovites had headed out of town last weekend—and that most of these people were not
permanent residents of satellite settlements or even dachniki but day trippers.[79] The increased scope for leisure came to be seen as an important symptom of the general well-
being of Soviet society; the history of dacha locations was mentioned only to contrast the
vanity and frippery of the prerevolutionary leisured classes with the wholesomeness of
Soviet recreational activities.[80]

The new approach to leisure had a parallel in public discussion of housing and settlement. Debates on architecture and town planning in the first half of the 1920s had been

74. Note, e.g., the efforts of the OMKh of the Leningrad oblispolkom to boost the Sestroretsk resort in 1930
(see TsGA SPb, f. 3199, op. 4, d. 14, ll. 381–83, 592–93, 632).

75. A. Ianvarskii, "Leto ne zhdet," *SP*, 30 Mar. 1934, 4.

76. E. Simonov, "Dom otdykha i otdykh doma," *VM*, 10 Mar. 1932, 1.

77. *Ekskursionnyi spravochnik na leto 1933 g.* (Moscow, 1933).

78. V. Baburov, "Prigorodnaia zona Moskvy," *Stroitel'stvo Moskvy*, no. 12 (1935), 27.

79. A. V., "Progulka za gorod," *VM*, 25 May 1936, 2.

80. *Otdykh pod Moskvoi: Spravochnik po lodochnym pristaniam i pliazham na leto 1940 goda* (Moscow,
1940); V. L. Nekrasova, *Putevoditel' po severnym okrestnostiam Leningrada* (Leningrad, 1935).

138    dominated by a generation that took seriously Marx's promise of a communist lifestyle that would harmoniously integrate urban and rural environments. The three main models proposed (linear urban growth, the compact city [*sotsgorod*], and deurbanization) had something very important in common: they all presupposed the thoroughgoing resettlement of the Soviet population with the aim of eliminating urban agglomerations.[81] The implications of these projects were as negative for the prerevolutionary dacha as they were for the major cities: the idea was to break down the dualism whereby economically productive life proceeded in overcrowded urban settlements and recreation in the greenbelt.

At the end of the 1920s, however, it was decided that the Soviet Union should not aspire to the harmonious, integrated life of the small town. As before, people would have to live in city centers or in densely populated industrial suburbs. The reasons for the abandonment of "utopian" planning projects were in large part economic: a spread of low-density settlement required too high and even a level of infrastructure, and it did not square with the absolute commitment to headlong industrialization.[82] But the more traditional planning policies of the 1930s also reflected a new concern with everyday life and the individual. The conflict between the culture of the 1920s and that of the 1930s forms the subject of a 1931 story by Konstantin Paustovskii in which an avant-garde architect named Gofman leads a ski party to a part-built vacation camp that he has designed. The main building is cylindrical, its curved windows are made of unbreakable glass, the climate inside is artificially controlled so as to be summery all year round, and its walls are so thin that they let in the sounds of the natural world from outside. As Gofman combatively explains: "Cities have had their day. If you . . . think that this is incorrect, then Engels thought otherwise. Each state system has its own particular forms of human settlement. Socialism doesn't need cities." The accompanying journalist, however, finds the design cold and impersonal: "In every house . . . there should be a certain stock of useless objects. In every house there should be at least one mistake." Gofman is duly summoned to a committee meeting, where he is accused of "unnecessary functionalism" and objections are made to the costliness of his design. At the end of the story he goes swimming and conveniently drowns before the Soviet architectural community has had time to show him the error of his ways (and before the author has had to face up to the moral implications of the conflict he has outlined).[83]

Paustovskii's story accurately reflects the movement away from deurbanizing projects, a tendency that enabled the dacha to regain some of the positive connotations it had lost in the 1920s. The Soviet Union, it was commonly argued, must avoid the suburban sprawl so characteristic of England and America, and dachas could help to preserve the greenbelts around the major cities. They had the further virtue of lessening the pressure on rest homes and sanatoria, of which the provision was inadequate throughout the Soviet period and es-

81. On the debates of the 1920s, see Bliznakov, "Soviet Housing," 85–148.

82. A critique of the Sokol settlement on economic grounds is to be found in N. Markovnikov, "Poselok 'Sokol,'" *Stroitel'naia promyshlennost'*, no. 12 (1929), 1071–76. Ironically, Markovnikov one year earlier had published a short book in which he presented a sympathetic analysis of garden city projects abroad; in 1929, presumably, he buckled under the pressure of incipient Stalinism.

83. K. Paustovskii, "Moskovskoe leto," in his *Sobranie sochinenii v deviati tomakh* (Moscow, 1981–86), 6:90–111.

pecially in the 1920s. And summer houses were in fact more important to the Russians than to the British and the Americans, given the long winters, the short building season, and the unsanitary conditions that prevailed in cities. "*Dacha* in the narrow sense of the word is a purely Russian phenomenon," claimed the *Great Soviet Encyclopedia* in 1930.

Positive assessments of this kind could not, however, bring practical improvements on their own. The dacha's increasing public respectability was not matched by the pace of exurban construction. The Moscow city administration, when it took stock of the available dacha resources in 1933, found little to gladden the hearts of the vacationing masses: the municipal dacha stock was badly depleted (the basic unit of dacha allocation in this period was the room, not the house), and other organizations had not done much to improve the situation.[84] Leningrad faced very much the same problems. In July 1931, for example, the oblast ispolkom instructed various organizations to inspect properties (especially former palaces and estates) that might provide dacha space. The conclusion reached was quick and unequivocal: "The municipal dacha stock, after inspection on site, consists of isolated lodgings of the following types: mezzanines, small attic rooms, and small outbuildings. On transfer of the entire housing stock to the ZhAKTs [housing cooperatives], the latter have adapted accommodations formerly used as dachas to form winter housing."[85] Despite regular attempts to free up dacha space, it was clear that municipal provision, as in the 1920s, was not competing effectively with the private market.[86]

Given the inadequacy of the existing publicly administered dacha stock, the construction of new settlements became a matter of urgency. The Leningrad housing organization Zhilsoiuz was required to set up "dacha and allotment cooperatives" at the raion level and also under the auspices of particular factories. The production of prefabricated wooden dachas was to be stepped up; the housing department (Zhilotdel) was required to organize a competition for dacha design and to develop designs for cheap and simple furniture suitable for dachas. According to the stipulations of this competition, vacation accommodations were to come in three main types: the "single-apartment dacha" (*odnokvartirnaia dacha*) intended for summer use only, with a plot of 600 square meters; the *sblochennaia dacha* (i.e., two semidetached dachas) designed for use all year round; and the *pansionat* for fifty people, which was also destined for year-round use.[87] The plan was to put up no fewer than 5,000 standard dachas during 1932.[88]

The organization burdened with these considerable tasks was the Trust for Dacha and

84. TsMAM, f. 718, op. 8, d. 35, l. 96.

85. TsGA SPb, f. 2047, op. 1, d. 2, l. 284.

86. In 1933, for example, the Moscow-based dacha trusts were ordered to evict citizens who had moved into dachas without the necessary official permission and tenants who had been subletting rooms or not paying their rent on time; these measures were confidently expected to free up "not fewer than 300 substantial dachas." See "Spekulianty budut vyseleny," *VM*, 17 Feb. 1933, 2.

87. *Programma vsesoiuznogo otkrytogo konkursa na sostavlenie proektov* (Leningrad, 1934). The designs presented in this competition were intended to be used in Lisii Nos, Mel'nichii Ruchei, and other areas of current dacha construction. Further standard designs of the mid-1930s are to be found in Liudvig, *Rekomendovannye proekty*. This book advocates the standardized mass production of prefabricated dachas and claims to be presenting the best of the current design solutions.

88. A transcript of the relevant meeting of the presidium of the oblispolkom can be found at TsGA SPb, f. 2047, op. 1, d. 2, ll. 240–42.

This dacha at Lisii Nos, which faces directly on the Gulf of Finland, would have been the ideal of many 1930s dachniki.

Suburban Housing Construction in Leningrad oblast (operational from August 1931). Over the three years of its existence, the trust was beset with the problems that afflicted all areas of production in the Stalin era: a poorly trained, inexperienced, and ill-disciplined workforce; a shortage of resources and of ready cash, given that debtors were slow to pay; constant struggles with other branches of production for access to equipment and raw materials; the pressure of relentless and unrealistic production targets (including the construction of many houses of the "winter type," which were not the trust's prime responsibility); and the cumbersome bureaucracy that any branch of the supply system entailed.

Despite these difficulties, the Leningrad dacha trust helped to create a new, centralized model of dacha rental and ownership for its region. It did not rent houses to private individuals but worked only with organizations: dachas were to be rented through trade unions, factories, and other state and Party institutions at standard rates. By 1934 such organizations were sending in a steady stream of applications requesting accommodations for their employees.[89]

The dachas built by the trust were of two main types: individual (for one family) and collective. The former typically consisted of two rooms and contained the following standard-issue furniture: two beds with mattresses (cost 210 rubles), six chairs (60 rubles), two tables (80 rubles), two buckets (5 rubles), one washstand (5 rubles). A list compiled in

89. TsGA SPb, f. 2047, op. 1, d. 2, ll. 271, 317, and d. 78.

1933 gave a total of 108 families resident in the trust's flagship building developments at Mel'nichii Ruchei (just beyond Vsevolozhsk, on the railway line heading toward Lake Ladoga) and Lisii Nos (on the north side of the Gulf of Finland). The size of the houses they inhabited varied from one to six rooms, but the average was around two. Canteens were to provide meals for the regular dacha population, as well as for shorter-term visitors from the same kinds of organization. The tenants included employees of the following institutions: the dacha trust itself, the OGPU (the political police), banks, supply organizations, and various factories (including the Karl Marx, Sverdlov, and Stalin works).[90]

Many members of this middling stratum of the Soviet elite, however, were dismayed when they arrived at their dachas. The houses (especially their interiors) were often not completed, rubbish was still lying about the building sites, and amenities were very basic (and sometimes nonexistent). The canteens had not opened and there was little sign of a compensating supply of basic foodstuffs to the dacha settlements. In a report compiled at the end of 1932, the newly appointed head of the trust's operational department was frank about the problems he faced: building standards were low, as was morale among the construction workers, given the abysmal conditions in which they worked; denied adequate temporary housing, workers had put up in semiconstructed dachas and left them in a wretched state.[91] The press relentlessly kept such failings in the public eye.[92]

Newspapers also alleged that municipal dachas in the more desirable locations were allocated by personal acquaintance (by *blat*, in Soviet parlance). One journalist commented in 1933:

> There are no rules for the distribution of dachas in the Moscow region. There are only memos [*zapiski*]. Memos come in three varieties: the friendly *blat* type, the string-pulling, and the naive, the last kind being written by organizations and enterprises that are appealing on behalf of their workers. The first kind is invariably successful, the second sometimes works, but the third—never.[93]

Although the trust was certainly a convenient target for accusations of corruption—one of the main Soviet techniques of governance, in the 1930s and after, was to attribute "popular" grievances to the failings of middle administration rather than to the Party elite or the system as a whole—there seems no reason to doubt that the administrative mechanisms of the time left ample scope for the practice of *blat*.[94]

In 1934 the trust was liquidated and replaced by local managing organizations

90. Ibid., d. 3, l. 87, and d. 46, ll. 251–52.

91. Ibid., d. 46, ll. 402–3.

92. See Radiukov, "Tish' i glad' vmesto dach," and D. Taver, "Propala programma dachnogo stroitel'stva," *VKG*, 2 Jan. 1932, 2, and 15 Mar. 1932, 2, respectively. Other examples in *VKG*, 14 Apr. and 8 and 10 May 1933; in *Moscow*, *VM*, 3 Apr. 1935. The question of dacha provision even found its way into the all-union press: e.g., S. Bogorad, "Khozhdenie po dacham," *Pravda*, 13 Apr. 1937, 6.

93. E. Bermont, "Ia khochu dachu," *VM*, 10 Apr. 1933, 3.

94. Corruption cases involving the acquisition of dachas by workers in the *blat*-ridden trade distribution system are described in E. Osokina, *Za fasadom "stalinskogo izobiliia"* (Moscow, 1999), 225, 226.

142   (*dachnye khoziaistva*) under the umbrella of Leningrad's housing administration (Lenzhilupravlenie). A parallel development took place in Moscow with the transfer of dacha management to the regional communal department in April 1934.[95] Control over the existing stock was further devolved by offering dachas for sale to factories and other organizations. But these administrative reshuffles did not change the general direction of policy: the trust had served as a means of transition from the chaotic situation of the 1920s to a more regulated system of distribution via state and Party organizations.

The prevailing trend was reinforced by developments in the cooperative movement. As we have seen, dacha cooperatives had existed since the 1920s, but in the 1930s their number and the strength of their institutional backing increased considerably.[96] Cooperatives were recognized by the Moscow soviet as a way of mobilizing the resources both of individuals and of enterprises and of easing problems that the dacha trusts alone were clearly incapable of tackling. By November 1935, the managing organization Mosgordachsoiuz was able to report that the number of cooperatives had risen from 61 to 114 in little more than a year. But this was not necessarily grounds for self-congratulation: the funds available for dacha construction had not risen proportionately, and there were now 6,000 cooperative members on the waiting list for dachas; the total number of completed dachas was only 378.[97] Individual settlements received grants (known as *limity*) out of the overall city budget, but this money went only a very small part of the way toward the costs of construction; the rest of the working capital was made up of members' preliminary contributions, bank loans, and whatever funds were forthcoming from the cooperative's sponsor organization (in many cases, the members' employer).

The houses built and administered by the cooperatives were reserved for people occupying positions of responsibility and influence in particular organizations. Even for these people, however, dachas were not easy to come by. As the waiting list for dachas lengthened and resources remained scarce, many prospective dachniki could not contain their frustration and gave vent to grievances at general meetings of the cooperative or in personal petitions to Mosgordachsoiuz or some other branch of the city government. The most common allegation was that the rightful order of priority had been outweighed by personal considerations: that managers of the dacha stock had been swayed by *blat*, by the corrupt rendering of personal favors, instead of observing the cooperative statutes. It is impossible to judge how legitimate these protests were, especially as many are couched in the language of denunciation.[98] What is clear, however, is that the prevailing economic conditions placed the managers of settlements in a position where they would have been hard pressed *not* to employ *blat*. To make use of contacts and to engage in practices that were not officially sanctioned was essential if construction work was to make any progress.

95. Text of the resolution by the Moscow oblispolkom in Portugalov and Dlugach, *Dachi*, 164.

96. For examples of public encouragement, see "Stroite dachi!," *VM*, 15 July 1932, 1, and "Zabota o sebe samom: Est' dachi, stolovye, detploshchadki," *VM*, 3 Apr. 1933, 2.

97. TsMAM, f. 1956, op. 1, d. 5, ll. 46–46ob. By mid-summer of 1937, the number of cooperatives had risen to 168, but only 85 had dachas completed and ready for use (ibid., d. 24, l. 30).

98. E.g., ibid., d. 42, l. 23; d. 378, ll. 49–51.

It is also clear that many members of dacha cooperatives served as unpaid "fixers" (*tolkachi*), or at least contributed a substantial amount of legwork, going from one institution to another to conduct the cooperative's business. To be a cooperative *aktivist* did not primarily imply political duties: it meant having to negotiate deliveries of timber, standing in line to get the cooperative's registration rubber-stamped, hiring casual laborers, and keeping an eye on them once they started work. It is hardly surprising, therefore, that many of these people, who had made a real practical contribution to the cooperative's activities, felt they deserved preferential allocation of dacha space.[99] Nor is it surprising that their claims often met an outraged response from other cooperative members: Stalin-era fixers by definition were not open and accountable in their actions, and the criteria for determining priority in the allocation of dachas were often unclear.

The suspicions of ordinary members were fueled by the murky closed-doors deals that the cooperative boards of administration seemed to be making with the sponsor organization. They were dismayed by a general trend of dacha settlements to become more organizationally (or "departmentally") based and less cooperative-like. That is to say, members tended to come from a single institution or a small number of linked institutions that retained close control over the construction and allocation of dachas. Settlements that had been established in the late 1920s were on the whole more heterogeneous. Mosgordachsoiuz complained in 1936 that at the Vneshtorgovets settlement, the sponsoring organization, the Ministry of Foreign Trade, was claiming a number of the dachas for its own people: "in such a situation the collective has no cooperative characteristics whatsoever and this construction is organizational under the cover of a cooperative."[100]

Dachniki without such organizational backing, still the majority, continued, as they had done in the 1920s, to rent from house owners in villages and settlements accessible from Leningrad and Moscow. As a representative of the dacha trust noted in a report to the Leningrad soviet of April 1932 regarding the continuing shortage of dachas: "If Leningraders do in spite of all this manage to get out to a dacha during the summer, this is because they get living space by virtue of the self-compression [*samouplotnenie*] of the permanent population of the suburban district and thanks to the modest private housing stock."[101] A further source of dachas for rent, especially in the second half of the 1930s, was cooperative settlements: subletting a cooperative dacha was forbidden by Mosgordachsoiuz, and some people were expelled from their cooperative for such an offense, but in many settlements this practice seems to have been tolerated.[102]

A middling white-collar family would typically rent a house in a village where the

---

99. For statements of people's perceived moral right to a dacha on these grounds, see ibid., d. 42, l. 117; d. 231, ll. 10–11, 60.

100. Ibid., d. 48, l. 238ob.

101. TsGA SPb, f. 2047, op. 1, d. 27, l. 151.

102. At a meeting of members of specific dacha cooperatives with representatives of Mosgordachsoiuz on 28 July 1937, several speakers complained that policy on subletting was formulated and implemented inconsistently; the head of the Moscow housing administration asserted that to forbid the practice would be foolish and counterproductive, given the drastic shortage of dacha accommodations in the region; cooperatives should, however, ensure that the prices asked were not extortionate (TsMAM, f. 1956, op. 1, d. 24, l. 16).

144   local population would keep them supplied with basic produce; the time-consuming task of running the household through the summer months could further be alleviated by hiring a local girl as a servant (especially after the violent onset of collectivization, there was no shortage of peasant women willing to enter the domestic service of city folk).[103] The dacha formed part of the way of life of overworked urban parents, who were able to send their children away for part of the summer. A Leningrad woman (born in 1929) recalled: "When I was a child we rented a dacha in Ozerki [very close to the city]. No kind of facilities, just a box of a room. And of course there was no space round about. . . . My mother was working almost without a break. . . . Meanwhile we spent the time at the dacha. . . . Our granny lived with us."[104] Similar were the experiences of Elena Bonner, who recalled spending one summer in the mid-1930s in a large house rented by her extended family in a village near Luga; as in the 1920s, the children and most of the women lived there all through the summer, while her politically active parents remained in the city.[105] And Mikhail and Elena Bulgakov packed their family off to dachas to which they would make only occasional short trips during the summer; for the most part they made do with swimming in the Moscow River.[106]

This pattern of life—to remain in the city over the summer but make regular forays into the surrounding countryside—was by no means unusual in the 1930s, judging by the increase in summer rail traffic.[107] On a typical day during the summer over 10 percent of Moscow's population would head for the forests and lakes surrounding the city. And they had plenty of territory to choose from: the "suburban zone" was taken up predominantly by agriculture and forest (48 and 42 percent respectively) and only very slightly by towns and urban settlements (2.4 percent). That said, leisure facilities were still underdeveloped: the problem of keeping up with the increasing demand for leisure—without, however, violating the forest zone—was discussed regularly in the 1930s and after.[108] Given the still inadequate leisure facilities in the Moscow area, it was argued that more land should be released for dacha construction in order to encourage workers to build. Settlements should not be allowed to grow too large (the proposed limit was 1,500 people), and dacha zones should be kept quite separate from other places of leisure. If construction was stepped up in this way, prices would be brought down.[109] Yet if dacha building was allowed to continue unchecked, there was a serious danger that urban settlements would

103. See, e.g., "'. . . I kazhdyi vecher za shlagbaumami . . .'" Servants were often employed in city apartments in the 1920s and 1930s by working couples with children, and at the dacha they may have been even more commonly encountered (because the need for child care was greater, given the prolonged absences of parents in the city, and because the labor pool—peasant women—was closer at hand).

104. Irina Chekhovskikh's interviews, no. 2, 6. (See "Note on Sources.")

105. Bonner, *Dochki-materi*, 184–85.

106. E. S. Bulgakova, *Dnevnik* (Moscow, 1990).

107. The number of suburban passengers was reported to have gone up by 39.3% from 1931 to 1932 ("V poezde na dachu," *VKG,* 22 Mar. 1933, 4).

108. The problems (as well as the achievements) are registered in A. I. Kuznetsov, "Arkhitekturnye problemy planirovki prigorodnoi zony," *Stroitel'stvo Moskvy,* no. 21–22 (1940), 3–7.

109. P. Sokolov, "Prigorodnaia zona i problema otdykha naseleniia Moskvy," *Sotsialisticheskii gorod,* no. 5 (1936), 16–21.

expand unacceptably, or that smaller dacha settlements would spring up in inappropriate places. Recent experience had shown that dacha plots were often too big (up to 2.5 hectares) to be ecologically sustainable.[110]

It seems that the greater part of the expansion of dacha settlements in the Moscow region in the 1930s can be put down to a process of creeping suburbanization: in 1936 it was estimated that 70 percent of the population of such settlements was made up by commuters (*zagorodniki*). As the *Great Soviet Encyclopedia* explained in 1930, dachas had "changed their function: they are not so much a summer dwelling for city people in need of a summer break as a dwelling for urban toilers, thus increasing the housing stock of the latter."[111] As for dachas proper (i.e., dachas as places for summer leisure), in 1934 there were places for 165,000 people (around 5 percent of the city's population) in the Moscow region (compare this with 86,000 for rest homes, 35,000 for Pioneer camps, and 28,500 for preschool colonies). These 1930s dachniki were predominantly women (75 percent), presumably because draconian labor legislation kept men tied to the workplace (two weeks' annual vacation was the norm in this period). Their class origin was likewise clearly marked: "There are no single dachniki. Very few workers. In the main, they are the families of employees [*sluzhashchie*]."[112] In December 1934, Mosgordachsoiuz reported to Nikita Khrushchev, then Moscow Party boss, that of the 6,400 members of dacha cooperatives in the Moscow area only 455 (that is, 7 percent) were workers.[113] But while the underrepresentation of proletarians was common knowledge, it rarely occasioned any public soul-searching.[114] Rather, the Soviet press emphasized how urban "toilers" were benefiting from the new Soviet social welfare contract with the state: they were offered subsidized trips to rest homes, and the luckier ones might enjoy a full-blown vacation at a resort in the Crimea or the Caucasus.

The notion of a social divide between dacha residents and "mass" vacationers is supported by memoir accounts. One Muscovite's recollections of childhood in the 1930s included walks past charming old dachas beyond the Sokol'niki gate that outwardly were unchanged since prerevolutionary times. "It seemed to us that these were some kind of 'former people' who were quietly living out their time behind tulle curtains."[115] The actress Galina Ivanovna Kozhakina recalled her 1930s experiences of dacha life in a similar light: "The dachas on neighboring plots were occupied by princes, former priests, and ru-

110. V. Baburov, "Prigorodnaia zona Moskvy," *Stroitel'stvo Moskvy*, no. 12 (1935), 27–31. The same author reiterates his agenda with a view to the third five-year plan in "Osvoenie lesoparkovoi zony," *Stroitel'stvo Moskvy*, no. 9 (1937), 17–18.

111. See *BSE*, 1st ed., s.v. "Dacha." By effectively redefining "dacha" as any form of suburban habitation, this entry made the claim that "up to 84%" of people living in dachas were "toilers."

112. Sokolov, "Prigorodnaia zona," 17.

113. TsMAM, f. 1956, op. 1, d. 10, l. 1. This picture of the dacha's class profile is confirmed by the available lists of cooperative members (assembled ibid., dd. 26, 27, 28).

114. In one *Pravda* commentary, for example, the growth of dacha settlements was seen as indicative of the "enormous demand for a dacha by people who previously couldn't even have dreamed of it," and hence of the rising cultural level of Soviet society: see "Dacha," *Pravda*, 23 Apr. 1935, 3.

115. Ia. M. Belitskii, *Okrest Moskvy* (Moscow, 1996), 22.

146  ined nepmen. Our neighbor, once a noble lady, bred a huge flock of turkeys."[116] The presence of "former people" in dacha settlements was evidence not of privilege but of stigma. Nadezhda Mandelstam, for example, recounted how social undesirables such as her husband were commonly forbidden to live within a hundred-kilometer radius of Moscow. For this reason, they tended to cluster in village settlements just beyond that limit.[117] Closer to the city, conditions were often no better for less oppressed dacha residents: the more spacious dachas were turned into multiple-occupancy dwellings, the suburban equivalent of the communal apartment.

Such ad hoc arrangements were made possible by the still rather low penetration of outlying areas by the municipal authorities: private owners in former dacha settlements accounted for 59 percent of the total stock, while kolkhoz and peasant ownership was 28 percent. Cooperatives managed only 11 percent. Of the 274 population centers inhabited by dachniki in the Moscow region in the mid-1930s, 51 were "old" settlements, 55 were "new," and the rest were ordinary villages. Prices for the season varied spectacularly, from 70 to 1,000 rubles.[118]

Once again advertisements can provide some information on the state of the dacha market. The back pages of newspapers in the 1930s were filled with notices concerning apartment swaps, lost dogs, household help, music lessons, and pieces of furniture, yet dachas were also featured. (As in the 1920s, we must assume that it was primarily a sellers' market, and that most potential landlords had no need to go looking for tenants.) Dacha advertisements began to appear very early in the year—in the middle of the winter—and continued through to May and June, when they gave way to notices concerning the rental of rooms in city apartments (generally sublet by departed dachniki).[119] Perhaps the most common type of dacha advertisement from February to May was that placed by institutions looking to rent or buy accommodations. Many organizations urgently needed to find living space for specialists arriving from other cities (hence the frequently encountered formula "Corners, rooms, dachas"). The demand for dachas was paralleled by the significant numbers of people who were trying to swap houses outside the city for central apartments, though it seems unlikely that these two types of demand were complementary: housing of all kinds—urban, suburban, and exurban—was in short supply.

The dacha shortage was exacerbated by the reluctance of many villagers to let out rooms because of concern that they would be liable for extra taxes. In Leningrad in 1932 it was noted that ordinary people could obtain dachas only through acquaintances, and even then at ridiculously high prices; the local authorities were often blamed for imposing extra charges that discouraged villagers from renting out their property and ultimately resulted in inflation.[120] The ispolkom of Moscow oblast had already (in May 1932) taken the

116. I. N. Sergeev, *Tsaritsyno. Sukhanovo: Liudi, sobytiia, fakty* (Moscow, 1998), 80–81.

117. N. Mandelstam, *Hope against Hope: A Memoir*, trans. M. Hayward (London, 1971), 293.

118. Sokolov, "Prigorodnaia zona," 17.

119. Muscovites away at the dacha between 15 Apr. and 30 Sept. retained rights to their living space in the city and were also entitled to sublet this space for the summer, as long as the prices asked were not "extortionate" (*spekuliativnye*): see "Nakanune dachnogo sezona," *VM*, 9 May 1933, 1.

120. *VKG*, 15 May 1932, 4.

initiative in this matter by allowing collective farm workers and all other non-"kulak" landlords 300 rubles of untaxed nonagricultural income, by giving the dacha economy full exemption from the agricultural tax, and by forbidding local soviets to impose any unauthorized new charges on landlords and tenants. In the wake of the Great Leap Forward, village people needed much convincing that they would not be treated as kulaks if they rented out their property over the summer.[121]

At the same time that they offered encouragement to peasant landlords, the Leningrad city authorities tried to cap dacha rents by imposing pricing norms. According to this system, dacha locations were divided into four categories, from the highly desirable northern side of the Gulf of Finland to more remote and less attractive locations. The norm for living space per person was 6 square meters; tenants were charged double for anything above that. A discount of 10 percent was given for dachas more than three kilometers from the nearest station. Rents were partially means-tested.[122] Summer train timetables were introduced to make travel to and from the dacha more attractive. On one suburban Moscow line, a "model train" was supposedly introduced: clean and welcoming, it was bedecked with curtains and portraits of political leaders; music was permanently turned on in a special "radio compartment"; the conductor dispensed reading matter; and a particularly comfortable carriage was reserved for mothers and children.[123]

But these reports of measures to regulate and improve the quality of dacha life brought dachniki little practical benefit. In many settlements the promised canteens had failed to materialize, and in their absence there was nowhere to buy even the most basic foodstuffs. Supply organizations had failed to account for the annual dacha exodus and continued to send food to the cities when it was needed much more in exurban settlements.[124] It was forbidden to transport paraffin by suburban train, a rule that even the most law-abiding Soviet dachniki were forced to flout, given the absence of alternative supply channels.[125] The transport of furniture and bulkier household items to the dacha was extremely complicated and time-consuming.[126] Leaky roofs, glass-free windows, and unplastered walls were commonly encountered on arrival.[127]

To cope with the dacha shortage, a typical Soviet solution was attempted: to shift the burden of construction to the population. Articles in the Leningrad press in 1935 told "individual builders" that they could expect to obtain credits from various organizations as

121. "Na dachu! Novyi poriadok naima dach!" *VM*, 12 May 1932, 3. This policy had to be reiterated in the press the following year, because peasants were unwilling to believe that it remained in force (see "V mae na dachu. L'goty ostaiutsia," *VM*, 30 Apr. 1933, 2).

122. "Skol'ko platit' za dachu?" *VKG*, 7 Apr. 1932, 2.

123. A. Vetrov, "Kontsert v dachnom poezde: Obraztsovyi prigorodnyi poezd," *VM*, 4 Apr. 1934, 3.

124. M. Iv., "Dachnikov eto interesuet!" *VKG*, 23 May 1933, 2. In 1935 it was estimated that dacha areas needed to be supplied with 20 tons of bread daily ("Chto zhdet dachnika?" *VKG*, 16 May 1935, 3). For a survey of supply problems in Moscow dacha locations, see V. Starov, "Ot dachnika trebuiut podvigov, a on ishchet otdykha," *VM*, 27 Apr. 1933, 2.

125. D. Maslianenko, "Dachnye kontrabandisty," *VKG*, 2 June 1935, 3.

126. "Kak perevezti veshchi na dachu?" *VM*, 22 Apr. 1935, 2.

127. A rhymed reflection on the imperfection of the Lisii Nos development is A. Flit, "Razmyshlenie na Lis'em nosu," *VKG*, 3 June 1933, 2.

148   well as practical assistance and building materials from the housing section of the city soviet (no help would be provided, however, for window and door frames, windowpanes
and interior decoration).[128] Citizens were advised that if they pooled the family's earnings,
they could save themselves the bother of a rented dacha and build their own modest out-
of-town house.[129] The dacha was now, in the mid-1930s, presented as an amenity to which
the ordinary Soviet worker could legitimately aspire. One exemplary article features a
shop superintendent from the Stalin Car Factory by the name of Iakov Rafailovich
Fainshtein, along with his friend, colleague, and dacha neighbor Rustem. The factory has
given both of them cars, which at first were objects of enormous fascination but are now
taken for granted. Fainshtein has brought back a vacuum cleaner and a phonograph, and
these have taken their places in the household alongside the "bicycle, car, radio, electrical
appliances, and other new things that have been acquired by the family in recent years."
Clearly Stalin-era culture circa 1935 placed a premium on a comfortable standard of living
and lifestyle for those who were held to deserve them. And here the dacha had an important role to play:

> While they're drinking tea on the terrace, Iakov Rafailovich reads the second vol-
> ume of *Peter I* while his wife reads *Engineer Garin's Hyperboloid*. They plunge into
> a little discussion of the works of the author of these books, Aleksei Tolstoi. Liusia
> Kharitonovna [Rustem's wife], turning over the latest issue of the newspaper, in-
> terrupts the discussion by asking: "What is a stratosphere balloon made of?"
> Then the two friends—the engineer Rustem and the head of section Fainshtein—
> share the latest factory news. When there is nothing left to tell and the tea has
> been drunk, silence falls. Some of them carry on reading, others just "breathe," as
> this pursuit in a pine wood in the freshness of the night itself offers no little en-
> joyment.
>    "It's so quiet," someone quips, "that you can hear the onions growing in our
> vegetable plot."
>    "I should hope so too! We gave it a good enough watering at the end of the
> day. But look how the potatoes have got going! They're surging up from the
> ground!" . . .
>    When the light goes out in the windows, this dachlet is completely swallowed
> up by the woods. Near Moscow there are lots of woods like this, lots of dachas like
> this, and lots of people like this relaxing in them. But the people who enjoy their
> rest most are those who work hardest![130]

This account is highly representative of the time in its mixture of legitimizing strategies: a
trip to the dacha is unashamedly a leisure activity and is quite explicitly linked to material

128. A. Kagan, " 'Samostroi,' " *VKG*, 28 Mar. 1935, 3.
129. I. Girbasova, "Sem'ia stroit dachu," *VKG*, 26 Apr. 1935, 3.
130. A. Gerb, "Dacha v lesu," *VM*, 3 July 1935, 2.

aspirations, yet at the same time it is linked to a rural "good life," to the values of "cultured" and purposeful work.

The model of dacha life fostered by the Stalin era comes over clearly in architectural handbooks of the 1930s. As Vladimir Papernyi observes, "individual wooden houses, cottages, and dachas became an increasingly legitimate category for architectural design and probable architectural commission."[131] A book published in 1939 identified 200 basic types of dacha design (the variation depended on climate and function) but advocated above all "communal" plots with shared or "paired" dachas, thus implying a criticism of a ministry regulation of the same year stipulating that buildings should take up no more than 10 percent of the territory of any plot of land.[132] The "mass" dacha generally lacked running water and other basic amenities, but for people with greater resources the legal restraints were fewer than later in the Soviet period:

> There are no restrictions on the design of the accommodation, and dachas can have verandas (either open or with windows), terraces, balconies, oriel windows, galleries, bathrooms, washrooms, various other facilities (such as a cellar, a boiler for central heating, or a laundry room and so on), rooms for special purposes (a darkroom) and so on.
>
> To provide parking space for cars arriving at the dacha it is possible to attach to the house a carport or a lightweight summer garage.

The recommended exterior was simple and unshowy; light building materials (other than brick) were to be used in order to reduce the cost of construction; nor was the dacha to approach a town house in its external features. The "pretensions to originality" and "tackiness" of prerevolutionary dachas were now quite out of place—even if, regrettably, they persisted in some locations.[133]

But normative documents such as architectural and planning handbooks have an extremely problematic relation to social practice throughout the Soviet period, and perhaps never more so than in the Stalin era, which may be said to have institutionalized a disjuncture between rule and action, word and deed. The reality of "individual construction" in the 1930s was, of course, very different from the moderate material gratification promised in the pro-consumerist public campaign of 1935; to build a dacha without the

---

131. V. Paperny, "Men, Women, and the Living Space," in Brumfield and Ruble, *Russian Housing*, 162. Some published materials of the 1930s called for increased public coverage of dacha construction projects and for greater architectural experimentation. One article recommended hexagonal clusters instead of the usual rectilinear street plans of dacha settlements: see V. P. Kalmykov, "Dachnye poselki," *Sovetskaia arkhitektura*, no. 1 (1934), 46–51. The same article criticized the "architectural conservatism" of the izba-style dacha.

132. That the "communal" dacha lifestyle was unpopular can be surmised from the construction policy of the Moscow dacha cooperative, which by the mid-1930s had amassed 3,081 dachas with only 3,791 sets of living quarters (Sokolov, "Prigorodnaia zona," 18).

133. Bobov, *Arkhitektura i stroitel'stvo dach*, 12, 21.

# Проект № 29. Дача спаренная

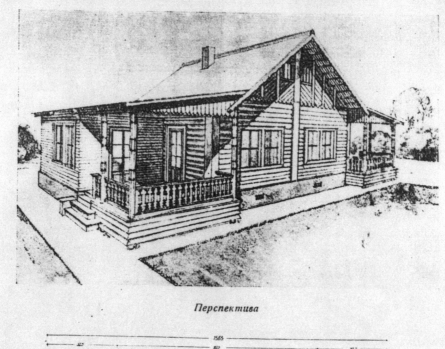

Перспектива

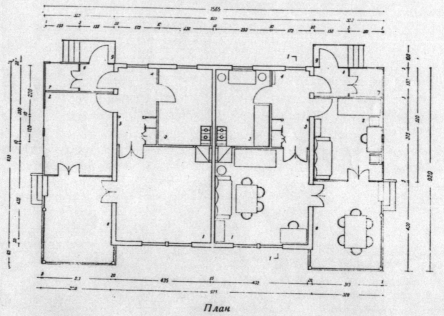

План

Soviet design for a "paired" dacha (from G. M. Bobov, *Arkhitektura i stroitel'stvo dach* [Moscow, 1939])

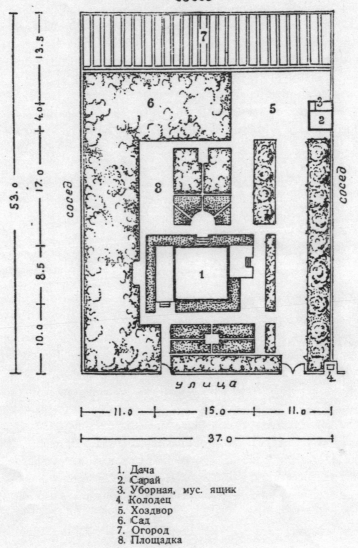

# СХЕМА 7

### застройки дачного участка

### размером 37 × 53 = 1961 м² (средний размер)

Площадь застройки — 117 м² (6%)
Жил. площадь — 56 м²
Полезн. площадь — 68 м²

1. Дача
2. Сарай
3. Уборная, мус. ящик
4. Колодец
5. Хоздвор
6. Сад
7. Огород
8. Площадка

Layout of a medium-sized prewar dacha plot (from *Vremennye tekhnicheskie pravila* [Moscow, 1940])

152 direct and explicit protection of an organization was one of the greatest feats that could be achieved by 1930s *blat*.[134]

Contemporary published sources also fail to mention the dachas reserved for the upper echelons of the Party and leading figures in other areas of Soviet life (notably, favored writers, artists, performers, scholars, and scientists). The provision of elite settlements of this kind had begun in the 1920s (Serebriannyi Bor, Malakhovka, Kratovo, Nikolina Gora, Zubalovo, and others), but in the 1930s it proceeded more intensively and systematically. Top Party and government cadres in Moscow and the corresponding regional elites had virtually carte blanche to build themselves enormous—by Soviet standards—country residences. The most sought-after dacha locations of the 1930s were to the west of Moscow, where heavily policed and intensively maintained compounds began to take over from the more ad hoc elite enclaves of the 1920s.[135] Stalin, for example, moved to a new dacha at Kuntsevo in 1934. This move marked a change in lifestyle quite consistent with the estrangement from his extended family that resulted from the suicide of his wife in 1932. When Svetlana Allilueva recalled her father's behavior at the earlier dacha at Zubalovo, she remembered a peasantlike feeling for nature, modest tastes, and an easy way with the servants. Now, however, Stalin's down-to-earth lifestyle was demolished piece by piece: members of the domestic staff who had known Allilueva's mother were soon laid off, the number of servants and guards was greatly increased (there were always two sets of cooks and cleaners so that they could work around the clock, in two shifts), and Stalin's entourage conducted a purge of old artifacts and furniture. The dacha interior became faceless and official. One observer who visited Kuntsevo in the spring of 1953, just a few weeks after Stalin's death, gave the following description of the main area for meetings:

> A room about 30 meters long. The far end was oval, as in noble families' residences of the century before last. Lots of identical windows securely sealed with heavy white curtains such as you find in all major institutions in the center of Moscow.
> The lower part of the walls, about a meter and a half off the ground, was brown and covered with Karelian birchwood, which looked rather official [*kazenno*]. Under the windows there were electric radiators cased in the same birchwood.[136]

Although Stalin had several dachas, in the Moscow region and elsewhere, all kept in a state of constant readiness, he chose to make the Kuntsevo dacha his main residence, a decision that both fed and reflected his growing suspiciousness and disengagement from people. Kuntsevo provided a new model for the elite dacha not only in its interior furnishings: Stalin actually chose to conduct a lot of his business there, regularly summoning colleagues to give briefings. Meetings of the Politburo would be conducted in the dacha's large egg-shaped con-

---

134. Examples are given in Fitzpatrick, *Everyday Stalinism*, 100–101.

135. One example was the village of Zhukovka, where many peasants were dekulakized and exiled and their land was made available for the construction of elite dachas: see L. M. Trizna, "Zhukovka," in *Istoriia sel i dereven' podmoskov'ia XIV–XX vv.*, vol. 5 (Moscow, 1993), 10.

136. Iurii Druzhnikov, quoted in L. Vasil'eva, *Kremlevskie zheny* (Moscow, 1994), 109.

ference room adorned with portraits of major Soviet political figures, and Stalin's associates would be placed so that each man was seated underneath his painted image.[137]

The case of Stalin's dacha has great historical resonance: the Leader's move from the family dacha at Zubalovo to a gray official residence at Kuntsevo may be seen as emblematic of his break with the values of the Old Bolsheviks and his repudiation of revolutionary asceticism. As might be expected, Stalin's comrades were quick to follow their boss's lead: by the mid-1930s it was rare for senior Party figures to be making their own dacha arrangements; most of them had "personal" dachas that were officially state-owned but were rented out indefinitely to members of the political elite.[138]

Yet privileged dachniki could be as vulnerable as anyone else in the 1930s to the changing political winds. In 1933, for example, the village of Roslovka (Moscow region) had been developed as a comfortable dacha settlement for the managerial elite of the baking industry, but in 1937 and 1938 its character changed again: most of its residents disappeared in the purges, and other members of the elite were reluctant to take their place. As a result, the settlement was in due course occupied by factory workers (with five or six families to each house).[139]

Dacha settlements were almost certainly affected even more severely by the Terror than the cities where their residents had their main dwellings. For one thing, they were populated by precisely the categories of people—above all, Party/state functionaries and middle managers—who were most vulnerable to unmasking as "enemies of the people." And the unofficial channels through which the governing boards of dacha cooperatives were forced to operate gave ample material for conspiracy theorists among the rank-and-file membership. As economic bottlenecks remained tightly sealed, there may well have been a tendency to admit to cooperatives "random people" (*sluchainye liudi*) whose relation to the sponsor organization might be tenuous but who were well equipped to negotiate the shortage economy and obtain building materials.[140]

But, for as long as they remained in favor, men highly placed in the apparat could allow themselves almost anything. Kliment Voroshilov, Anastas Mikoyan, and of course Stalin wasted little time in carving out plots in elite locations and having spacious residences built at public expense.[141] By the mid-1930s, all semblance of self-restraint had

137. Ibid. Other details on Stalin's dacha taken from Allilueva, *Dvadtsat' pisem*. A map of elite dacha settlements in the Moscow region is given in T. Colton, *Moscow: Governing the Socialist Metropolis* (Cambridge, Mass., 1995), 512.

138. Bonner, *Dochki-materi*, 196.

139. E. N. Machul'skii, "Roslovka," in *Severo-zapadnyi okrug Moskvy*, 312–13. The dacha was, from the point of view of the secret police, a perfectly convenient working location: Nina Kosterina, for example, saw her family's dacha landlord arrested in the summer of 1937 (*Diary*, 42–43).

140. In July 1937 a representative of Mosgordachsoiuz reported that in the past year thirty-four members of the Podpol'shchik cooperative (run by Old Bolsheviks) had been arrested, and that a similar pattern of events could be observed in many other cooperatives. His conclusion was that "anyone who feels like it can infiltrate our cooperatives. We have provided enemies of the people with dachas" (TsMAM, f. 1956, op. 1, d. 24, l. 29).

141. On the *nomenklatura* dacha prerogative, see Michael Voslensky, *Nomenklatura: Anatomy of the Soviet Ruling Class*, trans. E. Mosbacher (London, 1984), 228–39. The personalistic nature of dacha allocation in the 1930s is suggested by archival materials from the Sovnarkom apparat: see, e.g., GARF, f. R-5446, op. 34, d. 1, ll. 12, 147.

154 gone. In one particularly unsavory episode, the state prosecutor, Andrei Vyshinsky, maneuvered to acquire the dacha of the Old Bolshevik Leonid Serebriakov even as he was demanding the death penalty for him at one of the Moscow show trials. Vyshinsky transferred the plot of land from cooperative to state ownership and in the process pocketed the money that Serebriakov had paid into the cooperative pool for his dacha.[142]

By the mid-1930s the net of privilege was cast wider to include new categories of beneficiary. In 1932 *Literaturnaia gazeta* noted pointedly that the only existing rest homes for writers could accommodate only fifteen people a month and were located an awkward fifteen-kilometer journey from a rail station two and a half hours' ride from Moscow. Fifty-six people (mainly writers' families rather than the writers themselves) were crammed into a building of seventeen rooms.[143] Construction of the famous writers' colony at Peredelkino started in 1934, shortly after the first congress of the Soviet Writers' Union, as a means of remedying this situation. Sovnarkom allocated 1.5 million rubles toward the cost of the first thirty dachas, and prominent writers and literary bureaucrats appealed successfully for further substantial injections of cash.[144] We have no reason to believe that the allocation of these funds was any more open, accountable, or equitable than in any other sector of the Soviet economy. As Gorky noted with alarm to a member of the Politburo in 1935:

> Money is often allocated without due attention, without consideration for the real needs of the union members. A needy writer can be refused help, but the sister of a writer receives 5,000 rubles. The government gave money for the construction of a dacha settlement, and 700,000 of this sum disappears like straw in the wind. There are many instances of generosity of this kind.[145]

Such doubts had earlier been raised from time to time by major Party figures.[146] But now, in the mid-1930s, Gorky's was a lone—and, given his own lavish accommodations, some-

142. Details in Arkady Vaksberg, *The Prosecutor and the Prey: Vyshinsky and the 1930s' Moscow Show Trials*, trans. J. Butler (London, 1990), 86–93. Nor was this Vyshinsky's only intervention in the life of dacha settlements during the Terror: in October 1938 he wrote to the manager of Sovnarkom affairs complaining that although several members of Ranis (a cooperative for representatives of academia and the arts) had recently been arrested, their dachas had been sealed up and their redistribution had been delayed (GARF, f. R-9542, op. 1, d. 41, l. 2).

143. "V Maleevke stalo luchshe, no eshche ne stalo khorosho," *LG*, 11 July 1932, 1, and E. Pel'son, "V Maleevke ne stalo luchshe," *LG*, 29 July 1932, 4.

144. D. Babichenko, *"Schast'e literatury": Gosudarstvo i pisateli 1925–1938: Dokumenty* (Moscow, 1997), 177–78, 197–98. Similar expenditure was sanctioned by other Soviet organizations: the Union of Soviet Architects, for example, resolved in 1936 to "increase funding for building and buy dachas from 100,000 rubles to 300,000 rubles" (Paperny, "Men, Women, and the Living Space," 162).

145. Quoted in Babichenko, *"Schast'e literatury,"* 202.

146. See, e.g., a letter of September 1933 in which Kalinin advises Voroshilov against setting up individual dachas in Sochi, given the expense of maintaining them, the potential for corruption in their allocation, and their impracticality: if a war were to erupt in the region, it would not be easy to turn them into hospitals; for this reason, collective rest homes should be preferred: RGASPI, f. 74, op. 2, d. 42, l. 38. The tendency of Party officials to affect "democratic" manners when on vacation is attested by Nadezhda Mandelstam, who recalls her hus-

Boris Pasternak's dacha at Peredelkino (from Natal'ia Poltavtseva)

what compromised—voice. Well-known writers had been petitioning the Central Committee for material privileges since the early 1920s, and by the mid-1930s the Party was coming to acknowledge their right to a peaceful creative environment in return for obedient membership in the union.

The state's encouragement of "creativity" by providing dachas gave rise to a new model of dacha life, which revived the prerevolutionary concept of the writer's retreat and underpinned it with the resources of the Soviet state. The result, in the words of one sardonic observer of Peredelkino, was a "feudal" settlement where the titans of Soviet literature took the role of lords of the manor.[147] Among the most prominent beneficiaries of these resources was Boris Pasternak, who in the second half of the 1930s took to spending large parts of the winter alone in Peredelkino (he visited Moscow about twice a month). Pasternak, like so many members of the intelligentsia, had been tormented by abysmal living conditions in his Moscow apartment in the 1920s; in Peredelkino he saw an opportunity to recreate the inspiring solitude of the student garret: "I am an incorrigible and convinced frequenter of bunks and attics (the student who 'rents a cubbyhole') and my

band's improbable encounter with Nikolai Ezhov, a future administrator of the Terror, in Sukhumi in 1930 (*Hope against Hope*, 322). A similar account of free-and-easy socializing is given by Anna Larina, who saw Bukharin in 1930 while staying in Mukhalatka "in a rest home for members of the Politburo and other leaders" (Bukharin, however, stayed at a separate dacha in Gurzuf) (*This I Cannot Forget*, 107).

147. L. Sobolev, *Neizmennomu drugu: Dnevniki. Stat'i. Pis'ma* (Moscow, 1986), 280 (a letter of May 1938).

156 very best recollections are of the difficult and modest periods of my existence: in them there is always more earth, more color, more Rembrandt content." Pasternak later confessed his discomfort after the substantial renovation and extension of the dacha in 1953–54: "I feel uncomfortable in these surroundings; it is above my station. I am ashamed at the walls of my enormous study with its parquet floor and central heating." So great was Pasternak's debt to his country retreat that his son saw fit to defend him against the charge of being a "dachnik" (perhaps he sensed an upsetting incongruity in the fact that his father had composed much of *Doctor Zhivago,* among other things a sprawling paean to nature as the life force of art, history, and Russia, while holed up in the pseudo-wilderness of the Soviet writer's village): "But if twentieth-century art is pre-eminently city art, it is quite natural for contemporary man to encounter nature in his country cottage; and for his reflection to derive from his impressions of genteel suburban rusticity."[148]

Soviet society was everywhere structured by hierarchies that governed people's access to goods and services. At the same time that the first dachas in Peredelkino were going up, slightly less favored writers were petitioning the authorities to obtain land for a dacha cooperative. Here the plan was for fifty modest wooden dachas of two to four rooms as well as one hostel for thirty people. The petition was signed by cultural figures little associated with collective actions of this kind: Osip Brik, Iurii Olesha, Iakov Protazanov, and, most surprising, Mikhail Bulgakov.[149] Galina Vladimirovna Shtange, social activist and wife of a professor whose position entitled him to build a dacha in the Academy of Sciences cooperative, was a typical upper-middling member of the intelligentsia. After three years of tense anticipation and frequent delays, the Shtanges were allocated a building lot in January 1938; while grateful for the chance to have "our own little corner to go to in our old age," Galina Vladimirovna was under no illusions about its level of comfort: "Like all these cooperatives, ours, the 'Academic,' turned out to be not the best quality and the dachas are not quite what we were promised. They're not equipped for winter, there's no stove, no fence, no icebox, no shed."[150] Nor were standards always much higher in prestige settlements like Peredelkino. Boris Pasternak complained in 1939 that his spacious retreat was rotting and collapsing a mere three years after it had been built; the new dacha to which he moved that year was supplied with gas and running water only in the winter of 1953–54.[151]

148. E. Pasternak, *Boris Pasternak,* 111–12, 209, 125. Pasternak's Peredelkino period coincided with his general withdrawal from and disgust with Soviet public life, his cultivation of a simpler prose style and authorial persona, his growing interest in Chekhov rather than Tolstoi as a model, and, not least, his engagement with the *usad'ba* tradition in Russian literature: see B. Zingerman, "Turgenev, Chekhov, Pasternak: K probleme prostranstva v p'esakh Chekhova," in his *Teatr Chekhova i ego mirovoe znachenie* (Moscow, 1988), esp. 145–67. Numerous other accounts echo Pasternak's attachment to his country retreat. Note, e.g., a 1938 diary entry where the alcoholic writer and literary functionary Vladimir Stavskii launches into an undistinguished but nonetheless rapturous description of the views from his dacha at Skhodnia: V. Garros, N. Korenevskaya, and T. Lahusen. eds., *Intimacy and Terror* (New York, 1995), 219–21.

149. TsGAMO, f. 7539, op. 1, d. 1, ll. 1–36.

150. Quotation from Shtange's diary, in Garros et al., *Intimacy and Terror,* 193.

151. E. Pasternak, *Boris Pasternak,* 111–12, 209.

The allocation of land for dacha construction, which surged in the years 1934–36, was by no means restricted to members of the Party elite and the arts intelligentsia. Any Soviet enterprise might put in an application for land, planning permission, and resources. In a typical case, the Moscow oblast ispolkom allocated eight plots of land to a dacha cooperative from a chemicals factory. At the time of its application for building permission, the cooperative had thirty-five members, most of whom had been working at the factory since 1929 or 1930. Half were Party members. The factory bosses were included in the cooperative, but so were senior workmen, electricians, and carpenters. The original request, sent in July 1934, had mentioned that the dachas were intended for "the factory's best shockworkers." Construction was to be subsidized to a total of nearly a million rubles (provided by the branch of the relevant ministry, by a trust, and by the factory itself). The remaining funds were to be supplied by the cooperative members themselves.[152]

The types of dachas built by cooperatives varied significantly from one settlement to another, and often within a single settlement. Some cooperatives were egalitarian to a fault, building well over one hundred low-cost plywood dachas of an identical standard design, each with two or three rooms and somewhere between 25 and 40 square meters in living space. Others chose the more expensive option of log cabins and built more spacious summer houses (of 70, 80, or 90 square meters). Still others had a mix of two or more standard designs. A few smaller settlements—mainly for people of the "free" professions—had no standard designs at all. But even the larger and more standardized cooperatives might have a handful of dachas that were substantially larger than the rest, presumably occupied by people in positions of particular importance either in the cooperative management or in the sponsor organization. Thus there appears to have been a distinct hierarchy of status in many dacha cooperatives, but such differentiation was obscured by the language used to categorize residents. As we have seen, very few of them could be called "workers"; the categories most widely used were "engineering and technical workers" (ITR) and (especially) "employees" (*sluzhashchie*). But this last category was a real catchall in Soviet Russia. In reality, the members of dacha cooperatives were not humble bottom-of-the-ladder clerks but bureaucrats and functionaries of middling and upper rank. And even within this band of employees there was a huge gulf in status between, say, the senior accountant at a minor Moscow publishing house and the director of a major industrial enterprise. Such differences between specific employees and between whole organizations were, it seems, amply reflected in the types of dachas built and in the speed with which they were built.[153]

All settlements, however, were forced to reckon with a Soviet government decree of 17 October 1937 that effectively brought an end to the cooperative housing movement in the major cities. Cooperatives stood accused of failing to manage their assets with the necessary efficiency and thus not justifying the considerable state investment made in them.

152. TsGAMO, f. 7539, op. 1, d. 5, ll. 1–21.

153. Conclusions in this paragraph are based on a study of the lists of cooperative members and dachas built in TsMAM, f. 1956, op. 1, dd. 26, 27, 28. Variation in the size and style of cooperative dachas is subject to disapproving comment in A. R., "Voprosy dachnogo stroitel'stva," *Zhilishchnaia kooperatsiia*, no. 6 (1935), 43–45.

158    For this reason, they were now forced to relinquish their quasi-independent status and come under the authority of local soviets or of organizations (enterprises, ministries, trade unions, and so on).[154] The 1937 decree is usually and with justification seen as having clinched the "departmentalization" of a crucial sector of the socialist welfare state.[155]

The decree mainly targeted high-density urban housing, but its strictures were extended to exurban locations too. Dacha cooperatives had been berated throughout the 1930s for overspending and choosing unrealistically expensive dacha designs. Now, the government asserted, the time had come to call in all debts and assess which cooperatives were financially self-sustaining. Dacha settlements where less than half of the capital had been generated by members' contributions were to be liquidated forthwith. In the days that followed the decree, Mosgordachsoiuz "activists" met with representatives of various cooperatives in efforts to clarify the situation. Of the many questions asked during these meetings, the most common and the most urgent was: What can I do to secure the right to continue using my dacha (or dacha plot, if the house was unfinished or partially built) even after the cooperative has been liquidated? The answer given was that each person should make a personal application to the Moscow city soviet; each case would be decided individually.[156] The standard procedure, later confirmed by practice, was that members of liquidated dacha cooperatives were allowed, at the discretion of the relevant soviet, to keep their dachas as "personal property" on condition that they repaid any outstanding loan within six months.[157]

A good many dacha cooperatives, however, remained intact after the decree of October 1937: the survival rate given by Mosgordachsoiuz for cooperatives in the Moscow region was 50 percent, and this is likely to be a conservative estimate, given this organization's interest in demonstrating its zealous execution of state policy.[158] However, the settlements that were financially secure enough to ride the storm were in practice likely to be those that already enjoyed a close working relationship with a sponsor organization. In other words, a great number of dacha cooperatives may indeed have survived the shake-up of 1937, but they arrived at this defining moment in a distinctly Soviet form: the October decree should be regarded as merely the culmination of the process whereby dacha cooperatives became ever more "departmentalized" and ever less cooperative-like.

It is worth dwelling on one other effect of October 1937: a significant number of dachas passed from cooperative into personal ownership.[159] This shift served to resolve an

154. "O sokhranenii zhilishchnogo fonda i uluchshenii zhilishchnogo khoziaistva v gorodakh," *Sobranie zakonov i rasporiazhenii raboche-krest'ianskogo pravitel'stva,* no. 69 (1937), art. 314.

155. This is the argument of, e.g., Andrusz, *Housing and Urban Development,* 36–37.

156. TsMAM, f. 1956, op. 1, d. 23.

157. See *Zhilishchnye zakony: Sbornik vazhneishikh zakonov SSSR i RSFSR, postanovlenii, instruktsii i prikazov po zhilishchnomu khoziaistvu* (Moscow and Leningrad, 1947), 9.

158. TsMAM, f. 1956, op. 1, d. 23, l. 102.

159. The rights of people who owned houses as personal property (e.g., the right to evict tenants once the term of their lease had expired if it could be proved the house was needed for the owner's personal requirements) are given due emphasis in an authoritative gloss on the October 1937 decree: see R. Orlov, "Poriadok primeneniia novogo zhilishchnogo zakona," *Sovetskaia iustitsiia,* no. 1 (1938), 20–24.

issue that had been moot for dacha cooperatives throughout the 1930s: Was it acceptable to allow members who had paid their initial contributions to go ahead and build dachas under their own steam if they had the necessary money, resources, and know-how? Confronted by the prospect of a long and frustrating wait for their turn to arrive, many people applied to the management of their cooperative or to Mosgordachsoiuz for permission to engage in "extrabudgetary construction" (*vnelimitnoe stroitel'stvo*). But in most cases, Mosgordachsoiuz, as the ultimate authority, denied permission. As the 1930s wore on, however, and the supply system failed to improve, this refusal came to seem all the more unreasonable. The matter was raised by several speakers at the meeting of the Mosgordachsoiuz activists in July 1937. The head of Moscow's housing administration was not unsympathetic but was unable to accede to their demands:

> I wrote a memo raising the issue of construction either wholly or partly at one's own expense, and at 70 percent, and at 50 percent [of the cost of the dacha]. I gave three options. The question was discussed three times. Three times meetings were called in Gosplan, but this question still wasn't resolved. There have been instances when Sovnarkom has allowed individual comrades to build dachas at their own expense. I think that if we continue to raise this issue in particular instances we will get permission.[160]

Quite in line with this policy, de facto private building continued into the period of the third five-year plan, even after the cooperative movement had been dealt a severe blow. This may seem paradoxical: the Soviet state undermined a form of collective undertaking and continued to support a form of individual activity. But actually this policy fits very nicely into a characterization of the Stalin-era system. First of all, it shows how apparently "nonnegotiable" ideological requirements could be waived in the interests of economy and expediency; how, in fact, ideology was never separate from economics. Second, it suggests how difficult it was for the regime to commit itself on matters of principle: the ad hoc resolution of problems was preferable to an unambiguous and realistic statement of policy. Third, the effective encouragement of individual construction was absolutely consistent with the Stalinist aim of eliminating "horizontal" social forms of cooperation and bringing state agencies into more direct contact with the individual. The "personal" builder may in theory have been free to construct a spacious five-room residence in an attractive part of the greenbelt, but in practice his success in this undertaking depended entirely on the discretion of his enterprise director, factory trade union committee, and a range of bureaucrats in the local and regional administrations.

A STUDY of published materials of the 1920s and 1930s suggests that the dacha fits perfectly the models that have gained most currency in social and cultural history as a means of differentiating those two decades: Timasheff's "Great Retreat" and Papernyi's "two cultures" model. In the early years of Soviet power dachas were commonly treated as an un-

160. TsMAM, f. 1956, op. 1, d. 24, l. 16.

160  desirable "remnant of the past" that had no place in a society informed by the principles of collectivism and Bolshevik self-denial. In practice, however, they were silently tolerated: partly because they served the important practical purpose of helping to alleviate the housing shortage in the major cities and partly because the overworked new state did not have the resources to administer them more closely. Then, after the first five-year plan had broken resistance to the Soviet social project and given rise to new, powerful interest groups, a significant change of orientation took place: individual property was relegitimized; prominence was given to symbols of material abundance; Soviet society became hierarchical and patriarchal. As a result, the dacha, that prime accoutrement of the comfortable prerevolutionary lifestyle, found favor once again.

This schema has many virtues, but it needs to be qualified. For one thing, public statements on the dacha, though in general softer in the 1930s, were by no means unqualified in their approval. For every writer, engineer, or skilled worker shown basking contentedly on a canopied veranda, there was an industrial manager subjected to public "indignation" for undue self-enrichment by the acquisition of a country retreat. And the collective forms of leisure with which the dacha is often contrasted—the parade, the expedition, the summer camp—became more, not less, prominent as the 1930s wore on.

But these are relatively small points that do not fundamentally undermine the "two cultures" account of interwar Soviet history. A more serious objection is that to view the 1930s as a step backward, as a kind of sociocultural Thermidor, is to underestimate the extent to which Soviet society was radically re-formed in the 1930s; such an interpretation runs the risk, moreover, of conflating public discourse and social practice. The Great Retreat was always much more a rejection of revolutionary utopianism than an enthusiastic adoption of "traditional" mores. The 1930s did much to establish what may now be seen as crucial characteristics of Soviet-style societies. At least two of these characteristics come sharply into focus in the history of the early Soviet dacha. First, the life chances of individual citizens, as we have seen, became firmly tied to their organizational allegiance. Second, access to and use of goods and benefits were valued more highly than ownership of them. Twenty years of Soviet life were more than enough to demonstrate both the risks associated with retaining property at all costs and the opportunities for status and well-being provided by regular, unproblematic access to basic necessities and to the objects of consumerly desire.

These two facets of Soviet society—the "organizational" principle and the emphasis on consumption—were, of course, connected. By the mid-1930s most Soviet people in the major cities (and it is of them alone that I am speaking) were fast learning the lesson that access could best be obtained and maintained by the protection of a sponsoring organization: a factory, a trade union, a creative union, or the Party apparat.

Although these twin characteristics would figure large in any ideal-typical account of the Soviet experience, their real implications for the lives of Soviet people varied over time. In the 1930s the regime's attempts to recast the relationship between state institutions and the individual were carried out in the face of various preexisting forms of social relationship. Institutions are, after all, made up of people, and Soviet citizens of the 1930s found their own ways of operating within new structures. The system was much more personalistic than the large volume of contemporary normative statements would allow; people were forced constantly to problematize the relationship between written rules and actual social practice, between public and private statements and values. The ways in which dachas were allocated and received may be seen as both symptoms of and contributions to the networks that gave Soviet society structure: ties that were neither properly bureaucratic nor wholly clan-based and particularistic, networks where the horizontal and vertical dimensions were rarely separate.

That is not to suggest that the vertical and the horizontal were ever wholly conflated, either in people's social practice or in their understanding of that practice. Soviet hierarchies of status were quick to emerge in the Stalin era, and they are palpable in the distribution of dacha space. Moreover, the informal social practices that people engaged in may have helped them to cut themselves some slack under an authoritarian regime and to get by in their everyday lives, but they also had human costs. Social relationships had been severely fractured by the social warfare waged by the Soviet regime, and they had not reformed to any adequate extent. According to one persuasive sociological account, *blat,* glossed as the "informal exchange of favors," was both social glue and lubricant in the later Soviet period.[161] But it is difficult to put the phenomenon in the 1930s in such a benign light. Even if the horizontal and the vertical were rarely separate, the vertical tended to overshadow and constrain the horizontal. *Blat* was oriented less toward ongoing sociability than toward the accomplishment of specific tasks. As the constant bickering in dacha cooperatives demonstrates, *blat* was a source of tension and fragmentation, not of cohesion.

Perhaps the most disastrous result of the collision between old social practices and new ideological goals and institutional structures was that it left people quite unsure of what the rules of social life were. Here the dacha sheds light on Soviet society for one other reason: it was a product and a symbol of hierarchical networks that were vulnerable. In the 1930s it reclaimed something of its medieval and Petrine meanings: a piece of property that was bestowed at the discretion of the leader and could just as easily be taken away. Now, however, the role of leader was taken by Soviet ideology, a notoriously fluid mélange of beliefs, programs, and practical policies that in turn was interpreted and administered by an equally fluid body of state officials. The dacha, then, can serve as a specific example of the mingling of modernization and traditionalism that has plausibly been seen as characteristic of the Soviet and other communist systems: it was valued as a symbol of material progress and for its association with "civilized" values (specifically, those of the officially approved Russian intellectual tradition); but it also reflected the particularistic and personalistic realities of Soviet society. On the one hand, the Soviet dacha gestured toward the older meaning of the term—a plot of land handed out entirely at the discretion of state authorities—yet it was also bound up with markedly modern phenomena: the bureaucratization of the distribution system, the emphasis placed on leisure as an attribute of the Soviet way of life, and an emerging (if tortuous) discourse on property rights.

161. See A. Ledeneva, *Russia's Economy of Favors: Blat, Networking and Informal Exchange* (Cambridge, 1998).

162      But the balance between the modernizing impulses of the Soviet regime and other social inputs was never fixed. As we survey the later Soviet period, it becomes clear that traditional practices (that is, practices deriving their strength from patterns of behavior
more long-standing or deep-seated than the socially transformative Soviet project)
should be seen not as a dead weight of passive resistance to state violence but rather as a
dynamic set of responses that were, in the long run, transformative in their own right. As
we survey developments of the later Soviet period, we will find new forms of social relationship (including a new kind of *blat*), a new intelligentsia, new attitudes toward property, and a new form of dacha that hybridized the country retreat of the Soviet leisure
class with the humble allotment.

# 6

## Between Consumption and Ownership

### Exurban Life, 1941–1986

The history of the dacha from the 1940s to perestroika is in large part a story of continuing growth: from being very much a minority privilege on the eve of the war, summer houses had become commonplace by the mid-1980s in most of Russia's major cities. But even a cursory comparison of dachas in 1940 and 1990 reveals to what extent the concept had been reshaped by four decades of relatively stable Soviet life. In the former case, we can still speak of a summer retreat intended primarily for leisure; in the latter, primarily of an ersatz homestead for underprovisioned urbanites. It was thus not only the social constituency of the dacha that had expanded but also its semantic field. When we speak of the postwar era it becomes impossible to keep the story of the dacha separate from that of the garden plot. So one narrative that instantly springs to mind—that of a consumer boom making second homes ever more accessible to urban Russians—needs to be qualified by an awareness of the pronounced social and political pressures that directed the dacha's development and by a careful consideration of the postwar dynamic between the main perceived attributes of the dacha: recreation, consumption, ownership, domesticity, and, not least, subsistence.

### The War and Its Aftermath

In the history of the dacha, the Great Patriotic War stands out as a chronological marker more significant than the death of Stalin. It was during the years 1941–45 that millions of Soviet people took part in an exurbanizing movement that prepared the ground (literally) for the "mass" dacha of the later Soviet period. They had little choice in the matter: facing starvation, city dwellers all over the country were forced to seize any available land to engage in subsistence agriculture. In Julie Hessler's apt phrase, Soviet society

164  in those years was characterized by a "survivalist ethic" that legitimated grassroots initiatives even without explicit official authorization.[1]

Not that such authorization was necessarily withheld. Very early in the war the Soviet government signaled its readiness to shift responsibility for food production and distribution from centralized planning to Party-state organizations at the local level. "Subsidiary farms" (*podsobnye khoziaistva*) attached to enterprises and institutions received active encouragement: the area sown in them rose from 1.4 million hectares before the war to 5 million by its end. The allotment movement, which had received much public attention as early as the 1930s, was boosted by *Pravda* articles and a joint Party-state resolution in March and April 1942; by the spring of 1943 trade unions and city soviets were taking a leading role in the distribution of land to workers.[2] Action was especially strong and decisive in the major cities, which stood to suffer even more than the rest of the country from the breakdown of the supply system. Even Leningrad's Summer Garden, laid out under Peter the Great, was dug up as potato patches.[3] The various forms of noncollectivized growing had a real effect on people's chances of survival. Official rations, often set near starvation level, were supplemented by produce from collective farm markets (though prices here were well beyond most people's means), subsidiary farms, and individual plots. In 1944, for example, over 12 percent of the average daily calorie intake was provided by food grown on private allotments.[4] The scale of the wartime allotment movement is reflected in the lengthy entry under "Gardening" (*sadovodstvo*) in a late volume (published 1944) of the first edition of the *Great Soviet Encyclopedia*. It is given statistical expression in the second edition: according to the entry "Allotment Gardening [*ogorodnichestvo*] by Workers and Employees," 5 million Soviet people were working the land in this way in 1942, but by 1945 that figure had risen to 18.5 million. This powerful trend continued through the hungry postwar years, when millions of people used allotments on the outskirts of the major cities, often to meet immediate subsistence needs. In April 1946, for example, the Moscow soviet proclaimed a total of 1.2 million allotment growers in the city: "tens of thousands" of Muscovites were producing enough to "guarantee their whole year's supply of potatoes and vegetables."[5]

1. J. Hessler, "A Postwar Perestroika? Towards a History of Private Enterprise in the USSR," *SR* 57 (1998): 524.

2. See U. G. Cherniavskii, *Voina i prodovol'stvie: Snabzhenie gorodskogo naseleniia v Velikuiu Otechestvennuiu Voinu (1941–1945 gg.)* (Moscow, 1964), 130–50, and William Moskoff, *The Bread of Affliction: The Food Supply in the USSR during World War II* (Cambridge, 1990), chap. 5. Cherniavskii (p. 142) relates that in 1942 almost a third of urban people had individual allotments or helped to cultivate collective allotments; in 1943 that figure rose to two-fifths; in 1944, to half.

3. A brief account of "food gardens" during the siege of Leningrad is given in Moskoff, *Bread of Affliction*, 201–3. The decision to grow vegetables in every available space within the city was taken in February 1942; by late summer of that year about 270,000 Leningraders were engaged in private vegetable gardening.

4. J. Barber and M. Harrison, *The Soviet Home Front, 1941–1945: A Social and Economic History of the USSR in World War II* (London, 1991), 83.

5. *Moskva poslevoennaia, 1945–1947: Arkhivnye dokumenty i materialy* (Moscow, 2000), 384. For more on the desperate food shortages of the postwar years, see V. F. Zima, *Golod v SSSR, 1946–1947 godov: Proiskhozhdenie i posledstviia* (Moscow, 1996), and E. Zubkova, *Poslevoennoe sovetskoe obshchestvo: Politika i povsednevnost', 1945–1953* (Moscow, 2000), 69–78.

Official encouragement of individual gardening continued in the late 1940s, when
local ispolkoms were ordered to make land available and trade unions began to distribute
allotments among their members. This policy was particularly marked in the wake of the
catastrophic famine of 1946–47: the government was forced once again to recognize the
expediency of devolving agricultural production to the urban population—of letting
people feed themselves. Growers were exhorted to emulate the feats of heroic allotment
cultivators such as the man who grew 2.5 tons of vegetables on a plot of 150 square meters.[6] Factories negotiated with regional and local authorities and with collective farms to
provide their workers with land; the bigger enterprises provided transport for their workers to visit their allotments on days off. Yet at the same time problems were acknowledged. Allotment collectives often had to fend for themselves, receiving little support
from factories and trade union organizations; seeds and tools were in short supply; and
the land people cultivated did not belong to them even de facto (let alone de jure), but
rather was reallocated to them each year on a temporary basis.[7]

However slim the prospects for long-term ownership, allotments still offered the Soviet urbanite significant benefits. They guaranteed a supply of basic vegetables and provided the opportunity for limited side earnings, as surplus produce could be sold at the
market: the immediate postwar period was marked by a relative tolerance of individual
economic activity and private trade.[8] Digging a potato patch was, moreover, a form of
"active leisure," and as such was encouraged in public discussions. It also enabled Soviet
citizens to engage in a healthy form of "socialist competition": to strive, in typical volun-
tarist fashion, for the maximum yield from their plot of a few dozen square meters. In
1949, allotment gardening was still common enough for one agricultural expert to observe with dismay that many trees on the outskirts of Moscow were dying because vegetables had been planted too close to them.[9] The number of growers remained reasonably
stable in the early 1950s. In 1952, for example, 903,000 families in Moscow were reported
to have allotments, an increase of 56,000 families over the previous year; in 1953 the number fell back to the previous level, and in Leningrad (both city and oblast) there was a similar slight decline.[10] Numbers also held up well outside the major cities: allotments were a

6. "Prakticheskie sovety ogorodnikam," *Ogonek*, no. 20 (1948), 29. There are numerous similar examples
in *Ogonek* and *Rabotnitsa* in the second half of the 1940s.

7. M. Basin and I. Shmelev, "V sadakh i ogorodakh odnogo zavoda," *Trud*, 21 May 1949, 4.

8. See Hessler, "Postwar Perestroika?" Contrast the "liberalization" of 1946–48 with the crackdown on individual peasant plots in 1939–40: see Osokina, *Ierarkhiia potrebleniia*, 220. The size of peasants' private plots
(*priusadebnye uchastki*) had been an incredibly sensitive public issue in the first few years of collectivization, and
in these debates we can see prefigured (albeit on a much larger and socially destructive scale) the arguments over
legitimate use of a garden plot in the post-Stalin period. On peasant plots in the 1930s, see S. Fitzpatrick, *Stalin's
Peasants: Resistance and Survival in the Russian Village after Collectivization* (Oxford, 1994), 134–36.

9. TsMAM, f. 718, op. 12, d. 37 (transcript of a meeting held to discuss the results of the allotment movement in the Moscow region, 12 Apr. 1949); the question of the danger to trees is raised on l. 24; the opportunity
to sell surplus produce is mentioned as one of the benefits of allotment gardening by an exemplary *ogorodnik*
and war invalid on l. 10.

10. Ibid., d. 231; GARF, f. R-5451, op. 30, dd. 269, 370.

166   truly national phenomenon, and progress reports poured in to the central trade union authorities from all corners of the Union.[11]

Cultivation of the land by factory workers had received further encouragement in the form of a government decree of February 1949, which, besides reiterating official support for allotments (*ogorody*), boosted a related but distinct activity: food gardening (*sadovodstvo*).[12] The Moscow city and regional authorities responded in August 1949 with a resolution urging that available agricultural land be allocated for "collective gardens" with plots ranging from 400 to 800 square meters. By the start of 1952, the Moscow trade union organization was able to report that 162 such gardens had been set up on 762 hectares; moreover, the 7,885 members of these collectives contained a healthy proportion of proletarians.[13]

But there were grounds for dissatisfaction nonetheless. Disagreements had arisen concerning the permissibility of building small shacks on individual garden plots. Gardening collectives argued strongly that their plots required hard work and regular attention: inasmuch as many plots were located inconveniently far from people's apartments (and thus differed significantly from allotments, which for the most part were located within or very close to the city limits), a small structure in which to store tools and take shelter from bad weather was simply essential. The Moscow soviet partially recognized this point by allowing the construction of watch booths and toolsheds in its resolution of August 1949. In what was perhaps a rather loose interpretation of this provision, many organizations then contacted the appropriate ispolkom and obtained permission to build summer shacks (*letnie domiki*); the maximum dimensions of these structures were at the discretion of each particular ispolkom. Two years later, however, it was found that garden collectives had abused the freedom they had been granted: some "watch booths" were as large as 28 square meters, and garden settlements almost everywhere had been building without the necessary strict supervision. As a result, the Moscow oblast ispolkom and the Moscow city soviet resolved in November and December 1951 that *all* buildings contravening their original instructions should be removed. Members of the garden collectives were, predictably, dismayed, and through their trade union organizations petitioned the municipal and regional authorities for permission to build summer shacks in the range of 6–10 square meters.[14] Similar pleas were heard in Leningrad, whose ispolkom in August 1951 forbade all construction on individual plots and prescribed instead collective "pavilions," each to accommodate 70 to 80 people.[15]

The collective nature of garden settlements was similarly in many cases open to dis-

11. A collection of these reports for 1951 can be found in GARF, f. R-5451, op. 30, d. 178.

12. See "O kollektivnom i individual'nom ogorodnichestve i sadovodstve rabochikh i sluzhashchikh" (24 Feb. 1949), in *Sbornik zakonodatel'nykh aktov o zemle*, 2d ed., expanded (Moscow, 1962), 99–100. There were still provisos, however: recipients of a plot of land had to work at their enterprise for five consecutive years before they gained the right to "permanent use" (*bessrochnoe pol'zovanie*).

13. TsMAM, f. 718, op. 12, d. 178, ll. 58–62.

14. TsMAM, f. 718, op. 12, d. 178. Factory representatives also complained that people who already had allotments were precluded from joining garden collectives: see GARF, f. R-5451, op. 30, d. 161, l. 26.

15. GARF, f. R-5451, op. 30, d. 282, l. 17. This file contains numerous similar protests, including several from garden collectives sponsored by Moscow enterprises.

pute. The original idea was for them to consist of large "production plots" of 600 or more square meters, but in practice most organizations, even if they did ensure that certain zones were allocated for collective cultivation, gave their workers individual plots. In 1951, for example, machine-building factories reported that they had nine strictly collective gardens occupying 223 hectares and cultivated by 1,130 workers; individual plots, by contrast, were worked by 7,563 people on 265 hectares. Reports of the early 1950s consistently reported significant increases in numbers of gardeners, who tended to fall into the "individual" rather than the "collective" category (where a distinction was made between the two). Quite often, however, the "individual" reality of the garden collective was passed over in silence: the "collective" tag was used consistently, even when it clearly gave a misleading impression of the gardeners' real activities.[16]

The mass return to the land in the late 1940s conformed to a pattern of behavior all too familiar in Russian history: the population, confronted by yet another social cataclysm, looked to the land for temporary survival and perhaps longer-term security. This change in orientation was reflected not only in factory-sponsored allotment areas but also in dacha settlements proper. One memoirist recalls "the spirit of the farm" in the settlement of Firsanovka (in the Moscow region, on the Leningrad railway line), where she lived with her parents in 1947 and 1948. The family's dacha landlords were Old Bolsheviks, and the settlement was populated largely by architects and musicians; their next-door neighbors were a "conservatory dynasty." In the evening the village fell silent as music wafted out of the neighbors' dacha, but in the daytime things were quite different: "The maestro often stood in 'dacha regalia' on the roof of the barn and shouted to his helper, so loud that the whole settlement could hear, 'Ivan! Don't forget to put the dung on the vegetable patches!' "[17] The demands of subsistence did not leave untouched even an exalted cultural enclave such as Peredelkino. Early in the war, in September 1941, the author Vsevolod Ivanov wrote to his wife and children (who had already been evacuated) that he and the few remaining locals were salting their own cucumbers, picking their own berries, and digging their own potatoes; the dacha settlement was beginning to resemble an underinhabited island, and Ivanov already felt like "Robinson Crusoe."[18] Just after the war, the poet Nikolai Zabolotskii, until recently an inmate of the gulag, found refuge at the dacha of an acquaintance in Peredelkino. Devoid of any regular source of income, he gained permission from the owners to grow vegetables on the dacha's land.[19] Zabolotskii's need was doubtless exceptionally great, but he was not alone among Peredelkino dwellers in cultivating more than just his poetic gift; Boris Pasternak, for one, was well known for digging his own potato patch.[20]

In the immediate postwar years, then, we can already see signs of the convergence be-

---

16. Ibid., d. 161, ll. 24–25; d. 167.

17. Such unreferenced examples are drawn from my own archive of dacha memoirs: see the "Note on Sources."

18. V. Ivanov, *Sobranie sochinenii v vos'mi tomakh* (Moscow, 1973–78), 8:669. Another letter of similar content, written two weeks later, can be found in the memoirs of Ivanov's widow: T. Ivanova, *Moi sovremenniki, kakimi ia ikh znala: Ocherki* (Moscow, 1984), 117.

19. N. Zabolotsky, *The Life of Zabolotsky*, ed. R. R. Milner-Gulland (Cardiff, 1994), 239.

20. See, e.g., Ivanova, *Moi sovremenniki,* 418.

168   tween dacha and allotment. Dacha owners were more likely now to work the soil with their own hands; more important, allotment cultivators were beginning to refashion their plots in the manner of dachniki, to use or at least envision them as dwelling places. For this potential to be realized, a great many social and ideological changes still had to take place. But some of these changes, as we shall see, also had their roots in the postwar period.

## The Dacha as Dwelling: The Property Issue in Postwar Russia

The extreme circumstances of the war can be seen to have triggered both quantitative and qualitative change in the relation of Soviet city dwellers to the land. But this was not the only large consequence of wartime experiences that had significance for the history of the dacha: there were also profound implications for the dacha as a piece of property, as a house and a domestic environment rather than simply as a plot of land for cultivation. In the late 1940s, single-family dwellings began to enjoy greater respectability than previously. More relaxed policies on land use were accompanied by a new encouragement of individual building.[21] As in the 1920s, the private sector was called on to repair the devastated housing stock. Land was distributed by local soviets. Resources (in the form of building loans) were handed out by ministries to enterprises under their control, and the enterprises then distributed the money among their workforce in consultation with the trade union organizations. The single-family *kottedzh* gained new prominence in design and planning.[22] At the same time, however, regulations pertaining to construction remained strict. Agreements were signed between the individual builder and the local soviet, and if the builder deviated from them in any way—for example, by bringing in someone else to help with the building work—the documents had to be redrawn. Often people did not bother to make the necessary adjustments and disputes arose between the legal owner and other people who, because of the labor they had contributed, had a moral right to a share in the dwelling.[23]

And so we come to another postwar innovation: renewed and more purposeful discussion of the nature and the limits of the right to property. Public debate on these matters was fueled by the large number of specific cases that needed resolution. Property disputes were less common in sites of new construction than in areas already provided with housing where people returned from the front or from evacuation. As can be imagined, the question of ownership was especially hard to resolve in former zones of occupation.

---

21. See the Soviet decrees "O meropriiatiiakh po vosstanovleniiu individual'nogo zhilishchnogo fonda . . ." (29 May 1944) and "O prave grazhdan na pokupku i stroitel'stvo individual'nykh zhilykh domov" (26 Aug. 1948).

22. See, e.g., V. G. Kalish, "Kottedzhi dlia gorniakov," *Arkhitektura i stroitel'stvo,* no. 4 (1947), 24–25: this article announces a design competition in Tula for "cottages" of between four and six rooms. Designs for individual houses are mentioned briefly as a feature of Soviet architecture in the late 1940s in V. Papernyi, *Kul'tura "dva"* (1985; Moscow, 1996), 152.

23. For a discussion of these issues, see L. Iurovskii, "O prave sobstvennosti na sovmestno vozvedennye doma," *SIu,* no. 4 (1958), 54–56, and I. Braude, G. Orlinskii, and A. Serebriakov, "O prave sobstvennosti na stroenie," *SIu,* no. 7 (1958), 65–69.

These grave practical difficulties provided the stimulus for a rather more inclusive definition of property rights in legal policy of the 1940s.[24] Much discussion was devoted to the
concept of "personal property" (*lichnaia sobstvennost'*), which differed from private
property (as found in the capitalist West) by being limited to people's personal use. As one
jurist explained, "personal property is property involving objects and products of consumption, that is, things that do not include weapons and means of production, which
have become public, socialist property."[25] The new term had been catapulted into Soviet
legal discourse by the 1936 Stalin Constitution, but it did not gain a secure place as part of
the Civil Code's basic typology of property until the post-Stalin era, when a basic distinction came to be made between "socialist" and "personal" property. In the meantime, it
represented a big gray area for Soviet legal theory. Article 10 of the Civil Code in the late
1940s mentioned that personal property was "protected by law" and presented a short list
of items and sources of income that might fall into this category, but this brief treatment
of the issue raised more questions than it answered. Debate was especially fierce with regard to ownership of housing. Was it permissible, for example, for Soviet people to own
more than one house? Some argued categorically that it was not. Others took the same
basic view but allowed certain exceptions (the acquisition of second houses by marriage
or by inheritance). Still others asserted that the injunction against second houses related
only to sale and purchase. But all tended to agree that to rent out a part of a house was not
illegal, and that houses put up since 1921 on the basis of a mere "right to build" could now
be reclassified as "personal property."[26]

In the postwar period, then, the uncertainty of Soviet property relations—which had
of course been exacerbated by the huge upheavals of the previous few years—was confronted by a new urge to codify, a new (albeit partial) commitment to abstract principle.
The dacha was a particularly ambiguous case for Soviet legal theory. It combined characteristics of a piece of property with those of an item of consumption; it was both a second
home—thus affording its occupant the opportunity for illegitimate unearned income—
and a wholly legitimate social and cultural amenity, the availability of which confirmed
the rising living standards of the Soviet people. This tension was never resolved in principle; it is hard to see how it could have been, given the constraints of Soviet ideology. The
precise nature of a dacha—the balance it struck between property and consumption—
could be established only in practice: by a detailed examination of a dacha's use in each
individual case.

As always, the surest way to ensure that such difficulties were overlooked was to enjoy
the protection of a powerful sponsor. "Legitimate" use differed significantly from one

---

24. For more on the impact of the war on revisions to the Civil Code, see S. Bratus, "Nekotorye voprosy
nauki grazhdanskogo prava i sudebnoi praktiki po grazhdanskim delam v period Otechestvennoi voiny," *SZ*,
no. 11 (1944), 30–37.

25. G. N. Amfiteatrov, "O prave lichnoi sobstvennosti," *SZ*, no. 8 (1945), 10–16.

26. For various points of view, see the following articles: P. Orlovskii, "Pravo sobstvennosti v praktike
Verkhovnogo suda SSSR," *SZ*, no. 9–10 (1944), 6–16; G. N. Amfiteatrov, "O prave lichnoi sobstvennosti"; D.
Genkin, "Pravo lichnoi sobstvennosti," *SZ*, no. 10 (1946), 18–21; I. Braude, "Neobkhodim li institut prava zas-
troiki v Grazhdanskom kodekse SSSR?" *SZ*, no. 6 (1947), 10–12.

170 organization to another. Certain branches of the government found themselves particularly favored in the late 1940s. The most prestigious dacha zones—mainly west and north
of Moscow—were colonized by ministries and Party organizations.[27] The army, understandably enough, was also among the main beneficiaries. General majors tended to receive plots of 0.75 hectares, while 0.5 was the norm for lower ranks within the officer
corps.[28] The leisure complex of the Central Committee and its ever-expanding apparat
was supplemented by new settlements. Spacious vacation homes in the south were built
for elite cadres.[29] In 1946 the dacha locations available for the Central Committee administrative machine were relatively few—Berezhki, Kratovo, Mamontovka, Skhodnia, and
Bykovo-Udel'naia—but their number soon grew to include such places as Usovo, Uspen-
skoe, Serebrianyi Bor, and Kuntsevo. The annual budget for maintaining these settlements in the late 1940s was in the region of 5 million rubles. All settlements were heavily
subsidized. The proportion of costs met out of the state budget varied from 70 to 90 percent; some residents did not pay even a nominal fee for their accommodations. The accounts for Kuntsevo and Barvikha in the early 1950s, for example, contained no receipts at
all. The budget for 1951 projected an average subsidy of 1,024 rubles for each of the 1,040
families due to be resident in Central Committee dachas. Besides running costs for the
dachas themselves, services included canteens where meals were available at cost, laundry,
medical care, and special bus connections. Electricity bills were unusually high because of
the large number of electrical appliances the residents owned and used. The dacha stock
in 1950 consisted of thirteen settlements with a total of 271 dachas and 1,569 rooms inhabited by 950 families.[30]

These figures clearly demonstrate, however, that the dacha—even for people working
in the Central Committee apparat—was not always a thing of luxury. A family was on average granted little more than a room and a half. In the mid-1950s, for example, the 90
families resident at the dacha settlement of Mamontovka had at their disposal a total of
1,865 square meters. Allocation of dacha space proceeded according to a particular institutional hierarchy. Just over 230 dachas were reserved for use by families in the most prestigious sectors of the apparat; the remaining 700 or so dachas had to be fought for by
other branches of the administration. The Services Department allocated dachas directly
to the higher cadres—to heads of departments, for example—while lower down the hierarchy space was allocated by the secretariats in question.[31] A similar hierarchy existed

27. Examples are given in T. Colton, *Moscow: Governing the Socialist Metropolis* (Cambridge, Mass., 1995),
511–13.

28. See TsGAMO, f. 2157, op. 3, d. 355, ll. 522, 528, and d. 345, l. 349. A Sovnarkom decree of June 1945 had
set the goal of improving living conditions for the senior ranks of the army. A particular instance was the settlement built for the Stalin Military Academy in 1947: see TsGAMO, f. 7974, op. 1-t, d. 12, ll. 1–39. Requests for
dachas and other privileges from high-ranking members of the Soviet army and their families are to be found in
GARF, f. R-9542, op. 1, d. 95.

29. According to Svetlana Allilueva, this policy can be traced directly to Stalin's trip south in the summer
of 1946 (for the first time since 1937): see her *Dvadtsat' pisem k drugu* (London, 1967), 182–83.

30. RGASPI, f. 17, op. 80, d. 107, ll. 121, 279; d. 110, ll. 106–7.

31. Ibid., d. 191, l. 9; d. 107, ll. 280–81.

with regard to the dachas of the Soviet government: members of the government were granted "personal" dachas equipped for year-round habitation, while leading workers in the apparat had the right to summer dachas.[32] The rest, the humble clerks of the government administration, could, we must assume, only hope for a room or two per family.

Middle-of-the-range institutionally sponsored dachas, such as those put up by the Ministry for Construction in the Oil Industry (Minneftestroi) in 1956, would have two or three rooms, be built according to a standard design, be equipped with electricity, plumbing, and central heating, and stand on a plot of 1,000 square meters. The cost, as the ministry stipulated to the designers, was not to exceed 25,000 rubles per dacha.[33] For certain categories of dacha client, however, the limits were much looser. In 1947 a Hero of the Soviet Union was built a dacha with a "hall-vestibule," a drawing room, a study, a kitchen, a servant's room, two bedrooms, and a nursery. The total cost was 250,000 rubles.[34]

The stratification of the dacha population even in a single location was noted by Stalin's daughter, Svetlana Allilueva. In Zhukovka, an unspoiled village to the west of Moscow, residents—who for the most part worked not at the nearby collective farm but rather commuted each day to factories on the outskirts of Moscow—would rent out their houses to academics and writers of modest means for the summer, as before the war. At the same time, however, special dachas were built for scientists working in "secret" fields (mainly atomic physics and the space program).[35] The third element in Zhukovka was a dacha settlement for the government. It was in this section that Allilueva lived as a privileged observer of its closed community: residents had special shops provided, and entrance into the settlement was by pass only. The only real place for the three dacha strata of Zhukovka to encounter one another was the local cinema, where the young people regularly brawled on weekends.[36]

State-owned "nomenklatura" dachas were, by Soviet standards, luxurious; they would often come complete with such desirable features as housekeeper, billiard table, and a real stone fireplace,[37] and they tended to be located in settlements equipped with a good shop, a canteen, even a cinema. The elite settlement of Gorki-10, for example, had a staff of 428 in 1949.[38] The mentality of the residents also differed fundamentally from that of "individual" dachniki. These privileged few were able to enjoy comfortable vacations while at the same time protecting themselves from charges of petty bourgeois materialism; for, after all, these dachas were not even their "personal," let alone "private," prop-

32. GARF, f. R-9542, op. 1, d. 130.

33. See TsGAMO, f. 7572, op. 1, d. 553.

34. TsGAMO, f. 7974, op. 1-t, d. 41.

35. Later on, the prominent people at Zhukovka came to include figures from a wider range of fields. In the summer of 1972, for example, Mstislav Rostropovich, Andrei Sakharov, and the guitar poet Aleksandr Galich lived on the same street in the settlement: see R. Orlova, *Vospominaniia o neproshedshem vremeni* (Ann Arbor, 1983), 286.

36. S. Allilueva, *Tol'ko odin god* (New York, 1970), 218–20.

37. The interior of one such dacha, witnessed in 1959, is described in some detail in M. Matthews, *Mila and Mervusya: A Russian Wedding* (Bridgend, 1999), 17–20.

38. GARF, f. R-9542, op. 1, d. 130, l. 5.

172   erty. They received their dacha perks, so the largely unspoken rationale went, not for who they were but for the post they held. In some settlements nomenklaturists were reminded of this fact by the official inventory numbers that were stamped on the furniture. It was apparently *mauvais ton* for them to buy their own dacha or even to show too proprietary a concern for the dachas provided for them by the state.[39]

The evidence suggests, moreover, that even nonnomenklaturists, if they felt the dacha privilege to be their right, were more active after the war in requesting it directly from powerful Party-state figures; such people—many of them prominent members of the arts or scientific intelligentsia—also seem to have been more successful with their requests than in the 1930s, when they more often had to rely on institutional "brokers" than on personal appeals to authority. Peredelkino residents, for example, were not afraid to go straight to Viacheslav Molotov (the head of the Soviet government) and ask for a car to facilitate their trips to the city or for financial assistance in renovating their dachas. In the 1940s, it appears, the regime established a more stable modus vivendi with the various institutional structures of privilege; state policy remained repressive in all spheres, but those writers and artists who knew the limits and did not overstep them found that rewards and privileges, once granted, could more easily be retained.[40]

Even so, it would be wrong to suppose that the residents of institutionally controlled settlements were able to remain loftily indifferent to the issue of property, which could be so thorny for most Soviet owners or occupiers of dachas. In the postwar period, questions arose regarding the transmission of privilege: the original recipients changed jobs or died, leaving their widows and children to fight to maintain the dacha as personal property. Over the period 1940–50, for example, N. A. Peshkova, the wife of Maxim Gorky's son, launched a series of appeals to authority in an effort to retain control of her late father-in-law's country residence. Gorky's dacha in the Gorki-10 settlement was converted into a rest home in 1940, but Peshkova, instead of accepting the new dacha she was offered in a different location, requested a plot of land in the same area on which to build a new dacha; in the meantime she asked permission to live in the smaller house on Gorky's plot that had formerly been used as the servants' quarters. A more acrimonious case came in 1946, when the widow of the prominent Soviet writer A. N. Tolstoi wrote to Molotov asking for permission to remain at the dacha in Barvikha occupied by Tolstoi and his family from 1938 until his death in 1945 and to oversee the creation of a literary museum in her husband's memory; she was not prepared to relocate to the alternative dacha she had been offered in Malakhovka (thirty-five kilometers from Moscow), which stood in what was by Soviet standards a manorial estate of 2,700 square meters. In a memo of March 1947, the Services Department gave its side of the story: the dacha had been given major repairs at state expense when Tolstoi returned from evacuation; since Tolstoi's death people had been living there "without authorization . . . who have no connection whatsoever to A. N.

39.  See M. Voslensky, *Nomenklatura: Anatomy of the Soviet Ruling Class* (London, 1984), 205–6.

40.  I draw here on V. Tolz, "Cultural Bosses as Patrons and Clients: The Functioning of the Soviet Creative Unions in the Post-war Period," paper presented at a seminar of the Soviet Industrialisation Project Series, University of Birmingham, U.K., December 2000. My own archival research suggests a similar picture.

Tolstoi or to his family"; and in any case, it was curtly pointed out, the dacha had never actually belonged to Tolstoi—he had rented it.[41]

Such cases served to remind even highly privileged members of Soviet society that the right to use or occupy was, despite much evidence to the contrary, not quite indistinguishable from the right to ownership. Occasionally it was argued that lengthy occupation of a state-owned dacha should be converted to personal ownership on the grounds that protracted state service precluded the acquisition of a house by ordinary means (that is, purchase). In 1947, for example, a resident of a dacha in the settlement administered by the state publishing network (OGIZ) complained that the new head of the organization was forcing him to vacate his summer house. Citing his long and dedicated service to Party and state, he insisted that the dacha should be confirmed as his personal property. "I was employed by the state without interruption. And as usually happens I have an official apartment, official transport, official dacha"—but as a result, he claimed, he hadn't earned enough money to build his own country retreat.[42]

Others, however, managed to avoid these problems by acquiring a house privately. It is easy, given the undoubted advantages of explicit institutional backing and the reticence of the sources, to overlook the fact that private dacha ownership endured all the way through the Soviet period. Some owners had retained property from before the Revolution by slipping through the net of municipalization in the 1920s; others had managed to build or purchase their own houses during the first half of the Soviet period. To be sure, such undertakings were not possible without a certain status in Soviet society (so as to ensure official permission to build or buy, or to secure the necessary building materials, or to raise the money necessary to buy the house outright), but the house thus obtained was largely independent of institutional control. In Iurii Trifonov's novella *The House on the Embankment* (1976), for example, the house owned by a Moscow professor and his family in 1947 has a run-down appearance that would not be tolerated by any moderately conscientious cooperative administration: it is "disorderly, on the point of falling apart, with a rotting porch and an unfinished second floor"; but even so, this house, with its enormous plot (4,000 square meters), its fence, pine trees, and wild vines around the veranda, and its little kitchen garden, represents the "private property" that in Soviet society was as highly valued by individuals as it was publicly decried.[43] One nonfictional owner of a spacious country property was the artist P. P. Konchalovskii, who bought a house with extensive gardens and outbuildings in 1929 and retained it until his death in 1956. All the while

41. GARF, f. R-9542, op. 1, d. 56; d. 18, ll. 10–13. Further examples include requests from the overachieving coal miner A. G. Stakhanov and from the family of V. V. Kuibyshev (Kuibyshev's first and second wives were for some time in competition for the privileges attendant upon an association with the great man): see respectively ibid., dd. 55 and 75. Such requests did not pertain only to dachas, of course: petitions concerning apartments, cars, and free Kremlin lunches were just as common.

42. Ibid., d. 18, l. 56. Examples from the 1970s and 1980s suggest that areas of uncertainty remained until much later in the Soviet period: appeals by widows of Soviet officials continued to be dutifully filed in the archives of the Services Department of Sovmin until the mid-1980s, when they finally began to fade out, presumably as a result of Andropov's and Gorbachev's campaigns against protectionism and patronage.

43. Iu. Trifonov, *Sobranie sochinenii v chetyrekh tomakh* (Moscow, 1985–86), 2:418.

174   he conducted himself like a true gentleman farmer; the property "remained miraculously intact as a fragment of the life of the prerevolutionary estate."[44]

Private dachas were not well documented and certainly did not receive much public attention, but surely they only benefited from this neglect. Owners were able to lie low and for the most part were left untroubled. Not only that, official silence left opportunities for manipulation of the regulations by sure-footed and well-connected citizens: privileged members of the system apparently were able to make use of state resources when they built their dachas and to enjoy a legitimacy derived from their association with the state, yet in reality to flout all planning regulations and to claim the dacha as private, not socialist or cooperative, property. The scope for such abuses seems to have increased significantly toward the end of the Soviet period (and, as we shall see, it reached its peak in the period of privatization of state assets in the early 1990s). The boundary between state and personal property remained conveniently blurred, and it is safe to assume that, as the Soviet period wore on, specially favored citizens and their families gained a surer sense of what they could get away with. A Politburo member observed in a discussion of elite privilege in 1983: "The size of dachas is not observed. There is no strict control. There are whole palaces built by certain academicians and figures in the arts in Nikolina Gora, all from materials obtained at state expense."[45]

To join a dacha construction cooperative (DSK) was a more accessible but considerably more arduous way to ensure long-term ownership. Even if postwar cooperative members were allocated land on which to build, many found that they were on their own when it came to putting up a house. The grandfather of one memoirist, a highly placed worker in the then prestigious railway sector, was offered the opportunity to join a DSK in 1949. He considered that acquiring property of this kind was dangerous, but his misgivings were overcome by the cooperative form of the settlement and by his concern to improve his family's living conditions. The land allocated to the prospective settlement was in a prestigious location, near the former Mamontov estate of Abramtsevo; but it was also densely wooded, and the dacha settlers had to clear the trees to make paths. For this project the necessary permission had to be obtained and foresters hired to fell the trees. After the cooperative members had joined forces to clear pathways and put up fences (in the process their treasurer disappeared with a large part of the money contributed), they were confronted with another enormous difficulty: how to obtain building materials. Even the simplest wooden boards could not be obtained through official channels—so dachniki here, as in so many other settlements, filched their wood from state building sites and hired a state-employed driver to transport it to their plot during his working hours. Even then, life was made difficult by fussy regulations passed on by the president of the cooperative from higher authority: dacha builders were, for example, required to plant sixty new trees on their plots to compensate for those that had been felled to clear the paths. Luckily, no serious effort was ever made to enforce such instructions.

This lack of strict administrative supervision was hardly untypical of the period. After

44. Ivanova, *Moi sovremenniki*, 125.
45. I am grateful to Jana Howlett for providing me with a transcript of this discussion.

A dacha built in the 1940s, located at Mel'nichii Ruchei (near Vsevolozhsk, east of St. Petersburg). This Soviet dacha plot has not been left unmarked by the post-Soviet era: it is overlooked by a "New Russian" residence that infringes all known planning regulations.

the cataclysm of the war, dacha settlements offered refuge, subsistence, and extra living space for many people, but often they became lawless and chaotic places. Andrei Sergeev, in his stylized memoir, *A Stamp Album,* recalls seeing a stream of beggars on suburban trains along the Kazan' line in the mid-1940s; this was a "bare, dull time without dachniki." In other words, settlements had filled up with permanent residents—who had every reason to fear for their property. "The half-empty houses were bolted up using all available locks, hooks, and bars."[46] According to another account, lawlessness remained a feature of dacha settlements for many years:

> Accounts of forced entries to dachas were passed on from mouth to mouth, each day acquiring fresh details. Dachas were burglarized frequently—very few people got by without experiencing this. The dacha thief was not, as a rule, a professional. In the 1950s and 1960s these were most often escaped or amnestied prisoners who were hungry and had absolutely nowhere to go. They forced their way into empty houses, not looking for riches but just hoping for a roof over their

46. A. Sergeev, *Al'bom dlia marok,* in his *Omnibus: Roman, rasskazy, vospominaniia* (Moscow, 1997), 206. Looting of dachas was also rife during the war, when settlements were left unattended: in 1942, for example, government-owned furniture from dachas at Gorki-10 was reported to have found its way into the homes of private citizens (GARF, f. R-9542, op. 1, d. 82).

176 heads and a bite to eat. They devoured fruit conserves left behind by the owners, the odd can of something or other, last year's dried crusts, and left behind them empty bottles, cigarette butts, and a big mess.

Other factors besides the threat of crime might make membership in a dacha settlement problematic. The cooperative form of property was liable to bring dachniki into conflict with one another, with the administration of their settlement, or with higher authorities. In the immediate postwar period especially, individual dachas seem quite often to have been subdivided into apartments; a government circular of December 1953 had to offer specific instructions on the correct way to proceed if land disputes arose between people sharing a single plot within a dacha cooperative.[47] The aim of 1950s legislation on dacha cooperatives was to regularize the procedures for acquiring and transferring their plots and houses and to put an end to "abuses" involving the de facto sale of patches of land or of rooms in a dacha. A building in a dacha cooperative could be transferred to another person on condition that that person was accepted as a member of the cooperative.[48] But the fact that proscribed informal arrangements persisted was reflected in the quantity of advice given on the legal resolution of conflicts arising from shared use of dachas.[49] In one publicly cited case of 1956, the wife of a cooperative member sold a room and part of a terrace to another family for 27,000 rubles; but she ran into difficulties when the new neighbors moved into another room in the dacha without relinquishing the first. The result of this awkward situation was three lawsuits: the first was brought by the member of the dacha cooperative, who sought the eviction of his unwanted neighbors; the second by the defendants in the first suit, who sought compensation for money they had spent on repairs; the third by the cooperative, which protested against the illegality of selling the room in the first place. The oblast court decided against all three parties, but in 1959 the Supreme Court of the RSFSR reviewed the case and concluded that the cooperative's appeal ought to be upheld in the interests of safeguarding the sanctity of "cooperative property."[50]

Other cases of the late 1950s supported adherence to a settlement's statutes in defiance of intuitive notions of justice. For example, in 1958 it was decided that people restored to a dacha cooperative after an earlier expulsion did not have the right to have their property

47. "O poriadke pol'zovaniia zemel'nymi uchastkami v dachakh DSK" (22 Dec. 1953), in *Zhilishchnye zakony*, 3d ed., expanded, ed. T. D. Alekseev (Moscow, 1957). The recommended procedure—that such disputes be settled before "comrades' courts" within the dacha cooperative—was discussed in more detail in a later article: see B. Erofeev and M. Lipetsker, "Sudebnye spory ob ustanovlenii poriadka pol'zovaniia zemel'nymi uchastkami," *SZ*, no. 4 (1959), 39–42.

48. This policy is spelled out in *SZ*, no. 5 (1950), 60–61. In the cautionary case cited (from the late 1940s), a cooperative member had sold an outbuilding on his plot without consulting the administration; it then transpired that the outbuilding was subject to removal, as it had been put up without the necessary permission. The original sale agreement was accordingly voided.

49. See "Iz praktiki prokuratury SSSR," *SZ*, no. 9 (1951), 93; Ia. Ianovskii, "Pravovoe regulirovanie zhiloi ploshchadi chlenov zhilishchno-stroitel'nykh i dachno-stroitel'nykh kooperativov," *SZ*, no. 8 (1955), 38–42; A. Mel'nikov, "Sudebnaia praktika po sporam s dachno-stroitel'nymi kooperativami," *SZ*, no. 10 (1958), 33–35.

50. *SIu*, no. 7 (1959), 83–84.

returned if the property had been legally occupied by another member of the cooperative in the meantime. This was a situation quite likely to arise after 1956, when hundreds of thousands of people were released from prison camps and some of them took steps to reclaim property that had been confiscated on their arrest. In one case, a former cooperative member by the name of Aronov, rehabilitated in 1956 after six years, was promptly reinstated as a member of his cooperative; a few months later he was allotted 450 square meters of land and two rooms on the second floor of the dacha that used to be his. Soon after, he and his neighbors were presenting rival suits to the local court. When his case was rejected at this level of the legal hierarchy, Aronov turned to the oblast court, which found in his favor. But Soviet legal commentary considered this decision misguided, as according to its statutes a dacha cooperative did not have the right to take over any part of a member's accommodation unless the member had been expelled from the cooperative.[51]

The dacha's relation to Soviet notions of property can further be explored through cases in which families broke down and spouses or relatives presented their rival claims for ownership. In one (by no means exceptional) example from the late 1940s, the breakup of the marriage of Anastasiia Shvaichenko and Aleksandr Gushcha led to a long-running dispute over entitlement to dacha space. The marriage was officially contracted in 1942, but it had fallen apart after Gushcha's return from the Red Army in 1943; Gushcha found himself a new woman in 1947, and the marriage was dissolved in February 1949. Gushcha and Shvaichenko managed to come to an agreement over the division of their city apartment (Shvaichenko took the larger of the two rooms, as was only fair, since she had had by far the better accommodations of the two before they married), but their dacha presented a much thornier issue: Gushcha claimed all of it, Shvaichenko half.

According to Soviet civil law, a wife was entitled to an equal share in all property acquired during the marriage, irrespective of whether this property was acquired by her money or her labor. Gushcha had received his dacha plot in 1938 and begun to build in April 1939, so Shvaichenko's case seemed initially to be weak. But here she alleged that they had initiated "marital relations" in 1937, and it was to this time that her right to property should be dated, not to 1942. After the Moscow city court denied her any right to the dacha, Shvaichenko appealed to the civil law division of the Supreme Court, which in June 1949 overturned the earlier ruling, deciding that the period of dacha construction had coincided with actual married relations (although it dated the start of these relations back to 1939, not to 1937). Even so, it judged, Shvaichenko's share should be somewhat less than half, as Gushcha had invested substantially in building materials for the dacha before the start of their relations. Shvaichenko appealed again, and after another few months of legal wrangling succeeded in obtaining more than a third share in the dacha (at some expense; the dacha was to be converted into two discrete dwellings).

Perhaps the most interesting aspect of this dispute is the way both parties—but especially the plaintiff, Shvaichenko—combined appeals to rights guaranteed by law with assertion of moral right. Strictly speaking, it was immaterial whether Shvaichenko took an active part in organizing the construction of the dacha: the crucial point was to establish

---

51. *SIu*, no. 6 (1958), 83.

178   whether she and Gushcha had conjugal relations at that time. But even so, in her petitions she laid great emphasis on the expertise she had brought to the project (she claimed, as a construction engineer, to have supervised all the building, which was carried out by hired workers, while her husband's involvement had been limited to obtaining the building materials through his contacts in the supply system). This dacha had been built with private resources on the basis of a "right to build" that Gushcha had obtained in 1937 under the assumption that it would translate into "personal" property for him. Of course, such perceived conflicts between moral and legalistic notions of rights are universal in societies with legal systems. But the Soviet system left unusually large scope for them, as the property issue was constantly fudged. It seems that the status of cooperative and "personally" owned dachas was perfectly clear to social actors until differences arose; at that point it emerged that there was little firm legal ground to stand on.[52]

## Property under Attack: The Khrushchev Era

In the late 1940s dachas were presented as a legitimate aspiration for ordinary Soviet people, albeit one that was unlikely to be satisfied in the immediate future. In the first half of the 1950s state-directed dacha provision proceeded more or less as it had done in the 1930s. The new ten-year plan for the reconstruction of Moscow was to create dacha space for 100,000 more people. This expansion of the exurban zone was to be centrally directed, inasmuch as cooperative settlements, in the view of the central planners, had failed to achieve the necessary coordination either with other construction projects or with the natural environment; architectural designs (even for outbuildings) were to be provided by central planning institutions. Dacha dwellers could show their individuality only by their choice of gates, decorative window surrounds, and door design.[53]

Much grander in its projections was the general construction drive of the late 1950s. As part of Khrushchev's ambitious program, Soviet citizens were presented with the opportunity to build their own (albeit very modest) houses. The seven-year plan from 1959 to 1965 aimed to build 15 million new apartments and 7 million small homes, the latter mainly for the rural population. The government resolved to encourage individual participation in this construction work by giving credits more freely and improving the infrastructure in potential settlement areas.[54] Specific instructions were delivered to do-it-

52. The file on the Shvaichenko and Gushcha case is TsMAM, f. 819, op. 3, d. 2. A rather similar case (arising from a divorce) of 1954–55 is ibid., d. 293. A dacha dispute between the plaintiff and his mother and three sisters is ibid., d. 192.

53. See N. Osterman and N. Reviakin, "Doma i dachi dlia prigorodnoi zony Moskvy," *Arkhitektura i stroitel'stvo Moskvy*, no. 12 (1953), 13–19. For more on postwar leisure provision in the greenbelt, see V. I. Vasil'ev and G. I. Makeenko, "Prigorodnaia zelenaia zona Moskvy," *Gorodskoe khoziaistvo Moskvy*, no. 5 (1952), 20–22, and P. Pomazanov, "Podmoskovnaia zona otdykha: O rekonstruktsii Khoroshevskogo Serebrianogo bora," *Arkhitektura i stroitel'stvo Moskvy*, no. 9 (1953), 18–22.

54. The crucial Central Committee resolution was "O razvitii zhilishchnogo stroitel'stva v SSSR" (31 July 1957).

yourself builders in dozens of books published between 1957 and 1960 that differed from one another only to take account of regional variations in climate and building materials.

These policies might have sounded liberal, but in reality access to land was strictly policed. Numerous bureaucratic mechanisms had to be engaged if permission to build were to be granted. Applicants were first to send a set of documents to the office of the chief architect of the town; if they were attached to an enterprise, they were also required to enclose letters of approval from their trade union organization and their workplace administration. A legal agreement was then signed with the communal department of the local soviet. The act of transferal (of land from public to personal ownership) stipulated that the applicant might construct a house on the plot as his or her "personal property." The house then had to be built within three years for the agreement to remain valid. Loans were generally available (for a sum not to exceed 50 percent of building costs) at an interest rate of 2 percent.[55]

The recommended size of an individual house remained modest: one room for a family of two or three people, two to three rooms for four or five people; the legal maximum was five rooms. The total living space was not to exceed 60 square meters. Prospective builders were urged not to trust their own judgment but to contact the Institute of Standard Designs in Moscow. The size of the plot of land was to be 300–600 square meters in the town, 700–1,200 "outside the town," and up to 2,500 in rural areas.[56]

New dacha sites were given similarly ambivalent treatment. On the one hand, achievements in dacha construction were given public coverage. On the other hand, restrictions, as with individual construction more generally, were quite severe. They specified the number of stories permitted (one) and the number of windows. Stoves were forbidden. Most do-it-yourselfers of this period ended up with a plain, functional dwelling.[57] Individual dacha construction could never be entirely respectable in the Soviet period, and everything was done to prevent "excess" in architectural forms and undue comfort in the interiors. Planners of the 1960s were consistently hostile to all dachas whose construction was not directed from the center: these they saw as pests guzzling a region's resources and polluting its environment.[58] As a slightly later handbook explained: "The dacha cottage is not the family's fixed place of habitation; it serves as a place to spend the summer vacation and weekends. For this reason any excessive and pointless ostentation is out of place here."[59]

A strong blow against "individualism" was struck in 1960–61, when the Soviet govern-

---

55. See, e.g., N. Gamov and M.I. Popov, *Sovety individual'nomu zastroishchiku* (Leningrad, 1959), and V.M. Ancheev, S.S. Kozhurin, and A.N. Korchuganov, *Spravochnik individual'nogo zastroishchika na severe* (Petrozavodsk, 1960).

56. For more details on regulations pertaining to land use, see *Sbornik zakonodatel'nykh aktov o zemle* (Moscow, 1962).

57. Designs for simple dachas of this kind are presented in L.N. Kreindlin, *Letnie sadovye domiki* (Moscow, 1967).

58. See, e.g., L. Karlik, "Na beregakh kliaz'minskogo vodokhranilishcha," *Stroitel'stvo i arkhitektura Moskvy*, no. 3 (1964), 30.

59. V.A. Kherkel', *Vasha dacha* (Moscow, 1972), 9.

180

A dacha at Abramtsevo, northeast of Moscow. This house was built in the early 1960s according to one of the standard designs of the time; the paneled facade especially is typical of Soviet dacha construction in the 1960s and 1970s. Since then, however, the dacha has undergone changes that were prohibited in the Khrushchev era: a heating system has been installed, windows have been added, and an extension has been built.

ment prohibited dacha construction outside some form of collective. The original Khrushchev legislation of 1957 had sanctioned the allocation of plots of land for individual construction, but three years later would-be owners of summer houses were forced to sign up in a dacha construction cooperative (DSK).[60] The change in the official line often caused great uncertainty, and its real impact seems to have varied from one settlement to another according to the actions both of individuals and of sponsor organizations. The dacha settlement to which one respondent belonged had been formed in the late 1950s on the basis of "individual construction," but the Khruschchevian twist in policy put its future on hold. After one year had passed, some members of the settlement lost patience and started to build their dachas without waiting for official clarification of the issue. In due course the settlement was converted quite painlessly into a DSK. Even settlements that adopted the cooperative format from the outset, however, were by no means guaranteed permission to proceed with building as they wished; they quite often ran into diffi-

60. See the following resolutions of the Council of Ministers: "Ob individual'nom stroitel'stve dach" (30 Dec. 1960) and (for garden plots) "Ob otmene zakrepleniia za rabochimi i sluzhashchimi v individual'noe pol'-zovanie zemel'nykh uchastkov, otvedennykh pod kollektivnye sady" (18 Sept. 1961).

culties at one or other level of the administrative hierarchy. Such delays sometimes led co-operative members to relinquish their plots before they had begun to build on them. Their plots were generally reallocated by personal approaches to potential replacements within the same organization.

Despite such potential hiccups, the general rules governing the new dacha settlements were clear enough. For a cooperative to be formed, a group of not fewer than ten people at a particular enterprise had to write to the administration; if sanctioned, the cooperative was then allocated land "for permanent use" (*v bessrochnoe pol'zovanie*). Its members were then required to put the building work out to contract (even if they themselves ended up taking part).[61] Building was expected to be carried out to standard designs, though special dispensation for individual designs could be obtained. All buildings became "cooperative property"; that is, they could not be sold or transferred to organizations or to individuals, although they could, with the approval of a general meeting of the cooperative, be passed on to parents, children, or spouses, and they could without qualification be inherited. The amount of space allocated to a member of the cooperative depended on the dues paid and the size of the family; living space was never to exceed 60 square meters.[62] In the Khrushchev era vigilance was heightened even with respect to state-run dachas. In 1958, for example, a set of charges were introduced for overhead and for depreciation of furniture and other household items in dachas owned by ministries and subordinate organizations. Prices were differentiated according to location and type of room.[63] In 1961, moreover, the senior ranks of the army were deprived of their privileged access to plots for building individual dachas.[64]

Legislative measures were backed up with publicized acts of surveillance. Investigative journalists of the late 1950s and early 1960s were in the habit of conducting "raids" on institutions and enterprises in order to uncover malpractice in various areas of Soviet life, and dacha locations were among the targets of their crusading vigilance. In 1959, two reporters from the satirical magazine *Krokodil* paid a visit to a new garden plot settlement for workers in the central planning organization (Gosplan). They quickly found that things were not being done in accordance with the *Gardener's Handbook*. Many plots were strewn with felled trees: the owners were clearly planning to convert their houses from the anonymous prefabricated design to a more prestigious log-cabin look. Worse still, a cistern for weed killer turned out to be a steam boiler to provide central heating for the dacha of the president of the gardening collective. The journalists concluded that under the cover of growing food, people were really busy putting up full-blown dachas.[65] Nu-

---

61. See the resolution of the USSR Council of Ministers "O zhilishchno-stroitel'noi i dachno-stroitel'noi kooperatsii" (20 Mar. 1958).

62. *Primernyi ustav dachno-stroitel'nogo kooperativa* (Moscow, 1959). Further explanation is provided in *Instruktsiia po bukhgalterskomu uchetu v zhilishchno-stroitel'nykh i dachno-stroitel'nykh kooperativakh* (Moscow, 1960).

63. *SPP RSFSR*, no. 15 (1958), art. 160.

64. *SPP SSSR*, no. 4 (1961), art. 23.

65. P. Vorob'ev and V. Temin, "Neuzhto sad?" *Kr*, no. 28 (1959), 10.

"Lady goldfish, turn my dacha into a smashed-up washtub! Just for half an hour, until the inspectors have gone . . .": a satirical cartoon alluding to a well-known Russian folktale (from *Krokodil*, no. 24 [1964])

merous other exposés of the same period drew attention to discrepancies between people's salaries and the luxurious residences they were having built.[66] More generally, the dacha was treated with great suspicion because it gave free rein to people's proprietary instincts; the definition of "personal property" implied by public discourse of the Khrushchev era seemed both to harden and to narrow.[67] Building regulations might on occasion be strictly enforced: tales abounded of "commissions" arriving to remove terraces and pavilions. Fences around individual plots were strictly forbidden. And land was generally vulnerable to unheralded state incursions—when territory needed to be reclaimed for an institution, for example.[68]

66. V. Kozlov and V. Titov, "O golubykh osobniakakh i khoroshem tone," *Kr,* no. 9 (1959), 8–9; L. Eliseev and V. Temin, "Il'ia Kandinov i drugie," *Kr,* no. 3 (1960), 11; D. Ivanov and V. Trifonov, "Grimasy kamennogo veka," *Kr,* no. 1 (1961), 4–5; cartoons in *Kr,* no. 25 (1961), 3, and "Kak mne obmanut' obshchestvennost'?" *Kr,* no. 5 (1963), 7 (woman boards up her villa to make it seem less luxurious).

67. See cartoons "Otgorodilis," *Kr,* no. 12 (1962), 13; the untitled sketch in *Kr,* no. 18 (1962), 13 (owner of large house and garage claims he has won all this in a lottery); "Byl chelovek . . . i net cheloveka," *Kr,* no. 26 (1962), 5 (man blotted out by the fence he has put up around his property); and front cover of *Kr,* no. 13 (1962).

68. For one such episode, see N. Anisimova, "Avtonomnoe khoziaistvo na shesti sotkakh," *SPb ved,* 26 May 1999.

The dacha also engaged Soviet anxieties about the operation of the market. Not for the first time in Russian history, peasants were the objects of especial disapproval (mixed with scorn) for obtaining rental income instead of living by the sweat of their brows.[69] But all private dacha landlords, not just peasants, were regularly attacked in the press.[70] Dacha "profiteering," moreover, formed a convenient target for mainstream literary satirists. In one far from untypical story, an impractical young couple who have just inherited a crumbling dacha invite a relative to help repair it, but he has all too eager an eye for its commercial possibilities (he wants to keep a pig, he grows flowers for sale, he even lets out the house for a meeting of evangelical Christians).[71] A more historically resonant treatment of the issue was *The Twelfth Hour* (1959), a play by the successful time-serving dramatist Aleksei Arbuzov, where the decline and fall of the nepmen is played out during a single evening at an opulent Pavlovsk dacha in 1928.[72]

The measures taken against the dacha market went much further than cultural disapprobation, however. In 1963 limits were imposed on the rent a private dacha owner could charge: no more that 3 rubles 60 kopecks per square meter in the Moscow and Leningrad regions.[73] The well-known practice of diversion of state property to private building sites also received attention; the risk of "speculation" was (correctly) assessed as being particularly high given the large number of state construction projects under way at this time.[74] According to resolutions at the republic level in 1962, dachas built or acquired by "nonlabor income" were subject to confiscation. In one case of 1963, a couple bought two cars and a spacious dacha (of 80 square meters; the price they paid was 8,000 rubles), partially concealing these transactions by registering the dacha and one of the cars in the names of family members. When challenged in court to explain how they had obtained so much cash, they were unable to do so. The husband worked as an assistant in a textile shop; his wife did not work. The clear implication was that he had earned his surplus money through involvement in the black market. Lottery winnings, interest on savings accounts, gifts, and inheritance were among the few permitted sources of income besides basic wages. Even money raised by selling produce from a kitchen garden was illegal unless it could be proved that such produce was grown primarily with the individual family's needs in mind.[75]

The public voice of the Khrushchev era was informed by an ethos of collectivist vigi-

69. See cartoon "Pered dachnym sezonom," *Kr*, no. 11 (1961), 14; and "K okonchaniiu dachnogo sezona," *Kr*, no. 25 (1965), 12; and front cover of *Kr*, no. 15 (1967).

70. See cartoons "Kak grazhdanin Chastnikov sadovyi uchastok osvaival," *Kr*, no. 5 (1962), 8–9; the untitled sketch in *Kr*, no. 9 (1965), 13 (man nailing "Dacha for rent" to a post; the dacha itself in the shape of a giant purse); "Sdal dachu," *Kr*, no. 16 (1965), 10; "Vesennii otlov," *Kr*, no. 17 (1965), 13; and in *Kr*, no. 19 (1970), 13.

71. See L. Lench, "Diadia Fedia," in his *Izbrannoe* (Moscow, 1975).

72. See A. Arbuzov, *Dvenadtsatyi chas*, in his *Dramy* (Moscow, 1969).

73. "Predel'nye stavki platy za sdavaemye v naem zhilye i dachnye pomeshcheniia v domakh i dachakh, prinadlezhashchikh grazhdanam na prave lichnoi sobstvennosti," *SZ*, no. 11 (1963), 89.

74. See cartoon "Levyi povorot," *Kr*, no. 29 (1962), 12; and *Kr*, no. 10 (1966), 11.

75. See Z. A. Fedotovskaia, "Sudebnaia praktika po delam ob iz"iatii u grazhdan stroenii, vozvedennykh imi na netrudovye dokhody libo ispol'zuemykh dlia izvlecheniia netrudovykh dokhodov," in *Nauchnyi kommentarii sudebnoi praktiki za 1963 god*, ed. I. Sediugin (Moscow, 1965).

"Dacha for Hyre": a cartoon targeting the rapacious (and illiterate) dacha landlord (from *Krokodil,* no. 5 [1962])

lance that was at times even more strident than that of the Stalin period.[76] Newspapers laid the same emphasis on monitoring construction and on collective forms of leisure in the late 1950s as they had done in 1935. Measures to provide more hotels, pensions, and sanatoria were given much greater publicity than encouragement of individual construction. Reports on the dacha were incongruous in this discursive context: not only did the dacha prioritize the individual over the collective, it also presented people with second houses that were indistinguishable from private property. That this development presented ideological problems is shown by the legal debates on the principles of inheritance within a dacha cooperative. In the 1970s, as in the 1950s, it was often unclear whether priority should be given to blood relatives or to those who had "used" the dacha most.[77]

It would be most accurate, however, to characterize the Khrushchev era as one of ambivalence; as a time when long-standing areas of tension in Soviet ideology and social policy were laid bare as never before. Published material on the dacha from the early 1960s betrays the confusion and inconsistency that was so characteristic of that period's "austere

76. Of course, one needs to distinguish between the forms and the consequences of public discourse. By Khrushchev's time, the threat of physical violence that lay (not very far) behind the discourse of the 1930s had substantially been removed.

77. See K. B. Iaroshenko, "Spory o prave na chlenstvo v zhilishchno-stroitel'nykh i dachno-stroitel'nykh kooperativakh," in *Kommentarii sudebnoi praktiki za 1975 god,* ed. E. V. Boldyreva and A. I. Pergament (Moscow, 1976).

consumerism."[78] On the one hand, individual dacha construction was deemed to be a good thing, as it helped to alleviate the housing shortage and raise the standard of living of Soviet people. On the other, it presented people with an opportunity to flaunt their influence and resources and indulge an unhealthy taste for comfortable living. This tug-of-war between promotion and proscription is amply reflected in Soviet journalism of the late 1950s and early 1960s. One 1959 issue of the prominent illustrated magazine *Ogonek,* for example, described in loving detail the dacha of a model worker at the Hammer and Sickle factory (acquired as a reward for thirty years' unremitting toil at the factory bench); a few pages later it launched into an exposé of bureaucrats in the distribution system who had abused building regulations in order to build themselves luxurious residences.[79] As usual, it was left to the vigilant and perceptive reader to deduce the limits of the legitimate in the spheres of consumption and ownership.

## The Intelligentsia Subculture

Against this political backdrop the intelligentsia ethos of dacha life made a strong comeback: the Khrushchev-era quest for moral activism and a repurified socialism ensured that the "spiritual" functions of the country retreat tended to be valued over its material attributes. The de-Stalinization campaign initiated at the Second Congress of Soviet Writers in 1954 forced a reassessment of the privileges that members of the intelligentsia had received in exchange for their contribution to Stalin-era culture. A state-allocated dacha in the writer's settlement at Peredelkino occasioned, in public at least, self-justification rather than self-congratulation. The wife of the writer Iurii Libedinskii recalled overhearing visitors to Peredelkino in the mid-1950s commenting enviously on the dacha residences they saw: "Look at what palaces they've been putting up! I was in Iasnaia Poliana [the ancestral estate of Leo Tolstoy] recently, the house there is a whole lot simpler. This lot live better than a count, but what are they up to as writers?"[80] Libedinskaia, on seeing her husband's pained expression, frog-marched these carping critics into her dacha and showed them the crowded interior: a mere three rooms for a large household of husband and wife, five children, a granny, and a nurse. As the coup de grâce, she directed the visitors' attention to the writer's desk, piled high with papers, folders, and books. Presented with such evidence of industry, dedication, and Bolshevik self-restraint, they withdrew in embarrassment.

But the change of emphasis in the dacha culture of the post-Stalin intelligentsia was

---

78. This apt oxymoron is borrowed from D. Crowley and S. Reid, "Style and Socialism: Modernity and Material Culture in Post-War Eastern Europe," in these authors' edited volume of the same title (Oxford, 2000), 12.

79. N. Mar, "Dlia sebia, detei i vnukov," and A. Spektorov and E. Veltistov, "Pauki," *Ogonek,* no. 32 (1959), 27, 30–31.

80. L. Libedinskaia, *Zelenaia lampa: Vospominaniia* (Moscow, 1966), 360. For a fictional work in which the dacha of a Soviet artist becomes a symbol of its owner's moral cowardice, see G. Shergova, "Zakolochennye dachi," *Novyi mir,* no. 3 (1978), 68–96.

186 not simply a self-protective response to the revelations of the de-Stalinizing 20th Party Congress. It conformed to a broader cultural movement whereby the intelligentsia became larger, more independent, and more vocal. And one of the best ways to find a voice was, as ever, to look to the past for a script: in this case, to the models of conduct provided by the nineteenth-century radical intelligentsia or the early Soviet "true Leninists." Thus, for example, Lidiia Libedinskaia and her husband, spending the summer at a rented dacha in Kuntsevo in 1948, read Aleksandr Herzen's *My Past and Thoughts* in the evenings and relived the spirited debates of the 1840s. In the 1950s and 1960s numerous other members of the cultural elite rediscovered and reaccentuated the forms of informal sociability that had been so culturally productive in the second half of the nineteenth century. In a gesture characteristic of the times, the "dacha" opened by the St. Petersburg Academy of the Arts in 1884 as a summer base for landscape artists was used for similar purposes in the second half of the Soviet period.[81] Increasingly the dacha came to be seen as a year-round retreat, not a temporary and luxurious amenity; in some people's understanding, it had experienced a complete transformation from vacation cabin to homestead. Nikolai Zabolotskii, perhaps Russia's most ecologically minded poet, is reported to have said in 1958: "At one time I couldn't stand life out of town. I laughed when people started looking for dachas in the spring. . . . But now, you see, I feel drawn to the land."[82] Dachas were now to be used, not merely to be enjoyed. Veniamin Kaverin, for example, a doyen of Soviet literature and long-standing Peredelkino resident, wrote disapprovingly of Konstantin Fedin's big, empty, unlived-in residence, while he recalled with obvious admiration Pasternak's potato patches.[83] Valentin Kataev went so far as to work Peredelkino into a myth of national origins: "I sometimes think that it was precisely here that what we are accustomed to call Rus' began. Even if that isn't true, because Rus' came from Kiev. But 'my Rus'' undoubtedly began here, in the forest outside Moscow."[84] For the post-Stalin intelligentsia more generally, the village house (*derevenskii dom*) became an approved alternative to a dacha in an institutionally sponsored settlement; as rural areas were gradually abandoned by the younger generation of the indigenous population, many such houses fell vacant in the 1960s and 1970s and were sold to educated urbanites. For their new owners, the remoteness and unkemptness of many of these "dachas" came merely as welcome confirmation of their cultural authenticity.

But the village model had already left its mark on the dacha settlements proper of the cultural elite. A new pattern of exurban life was established for several prominent members of the Moscow intelligentsia after the war, when they returned from evacuation or propaganda work and took up residence in Peredelkino. Some of the dachas were rebuilt

81. In the standard Soviet account of the dacha (located in Tver' oblast), the prerevolutionary tradition was held to have inspired Soviet artists in their "realistic" evocations of the popular spirit (*narodnost'*): see I. Romanycheva, *Akademicheskaia dacha* (Leningrad, 1975).

82. Libedinskaia, *Zelenaia lampa*, 355.

83. V. Kaverin, *Epilog: Memuary* (Moscow, 1989), 256 and 358, respectively.

84. V. Kataev, "Peredelkino" (1984), in his *Sobranie sochinenii v desiati tomakh* (Moscow, 1983–86), 10:458.

or refitted specifically for year-round use in the late 1940s (although Peredelkino had not been occupied by the Germans, it had been left in a poor state by the Soviet military personnel who had been stationed there).[85] The increase in the permanent population gave rise to new forms of sociability. Long-standing friendships remained important, to be sure, but the close-knit familiarity of the oldest residents was increasingly supplemented by other kinds of personal interaction. Informal home visits and shared strolls through the settlement gave opportunities for meetings that might cut across institutional affiliations, political allegiances, and artistic affinities.[86] Perhaps the most striking exponent of the impromptu visit was Aleksandr Fadeev, who, troubled by a deeply compromised past as high literary functionary under Stalin, sought fitfully to find common ground with writers less morally vulnerable than he.[87]

The 1960s intelligentsia inherited from their forebears not only a commitment to informal exurban association; they also shared their work ethic and their disdain for all the material trappings of life. The Soviet intelligentsia's model of the writer living modestly and industriously at the dacha was created in the 1930s, as I suggested in Chapter 5. But it received further literary development in Konstantin Paustovskii's "Empty Dacha" (1946), where a writer holes up to write a story and eventually reads it aloud to an audience of ordinary folk, who respond to it well; and in Andrei Bitov's "Life in Windy Weather" (1963), where a self-obsessed writer, trying to overcome his creative apathy, retreats to his top-floor study in a picturesquely decaying dacha owned by his wife's parents.[88] In Trifonov's *Another Life* (1975), moreover, an authentically rural dacha is the setting for a crucial row between the novella's protagonist and an unscrupulous colleague who subsequently does much to ruin his academic career.[89]

Dacha asceticism could be said to be exemplified by the shared dacha Anna Akhmatova, by then the grande dame of the literary counterculture, occupied at Komarovo (though not by choice). In Lidiia Chukovskaia's memoirs, Akhmatova's difficult circumstances are implicitly contrasted to the smart terrace and multicolored crockery of Margarita Aliger's Peredelkino dacha and even to the Pasternak residence (where Akhmatova

85. A brief account on the condition of Peredelkino in August 1942 was given by L. N. Seifullina (her letter is reproduced in Ivanova, *Moi sovremenniki,* 131–32). The Ivanovs' dacha had burned to the ground in the same year, apparently because an iron had been left on by one of the temporary occupants.

86. One must assume that informal sociability of this kind played an important role in dacha communities other than Peredelkino—in settlements for the government and Party elite, for example. The advantage of Peredelkino for the historian is that its inhabitants left a plentiful supply of memoirs.

87. Fadeev dropped in unexpectedly on Zabolotskii in 1946 and initiated a serious literary discussion (*Life of Zabolotsky,* 245). Tamara Ivanova's memoirs emphasize his neighborliness (*Moi sovremenniki,* 376–89). Kaverin describes Fadeev suddenly summoning him for a walk around Peredelkino in 1955 and hinting at some of his worries (*Epilog,* 308–11). Vsevolod Ivanov's son, Viacheslav, recalled hearing the pistol shot of Fadeev's suicide a year later as he sat working in his family's dacha: see his memoir "Goluboi zver'," *Zvezda,* no. 1 (1995), 191.

88. See K. Paustovskii, "Pustaia dacha," in his *Sobranie sochinenii v deviati tomakh* (Moscow, 1981–86), 6:372–77, and A. Bitov, "Zhizn' v vetrenuiu pogodu," in his *Imperiia v chetyrekh izmereniiakh* (Moscow, 1996), 1:99–128.

89. Trifonov, "Drugaia zhizn'," in his *Sobranie sochinenii,* 2:281–89.

188    paid a visit in 1955, only to be told that the Pasternaks were not at home).[90] Although Komarovo performed a role similar to that of Peredelkino in providing an exurban center for the intelligentsia, it acquired a rather different cultural profile, being seen as more detached from literary intrigue and urbanity than the Moscow writers' village. A poem by Joseph Brodsky, Akhmatova's protégé, gives the settlement its old Finnish name, shows it in winter, and strikingly plays off the poet's house against the harsh landscape: this is a remote northern hamlet, not a dacha settlement.[91]

When the intelligentsia turned their attention to the exurban habits of other sections of Soviet society, the dacha found itself the object of a distaste reminiscent of earlier periods of Russian cultural history and given racy expression in an "urban romance" by the guitar poet Aleksandr Galich in which a spurned lover lists the reasons for her rival's success:

> Don't pretend it's her wet lips have cast a spell on you—
> It's because her daddy's got a lot of privilege;
> He's got coppers on his gate, a nice place out of town,
> Dad has pretty secretaries and smooth young men around;
> Daddy's got a CC card to buy from closed foodstores,
> Dad can go to private films, that don't get shown around.[92]

> Тебя ж не Тонька завлекла губами мокрыми,
> А что у папы у ее дача в Павшине,
> А что у папы холуи с секретаршами,
> А что у папы у ее пайки цековские,
> И по праздникам кино с Целиковскою![93]

Iurii Trifonov, perhaps the most penetrating literary observer of the ways of Soviet urban society, tended to present the dacha in rather similar terms: as a symbol of self-serving materialistic values. In *The House on the Embankment,* the dacha at Bruskovo is the first of Professor Ganchuk's possessions that captures the imagination of his acquisitive, upwardly mobile, and ultimately treacherous protégé, Glebov. In *The Old Man* (1978), Pavel Evgrafovich Letunov, the pensioner of the title, has been a member of the

---

90. L. Chukovskaia, *Zapiski ob Anne Akhmatovoi* (Moscow, 1997), 2:358 (Aliger) and 2:135 (Pasternak). Further material is provided by Akhmatova's Komarovo neighbor Lev Druskin in his *Spasennaia kniga: Vospominaniia leningradskogo poeta* (London, 1984).

91. Io. Brodskii, "Kelomiakki," in his *Uraniia* (Ann Arbor, 1987), 140–44.

92. A. Galich, *Songs and Poems,* trans. G. S. Smith (Ann Arbor, 1983), 105.

93. A. Galich, "Gorodskoi romans (Tonechka)," in his *Pokolenie obrechennykh* (Frankfurt, 1972), 174. Another poem by Galich, "Za sem'iu zaborami," directs its scorn more specifically at the dacha compounds of the Party elite (ibid., 228–29). Ironically, Lidiia Chukovskaia found Galich himself to be disgustingly materialistic when she rode with him and his wife from Peredelkino to Moscow in the early 1960s. Raisa Orlova quotes Chukovskaia as saying: "They spent the whole way back chattering about some piece of Finnish furniture and about sideboards. I haven't had to take such self-satisfied vulgarity for ages" (Orlova, *Vospominaniia,* 278).

dacha cooperative Burevestnik (Stormy Petrel) for more than forty years.[94] Burevestnik (in 1973) is the backdrop for a typically Trifonovian generational conflict between the well-stocked memory and moral sensibility of an old revolutionary (Letunov) and the shortsightedness and materialistic values of his children and their spouses. The immediate cause of tension within the family is a dacha that has just fallen vacant after the sole remaining resident died without leaving behind any close relatives. Letunov's son Ruslan and daughter Vera urge him to go and talk to the chairman of the cooperative, Prikhod'ko: as the most prominent Old Bolshevik in the settlement, he commands considerable respect, and his extended family claims it badly needs extra living space. But Letunov is reluctant to oblige: in part, he is dismayed by his family's acquisitive instincts, but most of all he does not want to ask favors of Prikhod'ko, whom he has known and disliked for several decades (ever since he sat on the commission that expelled Prikhod'ko from the Party in the early 1920s). Letunov never does speak to Prikhod'ko about this matter, but the other main candidates for occupancy of the vacant dacha drop out of the running quite by chance. At the end of the novel, however, it appears that all the various parties' efforts to gain influence over Prikhod'ko may count for nothing: the site has been earmarked for construction of a new boardinghouse for vacationers.

As always, Trifonov is highly informative on the networks of personal contacts (and, correspondingly, the destructive envy and petty rivalries) that pervaded Soviet society. The importance of *blat* in obtaining building materials and in determining priority in the allocation of dachas is highly reminiscent of dacha cooperatives in the 1930s (with the crucial difference that no one, not even the most flagrant abuser of the Soviet system, is likely to be branded an "enemy of the people"). Take the following interior monologue by Oleg Vasil'evich Kandaurov, the most aggressive fixer in the novel:

> There is some character called Gorobtsov who's first on the list, not for this house specifically but for the first share that becomes available, and who's now in the running, but it won't be hard to compete with him, as he hasn't done anything for the cooperative. But Oleg Vasil'evich has. He sorted out the telephones. Brought along rubberoid for the office. A year ago he went through the Mossovet, via Maksimenkov, to make sure that Burevestnik got allocated its own stretch of land by the river with a cabana and a small area for mooring boats. This pathetic lot wouldn't have got a damn thing done without him.[95]

Kandaurov only states brazenly values that all too many of the cooperative members share. In fact, dacha life is presented as providing a focus for the spiritual corruption of

---

94. He has also known prerevolutionary dacha life: his family rented part of a house in the same settlement as the family of Asia, the object of Letunov's silent and unreciprocated love, who own their own property (see "Starik," in Trifonov, *Sobranie sochinenii*, 3:432–43 passim). The cooperative was set up in 1926 by "a few Moscow intellectuals of proletarian origins" (3:516) on the site of a country estate that burned down during a peasant uprising in the summer of 1917.

95. Ibid., 503.

190 "mature" Soviet society. Not only have the residents of Burevestnik long since forgotten their cooperative roots, they are also unfailingly indolent. In *The Old Man* a good deal of tea is drunk and jam eaten, but we never hear of anyone digging a vegetable patch; significantly, the positive character Letunov spent very little time at the dacha in his youth and middle age. Trifonov, of course, is far from being an unprejudiced observer. He is creating his own myth of dacha existence as sinfully empty, idle, and mean-spirited. As in Gorky's *Dachniki*, minor disputes thinly conceal more profound human failures.[96]

## The Garden-Plot Dacha

Trifonov's focus in *The Old Man* is one of the traditional dacha cooperatives that by the post-Stalin era were strongly associated with the material comfort, prosperity, and security of the families that lived in them. One of my informants recalled being embarrassed to tell her schoolmates in the 1950s that she spent the summer at a proper dacha, as this would have seemed suspiciously bourgeois; instead she took to saying that she went to visit her grandmother in the country (which was a wholly unremarkable pattern of life; in the eyes of her classmates, a couple of weeks at a resort would have been the most attractive and prestigious way to spend the summer). Cooperative housing was associated with privileged access to "collective" resources, material wealth (given the relatively substantial cash contributions required), and the sponsorship of an influential employer organization (locations allocated for cooperative dacha construction tended to be closer to the city and in more scenic spots).

But to join a dacha cooperative was possible only for a minority, and, especially in the Khrushchev period, it was not considered desirable to encourage such undertakings excessively, given the dacha's unhealthy association with private property. The most acceptable way of reconciling the aspiration to acquire a plot of land with the ideological animus against individual property was to promote the garden-plot movement. Garden collectives formed steadily during the 1950s, and to an even greater extent than in the late 1940s they tended to consist of individual plots rather than large territories for collective use.[97] In the first half of the 1960s, the rate of increase slowed significantly and existing settlements were subjected to closer scrutiny. After Khrushchev's removal, however, the garden

96. In *The Exchange* (1969), a rather better known story, Trifonov presents a slightly different take on Bolshevik dacha settlements. Here again the contrast is between "true Leninism" and upwardly mobile materialism; but the opposition of these two principles is complicated by the fact that they do not correspond to a division along generational lines. Moreover, the author's value judgments are more successfully concealed here than in *The Old Man*.

97. The general direction of policy was confirmed by the new standard statutes for garden associations approved by a resolution of the RSFSR Council of Ministers on 15 Oct. 1956 (*Sbornik zakonodatel'nykh aktov o zemle*, 102). On the move away from collective gardens, see B. Erofeev and M. Lipetsker, "Pravovaia organizatsiia kollektivnogo sadovodstva rabochikh i sluzhashchikh," *SZ*, no. 10 (1958), 37. Several of my respondents reported the common perception in the late 1950s (especially among white-collar workers) that garden plots were becoming relatively easily available.

association was revived once more. Encouraging signals were sent out to enterprises and organizations, and the authorities were soon inundated with requests for land. In 1967, for example, the Ministry of Agriculture reported that 3,870 workplaces in Moscow city and oblast had applied for allocation of a total of 38,000 hectares for new garden associations; in Leningrad, data had been received for only eight districts out of sixteen, but there were already 834 institutional applications for a prospective membership of 53,000 workers and employees. By this time 1.5 million Soviet families were already engaged in collective gardening.[98]

Reports on the development of garden associations compiled by the trade union authorities were far from being exclusively self-congratulatory, however. Goings-on in garden settlements often gave the lie to their "collective" label, as the first action of most garden administrations was to break up the available land into individual plots. But the most serious criticisms, as in the early 1950s, concerned the right to build houses on individual plots. Small summer dwellings were commonly built without due architectural control and with black-market building materials. And yet by the second half of the 1960s, no one seriously attempted to outlaw individual summer dwellings of some kind in garden collectives; the most that was done was to insist that such dwellings be built according to approved standard (and cheap) designs, to "recommend" that enterprises build collective hostels for the gardeners among their workforce, and to advocate the cooperative form of organization above the "association" (*tovarishchestvo*)—as if that would make any real difference to the way garden settlements were run.[99]

The garden settlement was the major new form of exurban life in the postwar era. It was presented as a new form of "active leisure," to be distinguished from the dacha by its more modest function of allotment gardening instead of extended summer habitation. Its legal status had the virtue of being tied to use of the plot, not to ownership of the house that stood on it.[100] Unlike dacha cooperatives, whose members were instructed to contract out construction work, garden settlements positively required members to contribute their own labor to the construction of a house. Yet the garden plot was still to be distinguished from the allotment on several counts. First, the amount of land allocated, though not enormous, was greater. Second, the house built on a garden plot, though not large or well equipped, did more than provide shelter and a place to store tools; allotments, by contrast, were typically provided from wasteland on the outskirts of the city and did not bring with them the right to build. Third, garden settlements were located

98. GARF, f. R-5451, op. 30, d. 543, ll. 1–5 (a report compiled by the central trade union administration for the Central Committee of the KPSS in 1967).

99. Ibid. Similar reports of construction of unwarrantedly large dwellings on garden plots are to be found in d. 564, esp. ll. 6–8 (a report compiled by a department of the central trade union administration in July 1968).

100. See K. B. Iaroshenko, "Spory o chlenstve v sadovodcheskikh tovarishchestvakh," in *Kommentarii sudebnoi praktiki za 1980 god,* ed. E. V. Boldyreva and A. I. Pergament (Moscow, 1981). An excellent social anthropological account of the garden-plot dacha can be found in Naomi Rozlyn Galtz, "Space and the Everyday: A Historical Sociology of the Moscow Dacha" (Ph.D. dissertation, University of Michigan, 2000). This work came to my attention too late for me to take account of it in my text.

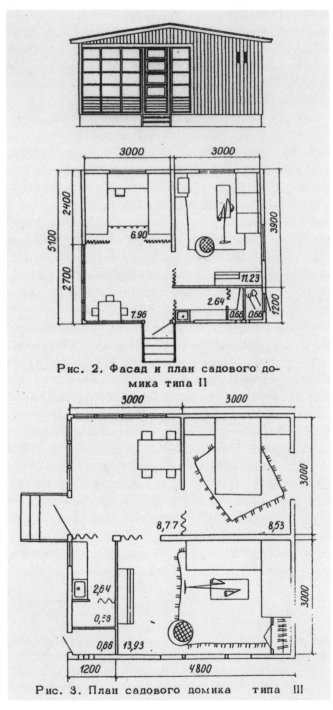

Рис. 2. Фасад и план садового домика типа II

Рис. 3. План садового домика     типа III

A standard design for a garden-plot house (from L. I. Kreindlin, *Letnie sadovye domiki* [Moscow, 1967])

A simple garden-plot house at Siniavino, one hundred kilometers east of St. Petersburg

farther away from cities than allotments. Fourth, the garden plot, though oriented primarily toward kitchen gardening, could have decorative flowerbeds and front lawn.[101]

Garden settlements came in two main varieties—the association (*tovarishchestvo*) and the cooperative. The only real difference between the two was that associations were created under the auspices of local trade union organizations, while cooperatives had a wider range of possible sponsor institutions. The method of land distribution, however, was generally the same in both cases: the local ispolkom would allocate land to a particular factory or institution, and the organization in question would distribute the land among its employees. Holders of garden plots were obliged to abide by the statutes of the cooperative. For an initial five-year period, members had to remain at the same enterprise (with certain commonsensical exceptions, notably retirement), but thereafter they received the plots for "permanent use." This was effectively private property disguised and made palatable to Soviet ideology by a collective form, and my interview material strongly suggests that people regarded it as such.

The land allotted to garden settlements was generally inhospitable, consisting (especially in the Leningrad region) of marshy or densely wooded terrain. Giving up collective farm land for individual gardeners within an association was regarded as deeply suspect, even if land was unproductive and neglected in collective agricultural use. In the late

101. This decorative function was given some emphasis in instructional literature: see Kherkel', *Vasha dacha*.

194  1960s, for example, local state organizations were proving so ready to distribute land for this purpose that they earned a public reproach from the RSFSR government.[102]

Such reproaches were more common and more forceful earlier in the decade, when the public hostility to private enrichment during the Khrushchev era was regularly extended to garden collectives. Local authorities were bombarded with instructions from on high. It would probably be futile to seek consistency or rationality in these multifarious interdictions, but local ispolkoms often took them seriously, either because they were too cowed to do otherwise or because they stood to gain something by asserting their power in this way (or, most likely, for a combination of these reasons). Some of my informants have made serious allegations of malpractice, asserting, for example, that ispolkoms harassed garden and dacha cooperatives with the intention of seizing plots that had fallen vacant. Such accounts fit very plausibly into the history of post-Stalin housing policy, which gave rise to periodic conflicts between the rival power bases of local government organizations (soviets) and workplaces (enterprises).

Whatever the mechanisms of the decision-making process, the overall effect was to make the life of the humble Soviet gardener more stressful. One such person was Grigorii Kravchenko, who acquired a plot in a garden cooperative at the least promising moment: in 1962, at the height of the campaign against individual property, a time when even very modest dwellings might be bulldozed if they infringed regulations. The statutes of Kravchenko's cooperative stipulated that members should absolutely not build houses, however small, on their plots; but this condition was universally disregarded, and log shacks (typically 4 x 4 m) quickly started to mushroom. What is more, the upper beams of such houses might intentionally be left to overhang the sides with a view to adding an extension at some later stage. In due course, the district authorities summoned the president of the trade union and the secretary of the Party bureau from the sponsoring organization and forcefully instructed them to bring the settlement into line. When the team of inspectors reached Kravchenko's plot, he was ordered to dismantle his house in the two weeks that remained of his vacation. Kravchenko nodded obediently, but when the inspectors had departed did nothing to comply with their instructions. And it seemed the trouble had blown over, until the settlement received another inspection, this time by the district architect. This second official visitor was even more literal-minded in his implementation of policy, demanding that all individual plots be liquidated and all land be turned over for collective use: he adhered rigorously to the official vision of garden associations as collective farms for city dwellers. Kravchenko was able to avert disaster only by giving what was effectively a bribe: he offered a plot of land in the cooperative to the ar-

---

102. In some regions, it was alleged in a central decree, kolkhoz lands had been handed over to individual gardeners without due attention either to agricultural productivity or to the environment. See "Ob ustranenii nedostatkov v rabote sadovodcheskikh tovarishchestv rabochikh i sluzhashchikh v RSFSR" (2 Aug. 1968), *SPP RSFSR*, no. 13 (1968), art. 69. The other point of view—that of gardeners faced with arduous weekly journeys to bleak and remote settlements—is presented in GARF, f. R-5451, op. 30, d. 543, ll. 8–12 (a 1967 trade union report on the development of collective gardening in Leningrad oblast).

chitect, who declined but mentioned an acquaintance who would be glad to have it. After that, Kravchenko and his fellow settlers heard nothing more from him.

Official strictures extended to many other activities at garden plots. One man in Kravchenko's settlement took to breeding rabbits covertly (livestock of all kinds was at the time strictly forbidden), and then took the further bold step of acquiring a pig. But he was so apprehensive of denunciations by his neighbors and of punitive administrative intervention that the unfortunate animal was kept cooped up in a tiny shack and so never got any exercise or even saw the light of day. The pork fat produced after the pig was slaughtered was revolting: mainly liquid in texture, with bunched globules of fat.

Even after a plot had been obtained and unwelcome interference from the local authorities had ceased, building a house and cultivating a garden plot were fraught with difficulties. The first was making the territory fit for settlement: the land had to be drained, roads built, and trees planted—and all this at an inconveniently long distance from the city. In the early days of a garden collective, employees of the organization in question were commonly bussed out on weekends for days of "voluntary" labor so as to help carry out labor-intensive preliminary tasks.

When garden-plot holders began to cultivate their land, they commonly found essential seedlings and fertilizer hard to obtain by normal means. In Kravchenko's words:

> I remember how we got hold of manure for our first vegetable patches when there were still no houses or roads. There was a collective farm field next to us where a small herd of cows was led out to graze. Sometimes the herdsman led the cows right up close to us and they lay there and rested. You had to keep watch to see when the herd went away and the cowpats were left behind. You couldn't afford to hang around, because by this time a few other manure lovers would always have turned up as well. And then we were off, a bucket and two plywood scoopers in our hands.

Even more persistence and ingenuity was required to build a house on a garden plot: this was often such an uncomfortably drawn-out process that people might remain without adequate shelter for two or three years. Over the summer, while toiling on their land, they could spend the night in a tent or in a house in a neighboring village; they might also put together a temporary hut (*vremianka*), but the only structure they were likely to have in the early stages was a flimsy lean-to encasing a short-drop toilet. This, according to one memoir account, was equivalent to marking out one's possession of the plot, planting one's flag on the territory.

Dacha construction was slowed most of all by the Soviet shortage economy. Even the simplest building materials were unavailable in state shops and so had to be obtained through unofficial channels. Constructing a dacha prompted Soviet people to engage in their full repertoire of *blat* practices—which, by the 1960s, seem to have been tied to ongoing social relations and circular networks to a much greater extent than in the 1930s, when the word *blat* had more disreputable overtones of corruption and criminality. The

A temporary hut (*vremianka*), made largely of old doors, at the Krasnitsy garden settlement, one hundred kilometers southeast of St Petersburg

ubiquity of such practices, as well as their relative freedom from stigma, is suggested by a play set in the late 1970s or early 1980s in which three men join together to build a dacha. They draw up a list of costs totaling 15,846 rubles (an enormous sum, given that two of them earn less than 150 rubles a month). When they take stock of their *blat* resources, however, the estimate is whittled down to a third of that figure.[103]

Other ways of making progress with dacha construction did not depend to any great extent on the intricacies of the Soviet "economy of favors." Members of Kravchenko's settlement were typical in filching bricks from Moscow building sites or picking up choice bits of timber (doors were an especially prized find) after a row of old wooden houses on the city's outskirts had been demolished. The materials thus obtained were then commonly transported to the dacha settlements by moonlighting state taxi drivers. In due course, a rumor spread through the settlement that inspectors were coming to demand invoices for building materials used in the construction of garden houses. (No one in the settlement could provide such documentation, of course, as they had all obtained their bricks, nails, and wood through unofficial channels.) Kravchenko did indeed receive such an inspection, but again thought quickly on his feet and claimed he had given money to the watchman to buy his materials; unfortunately, the watchman had since died. Anecdotal evidence of this kind is well corroborated by reports of official inspections, which sug-

103. S. Vasil', *Dacha na troikh*, in his *Dacha na troikh: P'esy zastol'nykh vremen* (Rostov-on-Don, 1989).

gest that infringements of the rules could be found wherever the authorities bothered to look. Yet even where "abuses" were exposed, retribution was by no means bound to follow: the restrictions were so unreasonable that even Soviet bureaucrats did not often insist on their precise observance. One string of reports from 1958 soberly listed the number of houses that had broken the rules in various settlements but also mentioned the achievements of these same garden collectives in making their territory fit for habitation and equipping it with various amenities. Only in one case was any indication given of what action might be taken to correct the failings identified.[104]

Stringent official policies were to a large and increasing extent ineffectual, and therefore tended both to discredit themselves and to transfer the real elaboration of policy to the local level (where, as we have seen, considerable negotiation went on among individual dachniki, settlements, sponsor organizations, and agents of the state). They also strengthened the self-organizing resolve of dacha communities. One woman recounted how members of her garden cooperative (set up in 1957 and located fifty-five kilometers from Moscow) pooled their resources to buy essential building materials, then drew lots to determine who would get the best logs. Grigorii Kravchenko recalled that when someone applied to join the cooperative of which he was then brigade leader, the first question asked was: "What will you do for the cooperative?" New members were, in other words, expected to place their contacts or expertise at the disposal of the settlement as a whole. In return, they would benefit from everyone else's know-how and access to particular goods and services.

Communal self-help practices, along with the shared difficulties they were designed to overcome, bound together garden settlements more effectively than any collectivist ideology and turned them into a new form of community with its own set of values and established models of behavior (not to say stereotypes). Dacha folk were acquiring a cultural prominence they had not enjoyed earlier in the Soviet period.

## Dachas as a Sociocultural Phenomenon in the Late Soviet Period

By the 1970s, dachas had grudgingly been accepted in public discourse as a fact of life. Summer houses—both owned and rented—were a crucial part of the routine for millions of urban families. It was estimated that one-quarter of people in Moscow and Leningrad used dachas, and that in Leningrad oblast alone city dwellers paid out between 25 and 30 million rubles to private dacha landlords. A journalist who cited these figures concluded with a rhetorical flourish: "So what does all this mean—am I for dachas or against them? Well, this is one of those cases when you can't say yes straight out, nor can you say no. I should rather give the reply that most people gave me: So what do you suggest instead of dachas?"[105] This was a serious question for Soviet urban planners and regional geogra-

104. See GARF, f. R-718, op. 12, d. 768.
105. L. Kuznetsova, "Snimu dachu!. . . ," *LG,* 2 July 1975, 13.

198   phers, especially after the introduction in the second half of the 1960s of the two-day weekend, which suddenly gave Soviet citizens significantly more leisure time.[106]

From the 1970s on, an important source of dachas for Moscow residents was rural houses bought or inherited from relatives: their acquisition was made possible by the increasing depopulation of certain rural sections of Moscow oblast (mainly those lying between the main railway lines and hence accessible only with some difficulty). One great advantage of the village house was that the attached land might be greater (up to 1,500 square meters, instead of the regulation 600 for garden associations). At the start of the 1980s, 15 percent of houses in rural areas of Moscow oblast were dachas belonging to inhabitants of Moscow and other cities. Urbanites who did not have a dacha of their own and could not afford to build one were catered to by a widespread (if semi-illicit) housing market that operated throughout the 1960s and 1970s: villagers would rent out their homes for the summer, without, of course, declaring this income to the Soviet tax collector. Muscovites who rented dachas in the 1960s and 1970s recall that such houses had to be booked as early as January or February, such was the demand. The accommodations varied enormously, from single rooms to whole houses, from the simplest of rural dwellings to dachas proper.[107]

The Moscow region was far ahead of the rest of the country in respect to exurban life. By the 1960s, despite restrictive legislation, out-of-town summer dwellings had become a genuine institution for the capital city.[108] Traffic between city and surrounding areas grew enormously: in 1935, half a million Muscovites might leave the city for the day on a weekend in summer; by 1967, this figure was pushing up toward 2.9 million. Of these people, approximately 450,000 were visiting their own dachas, while a further 400,000 were renting accommodations from the rural population.[109] The garden-plot drive steadily gained momentum through the postwar decades. A study conducted in the 1970s found that garden settlements had developed intensively in the 1950s and 1960s along all the main railway lines out of Moscow (except the Iaroslavl' line, which, as the first to be electrified, had been colonized by dacha settlers in the 1930s), and that garden cooperatives had now

106. Note, e.g., the roundtable "Vremena goda: Problemy otdykha," *LG*, 18 July 1973, 12, where one of the contributors, Iu. N. Lobanov, reported the results of a survey of leisure habits in Leningrad: "Before we began the study many of us held the conviction that 'dachas are on the way out.' But the figures show the reverse, and people's responses confirm that 'we'd like to have a place out of town!' "

107. Renting out private houses as dachas was permitted by the Civil Code in the 1960s, on condition that rents were capped. Even so, it is hardly surprising that private landlordism received plenty of negative coverage in the Soviet press: see G. D. Andrusz, *Housing and Urban Development in the USSR* (Albany, 1984), 104–6.

108. Published information on dacha construction in the 1960s–70s is scanty; some of it is summarized in D. Shaw, "Recreation and the Soviet City," in *The Socialist City: Spatial Structure and Urban Policy,* ed. R. A. French and F. E. I. Hamilton (Chichester, 1979), esp. 129–31. A survey of workers and employees at a Leningrad engineering works in 1965 found that 87.9% of respondents did *not* have a dacha, plot of land, or kitchen garden; by 1970 there was a slight but marked increase, and "mental workers" outnumbered physical laborers by 2 to 1. See I. Trufanov, *Problems of Soviet Urban Life,* trans. J. Riordan (Newtonville, 1977).

109. S. Kozlov, "Puti organizatsii massovogo otdykha v prigorodnoi zone," in *Sozdanie krupnykh kompleksov kurortov, mest otdykha i turizma,* ed. A. V. Roshchina (Moscow, 1972), 54, 56.

begun to spring up around smaller towns in Moscow oblast.[110] By 1980 there were 1,897 garden associations and 210,000 plots of land in Moscow oblast; for dacha cooperatives the equivalent figures were 256 and 20,000.[111] Regulations concerning the construction of summer dwellings and outbuildings had been significantly relaxed since the Khrushchev period.[112] And the garden plot became still more dacha-like in 1981 with the introduction of legislation that gave the prime inheritance claim in garden cooperatives to blood relatives.[113]

By this time, too, the authentic dacha-plot dacha and the upstart garden-plot dacha had begun to merge in people's understanding, even if the former retained a higher status. Many of my informants date a change in linguistic usage ("dacha" denoting both dacha proper and garden plot) to the 1960s, although it seems it became near-universal only in the late 1980s or early 1990s. The inclusion of garden-plot houses under the conceptual umbrella of "dacha" was suggestive of a new, more domestically minded attitude toward modest exurban landholdings; it implied a lifestyle as well as a commitment to toil in the vegetable patches. Dachas (of whichever type) were a rare opportunity for Soviet citizens to enjoy de facto private ownership of immovable property. The ability to overcome the problems thrown up by the shortage economy brought with it, moreover, a healthy rise in social status: the owner of a dacha was a person who "knew how to live." The achievement of post-Stalin dachniki was all the greater given that in general they did not bring in workmen even for the more specialized jobs: the members of dacha and garden cooperatives tended to do all the building themselves. In fact, for two generations of Soviet men, the ability to construct and equip the family dacha was an important means of self-validation. It also enabled them to measure themselves against their peers: given that the size, shape, and design of the house were restricted by legislation, "good" dachas would be distin-

110. See Iu. A. Vedenin, S. I. Panchuk, L. S. Filippovich, and E. G. Iudina, "Formirovanie dachnykh poselkov i sadovykh kooperativov na territorii moskovskoi aglomeratsii," *Izv. AN SSSR: Seriia geograficheskaia,* no. 3 (1976), 72–79.

111. V. S. Preobrazhenskii, Iu. A. Vedenin, N. M. Stupina, L. S. Filippovich, and I. Chalaia, "Problemy territorial'noi organizatsii rekreatsionnoi deiatel'nosti v Moskovskoi oblasti," *Izv. AN SSSR: Seriia geograficheskaia,* no. 6 (1982), 90. In 1982 the Moscow trade union organization reported that over 1,000 enterprises and organizations in the city had garden associations; in 1980 a "Moscow voluntary society of gardeners" had been set up (TsMAM, f. 718, op. 1, d. 2528, ll. 6–7). The available evidence suggests that demand for garden plots remained high in the provinces too during the 1970s: see GARF, f. R-5451, op. 30, d. 646 (trade union reports from 1979).

112. A. Denisov, "Lichnoe podsobnoe khoziaistvo," *Ekonomika sel'skogo khoziaistva,* no. 4 (1978), 125. According to this article, garden plot occupiers in the RSFSR were allowed to build summer houses with solid-fuel heating of between 12 and 25 square meters in "useful area" with a terrace of up to 10 square meters; the outbuilding could be up to 15 square meters, and rabbits and chickens could be kept there. This does not mean, of course, that official attitudes were by any means laissez-faire in the 1970s. There was still the occasional sally against garden settlements as hotbeds of private property and the unofficial economy. But it is perhaps significant that a crude example of this genre (K. Kozhevnikova, "Sad za gorodom," *LG,* 10 Nov. 1976, 11) met a response from more than 150 irritated readers, some of whose letters were published the following year (ibid., 26 Jan. 1977, 11).

113. Iaroshenko, "Spory o chlenstve v sadovodcheskikh tovarishchestvakh."

A garden-plot house at Krasnitsy. This garden plot might be called exemplary: every inch of land is used, and the house, with its many extensions and refinements, testifies to the owner's many years of devoted care and attention. Out of view is a second dwelling: a former *vremianka* that has grown into a well-equipped annex of the main house.

guished from "bad" dachas not by the number of floors or rooms but by how the windows had been fitted or the cement laid. One St. Petersburg man, born in 1933, recalled in the late 1990s the satisfaction he had gained from joining a garden cooperative relatively late in life (at the age of fifty):

> You go along, have a look, there are plenty of people you know in the cooperative, they're building houses, so you go up to them, take a look, ask them about how they do things. It's a real job building a dacha yourself, you lay the bricks, you mix the cement, you do the carpentry. Makes you both academician and hero, as they say. . . . It gives you a kind of moral satisfaction when you're making something with your own hands.[114]

The positive self-image of many late Soviet dachniki is beyond question. As one of my informants proclaimed, after decades of experience: "The owner of a dacha stands out from those around him: he is practical, industrious, determined, and full of optimism in his anticipation of regular contact with nature."

114. Irina Chekhovskikh, interview no. 4 (see "Note on Sources"). The involvement of men in home repairs and in cultivation of the "personal subsidiary farming plot" was noted by Soviet sociologists in the 1960s and 1970s: see L. Gordon and E. Klopov, *Man after Work* (Moscow, 1975), 91.

Such sentiments and the stock narratives of dacha life to which they gave rise can be traced not only in interviews and memoirs but also in mainstream Soviet fiction, which in the post-Stalin era became increasingly concerned with and informative on questions of everyday life. The same gendered proprietary impulse is reflected in a short story of the 1980s in which the hero, a welder at the local factory, finds his vocation (and thereby abandons the bottle) by building his own house:

> Three years Kondrat spent building his allotment house, building it thoroughly and without haste, and the house came out a real marvel: it was spacious, light, and cozy. It reminded you of a traditional Siberian izba, where there's nothing superfluous, where everything has been thought through and made to last. . . .
>
> He'd done the house, the gates, the little veranda, and the greenhouse according to his own taste: solidly, in the peasant manner, without any excessive dacha-style showiness. Next to overelaborate two-story mansions and houses with strange roofs cut away to make room for attic windows, his homestead was most likely the finest of all, in the way a person with inner spiritual grace is fine.[115]

Here an attempt is made to reclaim the country house as an attribute of an authentic, patriarchal rural world; the dacha, persistently feminized in Russian culture since the nineteenth century, is associated with spartan male virtues. It now regains some of its much earlier connotations—as a plot of land to be looked after, not as a place of idle repose. But the author, understandably enough, tends to avoid the word "dacha" in his text, preferring the more agriculturally resonant *usad'ba*.

Kondrat steadfastly resists any incursion of cluttering "feminine" artifacts into his austere new home. His wife tries to prettify their dwelling by spreading a flowered oilcloth on the table, but is told off severely for doing so: "Don't even think of it! You hold sway at home in the apartment, but don't go setting up a stupid perfumery [*sic*] here."[116] But she is happy to be submissive: the dacha has cured Kondrat of his alcoholism and given him a sense of purpose and pride. As another fictional character reflects in a moment of villagerly revelation, as her family is about to revoke its decision to place its dacha on the market, "City apartments don't seem to be for living in but for passing time"; the dacha, by contrast, brings a sense of purpose and participation in community life. Neighbors in urban apartment buildings are largely indifferent to one another, but dacha owners form a mutual-aid brotherhood that cuts across social boundaries to embrace manual and intellectual workers.[117]

We see here how the dacha could be accommodated within perhaps the most powerful cultural trend of the post-Stalin decades: a growing awareness of the economic predicament and cultural potential of the Russian village. In its literary manifestations

---

115. V. Zikunov, "Kondratova dacha," in his *Rodinskie kolodtsy: Rasskazy* (Krasnoiarsk, 1990), 41, 44.

116. Ibid., 42.

117. These quotations are taken from another piece of standard-issue late Soviet fiction: T. Nikolaeva, "Prodaetsia dacha," in her *Na malen'koi stantsii: Povesti i rasskazy* (Gor'kii, 1987), 114 and 94, respectively.

This dacha at Abramtsevo illustrates the appeal of the vernacular style for the late-Soviet dachnik

this was known as "village prose" (derevenskaia proza). Narratives infused with this rusti-cizing spirit treated dachas approvingly if they could be construed as a return to village roots or as an adoption of patriarchal values.[118] But dacha folk qua vacationers were con-sistently contrasted unfavorably with year-round residents in the same settlements. On occasion authors were led to conclude that dachas were doomed not only morally but physically: one conventional way of bringing closure to narratives of exurban life was to reveal on the last page that the settlement in question was shortly to be removed to make way for a rest home or a suburb.[119]

Dacha texts tended nonetheless to treat the exurban impulse with sympathy: the will-ingness of city dwellers to confront serious obstacles in order to satisfy their thirst for land was viewed as praiseworthy, and their urge to own property was assessed in various ways but rarely subjected to outright censure. One exemplary case is Dacha for Immediate Sale, a lengthy story set in a provincial city in the 1970s or 1980s. Nina Pavlovna Kalugina, re-cently retired, leaps at the chance to snap up a dacha put up for sale cheap when the own-

118. Examples include G. Popov, "Dacha" (1965), in his Gusi-lebedi: Rasskazy (Minsk, 1968), and A. Chernousov, "Vtoroi dom," Nash sovremennik, no. 1 (1983), 3–97.

119. On the counterposing of dachniki and permanent residents, see V. Lukashevich, "Zimniaia dacha" (1964), in his Doroga cherez zarosli: Povesti i rasskazy (Moscow, 1972); Chernousov, "Vtoroi dom"; N. Kozhevnikova, "Dacha: Povest'," Oktiabr', no. 12 (1983); G. Shergova, "Zakolochennye dachi," Novyi mir, no. 3 (1978), 73–133; Trifonov, "Starik"; V. Nasushchenko, "Dachnik Iakovlev," in his Belyi svet: Rasskazy (Leningrad, 1988). Chernousov, Kozhevnikova, and Trifonov wind up their stories by announcing the imminent demolition of the dacha settlement in question.

ers suddenly leave. Her husband, Igor' Petrovich, stuck in a middle-aged rut of television and detective novels, is unenthusiastic. Nina Pavlovna gets to work on him by stressing the benefits of the dacha for their health and domestic economy, but also by pointing out that a dacha is quite accessible even to ordinary people like them: "Here [i.e., in this town] what people call dachas aren't just suburban villas or izbas bought up in village but also the most ordinary little houses in collective garden associations."[120]

Nina Pavlovna eventually wins her husband over. They buy a house on a plot, having viewed it only in winter covered in snow. In the spring they are dismayed to find that it is in wretched condition. And the settlement itself is a disorderly sight:

> And what about the houses?! Well, they were an open-air museum of folk architecture, no more, no less. . . .
>
> Plots were handed out right after the war for growing potatoes: there was no documentation, no planning. Then, when an official inventory did take place, everything was frozen as it was.[121]

Despite all these apparent drawbacks, Igor' Petrovich quickly finds himself forming a bond with the soil. Then, amazingly, he hits on the idea of building a new house from scratch himself. As he ponders his options on a walk around a neighboring settlement, he spots a dacha that embodies his ideal:

> The house contained an unimaginable variety of architectural styles of different eras and peoples. There were European blinds on the windows, the roof was crowned by a Gothic tower, there were north Russian carved window surrounds and cornices, a porch under an awning, once again carved. And all this had been painted as if the decorator, finding that one can of paint had unexpectedly run out, had grabbed another, the first one that came to hand, and when he'd finished that, took yet another, and carried on painting without thinking about how the colors sky blue, orange, green, and raspberry were coordinated. But the point was that the color coordination lay precisely in this apparent lack of coordination. The house was alive, it breathed, it made inspired play with the colors, entrancing passers-by even at a fleeting glance.[122]

This passage is extremely expressive not only of Soviet Russian standards of taste but also of an ostensibly un-Soviet concern with domestic space and pride in personal property. The owner of this dacha—who, it transpires, is a mouselike co-worker of Igor' Petrovich's—has, like another fictional dacha owner mentioned earlier, been saved from alcoholism by the acquisition of a plot of land. In a conversation with Igor' Petrovich, he ex-

---

120. O. Pavlovskii, "Srochno prodaetsia dacha," in his *Srochno prodaetsia dacha: Povesti* (Kaliningrad, 1989), 7.

121. Ibid., 25.

122. Ibid., 63.

204 pounds on the destructive effects of *beskhoziaistvennost'* (the neglect of property brought on by the absence of ownerly instincts), claiming that no word for this concept can be found in non-Soviet dictionaries.

Igor' Petrovich himself joins the narrow but swelling ranks of capable and responsible Soviet dacha proprietors. He overcomes his scruples and has the friend of a friend deliver to him leftover building materials stolen from a construction site. With enormous determination, he sets about building a house. He even breeds rabbits. At the same time, he faces considerable obstacles: he is burglarized and he lives in fear of an inspection commission, which is rumored to be planning a visit to check on the provenance of building materials.

Soviet dachniki had good reason to consider these risks worth running. Dacha settlements may not have been the only places where Soviet citizens could indulge their proprietary urges, but there such urges took unusually visible, tangible, and individualized form. The attendant opportunities for self-fulfillment are abundantly evident in another piece of dacha fiction in which the hero, deeply offended by his wife's less than enthusiastic response to the house he has gone to enormous trouble to build, explains to himself the attraction it has for him. In contrast to the rented accommodations where he has spent his whole life up to now,

> here he had built a dwelling himself, with his own hands, he'd poured his own soul into this house. And even if it wasn't much to look at, even if it wasn't a grand residence or a villa, it was at least his, every last log in it had been nurtured by him, every detail had been polished and warmed in his hands a hundred times over. And this house wasn't official [*kazennyi*], nothing here was slapdash. The desire to have your own house, either held openly or kept to yourself, can probably be found in every person, and it is indestructible.[123]

Yet the same character who here so passionately defends the dignity of personal ownership is tormented just a few lines later by the various deceptions he has had to perpetrate in order to complete his house. He has committed theft of state property many times over, which makes him no different from millions of other Soviet citizens, but which he nonetheless finds deeply shameful to admit. Dachniki, as we see clearly in this story, were caught between their aspiration (by the 1970s generally regarded as legitimate) to build a house of their own and the wholly illegitimate means that were required if this aspiration was ever to be met.[124]

This is by no means to say that all late Soviet summerfolk were similarly motivated. Interviews and memoirs suggest that the new opportunities for dacha construction and ownership met a mixed reception from the Soviet population in the 1950s and 1960s, and

---

123. Chernousov, "Vtoroi dom," 90.

124. Two contrasting treatments of the theme are I. Davydov, "Dacha v Malakhovke," in his *Devushka moego druga* (Saratov, 1965), where the urge for dacha property is seen as wholly destructive and debasing, and Lukashevich, "Zimniaia dacha," where it is treated with considerably more sympathy.

that the most significant variable was age. People who were adults setting up a home or returning to domestic life immediately after the war eagerly seized on the plots of land they were offered. Their children, however, were much less enthusiastic: members of the '60s generation took more interest in tourism than in settling down to develop their own landholding. In their eyes, to receive a plot of land in a garden collective implied not relaxed enjoyment of one's property but rather lengthy weekly round trips to inconveniently located and inadequately provisioned settlements followed by hours of backbreaking toil. For them ownership implied not status and security but responsibility and hard work.

It is tempting to see in these generational differences mere confirmation of a common life-cycle pattern: a young person values diversity and novelty, but by the time old age arrives he or she will positively welcome being restricted to a narrower and more stable set of experiences. In the Soviet case, however, other social factors were at work. Older people on the whole enjoyed far fewer educational opportunities than their children and performed much more than their fair share of household tasks. They were also much more likely to have personal experience of village life, and hence often retained a set of peasant attitudes even after several decades in the urban workforce: a belief in the importance and the dignity of physical activity, a commitment to working the land, and a desire to acquire a landholding where that commitment could be pursued.

Younger people were by no means certain to share these values, and they found a convenient bone of contention in the garden plot. The generation gap, accordingly, is one of the commonplaces of late Soviet dacha fiction. In one story, a thirty-year-old economist in Baku finds himself using up his spare time chasing up a mason to fix the roof of the dacha that his infirm mother is having built. Not until very recently, as she neared pensionable age, has his mother shown any inclination to work the soil, but now she is clinging stubbornly to the dacha idea—which in Azerbaijan takes the form of a cozy white house by the sea, surrounded by vines, with a veranda, a well, and a few chickens. Once the family has acquired a plot of land, however, they find that they do not really have time to build a house on it, especially given the difficulty of obtaining building materials and transporting them to the site. The son makes known his dissatisfaction with his mother's "fanaticism," but the story ends with a truce: she massages his overheated temples and he resolves to keep his misgivings to himself.[125]

Other stories show people of the war generation experiencing in late middle age a sudden conversion to the delights of fresh air and agricultural labor. In one typical narrative, a war veteran suddenly decides that he is neglecting his grandchildren's future by not acquiring a gardening plot. Thanks to his iron willpower, the plot is soon cultivated and a house is built; further plans include verandas and a sauna. The younger members of the family, unwilling to continue contributing what they see as slave labor, are driven to such desperation that the veteran's son-in-law secretly burns down the dacha, leaving the distraught old man to imagine he has started the fire by forgetting to turn off an electric burner.[126] The value of the garden plot was called into question more openly, if less dras-

---

125. R. Ibragimbekov, "Dacha," in his *Dacha: Rasskazy* (Moscow, 1988).
126. V. Grechnev, "Dacha," in his *Sueta suet* (Moscow, 1994).

206 tically, in the post-Soviet period, when many young people demonstratively rejected the "summer slavery" of dacha life, which they saw as mere "playing at being peasants."[127]

The crucial role of older people in maintaining the dacha is a constant in Soviet dacha culture and is confirmed by memoirs and sociological research. Yet it would be no less accurate to reverse the terms and speak of the role of the dacha in smoothing people's transition from active work life to retirement. This shift in status is problematic at the best of times, but in late twentieth-century Russia it had the potential to become traumatic, given the lack of adequate state provisions for the elderly. But in the late Soviet period it was not only pensioners who felt undervalued and underemployed: enormous sections of the population could expect little fulfillment and even less reward from their work. In the failure of the Soviet state to provide adequate incentives and suitably stimulating employment for its people, especially its white-collar workers, we find by no means the least important cause of the dacha's enormous success in the latter decades of the Soviet period.

IN THE postwar era the dacha phenomenon found a much broader social constituency than it had enjoyed in the 1930s. By the late 1980s, millions of ordinary urban families were feeling the benefits of a modest second home. For them, as for many prewar dachniki, summer migration was a way of creating extra living space, of relieving the desperately cramped conditions in urban apartments. It is hardly by chance that the dacha boom came about in a period when many people's aspiration to have a separate apartment for their nuclear family was frustrated by the enduring housing shortage. A typical pattern of life was for middle-aged parents to move out to the dacha for the summer, leaving their children free to enjoy the relatively unencumbered city apartment. Or if parents and children were still young, children might be farmed out to their grandparents for three months, leaving the parents free to continue their jobs in the city.

But if the social composition of the dacha had undergone a transformation since the 1930s, so had its functions and meanings. The most obvious change was the increasingly important role of the garden plot in adding quantity and variety to the diet of postwar dachniki. For many families (especially those in small provincial cities), the dacha was a way of combating the shortages—of guaranteeing a supply of fruits and vegetables that were not always seen on open sale. In some localities in the 1960s and 1970s even potatoes were on occasion hard to get hold of in state shops. And the vegetables that could be bought were in general so unappetizing as to give the concept of "home-grown" produce a positive resonance that could never be matched in the West. This psychological reflex—to view the dacha as a survival strategy—was, as we shall see, greatly strengthened by the supply crises of the perestroika and post-Soviet periods. As Nancy Ries writes, "In Russian dacha did not signify a place of summer 'recreation'—at least for adults—so much as it did the headquarters of a family's self-provisioning efforts, as well as the place for an indispensable annual recuperation of mind, body, and soul from the effects of the city."[128]

Dachas in the 1930s were not wholly devoid of a subsistence function, but for the most

---

127. These quotations are taken from the St. Petersburg student newspaper *Gaudeamus*, 9 May 1999.
128. Nancy Ries, *Russian Talk: Culture and Conversation during Perestroika* (Ithaca, N.Y., 1997), 133.

part a clear distinction was maintained between "dacha" and "allotment" (*ogorod*). In the postwar era, however, an intermediate form of land use became ever more prominent: the garden plot (*sadovodcheskii uchastok*). To begin with, in the late 1940s and early 1950s, efforts were made to keep such plots entirely separate from the dacha concept—to forbid the construction of even the flimsiest shacks and to impose as far as possible collective forms of cultivation. But such a policy was woefully out of touch with the practical situation in the new garden settlements, where growers were expected to labor all day in barren fields without any kind of shelter; more important, it underestimated the ability of Soviet people to appropriate and manipulate official categories for their own ends. In time the garden plot took on characteristics of the summer retreat, becoming, in effect, the poor man's dacha. Eventually this elevation in cultural status achieved linguistic recognition: many Soviet people started to call their summer shacks "dachas," initially with perhaps a touch of self-deprecating irony, but with growing cultural assertiveness as the years passed.

And it is here that we find a further qualitative difference between the dachas of the 1930s and those of the 1980s. To be sure, dachas had enormous significance in alleviating some of the hardships faced by Soviet people even in the relatively prosperous major cities. But they also had positive value, as homes in their own right. The postwar era saw a broad change in the orientation of Soviet society as the rural migrants to the cities in the 1920s and 1930s settled more securely into urban life and brought up second and third generations. In the 1960s and 1970s their attention could for the first time wander from the urgent task of urban adaptation to the development of a more comfortable lifestyle. Yet would-be Soviet consumers were still starved of suitable goods, and here the mass dacha gained great appeal for its relative accessibility: to acquire a garden plot was not always a straightforward proposition, but still it was often easier than buying a car or a high-quality television set. Once established as a member of a garden collective, a Soviet family could make of its modest landholding whatever its resources and energy permitted. To an uninformed observer, perhaps, garden-plot dwellings differed little in their external aspect or in their use of space: houses were built to strict regulations (which, as we have seen, were not always so strictly enforced), and the same basic range of fruits and vegetables was found on most plots. Yet to build even a modest dwelling was an achievement in itself under the shortage economy; and the dacha interior was individualized and made domestic by the addition of furniture and other artifacts recycled from city apartments.

As we have seen, the discourse and practice of the 1930s left much more scope for consumption than for ownership. Most dachniki, for example, either rented a dacha on the private market or were allocated accommodations by their organization: in both cases, use of a dacha was markedly temporary and active engagement with it as a domestic environment was minimal. By the second half of the 1960s, if not earlier, Soviet citizens were able to feel a much greater sense of ownership, even if they usually achieved it under the cover of a cooperative or garden association. The history of the dacha in the postwar period points, in fact, to an important mechanism that Soviet citizens could use to acquire and transmit property rights. Soviet law had firmly established the principle that legitimacy of individual ownership of an object depended in large measure on the nature of its

208 use. Every Soviet family had the right to living space, but to acquire and profit from living space that exceeded one's personal requirements was strictly forbidden. Dachas were a particularly gray area: as a second dwelling, they were by definition not "necessary" items in the strictest sense of that term, yet in practice dacha ownership was permitted, as summer houses were classified as an item of consumption; as a recreational facility, not a second home.[129] So in the case of the dacha we see that consumption, besides being a source of difficulty for citizens whose wants were deemed to exceed their needs, might also be an effective guarantee of property rights in Soviet society.

The postwar period was associated with an important set of changes in people's attitudes toward land, property, leisure, consumer culture, and, not least, domesticity; all these may be seen reflected in the garden-plot movement and its gradual convergence with the dacha proper. With the fall of the Soviet system this convergence became all but total; the dacha became even more of a mass phenomenon, but its social and cultural significance underwent a further shift in line with the traumatic uncertainty that so many Russians experienced in the 1990s.

129. William Butler accords special prominence to the dacha in the discussion of personal ownership in his *Soviet Law,* 2d ed. (London, 1988), 185.

# 7

# Post-Soviet Suburbanization?

## Dacha Settlements in Contemporary Russia

In the history of the modern dacha and its social catchment area there have been several important shifts: from the court society of the Peterhof Road to a more widely dispersed and more city-oriented aristocratic elite; from this aristocratic elite to the larger constituency of urban middling people; the emergence of a mass dacha market in the later nineteenth century; the sudden and drastic reclassification and reallocation of the dacha stock under the Soviets; the convergence of the dacha-plot dacha and the garden-plot dacha in the postwar era.

When we arrive at the 1990s it seems right to inquire whether another such shift might have taken place. In the West, most large industrialized urban centers have entered— perhaps even passed through—a stage beyond urbanization and industrialization: with the improvement of transport connections, the general rise in living standards, and the activization of the land market, many people—often, but by no means always, the more prosperous sections of the urban population—choose to relocate to areas safe from urban encroachment and establish new settlements, new values, and new lifestyles. In Russia this shift never quite happened, despite the attempts made in the late imperial period to establish exurban settlements with a new sense of community. The failure of such initiatives was grossly overdetermined: the harsh climate made problematic the extension of settlement to a low-density periphery; transport provision was inadequate and expensive; urban administration remained extremely centralized; the social unrest that intensified from the 1890s on made life in underpoliced exurban settlements unattractive. As regards the Soviet period, we can point to a whole new set of factors that inhibited suburban development—above all, the powerful resistance of Soviet planners to do anything that might be construed as emulating the West. Soviet policies placed great emphasis on urbanization and on maintaining a

210    greenbelt around cities within the framework of a "unified system of settlement." The intended result was that there should be a sharp urban/rural divide, not a grubby fade-out of city sprawl into countryside. The internal arrangement of Soviet cities also disposed them to patterns of settlement quite distinct from the Western suburbanization model. Urban functions were to be widely dispersed throughout the city space; cities were to be zoned so as to rationalize the deployment and use of infrastructure; social segregation was thereby to be minimized. These measures, combined with the total rejection of market principles in land pricing, ensured that there was at best a very shallow density gradient from city center to periphery. The urban population itself had no interest in moving out of the city. Given the concentration of resources in the major cities and the overwhelming importance of an urban residence permit in ensuring access to goods and services, it would have been foolish to contemplate such a move. In short, just as in prerevolutionary times, the metropolis lorded it over the surrounding region.

Even so, by the 1980s there were signs that Soviet cities were entering a suburban phase. The efforts of Soviet planners were to little avail, given the activities of their comrades in the executive. The priority given to greenbelt conservation in the 1960 General Plan of Moscow came to seem little more than lip service, given the land-grab policies perpetrated in the 1970s and 1980s. In fact, it has convincingly been argued that the pressures on the swelling Moscow agglomeration in this period gave rise to a "socialist suburbanization" with three main distinguishing features.[1] First, constant expansion of the city boundaries without any concomitant decentralization of administrative authority. Second, an expansion of Moscow's outlying districts by large influxes of migrants from outside the urban agglomeration, *not* fueled by migration from the central districts of the city (as in the Anglo-American suburbanization of the postwar era). Third, the intensive development in Moscow's hinterland of Soviet forms of garden and dacha settlement, which have no exact equivalent in the West.

The post-Soviet period has taken these processes a stage further, which raises a new set of questions. Given the liberalization of land policy in the 1990s, the Russian population's acute concerns over subsistence, the continued overcrowding of the city, and the rise in the urban cost of living, have dacha and garden settlements fundamentally changed their character? Has suburbanization, with all it implies anthropologically as well as geographically,[2] finally made significant inroads into Russia's urban fabric?

---

1. The idea of "socialist suburbanization" is borrowed from Iu. Simagin, "Ekonomiko-geograficheskie aspekty suburbanizatsii v moskovskom stolichnom regione" (dissertation, Moscow, 1997).

2. "Suburbs" is a difficult term with different shades of meaning even in countries so apparently culturally congruent as Canada, Australia, the United States, and the United Kingdom. One cogent explication lists five main aspects of the concept (which may, however, be weighted rather differently from one country or city to another): (1) peripheral location in relation to a dominant urban center; (2) partly or wholly residential character; (3) low density; (4) distinctive culture or way of life; (5) separate community identity, often embodied in local government. See R. Harris and P. J. Larkham, "Suburban Foundation, Form, and Function," in *Changing Suburbs: Foundation, Form and Function,* ed. Harris and Larkham (New York, 1999), 8–14.

## Soviet Dachas in a Post-Soviet Context

By the 1970s, as we have seen, the word "dacha" covered a wide range of dwellings that varied greatly in function, appearance, and status. Four main types can be identified. First came the "departmental" dacha (*kazennaia dacha*), which was owned directly by a Party-state organization and was accessible only to those who occupied some position in that organization. Second was the Soviet-era "dacha-plot dacha," almost invariably built under the auspices of an organization, and very commonly under the umbrella of a cooperative. Third was the modest dwelling built on a plot of land in one of the many garden cooperatives or associations set up since the war. Fourth was the privately owned dacha, which was either inherited or built at a time and in a place where land was available for such individual undertakings, or else bought ready-made (most commonly in a depopulated and underresourced rural area).

Although state-owned dachas varied enormously in their size and level of amenities, they still included a pool of spacious and well-equipped accommodations for government employees. In a Politburo discussion of July 1983, Iurii Andropov, the disciplinarian general secretary of the time, alleged that many of his colleagues in government were "overgrowing with dachas": comrades in positions of responsibility were having spacious country retreats built for themselves, at the same time providing choice plots of land for their relatives. Speaking about the "leading workers in the Central Committee and government," the up-and-coming Mikhail Gorbachev commented that "everyone is speculating with dachas, throughout the country. There are a whole lot of disgraceful phenomena in evidence." He recommended that the Party control committee investigate such cases, but Andropov, although resistant to the bluster of other Politburo members, held back from this extreme measure.[3] Figures that came to light a few years later, near the end of Gorbachev's own period in high office, revealed the extent of official dacha holdings and the potential for abuse. In 1990 the Council of Ministers (the Soviet ministerial apparat) had at its disposal 1,014 dachas and two vacation complexes that in total comprised 55,000 square meters of living space; the annual subsidy was over 1 million rubles.[4] At the end of its existence, in 1991, the Party's Central Committee had dacha accommodations for 1,800 families in the Moscow region.[5] The crusading newspaper *Argumenty i fakty* revealed in the same year that a group of "inspectors," made up mostly of Soviet generals (numbering fifty-seven at the beginning of 1991) who had retired or been removed from their former posts, had a range of privileges—including access to the 142 dachas held by the Ministry of Defense—completely out of proportion to the scope of their present activities. Not only that, the "inspectors" had been actively abusing their privileges, in some cases unlawfully privatizing or selling off furniture held at state-owned dachas.[6]

Despite the populist campaign waged against elite privilege in 1990–91, the new polit-

3. Thanks to Jana Howlett for the transcript of this discussion.
4. See Sh. Muladzhanov, "Pomest'e po-ministerski," *Moskovskaia pravda*, 2 July 1991, 3.
5. S. Taranov, "Sobstvennost' KPSS: Koe-chto iasno, no daleko ne vse," *Izvestiia*, 27 Aug. 1991, 1.
6. A. Kravtsov, " 'Chtob ia tak zhil!' " *Argumenty i fakty*, no. 35 (1991), 6.

212 ical establishment in many cases simply took over the existing dacha accommodations. This was the case both at the apex of the political pyramid—Yeltsin and his changing cast of associates found themselves cozy retreats in Barvikha, Kuntsevo, and other resorts preferred by high Soviet cadres—and lower down. Statements of property and income made in January 1997 by administrators at the province (krai) level included spacious state-owned dachas of up to 600 square meters. Governor Evgenii Nazdratenko of the Far East, for example, with a (declared) annual income of $12,000, had a state-owned dacha of 257 square meters.[7] Private dachas owned by government figures might attain truly palatial dimensions (as much as 1,000 square meters). These, we must assume, constituted former state property that officeholders had either appropriated or built with their dubious side earnings. For example, the chief of the Federal Treasury's office in the same debt-ridden Far East province (Primorskii krai) was able to build himself a mansion outside Vladivostok that was valued at $645,000.[8] The taking over of elite dachas by their occupants was quite common practice—although (or more likely because) it was not specifically covered by privatization legislation.[9]

Largely because of the lack of clarity and the ineffectiveness of property law, some former state-sponsored dacha settlements acquired a complex and disputed status in the 1990s. One example is the writers' settlement at Peredelkino, run by the state-sponsored funding organization for literature, Litfond, from the late 1930s. On the collapse of the Soviet system, Litfond lost its subsidies and felt the pinch of market reforms. Legally, it did not even own the land on which the Peredelkino dachas stood. All it could do was rent out the existing accommodations. The central vacation home, the "House of Creativity," accordingly became a modest hotel where rooms could be rented for as little as $10 a night. But even this sum fell outside the price range of most post-Soviet writers. Residents apprehensively discussed privatization of the dacha stock in the settlement as a whole, as private ownership was sure to change the character of the place irrevocably—to lead to the displacement of writers by newly moneyed families or representatives of the nonliterary elite. Peredelkino was among the most desirable locations for such people, as it combined ease of access to the city, excellent ecological conditions, and prestige. Even in the absence of a thoroughgoing privatization program, it had been infiltrated by the post-Soviet military and governmental establishment and by the despised *nuvorishi*. The most striking new mansion there belonged to Zurab Tsereteli, effectively the court architect of the Yeltsin regime. Good contacts in high places were sufficient to obtain permission to build new residences even in heritage zones such as this. Peredelkino's vulnerability to the private building boom was accentuated by its uneasy administrative status: the settlement

---

7. Full details in "Bigwigs' holdings," at <http://vlad.tribnet.com/1997/iss153/text/table.htm >.

8. See "Outrage as deluxe dachas rise from rubble," at <http://vlad.tribnet.com/1998/iss171/text/news10.html>.

9. Early examples from journalism include Muladzhanov, "Pomest'e po ministerski," and E. Berezneva, "Kto, gde, kogda i pochem privatiziroval gosdachi," *Kuranty,* 7 June 1991, 1. There is an intelligent discussion of this issue in T. Colton, *Moscow: Governing the Socialist Metropolis* (Cambridge, Mass.), 713–14.

itself was located within municipal territory, but the adjoining lands were subject to oblast authority, and here new construction proceeded without adequate planning controls.[10]

## The Garden Plot as a Mass Phenomenon

The story of former state-sponsored dacha settlements in the 1990s is revealing of post-Soviet networks of power and patronage, but it sheds little light on the dacha's broader social significance. This significance, as we have seen, increased enormously with the postwar growth in cultivation of allotments and garden plots, and the years of Gorbachev's reforms brought a further giant step forward. A joint Soviet Party-government resolution of 7 March 1985 pledged support to the garden-plot movement. The immediate response of the RSFSR government was to formulate a program for boosting infrastructure in garden associations with a view to providing between 1.7 and 1.8 million new plots between 1986 and 2000.[11] In 1986, a recommended form for the statutes of such an association was approved. Traditional Soviet restrictions were still very much in force: buildings on garden plots were to be mere "summer garden huts" (*letnie sadovye domiki*) with a total living space of no more than 25 square meters; outbuildings (including huts for rabbits and poultry, sheds for gardening equipment, and outdoor toilets and showers) were to total no more than 15 square meters; the overall area of a plot was to fall between 400 and 600 square meters.[12] The RSFSR program for garden-plot development was by this time much more ambitious than the previous year's: now the plan was to increase the number of plots by more than 700,000 a year over the next five years and to improve the supply of building materials and the provision of services in garden settlements.[13] And in 1988 even the approved statutes were more relaxed: now garden houses could be heated, the area of land under construction could be 50 square meters (not even including terraces and verandas), and there was no stated limit on the area for outbuildings.[14] A 1989

---

10. On recent developments in Peredelkino, see N. Emel'ianova, "Nepriiatel' v Peredelkine," *Vechernii klub*, 25 Sept. 1999, and Robin Buss, "Letter from Peredelkino," *TLS*, 24 Sept. 1999, 14.

11. "O merakh po razvitiiu uslug po remontu i stroitel'stvu zhilishch, postroek dlia sadovodcheskikh tovarishchestv, garazhei i drugikh stroenii po zakazam naseleniia v 1986–1990 godakh i v period do 2000 goda" (21 May 1985), text in *SPP RSFSR*, no. 15 (1985), art. 71. The late 1980s were also a time when the Party finally gave its unqualified approval to the "personal subsidiary farm" (*lichnoe podsobnoe khoziaistvo*) that had for so long endured an equivocal and shifting legal status: see V. Ustiukova, *Lichnoe podsobnoe khoziaistvo: Pravovoi rezhim imushchestva* (Moscow, 1990), esp. 7–16, and Z. Kalugina, *Lichnoe podsobnoe khoziaistvo v SSSR: Sotsial'nye reguliatory i rezul'taty razvitiia* (Novosibirsk, 1991), esp. 4–7.

12. "Ob utverzhdenii Tipovogo ustava sadovodcheskogo tovarishchestva" (11 Nov. 1986), *SPP RSFSR*, no. 18 (1986), art. 132.

13. "O merakh po dal'neishemu razvitiiu kollektivnogo sadovodstva i ogorodnichestva v RSFSR" (5 June 1986), *SPP RSFSR*, no. 20 (1986), art. 149.

14. "Ob utverzhdenii Tipovogo ustava sadovodcheskogo tovarishchestva" (31 March 1988), *SPP RSFSR* no. 10 (1988), art. 45.

214   resolution promised to set up trading centers in garden settlements where dachniki could sell their produce and buy building materials and equipment.[15] All the while, the Moscow ispolkom was pledging to accelerate the creation of new settlements by searching out suitable land and taking less time over the necessary paperwork.[16] By 1987, more than 4.7 million citizens of the Russian Federation had "second homes" on garden plots (as compared to a mere 55,000 with dachas proper).[17]

The momentum accelerated in 1989 and 1990, when plots of land were easier to obtain than ever before. In January 1991, moreover, Gorbachev issued a decree on land reform that argued the need to conduct an inventory of agricultural territories and reallocate the land that was used inefficiently to peasant households, agricultural cooperatives, personal holdings, and dacha construction.[18] Research based on data collected in 1997 in four widely scattered urban locations (Samara, Kemerovo, Liubertsy, Syktyvkar) suggested that the median amount of time a household had been using the dacha was in the region of ten years. In other words, the dacha qua garden plot had historical roots (in the houses that people owned or inherited in the Brezhnev period) but still received a significant boost in the late 1980s and early 1990s.[19]

The Soviet government's encouragement of smallholding and garden-plot cultivation had an explicit rationale: to boost production of basic foodstuffs in the face of an impending supply crisis. Annual yields from individual plots were monitored and received comment in central government resolutions.[20] And problems, notably the reluctance of local soviets to allocate land for individual agriculture, were anxiously noted.[21]

The Moscow city administration, for example, was in 1990–91 keen to hand out less agriculturally productive land to garden cultivators, arguing that to do so would lessen the food crisis and reduce the pressure on housing in the capital. An RSFSR resolution of February 1991 noted that the supply situation in Moscow had deteriorated and set the target of providing not less than 300 square meters for each Moscow family in that year's growing season (the land was to come from collective farms and to be concentrated along the main railway lines).[22] The initiatives of the late 1980s had brought only partial success,

15. "O sozdanii kompleksnykh torgovo-zakupochnykh punktov v sadovodcheskikh i sadovo-ogorodnykh tovarishchestvakh" (6 Apr. 1989), *SPP RSFSR*, no. 11 (1989), art. 56.

16. V. S. Zakharov, "Ochered' na lono prirody," *Nedelia*, no. 40 (1988).

17. *Sotsial'noe razvitie SSSR: Statisticheskii sbornik* (Moscow, 1990), 207.

18. "O pervoocherednykh zadachakh po realizatsii zemel'noi reformy," in *Dachniki: Vash dom, sad i ogorod* (a newspaper published in the Moscow region), no. 1 (1991), 3.

19. Simon Clarke et al., "The Russian Dacha and the Myth of the Urban Peasant," paper posted at <http://www.warwick.ac.uk/fac/soc/complabstuds/russia/russint.htm>.

20. "O dopolnitel'nykh merakh po razvitiiu lichnykh podsobnykh khoziaistv grazhdan, kollektivnogo sadovodstva i ogorodnichestva," *SPP RSFSR*, no. 22 (1987), art. 135.

21. "O dal'neishem razvitii podsobnykh sel'skikh khoziaistv predpriiatii, organizatsii i uchrezhdenii" (14 Oct. 1987), *SPP RSFSR*, no. 21 (1987), art. 131. Hitches in the implementation of the policy were also mentioned in Ustiukova, *Lichnoe podsobnoe khoziaistvo*, 3–4; this book went on to note (5–6) that a more precise definition of "nonlabor income" (*netrudovoi dokhod*) was required.

22. "O pervoocherednykh merakh po obespecheniiu zhitelei g. Moskvy zemel'nymi uchastkami dlia organizatsii kollektivnogo sadovodstva i ogorodnichestva" (22 Feb. 1991), *SPP RSFSR*, no. 12 (1991), art. 159.

given the red tape involved in the allocation of land.[23] Near the major cities, where demand for land was at its most intense, there had developed "a battle for land between citizens desiring to obtain plots and the often reluctant local authorities, wishing to preserve the land for agriculture and other purposes."[24] At the beginning of 1991, more than one million people in Moscow were estimated to be on the waiting list for a plot of land. The oblast authorities, claimed the city administration, were frustrating the garden-plot initiative by agreeing to allocate only highly unproductive land belonging to state farms. Building materials were as difficult as ever to obtain; it was argued that construction needed to be reoriented from high-rises to small single-family homes. Land, however, was to remain cheap:

> Why should people have to buy [plots of land]? I believe that people should receive land free of charge: if they love the land and are able to cultivate it, let them work away and take as much as they can cope with. Not 100 square meters but 1,200 or 1,500, or even 2,000 if someone wants to have a minifarm on their plot with poultry and livestock. On the same plot they can build their family a house with a cellar, a garage, and various outbuildings. There isn't room for a family on 600 square meters.[25]

Although the speaker here—then president of the Moscow soviet—is presenting himself as a passionate advocate of progressive land reform, he uses a very traditional argument: economic value is less significant than use value. Research suggests that this attitude was shared by people who were unimpressed by receiving as private property land that they considered theirs anyway.[26] That said, the new land legislation did advance the cause of Russian private ownership: right to use (*pravo pol'zovaniia*) was firmly replaced by lifelong ownership with right of inheritance (*pozhiznennoe nasleduemoe vladenie*).[27] And the concerns of the city administration were addressed in one of the first presidential decrees of post-Soviet Russia, which set the target of 40,000 hectares to be provided for construction of individual houses in the Moscow region in the next ten years.[28]

23. See, e.g., the complaints referred to in the resolution of 5 July 1989 "O dopolnitel'nykh merakh po razvitiiu lichnykh podsobnykh khoziaistv grazhdan, kollektivnogo sadovodstva i ogorodnichestva . . . ," *SPP RSFSR*, no. 18 (1989), art. 104.

24. Research note contributed by Denis Shaw to "News Notes," *Soviet Geography* 32 (1991): 361.

25. Gavriil Popov, interviewed in "Khod konem?" *Dachniki: Vash dom, sad i ogorod*, no. 1 (1991), 2.

26. V.V. Vagin, "Russkii provintsial'nyi gorod: Kliuchevye elementy zhizneustroistva," *Mir Rossii*, no. 4 (1997), 81.

27. The next step, however—from life ownership (*vladenie*) to unconditional ownership (*sobstvennost'*)—was considerably more problematic and caused fierce political debates in the Yeltsin-era Duma: see the account in S. K. Wegren, *Agriculture and the State in Soviet and Post-Soviet Russia* (Pittsburgh, 1998), 160–66.

28. "Ob otvode zemel'nykh uchastkov v Moskovskoi oblasti dlia maloetazhnogo stroitel'stva i sadovodstva dlia zhitelei g. Moskvy i oblasti," in *Dachnoe khoziaistvo: Sbornik normativnykh aktov* (Moscow, 1996). A subsequent presidential decree gave renewed support for provision of land to individual builders around the Russian Federation: see "O dopolnitel'nykh merakh po nadeleniiu grazhdan zemel'nymi uchastkami" (23 Apr. 1993), ibid.

216      Millions of Soviet people, in Moscow and dozens of other cities, seized the opportunity to begin life as a garden-plot cultivator (*sadovod*). Here again, *use* of the land, not ownership, was the primary concern. As economic reform stumbled, Soviet citizens began to lose faith in the state's ability to feed them, and so invested more time and energy in the productive function of their dachas. If garden cooperatives in the 1970s had tended to have a rather horticultural feel, by the late 1980s their inhabitants were taking a subsistence-oriented approach to cultivation of their land.[29] In the 1980s and 1990s the term "dacha" underwent further expansion so as to connote the two very different functions— leisure and subsistence—that a plot of land in post-Soviet Russia might serve. In other words, the dacha continued to converge with the garden plot in people's understanding; it was, in the words of one self-help book, a "minifarm."[30]

     Muscovites' colonization of their oblast was remarkable. By 1995, garden associations numbered more than 7,000 in the region (the total number of plots was 1.5 million). And the average size of a holding had grown significantly, as the area of a new plot was often 1,000 square meters rather than the 600 that had been standard in Soviet times. In thirty-four of the thirty-nine districts (*uezdy*), the number of *sadovody* exceeded that of the local rural population. The "old" dachas were privatized (often with a reduction in the size of adjoining plots of land). The total number of urban families with some sort of second home in the Moscow oblast was around 1.65 million (75 percent were Muscovites; the rest were from smaller towns in the oblast).[31] In St. Petersburg, it was estimated in 1997 that between 60 and 80 percent of families had some kind of landholding; the time spent there ranged from twenty-seven days annually to virtually the whole of the owners' spare time.[32] In Leningrad oblast in 1999, 2.5 million people went to the dacha every weekend; 500,000 lived at the dacha all through the summer.[33] A 1993–94 survey conducted in seven Russian cities found that 24 percent of households owned a dacha (the proportion with some form of landholding would have been much greater). The garden-plot dacha was comfortably the most prevalent variety, forming just over half of the overall dacha population.[34] The rural house, by contrast, had suffered a decline in popularity, as people aspired to build their own houses, both better equipped and more conveniently located.[35] Overall, the number of owners of plots in the Russian Federation rose from 8.5 million at the start of land reform in 1991 to 15.1 million in 1997.[36] In 1999 came the ultimate recognition of the centrality of the garden-plot dacha to the nation's experience: a public holiday—Gardener's Day (*den' sadovoda*)—was instituted in its honor.[37]

    29. See Vagin, "Russkii provintsial'nyi gorod," 72, 86n.

    30. *Dacha—mini-ferma* (Moscow, 1993).

    31. Simagin, "Ekonomiko-geograficheskie aspekty," chap. 2.

    32. Iu. Nikiforova, "Mesto pod solntsem na 111-m kilometer," in *Peterburg*, supplement to *Argumenty i fakty*, no. 31 (1997), 2.

    33. V. Sergachev, "Dacha: Ot neveroiatnogo do ochevidnogo," *Birzha truda*, 17–23 May 1999, 1.

    34. R. Struyk and K. Angelici, "The Russian Dacha Phenomenon," *Housing Studies* 11 (1996), 233–50.

    35. Vagin, "Russkii provintsial'nyi gorod," 73.

    36. *Rossiiskaia gazeta*, 8 Aug. 1997, 8.

    37. A. Simonenko, "Na ogorode vse ravny!" *Nevskoe vremia*, 15 May 1999.

Subsistence-oriented dacha life expanded most rapidly in the Moscow and Petersburg regions, but it was by no means limited to them. Towns and medium-sized cities had never had much need of the dacha concept or the out-of-town leisure it entailed. Most families had at least a small plot of land within easy reach of their apartment. But now even such modest plots were often reclassified as "dachas."[38] There was some regional variation in vocabulary: in the Urals, for example, a garden plot (with or without a house) tended to be called a *sad* (garden), while in the northwestern region of Russia it was likely to be referred to as a "dacha."[39] The word "dacha" seems to have made relatively few inroads into the Black Earth region and the south of Russia, where the urban population's ties to the land were rooted firmly in an alternative tradition. In the provincial city of Lipetsk, some 500 kilometers south of Moscow, local people commonly spoke of making trips not "to the dacha" (*na dachu*) but "to the garden" (*na sad,* instead of the neutral *v sad*), which suggests that they conceived of their plot of land neither as a dacha proper nor as a garden plot but as an independent agricultural landholding.

## Post-Soviet Dachniki: Social Profile, Attitudes, Ways of Life

Although garden-plot cultivation in contemporary Russia is often viewed as a survival strategy, it is not generally practiced by the poorest families. Post-Soviet dachniki are drawn mainly from the thick middle strata of urban society. Large families with adequate material resources are the most likely to grow their own produce, even if their adult members are in paid employment. As Simon Clarke writes: "Like secondary employment, it seems that rather than being the last resort of those on the brink of starvation, domestic agricultural production provides an additional form of security for those who are already quite well placed to weather the storm."[40] This general observation can be supplemented by certain minor correlations. A household is much more likely to cultivate a garden plot if at least one member has grown up in a rural area or if its head is married. The age of the household head is also significant, thirty to sixty being the peak range for gardening activ-

---

38. Interesting material on the dacha habit, especially its role in the lives of a small-town intelligentsia marooned in post-Soviet conditions, can be found in A. White, "Social Change in Provincial Russia: The Intelligentsia in a *Raion* Center," *Europe-Asia Studies* 52 (2000): 677–94 (this article takes as its case study a town in Tver' oblast, four hours by bus from Moscow). Iaroslavl' is a city known to me where the word "dacha" seems to be used exactly as it is in Moscow (most of the dwellings thus denoted are garden-plot houses in crowded settlements on the far bank of the Volga). The weekly publication that carries small ads in Petrozavodsk also refers to "dachas": see *"Vse"—ezhenedelnik besplatnykh chastnykh ob"iavlenii,* at <http://vse.karelia.ru>. And to judge by one other Web page, the term "dacha" has made inroads as far east as Amursk: <http://www.amursk.ru/lschool/dachas.htm>.

39. Vagin, "Russkii provintsial'nyi gorod," 72. It is telling that the most in-depth of the dacha periodicals in the early 1990s took "Dachniki" as its main title, even though its focus was exclusively the garden-plot dacha (and this point was specifically mentioned in the editorial of the first issue: "Obrashchenie k chitateliu," *Dachniki: Vash dom, sad i ogorod,* no. 1 [1990], 2).

40. In 1998 the Center for Citizen Initiatives showed awareness of those less well equipped by pioneering a roof-top gardening scheme in St. Petersburg to help urban residents with no access to dacha plots: see <http://www.fadr.msu.ru/mirrors/www.igc.apc.org/cci/agirof.htm>.

218 ity. And male-headed households are less likely than female-headed households to grow all or most of their own vegetables. This finding matches abundant anecdotal evidence that women tend to take charge of managing the dacha landholding.[41]

So, as Clarke points out, the question why people produce ought to be rephrased as why people acquire land in the first place. And here again there is a strong correlation with earnings and occupational status. On the whole, it was families with a reasonable level of material security that took up the state's offer of a garden plot in the 1970s, 1980s, and early 1990s; the cultivation and upkeep of a plot (not to mention the construction of a house) implied considerable expenditure and little, if any, income. Dacha produce was not usually sold: only 1 percent of all households had any net positive monetary income from subsidiary agriculture. Vegetables surplus to the household's requirements were commonly distributed among friends and relatives at the end of the dacha season. The food bills of families with a dacha were no lower than those of people without a plot of land.

Subsistence, then, usually cited as the prime motivation behind the dacha boom of the 1990s, is only part of the story. It is worth noting that the powerful garden-plot movement, mostly seen as a pragmatic response to severe food shortages, coincided with a broader deurbanizing trend. Ever since 1927 the Soviet Union had been increasing its level of urbanization; and in the period 1979–88 there had been a distinct leveling up as the less urbanized regions caught up with the others. In 1989–90, however, urban development slowed, and in 1991–94 it actually went into reverse. This trend was particularly marked in the southern agricultural regions, but it also touched major cities in central Russia. Net migration between the city of Moscow and the surrounding oblast by 1994 favored the oblast. The major cities were in this sense becoming provincialized.[42] It seems that a significant part of this out-migration was due to rising rents in the city. Trapped in tiny apartments and unable to afford better ones, many Muscovites chose to make their dachas their primary residences.

The Moscow region had been subject to creeping suburbanization (or proto-suburbanization) for several decades. The sheer volume of commuter traffic into the city from the surrounding oblast was telling: 600,000 people a day by the early 1990s.[43] In 1979, 120,000 people lived in the most remote peripheral areas of Moscow (beyond the Outer Ring Road); by 1995 that figure had risen to 500,000. In theory, of course, suburbanization was something that Soviet planning was designed to avoid: the Soviet model of the city aimed for a far more even spread of population and function than its Western counterpart.[44] A greenbelt was to be preserved around the city, and satellite settlements were to be built beyond this forest zone. In the case of Moscow and several other major Soviet

41. Details in this and the next paragraph are taken from Clarke et al., "Russian Dacha." Fully compatible with Clarke's conclusions is H. T. Seeth, S. Chachnov, A. Surinov, and J. von Braun, "Russian Poverty: Muddling Through Economic Transition with Garden Plots," *World Development* 26 (1998), 1611–23.

42. Vagin, "Russkii provintsial'nyi gorod," 55.

43. Simagin, "Ekonomiko-geograficheskie aspekty," chap. 2.

44. For a definition of the Soviet city as an "entirely separate category of urban settlement," see R. A. French, "The Individuality of the Soviet City," in *The Socialist City: Spatial Structure and Urban Policy*, ed. French and F. E. I. Hamilton (Chichester, 1979), esp. 101–2. For a succinct "typology of socio-economic and environmental differentiation in the larger Soviet city," see D. M. Smith, "The Socialist City," in *Cities after Social-*

cities, however, this model did not shape reality. Although lip service was paid to keeping distinct the urban-rural boundary around Moscow, in practice this policy was not observed.[45]

In the mid-1990s the suburbanization of Moscow began to conform a little more closely to the Western model. Very little effort had been made in the first half of the decade to keep the greenbelt intact; even unspoiled park areas in the city's closer environs had been given over by feckless or corrupt bureaucrats to development as garden or dacha settlements.[46] In addition, the ever-expanding agglomeration seemed to be changing its character somewhat. For the first time ever, significant numbers of Muscovites started to exchange their centrally located apartments for small houses on the outskirts of the city. And even those who stayed put for the time being were more ready to contemplate such a move. The ambiguous status of many contemporary dacha settlements was confirmed by a survey conducted in the summer of 1997, which found that 40 percent of respondents regarded the dacha as "true country life," 55 percent as "suburb" (*prigorod*), and 5 percent as a no-man's-land.[47]

Housing construction in the private sector was encouraged by a presidential decree of 1992, and in 1993 the Moscow city administration announced a plan for the development of the suburban zone.[48] Boris Yeltsin's decree on land reform of October 1993 established a basis for a rudimentary land market. Restrictions and gray areas remained—it was specified, for example, that land use was not allowed to change after a transaction unless "special circumstances" obtained—but they affected the dacha market relatively little. Local authorities were concerned principally to prevent the sale of large chunks of agricultural land for nonagricultural purposes; small-scale transactions involving allotments and garden plots were unlikely to fall foul of the regulations (although they might still be bureaucratically complicated, especially where land hitherto owned "collectively"—notably in cooperatives—was at issue).[49] Comparative analysis of the housing market in 1994 and 1996 revealed a great increase in the number of advertisements, a slight fall in prices, and a much greater differentiation of prices according to location and distance from Moscow (the most expensive regions were to the west of Moscow, in the directions of Minsk and

*ism: Urban and Regional Change and Conflict in Post-Socialist Societies,* ed. G. Andrusz, M. Harloe, and I. Szelenyi (Oxford, 1996), esp. 82–84.

45. On the steady erosion of the greenbelt in the 1970s and 1980s, see Colton, *Moscow,* 468–85.

46. For an early example, see A. Neverov, "Chem pakhnet na Medvezh'ikh ozerakh?" *Moskovskii komsomolets,* 15 Sept. 1990, 2. For an inside account of the boom in the dacha plot market, I am indebted to an unpublished memoir by Vadim Kulinchenko, who between 1988 and 1991 served on the ispolkom of a settlement in an area that was especially attractive to the unofficial property developers of late Soviet Russia. According to Kulinchenko, in these years the dacha "was a matter not of relaxation in the country but purely of property. The local authorities were showered with blows from everyone up to the very highest levels of state power . . . , and in the localities people buckled."

47. I am grateful to Rachael Mann for showing me her B.A. dissertation, "Moscow's Suburbia or Exurbia?" (University of Glasgow, 1998), where these results are laid out. My own interviews and questionnaire results suggest a similarly mixed picture.

48. See J. Bater, *Russia and the Post-Soviet Scene: A Geographical Perspective* (London, 1996), 150–51.

49. See Wegren, *Agriculture and the State,* esp. 163–64.

220 Kiev). On the eve of the ruble's devaluation in the summer of 1998, monthly rents in the Moscow region ranged from two hundred to several thousand dollars.⁵⁰ But newspaper advertisements were only part of the story: in time-honored fashion, rental tended to be arranged by personal acquaintance or through fixers; real estate agents were reluctant to involve themselves in the short-term dacha market.⁵¹

Alongside traditional summer-only dachas there appeared a new type of year-round out-of-town house that was often called a *kottedzh* to emphasize its Western pedigree. The size and degree of comfort of such dwellings varied enormously. Many of them, contrary to general perceptions, were extremely modest, lacking such basic amenities as electricity and standing on the same 600-square-meter plots that held the dachas built by individual families in the 1950s and 1960s. They differed only in that they were normally made of brick rather than wood, had two stories, and had slightly more room inside (the average size of a winterized dacha, according to the fullest survey of the mid-1990s, was 44.6 square meters, as opposed to just over 30 square meters for summer-only constructions).⁵² At the other end of the market were the "New Russian" mansions beloved of glossy magazines. Many of these houses were hidden behind lofty fences in locations favored by the Soviet elite; but the more elaborate of them might also stand, incongruously, in old settlements alongside wooden shacks rather than in new ghettos for the superrich. Various attempts have been made to account for the apparent indifference to visible disparities of this kind: some say the owners of spacious villas want to display their wealth as publicly as possible; others assert that their choice of location is dictated by the impossibility of obtaining planning permission to build elsewhere. The second explanation is, to my mind, improbable: inasmuch as many New Russian houses in preexisting settlements themselves infringe multiple planning regulations, it appears that buying off the regional authorities is not so very difficult. Perhaps the reason is simply that New Russians are in a desperate hurry to convert their wealth into immovable property.

This incursion of new money certainly changed the atmosphere of many settlements. It had the effect of quickly redistributing land, as long-standing residents of prestigious settlements such as Peredelkino found new neighbors in unwelcome proximity. Often the new houses were built on formerly sacrosanct wooded land or green fields that had been signed away at a stroke of the bureaucrat's pen, but in some cases large Soviet-era plots were subdivided and portions sold off by owners impoverished by the collapse of the old regime and devoid of any better source of income. The arrival of New Russian *kottedzhi* also brought a reassertion of the dacha's leisure and ornamental functions. Gardening firms, for example, noted an increase in orders for junipers and cypresses, plants that were hardly suited to the harsh Russian climate but were nonetheless symbolic of a new lifestyle.⁵³

50. O. Kostiukova, "Dachi sovetskikh pisatelei po-prezhnemu v tsene," *Segodnia,* 8 June 1998.

51. D. Zhelobanov and A. Grigor'ev, "Dachniki i dachevladel'tsy ishchut drug druga bez posrednikov," *Delovoi Peterburg,* 26 May 1999.

52. The statistical comparison is made in Struyk and Angelici, "Russian Dacha Phenomenon," 247.

53. A. Aleksandrova, "Novoe dachnoe myshlenie," *Obshchaia gazeta,* 31 July 6 Aug. 1997. Note also glossy lifestyle magazines such as *Dom & dacha* (put out by the Burda publishing house from 1995), and the dacha furniture advertised at <http://www.dos.ic.sci-nnov.ru/gorodez/english/str31.htm>. The commitment of New Rus-

A New Russian dacha at Mozhaiskoe, southwest of St. Petersburg. The architectural pretensions of this house are undermined by its grubby surroundings. This is hardly a scenic spot, nor is it secluded: the dacha stands in full view of the local train stop.

Most dachas, however, fell between the extremes of solid, centrally heated *kottedzh* and 1960s garden shack. In the Moscow and Petersburg regions in the mid-1990s just over half of dacha owners had built their country houses on their own or with a small amount of help from hired workers. And the proportion of do-it-yourself dacha builders in smaller cities was even greater (in Moscow and Petersburg the inheritance figures were substantially higher).[54] Building work, as in the Soviet period, was generally extremely time-consuming and physically demanding; it often involved felling timber and slowly and painfully extracting tree stumps from the marshy or wooded land that was allotted to the new settlements. When family resources permitted, owners would try to profit from the relaxation of Soviet-era restrictions to build themselves a slightly more spacious house.[55] But many people who did not have time to build their dacha in the last years of the Soviet era found that after price liberalization they simply could not afford to do so. For aspiring dacha owners in the 1990s, timing was crucial: the people most advantaged were those who had time to take out loans and lay in supplies of building materials before

sians to what they probably thought of as a manorial way of life at the dacha is suggested by their common insistence on wood-fired heating rather than the much more low-maintenance gas (thanks to Judith Pallot for this observation).

54. Struyk and Angelici, "Russian Dacha Phenomenon," 243.

55. In 1999, for example, dacha designs were displayed at an exhibition in Saratov (a selection of the designs were posted at <http://www.expo.saratov.ru/rism>).

A house near the Zelenogradskaia stop on the Moscow–Iaroslavl' line, between Pushkino and Abramtsevo. Although this dacha is located in a garden settlement, its large and well-maintained lawn bespeaks a rejection of the Soviet agricultural imperative and a turn toward Anglo-American civilization. Only the turret betrays the owner's Russianness.

A dacha at Mozhaiskoe. Contemporary dachniki frequently invoke the English saying "My home is my castle."

Locals dubbed this dacha at Zelenogradskaia "the crematorium."

January 1992. For those who were unable to take such action, dacha construction often became a long and frustrating slog. Even a very simple dwelling might take ten or fifteen years to complete. Some partially built houses were simply abandoned, their owners having lost all hope of finishing the job: in a reference to the economic crisis and currency devaluation of late summer 1998, these were commonly known as "August [1998] dachas."[56]

Post-Soviet dachas had a rather basic level of home comforts. Research carried out in the mid-1990s suggested that just over half of dachas were equipped with gas—generally a ring with a cylinder—but only 5 percent had plumbing.[57] The average floor area of a garden-plot dacha was a modest 29 square meters.[58] Nor was the level of amenities in the settlement as a whole any better—especially given the size of settlements, which might reach that of a small regional center. For the 200,000 people crammed into Mshinskaia (110 kilometers from St. Petersburg) there were only ten policemen and one first aid brigade, and the nearest shop was 4 kilometers away. The result of the population compression that had taken place over the last fifteen years was, in the assessment of one journalist, an enormous open-air communal apartment.[59]

Distances, too, had grown enormously. In the 1960s, the dacha belt rarely extended

56. On abandoned plots in Leningrad oblast, see R. Maidachenko, "Est' svobodnye uchastki," *SPb ved*, 27 Apr. 1999.

57. Vagin, "Russkii provintsial'nyi gorod," 75–76.

58. Struyk and Angelici, "Russian Dacha Phenomenon," 240.

59. Nikiforova, "Mesto pod solntsem," 2.

A post-Soviet garden-plot house at Krasnitsy. In June 1999, when this picture was taken, the house had been under construction for ten years.

This dacha at Mel'nichii Ruchei is a not untypical post-Soviet architectural hodgepodge; the "Beware of the dog" sign is a further reminder of contemporary realities.

This garden settlement (Zelenogradskaia) was established as a garden cooperative in 1987, though dacha construction did not get under way until two or three years later. Although members of the cooperative were given equal shares of land, ten years of mainly post-Soviet life have brought striking variation in the ways people use their plots.

more than 60 kilometers from the city; in the 1990s, however, families commonly went to the very end of a suburban rail line (around 120 kilometers). And areas for settlement were not often within easy reach of the railway: they might easily be as much as forty minutes' walk away. The rise in car ownership has also done much to enable city dwellers to colonize broad territories between the radial railway lines. In 1993–94, 50 percent of people in the Moscow region were commuting 75 kilometers or more to the dacha, which represented no small investment of time, especially if buses and suburban trains were the only available means of transport. Distances in the Petersburg region were somewhat shorter, in provincial cities shorter still.

The liberal land policy of 1990–92 had the great virtue of giving millions of Soviet citizens a plot of their own, but it also illustrated the problems associated with liberal property legislation in the absence of adequate means of enforcing property rights. Disputes between neighbors were frequently provoked by the unlawful seizure of land by one party.[60] Since 1991 exurbanites have been plagued by burglars, just like earlier dachniki. A newspaper feature in 1992 told of residents who had taken the law into their own hands after discovering thieves on their land. While admitting that turning a rifle on someone for stealing a few cucumbers might be excessive, the article argued that such cases would

60. "Iuridicheskaia konsul'tatsiia," *Dachnyi kaleidoskop,* no. 7–8 (1992), 1.

226 continue to be common until state law enforcement was more adequate.[61] In 1999, people with long memories of dacha life were asserting that such a crime wave had not been seen since the hungry year of 1948. Thieves would take anything, from televisions to bed linen, doors, and window surrounds; metal items were a particular favorite, as they could be handed in for money at recycling points.[62]

A further problem concerned not the enforcement of the right to property but the nature of this right. In December 1992 a federal law on housing specifically indicated that houses built on dacha and garden plots were to be covered by privatization legislation, but until new legislation in 1997 the procedure involved was not regularized, so that local authorities were free to impose their own bureaucratic procedures (with corresponding charges).[63] The law on ownership was appallingly cumbersome; often it was impossible for people to sell a small plot without actually taking a loss on the transaction. And the legal distinctions between the various forms of gardening association—association (*tovarishchestvo*), cooperative, society (*obshchestvo*)—were not at all clear.[64] One woman observed:

> Our cooperative fell apart, of course, and it was only after it was gone that we understood that in some ways it had made life simpler. For example, passing on a dacha used to be a formality: all you had to do was write a letter to the administration: "I request that my share [*pai*] be transferred to my son/niece/aunt." The meeting voted unanimously in favor and the aunt became a member of the cooperative—in other words, a dacha owner in disguise. Now you have to pay enormous inheritance taxes and people say it's better to sell the dacha to your auntie— that way apparently the taxes are lower. It's not clear who is supposed to repair the roads now—and there's a pile of other little things that the cooperative administration used to deal with.

The government, for all that it had been quick (especially on the eve of elections) to promise special measures in support of garden associations,[65] had been slow to make the necessary infrastructural provisions, to reduce the tax burden on growers, and to provide a stable legal framework for ownership.[66]

In short, Russia had a long way to go before it could create in dacha settlements the

---

61. "Voina na ogorodakh," *Dachnyi kaleidoskop*, no. 9–10 (1992), 1.

62. Vera Popova, "Zona vne zakona," *Chas u dachi*, no. 2, supplement to *Peterburgskii chas pik*, 6 May 1999.

63. "Ob osnovakh federal'noi zhilishchnoi sfery" (24 Dec. 1992), sec. 2, art. 9, in *Dachnoe khoziaistvo*, 80; N. Kalinin, "Dacha dolzhna byt' 'v zakone,'" *Trud*, 11 Nov. 1997.

64. A. Litvinov, "Kommunalki na bolote," *Rossiiskaia gazeta*, 8 Aug. 1997, 8.

65. Note, e.g., the presidential decree "O gosudarstvennoi podderzhke sadovodov, ogorodnikov i vladel'- tsev lichnykh podsobnykh khoziaistv" (7 June 1996), in *Dachnoe khoziaistvo*, 45.

66. An early discussion of the issues (which centers on the implications of the RSFSR Land Code for occupiers of garden plots) is to be found in "Nadezhnuiu zashchitu pravam sadovodov," *Dachniki: Vash dom, sad i ogorod*, no. 11 (1991), 3.

"moral order" of the suburb identified by one urban anthropologist.[67] "Moral minimalism"—that is, the avoidance of conflict and a reluctance to exercise social control against one's neighbors—may be the foundation of the order that prevails in many of the suburbs now inhabited by more than half of the U.S. population, but Russian dacha communities function rather differently. The American developments are characterized by fluid social relations (not least because of the much greater social and geographical mobility of their residents) and low levels of social integration.

Although Russians did not have the luxury of social indifference and the corresponding strategies of conflict avoidance, it could hardly be said that post-Soviet dacha settlements lacked a moral order of any kind. Geographical mobility was much more limited than in the United States, and for this reason Russians were drawn into long-term close-quarters relations with their dacha neighbors. Russians were denied the privacy afforded by the suburban crabgrass frontier; building and maintaining a dacha was, on the contrary, a very public (and generally prolonged) affair that drew people willy-nilly into new social networks. The result was that Soviet traditions of mutual aid in defiance of public administration and systems of distribution—the proverbial *blat*—lived on, even under newly monetarized post-Soviet conditions.

Similarly, a number of Soviet/Russian social identities persisted in adapted or attenuated form. The dacha (read: garden plot) explosion became truly a movement, with its own public profile, set of values, and subcultures; besides numerous publications, it had its own TV program, titled *600 Square Meters*. Physical toil was the moral centerpiece of all this publicity. The emphasis was placed on "healthy peasant physical labor," on the virtues of "cultivating one's own garden" and thereby achieving a self-sufficiency rooted in the soil and invulnerable to political or social upheaval.[68] One of my informants expressed a complementary but much less sympathetic view by as she reflected on the Russians' apparent magnetic attraction to the soil in the late Soviet and post-Soviet periods:

> Of course people are drawn to the soil. Of course there is something of a hobby and something of an adventure about it. But . . . ?! The best answer to this question I heard from my father-in-law. He made out that everyone wants to show their neighbors how well they can work. In other words, it's "Labor is a matter of honor, glory, valor, and heroism" all over again. But [you might think that] at the factory there is ample opportunity for this kind of activity! And everyone sees how everyone else works. But it turns out that this is something quite different. No one envies someone who fulfills or overfulfills the production plan. But a good harvest of cherries, for example, can make your neighbor burst with envy. It's not even material envy, but [a sense of] their own imperfection.

---

67. M. P. Baumgartner, *The Moral Order of a Suburb* (New York, 1988).

68. See the headline exhortation "Leto—eto otdykh, leto—eto trud," *Dachnaia gazeta* (Stavropol'), no. 11 (1992), 1; and M. Nikolaeva, "Pervaia zapoved'—khranit' i vozdelyvat' sad," *Dachnyi sezon: Gazeta dlia ural'skikh sadovodov i ogorodnikov* (Cheliabinsk), no. 9 (1998), 1.

Whatever role we ascribe to Soviet conditioning in the behavior of contemporary dachniki, they certainly seem to derive a positive self-image from purposeful and productive cultivation of their garden plots. In Russians' pronouncements on their dachas one can often sense an undercurrent of national identification, a worldview expressed approximately by the phrase "We may be poor, but . . ."[69] The dacha is presented as something quintessentially Russian, less luxurious and spacious than the vacation homes of Americans or Western Europeans but more authentically rural and representative of Russians' inborn bond with the soil and appetite for hard physical work. At the same time, the dacha is conceived of as meeting a universal human impulse to flee the city and work the land. Here the West may figure in people's discourse as supporting comparative material:

> Let's take a look at a country like England that is conservative, traditional, but conservative in the good sense. And what do we see? What did all political figures dream of, take Churchill, take who you like. What did they dream of doing when they got to have a rest, I mean when they retired? And what about our beloved Sherlock Holmes, what did he end up doing at the end of his life? They all dreamed of one and the same thing: to grow roses on their own plot of land.[70]

The dacha thus offers the opportunity for rest as opposed to mere lounging about (*rasslabukha*) or, more precisely, for "active leisure" (*aktivnyi otdykh*): judging by the frequency of its occurrence in my interviews, this term, born of the Soviet sociology of leisure, seems to have put down roots in the collective mentality.

But going to the dacha is also regarded as a pleasurable activity, largely because of the lack of alternative forms of entertainment: "What is there to do at home here? Sit in front of the TV, I suppose? There people chat with one another in the evening, they'll get together in the house, maybe have a barbecue, they'll have a drink before supper, then they have a chat."[71] Life out of town gives rise to forms of sociability that often blur into mutual aid and support. Russians on their garden plots affirm the importance of "friendship" as they would in their apartments, but here they do so with an anti-urban emphasis: members of dacha communities see themselves as more people-centered, more in touch with their feelings, and better able to enjoy themselves than pampered city folk. Favors are simpler and delivered more immediately than in urban *blat* relationships. Networks are less circular, in the sense that people may return a favor directly to the person who has done one for them (for example, in the exchange of surplus produce at the end of the dacha season). But perhaps more important than actual services rendered and received is the broader sense of a community united by common interests: advice on seedlings shared

69. This attitude is nicely captured by Nancy Ries, with specific reference to the Russian language: *Russian Talk: Culture and Conversation during Perestroika* (Ithaca, N.Y., 1997), 30.
70. Irina Chekhovskikh, interview no. 5, p. 7 (see "Note on Sources").
71. Ibid., interview no. 1, p. 6.

with strangers on the train ride back to the city fosters a belief in the garden plot as the main experience that post-Soviet citizens hold in common.

Although Russians' feeling of belonging (for better or worse) to a large garden-plot community is strong, just as striking is the satisfaction they gain from their own land-holding. As Nancy Ries comments, although subsistence gardening is a grind, "the pride with which people displayed their gardens, their colorful anthropomorphizing of the fruits of their labors, and their dedication to this lifestyle signaled the symbolic value and identity they derived from these practices."[72] Pride is also attached to the dacha residence itself and to the domestic environment associated with it. Despite restrictions on design, Soviet citizens were able to exercise far more choice in the internal arrangement of their dachas than in the layout of their urban apartments. Apartments were the outcome of a protracted and impersonal allocation process, while dachas were the result of one's own labors. Unsurprisingly, Soviet people were far more positively disposed toward their dachas—which in many cases they or their parents had built themselves—than toward their apartments. Dachas, in short, were the closest many Soviet citizens came to a private home, and brought a genuine improvement in their quality of life.[73]

But, although the contemporary Russian garden settlement richly deserves further anthropological investigation as an important, apparently antimodern alternative civilization, it should perhaps occasion not cultural celebration but profound regret as a symbol of the poverty and powerlessness of the bulk of Russia's population even in the relatively prosperous major cities. In the words of Simon Clarke: "The dacha makes no economic sense at all, providing the most meagre of returns for an enormous amount of toil, but it is much more than a means of supplementing the family diet or of saving a few rubles. It is both a real and a symbolic source of security in a world in which nothing beyond one's immediate grasp is secure."[74]

BACK IN 1991, Gavriil Popov had seen the garden plot as a means of achieving suburbanization. He anticipated that people would sell their apartments in the city once they had built their houses (a land bank would be able to advance them up to 60 percent of the price of their apartment while construction of the new house was in progress). In a further optimistic prognosis, he saw Russia emulating America's suburbanization:

the country will be in transition from a state reminiscent of America in 1929 or 1930 to that of America in the postwar era, when a house in the suburbs became

---

72. Ries, *Russian Talk,* 133–35. A more in-depth anthropological account of the post-Soviet dacha is R. Hervouet, "'Etre à la datcha': Eléments d'analyse issus d'une recherche exploratoire," in *Le Belarus: L'etat de l'exception,* ed. F. Depelteau and A. Lacassagne (Sainte-Foy, Québec, forthcoming). This article draws attention to the subjective, as opposed to economic, motivations that underlie the dacha habit, and to the opportunities it brings for individual agency and self-affirmation. Thanks to Ronan Hervouet for letting me see his work in advance of publication.

73. These points are argued well in A. Vysokovskii, "Will Domesticity Return?" in *Russian Housing in the Modern Age: Design and Social History,* ed. W. C. Brumfield and B. Ruble (Cambridge, 1993).

74. Clarke et al., "Russian Dacha."

In this settlement near Pavlovo, Leningrad oblast, can be seen some of the anomalies of the contemporary dacha. The attire and demeanor of the owners of this plot might seem to mark them out as typical ex-Soviet garden toilers, yet their house is immeasurably grander than anything conceivable in a Soviet garden settlement. (The size of the house turns out to have a simple explanation: the settlement was established under the auspices of a local brick factory, so good-quality building materials were both plentiful and cheap.) By the time this picture was taken (April 1999), the social composition of the settlement had diversified greatly since the early days, when all plots had been distributed to members of the factory's workforce. Several of the original recipients had lacked the resources to finish building their houses, and so had sold their plots to New Russians. But the couple in the foreground had avoided such material difficulties and insisted that they would maintain this house as their dacha, though it would clearly serve very well as a permanent dwelling.

> the basic modern form of life for a person working in the city. As a matter of fact, this is precisely what the forgotten classics of Marxism-Leninism were thinking of when they reckoned on the fusion of the city and the countryside. What we ended up with was not fusion but extreme separation.[75]

But, as we have seen, these "garden settlements" had very little in common with leafy suburbia in an American understanding. Far from liberating the Russian people from the yoke of socialism by fostering the values of individual initiative, civic association, and private property, the mass dacha of the 1990s may be seen to have had the opposite effect—of reinstituting reliance on cash-free mutual aid and primitive forms of subsis-

75. Gavriil Popov, interviewed in "Khod konem?" *Dachniki: Vash dom, sad i ogorod*, no. 1 (1991), 2.

tence farming. In support of this view we can cite an opinion just as forthright as
Popov's—that of Eduard Limonov, the eternal enfant terrible of contemporary Russian
literature:

> The dacha turns a Russian into an idiot, it takes away his strength, makes him im-
> potent. Any connection with property tends to make people submissive, cow-
> ardly, dense, and greedy. And when millions of Russian people are attached to
> dacha plots and spend their time planting carrots, potatoes, onions, and so on, we
> can't expect any changes in society.[76]

How are we to square two such radically opposed views? It is hard to disagree with
Limonov that the survival strategies that millions of Russians are forced to adopt place severe limits on their political and economic activism. Yet, although Popov's assessment
seems far too sanguine, it does identify a widely felt householder impulse that Limonov,
with his intransigent hostility to property, cannot appreciate.

Even so, it does seem possible to pull these two dacha pundits together and generate a
number of paradoxical hybrid descriptions. Thus contemporary dacha settlements may
be seen as a symptom of the provincialization of city life: in a reversal of modernizing
trends, the inhabitants of major industrial centers are opting for the smallholding way of
life that has for centuries prevailed in the Russian small town. Or alternatively, the dacha
boom can be taken as evidence of the peasantization of Russia's "middle class" (a thick
stratum of society defined merely by the fact that it is likely neither to starve nor, by the
standards that prevail west of Brest, to achieve a remotely acceptable level of prosperity).
And finally, dacha sprawl is, to coin a phrase, a form of shanty exurbanization. That is to
say, it is driven both by the urge to flee the expanding city and set up an independent community in a rural setting (the exurbanizing impulse) and by the imperative to provide for
one's basic needs in the absence of adequate legal protection and infrastructural provision
(the shanty predicament).

The truth, however, is that no single description will capture the diversity of forms of
settlement and habitation that go under the name of "dacha" in post-Soviet Russia; nor
will it adequately encompass the range of motivations that propel dachniki out of town
each summer weekend; nor, finally, can it serve as an accurate guide to the future. All of
which suggests that the dacha will remain culturally as well as horticulturally productive
for a while yet.

76. "Limonov khochet razbit' divan Oblomova," *Smena*, 5 Dec. 1996.

# Conclusion

As postcommunist Russia began to inventory the perquisites of the Soviet elite, the dacha emerged as one of the main accessories of the privileged class. There was no more high-profile commentary on this subject than Nikita Mikhalkov's Oscar-winning *Burnt by the Sun* (1994). In its mise-en-scène this film is a Chekhovian ensemble piece: a family assembles at the dacha, but soon the air is thick with tension as long-standing animosities and disagreements are discharged into the atmosphere. Conflicts—along social, generational, and emotional fault lines—threaten vaguely but persistently to erupt into acrimonious *skandal*.

But this is no cherry orchard. Rather, it is a dacha owned by a family from the old Moscow intelligentsia—the older generation remembers receiving here such illustrious guests as Boris Chaliapin and Sergei Rachmaninov—which has now been incorporated into a settlement for artists, writers, performers, and musicians (identified by the acronym KhLAM, which spells a Russian word meaning "junk"). The daughter of the family, Marusia, has married an Old Bolshevik and Civil War hero, Kotov, a rough-hewn national celebrity. This domestic milieu provides the setting for the entrance of Mitia, a former sweetheart of Marusia's, who, after compromising himself by siding with the Whites, was lured into becoming a Bolshevik agent. Now, in 1936, he is working for the NKVD and, as is revealed in the dénouement, has been given the task of arresting Kotov, who is to fall victim to the next wave of the Terror.

The film was deservedly admired for its fine acting and high production values. But, like so much of Mikhalkov's work, it aims for rather more than that, implying nothing less than an interpretation of modern Russian history and society. The broad-shouldered, potent, heroic, nationally rooted, ultimately martyred man of the people (Kotov) stands in opposition to the opportunist, cowardly, villainous, slightly built, childless cosmopolitan *intelligent* (Mitia). Kotov's manly qualities are in further contrast to the almost painfully Chekhovian family into which he has entered by marriage. His in-laws are as cultured, sociable, high-strung, and charmingly set in their ways as any Gaev or Astrov viewed with the softening hindsight of revolution and state terrorism. As one critic noted, "It's as if the old dacha folk of *Burnt by the Sun* are the heroes of *Mechanical Piano*[1] who've grown older and survived to the 30s."[2]

The case of *Burnt by the Sun* provides a fitting epilogue for this book, and not just in the sense that it offers a post-Soviet perspective on the dacha phenomenon. Rather more significantly, it illustrates the ease with which the dacha, over the past two centuries of its history, has been overlaid with social and cultural mythmaking. Mikhalkov could be accused of employing a kind of artistic sleight of hand in his portrayal of 1930s exurbia. For, as he himself has admitted, the dacha lifestyle depicted in his film is drawn from his recollections of a childhood spent in the milieu of the Soviet cultural elite. It does not necessarily have much to do with the ways of the prerevolutionary artistic intelligentsia.[3] Here, as in many other texts mentioned in this book, the single image of the dacha is made to bear a considerable cultural burden—in this case, to elide disjoined social and cultural worlds and to evoke a transhistorical Russianness that was in Mikhalkov's view severely damaged but not destroyed by the evil furies of the early Soviet period. The evil is conveniently externalized and objectified in the demonic Mitia, while Russianness resides in the unchanging rhythms of exurban life.

But the fact that Mikhalkov was tempted to make two such radically different eras coalesce, besides leading us to question the director's personal motives and wider ideological purposes, illustrates a complementary point that is also central to this book: much as we may want to drag the dacha out of the cultural responses it elicits, in practice it always remains mired in them. And this in turn suggests a large potential difficulty: how are we to disentangle social and cultural history? Or, to put it still more simply, how can we know things reliably about the history of a phenomenon such as the dacha?

To these questions I can offer two broad answers. The first is practical: the only way to begin to bridge the gap between social and cultural approaches is to consult as wide a range of sources as possible. One of the advantages of studying an everyday phenomenon is that it leaves traces—small, perhaps, but discernible—in many places. The second answer is theoretical: there is in fact often no need to disentangle social and cultural history. Cultural meanings do not float in some asocial stratosphere but are themselves tied to and articulated in social relations and practices. In no field of social history would this insight seem to have more obvious relevance than in the study of people's dwellings and habitats.

1. A reference to *Neokonchennaia p'esa dlia mekhanicheskogo pianino* (1976), an earlier Mikhalkov film set at the dacha that was loosely based on works by Chekhov.

2. A. Arkhangel'skii, "Desnitsa i shuitsa N. S. Mikhalkova," *Iskusstvo kino*, no. 3 (1995), 5.

3. As Mikhalkov commented in an interview, "*Burnt by the Sun* is in many ways bound up with personal feelings, with the image of my home": ibid., 10. He discusses his upbringing in an interview quoted extensively in his father's memoirs: S. V. Mikhalkov, *Ot i do . . .* (Moscow, 1997), 387–94. For a critique of Mikhalkov's easy equating of Chekhovian and Soviet intelligentsias, see, in the same issue of *Iskusstvo kino*, Iu. Bogomolov, "Kontsy v vodu—kompleksy naruzhu . . ."

234    Housing is so closely tied to people's identities and to their place in the community that it would be deeply unsatisfactory to make a study of bricks and mortar without inquiring as to people's subjective understanding of their dwellings. Many anthropologists have recognized the significance of the dwelling unit by making the household, rather than the family, the starting point for their work.[4] In this light, the pronounced subjectivity of many of the sources cited in this book should be seen not as a problem but as a small contribution toward a solution.

Yet this approach poses problems for inquiry into the historical long term; it is unclear, for example, how it accounts for and analyzes change over time. One consequence of the mixing of social and cultural history is the difficulty of establishing chronological cut-off points. Any history that is at least as much cultural as it is social will tend to undermine clear-cut periodizations, to subvert simplistic notions of historical causality, to stress continuity over rupture, and to divert attention from a historiography fixated on certain key dates and schematic arguments associated with them. In Russian history, of course, the biggest landmark is 1917, and the most schematic arguments concern the nature of the Soviet system.

All this is not to belittle the enormity of the Bolshevik coup as a factor in Russia's subsequent history or even to assert that it is not a watershed of some kind in the history of the dacha. In one sense, the October Revolution divides the present study neatly into two: it brought into being a society in which large and increasing numbers of urban office workers grew food on allotments or dacha plots; before 1917, by contrast, they did so only rarely. The extent of food gardening varied greatly through the Soviet period, and until the 1960s the plots of land where vegetables were grown were not generally called dachas; yet the Soviet takeover fundamentally rerouted Russian exurbia/suburbia toward the function of subsistence. In the 1980s and 1990s the dacha fused in many people's minds with the allotment shack.

Nor is 1917 the only date that can be used to punctuate a history of the dacha. My chapter titles imply and my argument in many places makes explicit that this history can meaningfully be divided into successive phases, even if they invariably overlap and remain blurred around the edges.

But it is equally possible to identify aspects of the dacha's history that are common to several epochs; to show that cultural meanings and social practices could straddle historical divides, even if people and buildings very often did not. Most obviously, for the last two hundred years the dacha has been easy prey for stereotypes that have been largely negative and have many common features. Reasons are not hard to find: Russia in the nineteenth and twentieth centuries can be called a consumer society only with qualifications immeasurably greater than are necessary in the case of Western Europe, and so the discursive space available for leisure and its appurtenances was much smaller than in England or France.[5] And the dacha's public image was always colored by Russian social cir-

4. See D. Birdwell-Pheasant and D. Lawrence-Zúñiga, eds., *House Life: Space, Place and Family in Europe* (Oxford, 1999).

5. On the importance of recognizing local variations in the extent and nature of consumption, see C. Clunas, "Modernity Global and Local: Consumption and the Rise of the West," *AHR* 104 (1999), 1497–511.

cumstances. The tendency to sec dachas as emblematic of shallowness and vanity, of rootlessness and mercantilism, has been remarkably enduring ever since summer houses were
identified as an essentially Petersburg phenomenon in the early nineteenth century. The
dacha was easily accommodated in an emerging bipolar typology that contrasted the cold
bureaucratic granite of the new capital with the warm familial earthiness of the old. In
time this contrast weakened, as Moscow acquired a prominent dacha tradition of its own,
but it set the tone for much subsequent commentary on exurbia. The drafty hut made out
of "barge timber," first exposed by Petersburg journalists in the 1840s, was a regular fall-
back for their later colleagues.

There have, however, been distinguished exceptions to the general rule of public disapproval of the dacha. The first is that country houses inhabited by members of the intelligentsia have received more sympathetic treatment than average. Many of the writers
who gave short shrift to dachniki in their articles and newspaper columns were themselves
contentedly ensconced in summer houses. The double standard of a typical purveyor of
doggerel was pithily laid bare by the prolific Soviet poet and translator Samuil Marshak:

> There once was a man quite perverse
> Whose practice was always to curse
> From his dacha's veranda
> With unabashed candor
> His neighboring dachniks in verse.[6]

> Он жил на даче,
> Но, одначе,
> Разил он дачников стихом.[7]

The most successful means of legitimization for dachniki was to stress the perma-
nence of their dwelling and their serious, long-term commitment to it both as a home and
as a landholding. In the nineteenth century, this commitment led some dachniki to adopt
the model provided by the country estate; in the twentieth, especially since the war, the
well-appointed peasant izba has also been the object of emulation. The occupier of such a
dacha, in the nineteenth century as in the twentieth, thought of himself as a *khoziain,* as
an owner whose legal right to his property were less significant than the moral right con-
ferred by his gainful use of it. Like so much else in Russia, the dacha has been caught between Westernizing and self-Orientalizing discourses. In the process, over the last two
hundred years it has tended to follow a curious cultural trajectory: on attaining prominence in the mid-nineteenth century, it was seen as imitating, for better or for worse
(usually, of course, for worse), Western models of civilized and leisured exurban life; but
by the late twentieth century, in many people's understanding, it had come to be the
repository of the national popular spirit (*narodnost'*). In this respect it can be seen as in-
heriting and then refashioning the cultural legacy of the elite country estate, whose aristo-

---

6. My thanks to Liz Leach for this justifiably free version.
7. S. Marshak, "Dachnik-oblichitel'" (1958), *Sobranie sochinenii v vos'mi tomakh* (Moscow, 1968–72), 5: 530.

236  cratic Westernism in the eighteenth century did not prevent it from later becoming the icon of a vanished national past. The *usad'ba* has long been championed as a crucible of Russian subjectivity and cultural activity; perhaps the time has come to recognize that for the last 150 years the dacha has played this role more intensively, extensively, and interestingly.

The history of the dacha can be seen as a whole not only in cultural terms but also in more tangible ways. Underlying the dacha form of settlement has been a set of broad geographical factors: countries with harsh winters and short, hot summers and plenty of space (such as Russia, Finland, and Canada) are more likely to opt for apartment living for eight or nine months of the year and log cabins for the remainder. And then there is the public-health aspect: urban Russians have mostly lived in crowded and unsanitary conditions, and an outlet into the greenbelt has commonly been considered essential to preserve mental and bodily well-being. The compromise solution of suburbanization has never been successful because of the prevailing politics of land sale and distribution and the retarded development of transport in Russian cities. Equally, we should recall the simple fact that Russia, in the nineteenth and twentieth centuries, was a country subjected to a high degree of political centralization whose elites and subelites had an overriding centripetal attraction to the metropolitan civilizations of St. Petersburg and (latterly) Moscow. Perhaps the greatest irony of Russia's exurban history is that, at bottom, the dacha does not represent estrangement from the city (or even ambivalence toward it) but rather is a way for people to guarantee themselves a foothold in the metropolis; a means of saving the money, gathering the strength, or (more recently) growing the food to sustain their next prolonged encounter with the big city.

Unsurprisingly, then, we can see a certain unity in the dacha's social constituency since the early nineteenth century. Summer houses, both owned and (more commonly) rented, have tended to be the attribute of a section of Russian society that is not much talked about: urban nonproletarians. As this rather clumsy formulation suggests, there is no easy way of conceptually isolating this group. In Russia the conditions necessary for the creation of a "middle class"—and they are social, economic, and institutional as well as cultural—have never come together. One of the all too justified commonplaces of historical analysis has been that in Russia the urban middle strata remained disunited and lacking in self-consciousness. For the last century and a half the only thing they have shared, to my knowledge, is the exurban habit; if the tag "middle-class" refers to anyone in Russia, it is to the dachnik. Not that this observation can bring us much moral or intellectual succor. One could have no stronger confirmation of the enduring social weakness and political marginalization of this putative middle than the fact that so many of its members are called, every Friday night or Saturday morning, to don rubber boots and depart for their plot of land. In the modern dacha, if we care to look closely enough, we find much of what has made Russia in the last century so incredibly resilient and so disastrously dysfunctional. What it does not do, unfortunately, is suggest how the symbiotic relationship between these two characteristics can ever be broken.

# Note on Sources

### INTERVIEWS

My account of postwar dachas is informed by numerous informal ethnographic interviews, a few of which are mentioned in the text and notes. My other source of oral history is a set of ten in-depth interviews conducted by Irina Chekhovskikh in St. Petersburg and Novaia Ladoga as part of her now completed dissertation on post-Soviet survival strategies. Wherever her transcripts have been used, she is cited accordingly.

### UNPUBLISHED MEMOIRS

In 1999 I ran "dacha biography competitions" in newspapers in Moscow and St. Petersburg (respectively, *Vechernii klub* and *Sankt-Peterburgskie vedomosti*). I invited readers to send in their reminiscences of exurban life and offered a cash prize as incentive. I collected twenty texts in this way and followed up the longer and more interesting entries in face-to-face interviews. I draw on these dacha memoirs in Chapters 6 and 7.

### ARCHIVES

The main archival holdings consulted were:

*Gosudarstvennyi arkhiv Rossiiskoi Federatsii (GARF)*

| | |
|---|---|
| f. R-5446 | Sovet Ministrov SSSR |
| f. R-5451 | Vsesoiuznyi tsentral'nyi sovet professional'nykh soiuzov |
| f. R-9542 | Khoziaistvennoe upravlenie upravleniia delami Soveta Ministrov SSSR |

*Leningradskii oblastnoi gosudarstvennyi arkhiv v g. Vyborge (LOGAV)*

| | |
|---|---|
| f. R-2907 | Leningradskii okruzhnoi otdel mestnogo khoziaistva |
| f. R-2946 | Otdel mestnogo khoziaistva pargolovskogo raiispolkoma |
| f. R-3731 | Upravlenie stroitel'nogo kontrolia Lodeinopol'skogo okrispolkoma |
| f. R-3758 | Upravlenie stroitel'nogo kontrolia Leningradskogo okrispolkoma |

*Rossiiskii gosudarstvennyi arkhiv sotsial'no-politicheskoi informatsii (RGASPI)*

| | |
|---|---|
| f. 17 | TsK KPSS, esp. op. 80 (Khoziaistvennyi otdel upravleniia delami) |
| f. 74 | K. E. Voroshilov |
| f. 78 | M. I. Kalinin |
| f. 124 | Vsesoiuznoe obshchestvo starykh bol'shevikov |

*Rossiiskii gosudarstvennyi istoricheskii arkhiv (RGIA)*

f. 23       Ministerstvo torgovli i promyshlennosti
f. 387      Ministerstvo zemledeliia i gosudarstvennykh imushchestv
f. 963      A. P. Kozhevnikov
f. 1152     Gosudarstvennyi sovet, Departament gosudarstvennoi ekonomiki

*Tsentral'nyi gosudarstvennyi arkhiv Moskovskoi oblasti (TsGAMO)*

f. 182      Otdel mestnogo khoziaistva moskovskogo okrispolkoma
f. 2157     Mosoblispolkom
f. 2591     Moskovskii uezdnyi otdel kommunal'nogo khoziaistva
f. 7539     Biuro planirovki i otvoda zemel' APU mosoblispolkoma
f. 7572     Arkhitekturno-planirovochnaia masterskaia im. akademika V. A. Vesina
f. 7974     Arkhitekturno-planirovochnoe upravlenie

*Tsentral'nyi gosudarstvennyi arkhiv Sankt-Peterburga (TsGA SPb)*

f. 78       Primorsko-Sestroretskii raiispolkom
f. 469      Pargolovskii volispolkom
f. 2047     Leningradskii oblastnoi trest dachnogo i prigorodnogo zhilishchnogo stroitel'stva
f. 3199     Otdel kommunal'nogo khoziaistva Leningradskogo oblastnogo ispolkoma

*Tsentral'nyi gosudarstvennyi istoricheskii arkhiv Sankt-Peterburga (TSGIA SPb)*

f. 722      Tsarskosel'skaia uezdnaia zemskaia uprava
f. 768      Kantseliariia Petergofskogo uezdnogo predvoditelia dvorianstva
f. 1205     Upravlenie Petrogradskogo udel'nogo okruga

*Tsentral'nyi istoricheskii arkhiv Moskvy (TsIAM)*

f. 64       Moskovskoe gubernskoe po delam ob obshchestvakh prisutstvie
f. 483      Moskovskoe uezdnoe politseiskoe upravlenie

*Tsentral'nyi munitsipal'nyi arkhiv Moskvy (TsMAM)*

f. 718      Moskovskii gorodskoi sovet professional'nykh soiuzov
f. 819      Moskovskii gorodskoi sud
f. 1956     Pravlenie gorodskogo Moskovskogo dachnogo soiuza "Mosgor-dachsoiuz"
f. 2311     Sokol'nicheskii raionnyi zhilishchno-zemel'nyi otdel

## PERIODICALS

The following newspapers and journals were sampled.

*Prerevolutionary*

*Dachnaia gazeta* (St. Petersburg), *Dachnik* (Moscow), *Dachnik* (St. Petersburg), *Dachnik rizhskogo vzmor'ia* (Riga), *Dachnitsa* (St. Petersburg), *Dachnyi kur'er* (St. Petersburg), *Dachnyi listok* (Warsaw), *Dachnyi vestnik* (Moscow), *Domovladelets* (Moscow), *Domovladelets* (St. Petersburg), *Gorodskoe delo, Khudozhnik, Lipetskii letnii listok, Losinoostrovskii vestnik, Moskovskie vedomosti, Moskovskii listok, Nashe zhilishche: Vestnik domovladeniia i domoustroistva, Novyi Satirikon, Ogonek, Oranienbaumskii dachnyi listok, Pargolovskii letnii listok, Peterburgskaia gazeta, Peterburgskii listok, Poselkovyi golos* (St. Petersburg), *Poselok* (St. Petersburg), *Poselok* (Samara), *Razvlechenie, Russkoe slovo, Sankt-Peterburgskie vedomosti, Sel'skii stroitel', Severnaia pchela, Sezonnyi listok* (Lipetsk), *Sovremennik, Stroitel': Vestnik arkhitektury, domovladeniia i sanitarnogo zodchestva, Stolitsa i Usad'ba, Vedomosti Sankt-Peterburgskogo gradonachal'stva i Sankt-Peterburgskoi gorodskoi politsii, Vestnik poselka Lianozovo, Zhivopisnoe obozrenie*

*Soviet*

*Biulleten' finansovogo i khoziaistvennogo zakonodatel'stva, Krokodil, Ogonek, Pravda, Rabotnitsa, Sotsialisticheskaia zakonnost', Sotsialisticheskii prigorod, Sovetskaia iustitsiia, Trud, Vecherniaia krasnaia gazeta, Vecherniaia Moskva, Zhilishchnaia kooperatsiia, Zhilishchnoe delo, Zhilishchnoe tovarishchestvo, Zhilishchnoe tovarishchestvo—zhilishche i stroitel'stvo*

*Post-Soviet*

*Dachnaia gazeta* (Stavropol'), *Dachniki: Vash dom, sad i ogorod* (Moscow oblast), *Dachnyi sezon: Gazeta dlia ural'skikh sadovodov i ogorodnikov* (Cheliabinsk)

# Bibliography

PRIMARY SOURCES

The bibliography does not include newspaper articles or articles published in the periodicals listed in the "Note on Sources."

Aksenenok, G. A. *Pravo gosudarstvennoi sobstvennosti na zemliu v SSSR*. Moscow, 1950.

Alekseev, T. D. *Zhilishchnye zakony*. 3d ed., expanded. Moscow, 1957.

*Alfavitnyi sbornik rasporiazhenii po S.-Peterburgskomu Gradonachal'stvu i Politsii, izvlechennykh iz prikazov za 1866–1885 gg*. St. Petersburg, 1886.

Allilueva, S. *Dvadtsat' pisem k drugu*. London, 1967.

———. *Tol'ko odin god*. New York, 1969.

Ancheev, V. M., S. S. Kozhurin, and A. N. Korchuganov. *Spravochnik individual'nogo zastroishchika na severe*. Petrozavodsk, 1960.

Andreev, L. *Sobranie sochinenii*. 13 vols. St. Petersburg, 1896–1911.

Andreeva, V. *Dom na chernoi rechke*. Moscow, 1980.

Andreevskii, D. "Dachemaniia ili Razve my khuzhe drugikh?" (1850), held at St. Petersburg State Theater Library, Department of Manuscripts and Rare Books, I.38.2.33.

Andreyev, Leonid. *Photographs by a Russian Writer*. Ed. R. Davies. London, 1989.

Annenkov, Iu. *Dnevnik moikh vstrech: Tsikl tragedii*. 2 vols. New York, 1966.

Annenkov, P. V. *The Extraordinary Decade: Literary Memoirs*. Trans. Irwin R. Titunik. Ann Arbor, 1968.

Arbuzov, A. "Dvenadtsatyi chas." In *Dramy*. Moscow, 1969.

*Arkhitekturnyi sbornik sel'skikh postroek i modnoi mebeli*. Moscow, 1873.

*Arlekin na dache: Letnii iumoristicheskii kalendar'*. St. Petersburg, 1888.

Arnol'd, Iu. *Vospominaniia Iuriia Arnol'da*. 3 vols. Moscow, 1892–93.

*Atlas proektov i chertezhei sel'skikh postroek*. St. Petersburg, 1853.

Babel', I. *Zabytyi Babel'*. Ann Arbor, 1979.

Babichenko, D. *"Schast'e literatury": Gosudarstvo i pisateli, 1925–1938*. Moscow, 1997.

Baburov, V. "Osvoenie lesoparkovoi zony." *Stroitel'stvo Moskvy* 9 (1937): 17–18.

———. "Prigorodnaia zona Moskvy." *Stroitel'stvo Moskvy* 12 (1935): 27–31.

Bakhrushin, Iu. A. *Vospominaniia*. Moscow, 1994.

Baranovskii, G. V. *Arkhitekturnaia entsiklopediia vtoroi poloviny XIX veka*. Vol. 4. St. Petersburg, 1904.

Barantsevich, K. *Kartinki zhizni*. St. Petersburg, 1892.

Batiushkov, K. N. *Polnoe sobranie stikhotvorenii*. Moscow and Leningrad, 1964.

Belinskii, V. G. "Peterburg i Moskva." In *Polnoe sobranie sochinenii*. 13 vols. Moscow, 1953–59. Vol. 8.

Benois, A. *Memoirs*. Trans. M. Budberg. Vol. 1. London, 1988.

Bernoulli, J. "Zapiski astronoma Ivana Bernulli o poezdke ego v Rossiiu v 1777 godu." *Russkii arkhiv* 1 (1902): 5–30.

242   Bertenson, S. *Vokrug iskusstva*. Hollywood, 1957.

Bespiatykh, Iu. N., ed. *Peterburg Anny Ioannovny v inostrannykh opisaniiakh*. St. Petersburg, 1997.

Bitov, A. "Zhizn' v vetrenuiu pogodu." *Imperiia v chetyrekh izmereniiakh*. 4 vols. Moscow, 1996. Vol. 1.

Blagovo, D. *Rasskazy babushki: Iz vospominanii piati pokolenii*. Leningrad, 1989.

Blinov, A. "Dacha na beregu kanala." *Peremena pogody: Povesti i rasskazy*. Moscow, 1967.

Blok, A. *Sobranie sochinenii v vos'mi tomakh*. 8 vols. Leningrad, 1960–63.

Blok, Iu. *Velosiped: Ego znachenie dlia zdorov'ia, prakticheskoe primenenie, ukhod za mashinoiu i pr.* Moscow, 1892.

Bobov, G. M. *Arkhitektura i stroitel'stvo dach*. Moscow, 1939.

Boikov, S. *Medovyi mesiats, ili kak provodiat vremia molodye*. St. Petersburg, 1850.

Bonner, E. *Dochki-materi*. Moscow, 1994.

Brodskii, I. *Uraniia*. Ann Arbor, 1987.

Bulgakova, E. S. *Dnevnik*. Moscow, 1990.

Bulgarin, F. *Letniaia progulka po Finliandii i Shvetsii v 1838 godu*. 2 vols. St. Petersburg, 1839.

——. *Sochineniia*. Moscow, 1990.

Bunin, A. V., et al. *Gradostroitel'stvo*. Moscow, 1945.

Bunin, I. A. "Na dache." In *Sobranie sochinenii v deviati tomakh*. 9 vols. Moscow, 1965–67. Vol. 2.

Bur'ianov, V. *Progulki s det'mi po S. Peterburgu i ego okrestnostiam*. 3 vols. St. Petersburg, 1838.

Buryshkin, P. A. *Moskva kupecheskaia*. Moscow, 1991.

Buturlin, M. D. "Zapiski Grafa Mikhaila Dmitrievicha Buturlina." *Russkii arkhiv* 9 (1897): 33–106; 10 (1897): 237–82; 11 (1897): 313–67; 12 (1897): 517–97.

Bykova, V. *Zapiski staroi smolianki*. 2 vols. St. Petersburg, 1898–99.

Chekhov, A. P. *Polnoe sobranie sochinenii i pisem v tridtsati tomakh*. 30 vols. Moscow, 1974–83.

Chekhova, M. P. *Iz dalekogo proshlogo*. Moscow, 1960.

Cherikover, S. *Peterburg*. Moscow, 1909.

Chernousov, A. "Vtoroi dom." *Nash sovremennik* 1 (1983): 3–97.

Chernyi, S. *Sobranie sochinenii v piati tomakh*. 5 vols. Moscow, 1996.

Chukovskaia, L. *Pamiati detstva*. New York, 1983.

——. *Zapiski ob Anne Akhmatovoi*. 3 vols. Moscow, 1997.

Chukovskii, K. I. *Dnevnik*. 2 vols. Moscow, 1997.

Custine, Marquis de. *Letters from Russia*. Trans. R. Buss. London, 1991.

*Dacha—mini-ferma*. Moscow, 1993.

*Dacha-koloniia Kievskogo Uchebnogo Okruga dlia uchenikov srednikh uchebnykh zavedenii g. Kieva*. Kiev, 1907.

*Dachi i okrestnosti Moskvy: Putevoditel'*. Moscow, 1928.

*Dachnaia biblioteka*. St. Petersburg, 1911.

*Dachnik: Dachnye mestnosti vblizi g. Kieva*. Kiev, 1909.

*Dachniki, ili Kak dolzhno provodit' leto na dache*. St. Petersburg, 1849.

*Dachnoe khoziaistvo: Sbornik zakonodatel'nykh aktov*. Moscow, 1996.

*Dachnye Don-Zhuany: Veselye rasskazy*. St. Petersburg, 1889.

Dal', V. *Tolkovyi slovar' zhivogo velikorusskogo iazyka*. 2d ed. 4 vols. St. Petersburg, 1880–82.

Dal'berg, A. *Prakticheskie sovety pri postroike dach*. St. Petersburg, 1902.

Dashwood, Sir Francis. "Sir Francis Dashwood's Diary of His Visit to St. Petersburg in 1733." *Slavonic and East European Review* 38 (1959): 194–222.

Davydov, I. "Dacha v Malakhovke." In *Devushka moego druga*. Saratov, 1965.

Del'vig, A. I. *Polveka russkoi zhizni: Vospominaniia A. I. Del'viga, 1820–1870.* Moscow and Leningrad, 1930.

Denisov, A. "Lichnoe podsobnoe khoziaistvo." *Ekonomiku sel'skogo khoziaistva* 4 (1978): 123–26.

Dershau, F. *Finliandiia i finliandtsy.* St. Petersburg, 1842.

Derzhavin, G. R. *Stikhotvoreniia.* Leningrad, 1957.

Dmitriev, M. A. *Glavy iz vospominanii moei zhizni.* Moscow, 1998.

Dobuzhinskii, M. *Vospominaniia.* Vol. 1. New York, 1976.

Domosedov, I. [pseud.]. "Peterburg zarechnyi." *Russkii illiustrirovannyi al'manakh*, 1858, 139–62.

Dostoevskii, F. M. *Polnoe sobranie sochinenii v tridtsati tomakh.* 30 vols. Leningrad, 1972–90.

Druskin, L. *Spasennaia kniga: Vospominaniia leningradskogo poeta.* London, 1984.

Dumas, A. *Voyage en Russie.* Paris, 1960.

Durilin, P. N. "Moskovskie prigorody i dachnye poselki v sviazi s razvitiem gorodskoi zhizni." *Arkhiv gorodskoi gigieny i tekhniki* 1–2 (1918): 63–101.

*Ekskursionnyi spravochnik na leto 1933 g.* Moscow, 1933.

Engel'gardt, S. "Iz vospominanii." *Russkii vestnik* 191 (1887): 690–715.

Eremeev, M. "Zagorodnyi dvukh-etazhnyi dereviannyi dom." *Sel'skii khoziain* 27 (1892).

Erlykin, L. A. *Individual'nyi dom i uchastok.* Moscow, 1989.

Eventov, I. S. *Russkaia stikhotvornaia satira, 1908–1917 godov.* Leningrad, 1974.

Fedin, K. *Sobranie sochinenii v desiati tomakh.* 10 vols. Moscow, 1969–73.

Fedotov, N. *Opisanie i podrobnye plany dachnikh mestnostei po finliandskoi zheleznoi doroge.* St. Petersburg, 1886.

———. *Putevoditel' po dachnym mestnostiam.* St. Petersburg, 1889.

Fedotovskaia, Z. A. "Sudebnaia praktika po delam ob iz''iatii u grazhdan stroenii, vozvedennykh imi na netrudovye dokhody libo ispol'zuemykh dlia izvlecheniia netrudovykh dokhodov." In *Nauchnyi kommentarii sudebnoi praktiki za 1963 god*, ed. P. I. Sediugin. Moscow, 1965.

Feigin, L. A. *Sputnik dachnika po okrestnostiam Moskvy.* Moscow, 1888.

Fon-Gernet, A. *Nemetskaia koloniia Strel'na pod S.-Peterburgom, 1810–1910.* St. Petersburg, 1910.

Furmann, P. *Entsiklopediia russkogo gorodskogo i sel'skogo khoziaina-arkhitektora.* 3 vols. St. Petersburg, 1842.

Gaidar, A. *Sobranie sochinenii v chetyrekh tomakh.* 4 vols. Moscow, 1959–60.

Galich, A. *Pokolenie obrechennykh.* Frankfurt am Main, 1972.

Gamov, N. P., and M. I. Popov. *Sovety individual'nomu zastroishchiku.* Leningrad, 1959.

Garros, V., N. Korenevskaya, and T. Lahusen, eds. *Intimacy and Terror.* New York, 1995.

Garshin, V. M. "Peterburgskie pis'ma." In *Sochineniia.* Moscow and Leningrad, 1951.

Geirot, A. *Opisanie Petergofa.* St. Petersburg, 1868.

Gensler, I. *Kullerberg, ili Kak guliali peterburgskie nemtsy na Ivanov den'.* St. Petersburg, 1909.

Georgi, I. G. *Opisanie rossiisko-imperatorskogo stolichnogo goroda Sankt-Peterburga i dostopamiatnostei v okrestnostiakh onogo.* St. Petersburg, 1996.

Gertsen, A. I. "Byloe i dumy." In *Sobranie sochinenii v tridtsati tomakh.* 30 vols. Moscow, 1954–66. Vols. 8–11.

Ginzburg, M. Ia. *Zhilishche.* Moscow, 1934.

Gnedich, N. I. *Stikhotvoreniia.* Leningrad, 1956.

Gogol', N. V. *Polnoe sobranie sochinenii.* 14 vols. Leningrad, 1937–52.

Gollerbakh, E. *Gorod muz.* Leningrad, 1927.

———, ed. *Sputnik po Petrogradu i ego okrestnostiam.* Petrograd, 1924.

Golovin, I. *Poezdka v Shvetsiiu v 1839 godu.* St. Petersburg, 1840.

244  Golovina, V. N. *Zapiski grafini Varvary Nikolaevny Golovinoi (1766–1819)*. Trans. E. S. Shumigorskii. St. Petersburg, 1900.

Goncharov, I. A. "Oblomov." In *Sobranie sochinenii*. 8 vols. Moscow, 1952–55. Vol. 4.

Gordin, A. M., and M. A.Gordin, eds. *I. A. Krylov v vospominaniiakh sovremennikov*. Moscow, 1982.

Gor'kii, M. "Dachniki." In *Polnoe sobranie sochinenii*. 26 vols. Moscow, 1968–76. Vol. 7.

Gornostaev, D. *Kak postroit' krest'ianskuiu kirpichnuiu izbu, chtoby ona byla prochna i predstavliala zdorovoe zhilishche*. Moscow, 1910.

Got'e, Iu. V. *Time of Troubles: The Diary of Iurii Vladimirovich Got'e*. Trans. T. Emmons. Princeton, 1988.

Grebenka, E. P. "Peterburgskaia storona." In *Fiziologiia Peterburga*. Moscow, 1991.

Grech, A. *Ves' Peterburg v karmane*. St. Petersburg, 1851.

Grechnev, V. "Dacha." In *Sueta suet*. Moscow, 1994.

Grimm, G., and L. Kashkarova. *Peterburg-Petrograd-Leningrad v proizvedeniiakh khudozhnikov*. Moscow, 1958.

Griundling, P. *Motivy sadovoi arkhitektury*. St. Petersburg, 1903.

Iakubovskii, I. A. *Istoriia zhizni Ivana Andreevicha Iakuboskogo, karlika Svetleishego Kniazia Platona Aleksandrovicha Zubova, pisannaia im samim*. Munich, 1968.

Ianishevskii, A. *Dacha na Volge*. Kazan', 1900.

Iaroshenko, K. B. "Spory o chlenstve v sadovodcheskikh tovarishchestvakh." In *Kommentarii sudebnoi praktiki za 1980 god,* ed. E. V. Boldyreva and A. I. Pergament. Moscow, 1981.

———. "Spory o prave na chlenstvo v zhilishchno-stroitel'nykh i dachno-stroitel'nykh kooperativakh." In *Kommentarii sudebnoi praktiki za 1975 god*, ed. E. V. Boldyreva and A. I. Pergament. Moscow, 1976.

Iaroslavtsev, A. "Na dache i na bale, eskiz iz pisem molodogo cheloveka." *Sbornik literaturnykh statei, posviashchennykh russkimi pisateliami pamiati pokoinogo knigoprodavtsa-izdatelia Aleksandra Filippovicha Smirdina* 5 (1859): 219–49.

Iastrzhembskii, S. B., I. B. Sambur, and S. M. Ginzburg. *Zhilishchnyi spravochnik dlia sudebnykh rabotnikov*. Moscow, 1935.

Ibragimbekov, R. "Dacha." In *Dacha: Rasskazy*. Moscow, 1988.

Ibragimbekov, R., and N. Mikhalkov. "Utomlennye solntsem." *Kinostsenarii* 4 (1994): 3–53.

Ignatieff, M. *Isaiah Berlin: A Life*. London, 1998.

*Illiustrirovannyi putevoditel' po okrestnostiam Moskvy*. Moscow, 1926.

*Instruktsiia po bukhgalterskomu uchetu v zhilishchno-stroitel'nykh i dachno-stroitel'nykh kooperativakh*. Moscow, 1960.

*Instruktsiia po stroitel'stvu i remontu dach i nadvornykh stroenii v dachno-stroitel'nykh kooperativakh i o poriadke priema vypolnennykh rabot*. Moscow, 1950.

Ivanitskii, N. I. "Avtobiografiia Nikolaia Ivanovicha Ivanitskogo." *Shchukinskii sbornik* 8 (1909).

Ivanov, V. *Sobranie sochinenii v vos'mi tomakh*. 8 vols. Moscow, 1973–78.

Ivanov, V. V. "Goluboi zver' (vospominaniia)." *Zvezda* 1 (1995): 173–99; 2 (1995): 192–207; 3 (1995): 155–97.

Ivanova, T. *Moi sovremenniki, kakimi ia ikh znala: Ocherki*. Moscow, 1984.

*Kak postroit' dachu za poltseny*. St. Petersburg, 1996.

Kalish, V. G. "Kottedzhi dlia gorniakov." *Arkhitektura i stroitel'stvo* 4 (1947): 24–25.

Kalmykov, V. P. "Dachnye poselki." *Sovetskaia arkhitektura* 1 (1934): 46–51.

Kalugina, Z. I. *Lichnoe podobnoe khoziaistvo v SSSR: Sotsial'nye reguliatory i rezul'taty razvitiia*. Novosibirsk, 1991.

Kamenogradskii, P. I. *Dachnyi sad: Razbivka i obsadka nebol'shikh sadov i parkov derev'iami, kus-* 245
*tami i tsvetami.* 3d ed. Petrograd, 1918.

Karlik, L. "Na beregakh kliaz'minskogo vodokhranilishcha." *Stroitel'stvo i arkhitektura Moskvy* 3
(1964): 29–31.

Karpovich, V. S., ed. *Motivy dereviannoi arkhitektury.* St. Petersburg, 1903.

Kataev, V. "Peredelkino" (1984). In *Sobranie sochinenii v desiati tomakh.* 10 vols. Moscow, 1983–86.
Vol. 10.

Katkovskii, Iu. B. *Zhilishchno-arendnye i zhilishchno-stroitel'nye kooperativy: Sbornik po zakono-*
*datel'stvu v voprosakh i otvetakh.* Moscow, 1936.

Kaverin, V. *Epilog: Memuary.* Moscow, 1989.

Keller, O. *St. Petersburg and Its Environs, Finland, Moscow, Kiev, Odessa . . .* London, 1914.

Kharuzina, V. N. *Proshloe: Vospominaniia detskikh i otrocheskikh let.* Moscow, 1999.

Kherkel', V. A. *Vasha dacha.* Moscow, 1972.

Khodasevich, V. *Stikhotvoreniia.* Leningrad, 1989.

Kholmogorov, M. "Komendantskaia dacha." In *Naprasnyi dar: Tri povesti.* Moscow, 1989.

*Khoziaika doma (domoustroistvo).* St. Petersburg, 1895.

Kil'shtet, K. E. *Vospominaniia starogo Petrogradtsa.* Petergof, 1916.

Komarovskii, N. E. *Zapiski.* Moscow, 1912.

Komelova, G., and I. G. Kotel'nikova, comps. *Peterburg kontsa XVIII–nachala XIX v. v proizvedeni-*
*iakh khudozhnika B. Patersena.* Leningrad, 1972.

Komelova, G., G. Printseva, and I. Kotel'nikova. *Peterburg v proizvedeniiakh Patersena.* Leningrad,
1978.

Koni, A. F. *Peterburg: Vospominaniia starozhila.* Petrograd, 1922.

Korolenko, V. G. "Smirennye (Derevenskii peizazh)." In *Polnoe sobranie sochinenii.* 9 vols. St. Petersburg, 1914. Vol. 3.

Korolev, F. N. *Rukovodstvo k vozvedeniiu v selakh ognestoikikh zdanii.* St. Petersburg, 1880.

———. *Sel'skoe stroitel'noe iskusstvo.* St. Petersburg, 1887.

Kosterina, N. *The Diary of Nina Kosterina.* Trans. M. Ginsburg. London, 1972.

Kozhevnikova, N. "Dacha: Povest'." *Oktiabr'* 12 (1983): 73–133.

Kozlov, A. N. *Proekty dach, zagorodnykh dereviannykh domov i khoziaistvennykh postroek, v planakh*
*i fasadakh, s detal'nymi risunkami.* Moscow, 1902.

Kozlov, P. S. "Puti organizatsii massovogo otdykha v prigorodnoi zone." In *Sozdanie krupnykh*
*kompleksov kurortov, mest otdykha i turizma,* ed. A. V. Roshchina. Moscow, 1972.

Kreindlin, L. I. *Letnie sadovye domiki.* Moscow, 1967.

Krestovnikov, N. *Semeinaia khronika Krestovnikovykh.* 2 vols. Moscow, 1903–4.

Krestovskii, V. "Dachi, kak poprishche zolotopromyshlennoi deiatel'nosti." In *Peterburgskie zoloto-*
*promyshlenniki.* St. Petersburg, 1865.

———. *Peterburgskie trushchoby: Kniga o sytykh i golodnykh.* St. Petersburg, 1867.

Kshesinskaia, M. *Vospominaniia.* Smolensk, 1998.

Kugushev, Kniaz'. "Stseny na chistom vozdukhe: Fotograficheskii snimok s natury." *Sbornik liter-*
*aturnykh statei, posviashchennykh russkimi pisateliami pamiati pokoinogo knigoprodavtsa-iz-*
*datelia Aleksandra Filippovicha Smirdina* 5 (1859): 147–218.

Kukol'nik, N. "Novye postroiki v Petergofe." *Khudozhestvennaia gazeta* 11–12 (1837): 173–77.

———. "Villa." *Khudozhestvennaia gazeta* 11–12 (1837): 178–90.

Kupffer, E. Iu. *Zhiloi dom: Rukovodstvo dlia proektirovaniia i vozvedeniia sovremennykh zhilishch.* St.
Petersburg and Moscow, 1914.

246  Kurbatov, V. Ia. *Strel'na i Oranienbaum.* Leningrad, 1925.

Kushchevskii, I. *Malen'kie rasskazy.* St. Petersburg, 1875.

*Kuskovo i ego okrestnosti.* Moscow, 1850.

Kutepov, A. *Proekty dlia stroenii domov i drugikh raznogo roda postroek vo vnov' priniatom vkuse.* Moscow, 1852.

Kuznetsov, A. I. "Arkhitekturnye problemy planirovki prigorodnoi zony." *Stroitel'stvo Moskvy* 21–22 (1940): 3–7.

Kuznetsov, E. *Russkie narodnye gulian'ia po rasskazam A. Ia. Alekseeva-Iakovleva v zapisi i obrabotke Evg. Kuznetsova.* Moscow and Leningrad, 1948.

Larina, A. *This I Cannot Forget.* London, 1993.

Leikin, N. A. *Na dachnom proziabanii.* St. Petersburg, 1912.

———. *Neunyvaiushchie Rossiiane.* St. Petersburg, 1912.

Lench, L. *Izbrannoe.* Moscow, 1975.

Lents. "Prikliucheniia Lifliandtsa v Peterburge." *Russkii arkhiv* 4 (1878): 436–68.

Leskov, N. S. "Sovmestiteli." *Sobranie sochinenii v odinnadtsati tomakh.* 11 vols. Moscow, 1956–58. Vol. 7.

*Leto v Tsarskom Sele: Rasskazy dlia detei.* St. Petersburg, 1880.

Levitov, I. *Putevoditel'.* Moscow, 1881.

Libedinskaia, L. *Zelenaia lampa: Vospominaniia.* Moscow, 1966.

Liubetskii, S. M. *Moskovskie okrestnosti, blizhnie i dal'nie, za vsemi zastavami, v istoricheskom otnoshenii i v sovremennom ikh vide, dlia vybora dach i gulian'ia.* Moscow, 1877.

Liudvig, G. M. *Rekomendovannye proekty: Al'bom dach.* Moscow, 1935.

Lobanov, Iu. N. "Otdykh i krov: Nekotorye voprosy organizatsii kratkovremennogo otdykha naseleniia Leningrada." *Stroitel'stvo i arkhitektura Leningrada* 5 (1973): 13–15.

*Losinoostrovskaia i ee okrestnosti.* Moscow, 1913.

Lukashevich, V. "Zimniaia dacha." In *Doroga cherez zarosli: Povesti i rasskazy.* Moscow, 1972.

Machinskii, V. D. *Kak postroit' deshevyi dom.* Moscow, 1927.

———. *Rabochii poselok.* Moscow, 1925.

Maiakovskii, V. *Polnoe sobranie sochinenii.* 13 vols. Moscow, 1955–61.

Mamin-Sibiriak, D. N. "Cherty iz zhizni Pepko." In *Sobranie sochinenii.* 10 vols. Moscow, 1958. Vol. 8.

Man'kov, A. G. "Iz dnevnika riadovogo cheloveka (1933–1934 gg.)." *Zvezda* 5 (1994): 134–83.

Mandel'shtam, E. "Vospominaniia." *Novyi mir* 10 (1995): 119–78.

Mandel'shtam, O. "Shum vremeni." *Sochineniia v dvukh tomakh.* 2 vols. Moscow, 1990. Vol. 2.

Mandelstam, N. *Hope against Hope: A Memoir.* Trans. M. Hayward. London, 1971.

Markovnikov, N. "Poselok 'Sokol.'" *Stroitel'naia promyshlennost'* 12 (1929): 1071–76.

———. *Zhilishchnoe stroitel'stvo za granitsei i v SSSR.* Moscow, 1928.

Marshak, S. *Sobranie sochinenii v vos'mi tomakh.* 8 vols. Moscow, 1968–72.

Mart'ianov, P. K. *Lopari i samoedy stolichnykh nashikh tundr.* St. Petersburg, 1891.

*Materialy k otsenke gorodskikh nedvizhimykh imushchestv v S.-Peterburgskoi gubernii.* St. Petersburg, 1904.

*Materialy o gorodakh pridvornogo vedomstva: Gorod Petergof.* St. Petersburg, 1882.

*Materialy po statistike narodnogo khoziaistva v S.-Peterburgskoi gubernii.* St. Petersburg, 1889–95.

Matthews, M. *Mila and Mervusya: A Russian Wedding.* Bridgend, 1999.

Mel'nikov, A. P. "Iz vospominanii o P. I. Mel'nikove." *Sbornik v pamiat' P. I. Mel'nikova.* Nizhnii Novgorod, 1910.

Mikhalkov, S. V. *Ot i do . . .* Moscow, 1997.

Mikhel'son, M. I. *Russkaia mysl' i rech': Opyt russkoi frazeologii.* St. Petersburg, 1899.

Mikhnevich, V. O. *Peterburgskoe leto.* St. Petersburg, 1887.

———. *Vsego ponemozhku: Fel'etonno-iumoristicheskie nabroski.* St. Petersburg, 1875.

Milashevskii, V. A. *Vchera, pozavchera . . .* 2d ed. Moscow, 1989.

Miliukov, A. *Rasskazy iz obydennogo byta.* St. Petersburg, 1875.

Mordukhai-Boltovskii, I. D. *Svod zakonov Rossiiskoi Imperii.* St. Petersburg, 1912.

*Moskovskaia guberniia po mestnomu obsledovaniiu, 1898–1900 gg.* 4 vols. Moscow, 1903–8.

*Moskva i ee okrestnosti.* Moscow, 1882.

*Moskva poslevoennaia, 1945–1947: Arkhivnye dokumenty i materialy.* Moscow, 2000.

Moskvich, G. *Prakticheskii putevoditel' po S.-Peterburgu i ego okrestnostiam.* Odessa, 1903.

Mukhanov, P. *Portfel' dlia khoziaev, ili Kurs sel'skoi arkhitektury.* Moscow, 1840.

Nabokov, V. *Pnin.* London, 1997.

———. *Speak, Memory: A Memoir.* London, 1951.

Nasushchenko, V. "Dachnik Iakovlev." In *Belyi svet: Rasskazy.* Leningrad, 1988.

Nazimova, M. G. "Babushka grafinia M. G. Razumovskaia." *Istoricheskii vestnik* 75, no. 3 (1899): 841–54.

Neelov, A. P. "Iz dal'nikh let." *Russkaia starina* 165 (1916): 111–17, 257–70.

Neigardt, P. *Spisok zemel'nykh vladenii S.-Peterburgskogo uezda.* St. Petersburg, 1865.

Nekrasova, V. L. *Putevoditel' po severnym okrestnostiam Leningrada.* Leningrad, 1935.

Nemtsov, N. M. *Zhilishchnye dela: Posobie dlia narzasedatelia, sud'i vydvizhentsa i sotssovmestitelia po zhilishchnym delam.* Moscow, 1932.

Nikitenko, A. *The Diary of a Russian Censor.* Trans. H. S. Jacobson. Amherst, 1975.

Nistrem, K. *Ukazatel' selenii i zhitelei uezdov Moskovskoi gubernii.* Moscow, 1852.

*Noveishii sbornik raznykh svedenii o S.-Peterburge i ego Okrestnostiakh na vse vremena goda.* St. Petersburg, 1861.

*Novye Sokol'niki. Dachnye uchastki. Imenie Anny Nikolaevny Kovalevoi.* Moscow, 1911.

Obodovskii, A. D. "Dachnaia epidemiia." *Dramaticheskie sochineniia: P'esy, stseny, monologi.* St. Petersburg, 1894.

Olenina, A. A. *Dnevnik Anny Alekseevny Oleninoi (1828–1829).* Paris, 1936.

*Opisanie edinstvennogo v Rossii blagoustroennogo podmoskovnogo poselka "Novogireevo" pri sobstvennoi platforme.* Moscow, 1906.

Orlova, R. *Vospominaniia o neproshedshem vremeni.* Ann Arbor, 1983.

*Ostankino.* St. Petersburg, 1897.

Osterman, N., and N. Reviakin. "Doma i dachi dlia prigorodnoi zony Moskvy." *Arkhitektura i stroitel'stvo Moskvy* 12 (1953): 13–19.

Ostrozhskii, K. *Dachnye baryshni: Letnie kartinki v 4–kh aktakh.* St. Petersburg, 1911.

*Otdykh pod Moskvoi: Spravochnik po lodochnym pristaniam i pliazham na leto 1940 goda.* Moscow, 1940.

Ozhe, I. "Iz zapisok Ippolita Ozhe, 1814–1817." *Russkii arkhiv* 1 (1877): 51–75.

Panaev, I. I. *Literaturnye vospominaniia.* Moscow, 1950.

———. "Novye zametki peterburgskogo turista." *Vek* 24 (1861).

Panaeva, A. Ia. *Vospominaniia.* 4th ed. Moscow and Leningrad, 1933.

Pasternak, A. L. *Vospominaniia.* Munich, 1983.

Pasternak, E. *Boris Pasternak: The Tragic Years, 1930–60.* London, 1990.

Patkul', M. A. *Vospominaniia Marii Aleksandrovny Patkul' rozhdennoi Markizy de Traverse za tri chetverti XIX stoletiia.* St. Petersburg, 1903.

248  Paustovskii, K. *Sobranie sochinenii v deviati tomakh.* 9 vols. Moscow, 1981–86. Vol. 6.

Pavlova, K. "Dvoinaia zhizn'." In *Polnoe sobranie stikhotvorenii.* Moscow and Leningrad, 1964.

Pavlovskii, O. *Srochno prodaetsia dacha: Povesti.* Kaliningrad, 1989.

Pelikan, A. A. "Vo vtoroi polovine XIX veka." *Golos minuvshego* 2 (1914): 104–41; 3 (1914): 155–99.

Persiianinova, N. L. *Bol'shie i malen'kie.* Moscow, 1912.

*Peterburg-Petrograd-Leningrad v russkoi poezii.* Leningrad, 1975.

*Peterburgskie dachi i dachniki.* St. Petersburg, 1867.

*Peterburgskie dachnye mestnosti v otnoshenii ikh zdorovosti.* St. Petersburg, 1881.

*Petergofskii sbornik: Sbornik neobkhodimykh svedenii dlia dachnika v g. Petergofe.* St. Petersburg, 1888.

*Petrograd i ego okrestnosti: Illiustrirovannyi putevoditel' i spravochnik.* Petrograd, 1915.

Petrov, P. N. *Istoriia Sankt-Peterburga s osnovaniia goroda, do vvedeniia v deistvie vybornogo gorod-skogo upravleniia, 1703–1782.* St. Petersburg, 1884.

Petrusheva, L. I., ed. *Deti russkoi emigratsii.* Moscow, 1997.

Pleshcheev, A. A. *Pod sen'iu kulis.* Paris, 1936.

Plotnikov, V. S. *Deshevoe dachnoe stroitel'stvo.* Moscow, 1930.

"Podgotovitel'nye rasporiazheniia pered pereezdom na dachu." *Domostroi* 1 (1892).

Polilov-Severtsev, G. T. *Nashi dedy-kuptsy: Bytovye kartiny nachala XIX stoletiia.* St. Petersburg, 1907.

Poluianskii, K. Ia. *Dachi: Temnye storony naemnykh dach i vygoda stroit' sobstvennye dachi.* St. Petersburg, 1894.

Polunin, V. *Three Generations: Family Life in Russia, 1845–1902.* London, 1957.

Pomazanov, P. "Podmoskovnaia zona otdykha: O rekonstruktsii Khoroshevskogo Serebrianogo bora." *Arkhitektura i stroitel'stvo Moskvy* 9 (1953): 18–22.

Pope-Hennessy, U. *Leningrad: The Closed and Forbidden City.* London, 1938.

Popov, G. "Dacha." *Gusi-lebedi: Rasskazy.* Minsk, 1968.

Portugalov, P. A., and V. A. Dlugach, eds. *Dachi i okrestnosti Moskvy.* Moscow, 1935.

"Posledniaia staraia dacha na Kamennom ostrove." *Starye gody,* July–September 1910, 182–85.

Pozdniakov, V. "Petrograd glazami rebenka." *Neva* 2 (1994): 281–93.

*Pravila svetskoi zhizni i etiketa: Khoroshii ton.* St. Petersburg, 1889; rpt. Moscow, 1991.

Preobrazhenskii, V. S., et al. "Problemy territorial'noi organizatsii rekreatsionnoi deiatel'nosti v Moskovskoi oblasti." *Izvestiia Akademii Nauk SSSR: Seriia geograficheskaia* 6 (1982): 87–99.

*Programma vsesoiuznogo otkrytogo konkursa na sostavlenie proektov.* Leningrad, 1934.

Pushkarev, I. *Putevoditel' po Sanktpeterburgu i okrestnostiam ego.* St. Petersburg, 1843.

*Putevoditel' k zamechatel'nym okrestnostiam moskovskim.* Moscow, 1855.

*Putevoditel' po dachnym okrestnostiam g. S.-Peterburga na 1903 god.* St. Petersburg, 1903.

*Putevoditel' po S.-Peterburgu, okrestnostiam i dachnym mestnostiam s planom stolitsy, imperatorsikh teatrov i tsirka.* St. Petersburg, 1895.

*Putevoditel' po Tsaritsynu.* Moscow, 1912.

*Putevoditel' po Vyborgu i okrestnosti* [*sic*]. Vyborg, 1915.

Pyliaev, M. I. *Staryi Peterburg.* St. Petersburg, 1887.

Raevskii, A. "Okrestnosti Moskvy." *Syn otechestva* 25, no. 40 (1815): 53–65.

Raevskii, F. *Peterburg s okrestnostiami.* St. Petersburg, 1902.

Reitlinger, N. *Putevoditel' po Reveliu i ego okrestnostiam.* St. Petersburg, 1839.

Rimskii-Korsakov, N. *Letopis' moei muzykal'noi zhizni (1844–1906).* 3d ed. Moscow, 1926.

Romanycheva, I. *Akademicheskaia dacha.* Leningrad, 1975.

Rudol'f, M. *Moskva s topograficheskim ukazaniem vsei ee mestnosti i okrestnostei.* Moscow, 1848.

Rudol'skii, A. *Arkhitekturnyi al'bom dlia khoziaev.* Moscow, 1839.

*Russia with Teheran, Port Arthur, and Peking.* London, 1914.

Safonovich, V. I. "Vospominaniia." *Russkii arkhiv* 1 (1903): 112–40; 2 (1903): 145–200; 3 (1903): 331–68; 4 (1903): 492–533.

Saladin, A. *Putevoditel' po prigorodnym i dachnym mestnostiam do stantsii Ramenskoe Moskovsko-Kazanskoi zheleznoi dorogi.* Moscow, 1914.

*Sbornik zakonodate'nykh aktov o zemle.* 2d ed. Moscow, 1962.

Semenov, V. *Blagoustroistvo gorodov.* Moscow, 1912.

Sergeev, A. "Al'bom dlia marok." *Omnibus: Roman, rasskazy, vospominaniia.* Moscow, 1997.

Severtsev-Polilov, T. "Iz dnevnika iunoshi 'tridtsatykh godov.'" *Vestnik Evropy* 7 (1908): 97–120.

Shalikov, K. P. *Puteshestvie v Kronshtat 1805 goda.* Moscow, 1817.

Shantarenkov, N., ed. *Russkii vodevil'.* Moscow, 1970.

Shchapov, N. M. *Vdol' Iaroslavskoi zheleznoi dorogi.* Moscow, 1925.

Shcheglov, I. *Dachnyi muzh (Peterburgskii anekdot).* Moscow, 1888.

Shchukin, P. A. "Iz vospominanii Petra Ivanovicha Shchukina." *Russkii arkhiv* 12 (1911): 544–51; 5 (1912): 82–130.

Shefner, V. "Barkhatnyi put': Letopis' vpechatlenii." *Zvezda* 4 (1995): 26–80.

Sheinis, D. I. *Zhilishchnoe zakonodatel'stvo.* 3d ed. Moscow, 1926.

Shemanskii, A., and S. Geichenko. *Kottedzh: Dacha Nikolaia I v Peterburge.* Leningrad, 1930.

Sheremet'ev, S. *Vospominaniia, 1853–1861.* St. Petersburg, 1898.

Shergova, G. "Zakolochennye dachi." *Novyi mir* 3 (1978): 68–96.

Shirokii, V. F. *Dacha A. S. Pushkina v Tsarskom sele (dom Kitaeva).* Leningrad, 1936.

Shklovskii, V. *Tret'ia fabrika.* Moscow, 1926.

Shramchenko, A. P. *Spravochnaia knizhka Moskovskoi gubernii.* Moscow, 1890.

Shreder, F. *Noveishii putevoditel' po Sanktpeterburgu.* St. Petersburg, 1820.

Shreider, K. *Illiuminatsiia.* St. Petersburg, 1856.

———. *Sobranie risunkov sadovykh i domovykh ukrashenii i vsiakikh prinadlezhnostei sego roda.* St. Petersburg, 1842.

Shteinberg, P. N. *Dekorativnyi dachnyi i usadebnyi sad.* Petrograd, 1916.

Shtorkh, P. *Putevoditel' po sadu i gorodu Pavlovsku.* St. Petersburg, 1843.

Shuvalova, I. N., ed. *Ivan Ivanovich Shishkin. Perepiska. Dnevnik. Sovremenniki o khudozhnike.* Leningrad, 1984.

Skalon, D. A. "Vospominaniia D. A. Skalona." *Russkaia starina* 131, no. 9 (1907): 516–26.

*Skol'ko let, skol'ko zim! ili Peterburgskie vremena.* St. Petersburg, 1849.

*Slovar' akademii rossiiskoi.* St. Petersburg, 1806–22.

*Slovar' russkogo iazyka XI–XVII vv.* Moscow, 1975–.

*Slovar' russkogo iazyka XVIII veka.* Leningrad, 1984–.

Smirnov, S. *Putevoditel' ot Moskvy do Troitskoi Sergievoi Lavry.* Moscow, 1882.

Smirnova-Rosset, A. O. *Avtobiografiia.* Moscow, 1931.

Smyth, C. Piazzi. *Three Cities in Russia.* 2 vols. London, 1862.

Sobolev, A. K. *Podmoskovnye dachi (Ocherki, nabliudeniia i zametki).* Moscow, 1901.

Sobolev, L. *Neizmennomu drugu: Dnevniki. Stat'i. Pis'ma.* Moscow, 1986.

*Sobranie Fasad i planov sel'skikh i sadovykh domov.* Moscow, 1829.

Sokolov, A. A., and N. Rinev. *Na ogonek: Ocherki zakulisnoi zhizni Peterburga.* St. Petersburg, 1885.

Sokolov, P. "Prigorodnaia zona i problema otdykha naseleniia Moskvy." *Sotsialisticheskii gorod* 5 (1936): 16–21.

250 Sokolov, P. P. "Vospominaniia akademika P. P. Sokolova." *Istoricheskii vestnik* 121 (1910): 378–418; 122 (1910): 885–917.

Sollogub, V. A. *Vospominaniia.* Moscow and Leningrad, 1931.

*Soobshcheniia stolitsy s okrestnostiami ee.* St. Petersburg, 1882.

*S.-Peterburg i ego okrestnosti (Tsarskoe Selo, Petergof i dr.).* 2d ed. St. Petersburg, 1881.

*Spravochnaia knizhka dlia lits, poseshchaiushchikh dachi i zagorodnye uveselitel'nye mesta.* St. Petersburg, 1858.

*Spravochnik po Leningradu.* Leningrad, 1925.

Stanislavsky, C. *My Life in Art.* Trans. J. J. Robbins. Boston, 1924.

Stepanov, P. V. "Derevenskii dom-dacha i glavneishie usloviia postroiki domov." *Sel'skii khoziain* 25 (1892).

Steveni, W. B. *Petrograd Past and Present.* London, 1915.

Stori, V. *Dachnaia arkhitektura.* 5 vols. St. Petersburg, 1907–17.

Sudeikin, G. M. *"Al'bom proektov" dach, osobniakov, dokhodnykh domov, sluzhb i t.p.* Moscow, 1912.

———. *Al'bom proektov zimnikh dach, izb (bez sluzhb), osobniakov-nebol'shikh domov dlia odnoi sem'i, rabochikh, gorodskikh, provintsial'nykh i kooperativnykh domov iz dereva i kirpicha.* Moscow, 1928.

Sverbeev, D. N. *Zapiski (1799–1826).* 2 vols. Moscow, 1899.

Svetlov, S. F. *Peterburgskaia zhizn' v kontse XIX stoletiia (v 1892 godu).* St. Petersburg, 1998.

Teffi, N. A. *Iumoristicheskie rasskazy.* Moscow, 1990.

Teleshov, N. D. *Zolotaia osen' i drugie rasskazy.* Moscow, 1915.

Tikhomirov, M. "Detskie gody: Moskva i podmoskov'e." *Moskovskii arkhiv* 1 (1996): 455–84.

Tilinskii, A. I. *Deshevye postroiki: 100 proektov, v razlichnykh stiliakh, dachnykh i usadebnykh domov, sadovykh besedok, ograd, palisadnikov, kupalen, sadovoi mebeli.* St. Petersburg, 1913.

Tiutcheva, A. F. *Pri dvore dvukh imperatorov. Vospominaniia, dnevnik, 1853–1882.* Moscow, 1928–29; rpt., Cambridge, 1975.

Toporov, S. A., ed. *Moskva: Ee proshloe i nastoiashchee.* Moscow, 1896.

Trifonov, Iu. *Sobranie sochinenii v chetyrekh tomakh.* 4 vols. Moscow, 1985–86.

*Trudy pervogo S.-Peterburgskogo s''ezda predstavitelei podstolichnykh poselkov, 28–31 avgusta 1909 goda.* St. Petersburg, 1910.

Tsvetaev, V. D. *Dubrovitsy: Iz dachnykh vpechatlenii.* Moscow, 1907.

Tsvetaeva, A. *Vospominaniia.* Moscow, 1971.

Tsvetaeva, M. *Sochineniia v dvukh tomakh.* 2 vols. Moscow, 1988.

Turgenev, A. I. *Pis'ma Aleksandra Turgeneva Bulgakovym.* Moscow, 1939.

Turgenev, I. S. "Pervaia liubov'." *Polnoe sobranie sochinenii i pisem v tridtsati tomakh.* 30 vols. Moscow, 1978–86. Vol. 6.

Tynianov, Iu. "Avtobiografiia." In *Iurii Tynianov: Pisatel' i uchenyi.* Moscow, 1966.

*Ukazatel' zakonov dlia sel'skikh khoziaev.* St. Petersburg, 1845.

Uspenskii, G. I. "Bez opredelennykh zaniatii." *Polnoe sobranie sochinenii.* 10 vols. Moscow, 1940–54. Vol. 7.

Ustiukova, V. V. *Lichnoe podsobnoe khoziaistvo: pravovoi rezhim imushchestva.* Moscow, 1990.

*Vash dom: Katalog proektov individual'nykh zhilykh domov usadebnogo tipa dlia stroitel'stva v sel'skoi mestnosti nechernozemnoi zony RSFSR.* Moscow, 1980.

Vasil', S. "Dacha na troikh." In *Dacha na troikh: P'esy zastol'nykh vremen.* Rostov-on-Don, 1989.

Vasil'ev, V. I., and G. I. Makeenko. "Prigorodnaia zelenaia zona Moskvy." *Gorodskoe khoziaistvo Moskvy* 5 (1952): 20–22.

Vedenin, Iu. A., et al. "Formirovanie dachnykh poselkov i sadovykh kooperativov na territorii Moskovskoi aglomeratsii." *Izvestiia Akademii Nauk SSSR: Seriia geograficheskaia* 3 (1976): 72–79.

Verlander, A. P. *Po Baltiiskoi doroge.* 2 vols. St. Petersburg, 1883–84.

Vershinin, A. P. *Dachniki: Shutka v odnom deistvii.* Viatka, 1891.

Viazemskii, P. *Staraia zapisnaia knizhka.* Leningrad, 1929.

Vigel', F. F. *Zapiski.* 2 vols. Moscow, 1928.

Viktorskii, V. A. *Dachnyi Romeo.* St. Petersburg, 1905.

Vil'chkovskii, S. N. *Tsarskoe Selo.* St. Petersburg, 1911.

Vistengof, P. *Ocherki moskovskoi zhizni.* Moscow, 1842.

*Vospominaniia o Vasilii Feduloviche Gromove s ego portretom.* St. Petersburg, 1870.

*Vremennye tekhnicheskie pravila i normy planirovki i zastroiki territorii dlia individual'nogo i dachnogo stroitel'stva v gorodakh, rabochikh i dachnykh poselkakh Moskovskoi oblasti.* Moscow, 1940.

*Vseobshchii putevoditel' i spravochnik po Moskve i okrestnostiam.* 4th ed. Moscow, 1911.

*Vsia Moskva na ladoni.* Moscow, 1875.

*Vsia Moskva na ladonke.* Moscow, 1857.

V-v, M. *Kak provodit' leto na dache (Dachnaia dietetika).* St. Petersburg, 1909.

Wassenaer, Cornélie de. *A Visit to St. Petersburg, 1824–1825.* Trans. Igor Vinogradoff. Norwich, 1994.

Wilmot, M., and C. Wilmot. *The Russian Journals of Martha and Catherine Wilmot.* London, 1934.

Zabolotsky, N. *The Life of Zabolotsky.* Cardiff, 1994.

Zagoskin, M. N. *Moskva i moskvichi.* Moscow, 1851.

Zagoskin, S. M. "Vospominaniia." *Istoricheskii vestnik* 81 (1900): 36–61, 416–34.

Zakharov, M. P. *Okrestnosti Moskvy za Sokol'nich'ei i Krestovskoi zastavami.* Moscow, 1887.

" 'Zakhvatchiki, imenuiushchie sebia "narod". . .': Neskol'ko dokumentov iz fonda P. P. Durnovo (1917–1919)." *Zvezda* 11 (1994): 156–68.

Zasosov, D. A., and V. I. Pyzin. *Iz zhizni Peterburga 1890–1910-kh godov: Zapiski ochevidtsev.* Leningrad, 1991.

Zazulin, I. P. *Dachnye shalosti v Lesnom.* St. Petersburg, 1884.

Zenzinov, V. *Perezhitoe.* New York, 1953.

Zheltukhin, N. *Prakticheskaia arkhitektura gorodskikh, zagorodnykh i sel'skikh zdanii.* St. Petersburg and Moscow, 1875.

Zhemchuzhnaia, Z. *Puti izgnaniia: Ural, Kuban', Moskva, Kharbin, Tian'tszin.* Tenafly, N.J., 1987.

*Zhilishchno-bytovaia rabota professional'nykh soiuzov.* Moscow, 1956.

*Zhilishchnoe zakonodatel'stvo: Spravochnik postanovlenii i rasporiazhenii tsentral'noi i mestnoi vlasti s prilozheniem sudebnoi praktiki za 1928 god.* Moscow, 1929.

*Zhilishchnoe zakonodatel'stvo (spravochnik): Svodka postanovlenii i rasporiazhenii tesntral'noi i mestnoi vlasti za 1927 g.* Moscow, 1927.

*Zhizn' v svete, doma i pri dvore.* St. Petersburg, 1890.

Zhukova, M. S. "Dacha na Petergofskoi doroge." In *Dacha na Petergofskoi doroge: Proza russkikh pisatel'nits pervoi poloviny XIX veka*, ed. V. V. Uchenova. Moscow, 1986.

———. *Vechera na Karpovke.* Moscow, 1986.

Zikunov, V. "Kondratova dacha." *Rodinskie kolodtsy: Rasskazy.* Krasnoiarsk, 1990.

Ziloti, V. P. *V dome Tret'iakova.* New York, 1954.

Znakomyi, G. *Dachi i okrestnosti Peterburga.* St. Petersburg, 1891.

Zotov, V. R. "Peterburg v sorokovykh godakh (Vyderzhki iz avtobiograficheskikh zametok)." *Istoricheskii vestnik* 39 (1890): 29–53, 324–43, 553–72.

252

SELECTED SECONDARY SOURCES

This list is limited to the few works most directly relevant to the history of the dacha.

Amburger, E. *Ingermanland: Eine junge Provinz Rußlands im Wirkungsbereich der Residenz und Weltstadt St. Petersburg-Leningrad.* 2 vols. Cologne, 1980.

Andrusz, G. D. *Housing and Urban Development in the USSR.* Albany, N.Y., 1984.

Antsiferov, N. P. *Prigorody Leningrada.* Moscow, 1946.

Bascmakoff, N., and M. Leinonen. *Iz istorii i byta russkih v Finljandii.* Vol. 1. Helsinki, 1990.

Bater, J. "Between Old and New: St. Petersburg in the Late Imperial Era." In *The City in Late Imperial Russia,* ed. M. Hamm. Bloomington, 1986.

——. *Russia and the Post-Soviet Scene: A Geographical Perspective.* London and New York, 1996.

——. *The Soviet City: Ideal and Reality.* London, 1980.

——. *St. Petersburg: Industrialization and Change.* London, 1976.

Belitskii, Ia. M. *Okrest Moskvy.* Moscow, 1996.

Borisova, E. A. *Russkaia arkhitektura v epokhu romantizma.* St. Petersburg, 1997.

——. *Russkaia arkhitektura vtoroi poloviny XIX veka.* Moscow, 1979.

Borisova, E. A., and G. Iu. Sternin. *Russkii modern.* Moscow, 1990.

Brumfield, W. C., and B. Ruble, eds. *Russian Housing in the Modern Age: Design and Social History.* Cambridge, 1993.

Cherniavskii, U. G. *Voina i prodovol'stvie: Snabzhenie gorodskogo naseleniia v Velikuiu Otechestvennuiu Voinu (1941–1945 gg.).* Moscow, 1964.

Chernykh, O. I. "Dachnoe stroitel'stvo Peterburgskoi gubernii XVIII–nachala XX vv." Dissertation, St. Petersburg, 1993.

Colton, T. *Moscow: Governing the Socialist Metropolis.* Cambridge, Mass., 1995.

Deotto, P. "Peterburgskii dachnyi byt XIX v. kak fakt massovoi kul'tury." *Europa Orientalis* 16 (1997): 357–72.

Dukov, E. V., ed. *Razvlekatel'naia kul'tura Rossii XVIII–XIX vv.: Ocherki istorii i teorii.* St. Petersburg, 2000.

Evangulova, O. S. "Gorod i usad'ba vtoroi poloviny XVIII v. v soznanii sovremennikov." *Russkii gorod* 7 (1984): 172–88.

Floryan, M. *Gardens of the Tsars: A Study of the Aesthetics, Semantics and Uses of Late Eighteenth-Century Russian Gardens.* Aarhus, 1996.

French, R. A. *Plans, Pragmatism and People: The Legacy of Soviet Planning for Today's Cities.* London, 1995.

French, R. A., and F. E. I. Hamilton, eds. *The Socialist City: Spatial Structure and Urban Policy.* Chichester, 1979.

Galtz, N. R. "Space and the Everyday: An Historical Sociology of the Moscow Dacha." Ph.D. dissertation, University of Michigan, 2000.

Gorbatenko, S. "Rastsvet Petergofskoi dorogi." *Leningradskaia panorama* 7 (1989): 37–40.

Gordin, A. M. *Pushkinskii Peterburg.* Leningrad, 1974.

Gordin, A. M., and M. A. Gordin. *Pushkinskii vek: Panorama stolichnoi zhizni.* St. Petersburg, 1995.

Hamm, M., ed. *The City in Russian History.* Lexington, Ky., 1976.

Hervouet, R. "'Etre à la datcha': Eléments d'analyse issus d'une recherche exploratoire." In *Le Belarus: L'etat de l'exception,* ed. F. Depelteau and A. Lacassagne. Sainte-Foy, Québec, forthcoming.

Ianush, B. V. *Neizvestnyi Pavlovsk: Istoriko-kraevedcheskii ocherk.* St. Petersburg, 1997.

Il'in, G. V. "Zelenograd (vozniknovenie i razvitie)." *Russkii gorod* 5 (1982): 37–50.

*Istoriia sel i dereven' podmoskov'ia XIV-XX vv.* Moscow, 1993–.

Iukhneva, N. V., ed. *Peterburg i guberniia: Istoriko-etnograficheskie issledovaniia.* Leningrad, 1989.

Jahn, H. F. "The Housing Revolution in Petrograd, 1917–1920." *Jahrbücher für Geschichte Osteuropas* 38 (1990): 212–27.

Kaganov, G. *Images of Space: St. Petersburg in the Visual and Verbal Arts.* Trans. S. Monas. Stanford, 1997.

Kataev, S. Reiman, A. "Upadok petergofskoi dorogi." *Leningradskaia panorama* 8 (1989): 36–39.

Kazhdan, T. P. *Khudozhestvennyi mir russkoi usad'by.* Moscow, 1997.

Kirichenko, E. I. *Arkhitekturnye teorii XIX veka v Rossii.* Moscow, 1986.

Konechnyi, A. *Byt i zrelishchnaia kul'tura Sankt-Peterburga-Petrograda XVIII–nachalo XX veka: Materialy k bibliografii.* St. Petersburg, 1997.

Korentsvit, A. "Dachi na Petergofskoi doroge." *Leningradskaia panorama* 4 (1988): 35–37.

Kornilova, A. V., ed. *Pamiatniki istorii i kul'tury Sankt-Peterburga: Sbornik nauchnykh statei.* St. Petersburg, 1994.

Kuznetsov, E. *Iz proshlogo russkoi estrady: Istorichekii ocherk.* Moscow, 1958.

Lebina, N. B. *Povsednevnaia zhizn' sovetskogo goroda: Normy i anomalii, 1920–1930 gody.* St. Petersburg, 1999.

Loseva, A. S. "Obraz Petergofa epokhi romantizma." Dissertation, Moscow, 1997.

Lotman, Iu. M. "Kamen' i trava." In *Lotmanovskii sbornik,* vol. 1. Moscow, 1995.

Lukomskii, G. K. *Pamiatniki starinnoi arkhitektury Rossii.* Petrograd, 1916.

Malafeeva, S. "Poltora veka Petrovskogo parka." *Moskovskii arkhiv* 1 (1996): 107–17.

Nashchokina, M. V. "Arkhitektura dachnykh poselkov kontsa XIX–nachala XX vv." In *F. O. Shekhtel' i problemy istorii russkoi arkhitektury kontsa XIX–nachala XX vekov.* Moscow, 1988.

——. "Dachnye poselki vtoroi poloviny XIX–nachala XX vv." In *Sel'skie poseleniia Rossii: Istoricheskii i sotsiokul'turnyi analiz,* ed. O. G. Sevan. Moscow, 1995.

——. "Poselok 'Sokol'—gorod-sad 1920-kh godov." *Arkhitektura i stroitel'stvo Rossii* 12 (1994): 2–7.

*Ot konki do tramvaia: Iz istorii peterburgskogo transporta.* St. Petersburg and Moscow, 1993.

Papernyi, V. *Kul'tura "dva."* Moscow, 1996.

Priamurskii, G. G. *"V Poliustrovo na vody i razvlecheniia . . ."* St. Petersburg, 1996.

*Prigorody i okrestnosti Peterburga-Leningrada: Katalog graviur i litografii v sobranii Gosudarstvennoi Publichnoi biblioteki im. M. E. Saltykova-Shchedrina.* St. Petersburg, 1968.

Punin, A. L. *Arkhitektura Peterburga serediny XIX veka.* Leningrad, 1990.

——. A. L. *Arkhitekturnye pamiatniki Peterburga: Vtoraia polovina XIX veka.* Leningrad, 1981.

Randolph, J. "The Old Mansion: Revisiting the History of the Russian Country Estate." *Kritika* 1 (2000).

Rayfield, D. "Orchards and Gardens in Chekhov." *Slavonic and East European Review* 67 (1989): 530–45.

Reinus, L. M. *Dostoevskii v Staroi Russe.* Leningrad, 1969.

Roosevelt, P. *Life on the Russian Country Estate: A Social and Cultural History.* New Haven, 1995.

Rozanov, A. S. *Muzykal'nyi Pavlovsk.* Leningrad, 1978.

Ruble, B. *Leningrad: Shaping a Soviet City.* Berkeley, 1990.

Ruzhzhe, V. L. "Goroda-sady." *Stroitel'stvo i arkhitektura Leningrada* 2 (1961): 34–36.

*Sadovo-parkovoe iskusstvo Leningrada v proizvedeniiakh khudozhnikov i arkhitektorov XVIII–XX vv.: Katalog vystavki.* Leningrad, 1983.

Seeth, H. T., S. Chachnov, A. Surinov, and J. von Braun. "Russian Poverty: Muddling through Economic Transition with Garden Plots." *World Development* 26 (1998): 1611–23.

254    Sergeev, I. N. *Tsaritsyno. Sukhanovo. Liudi, sobytiia, fakty.* Moscow, 1998.

*Severo-zapadnyi okrug Moskvy.* Moscow, 1997.

Simagin, Iu. "Ekonomiko-geograficheskie aspekty suburbanizatsii v moskovskom stolichnom regione." Dissertation, Moscow, 1997.

Smith, D. M. "The Socialist City." In *Cities after Socialism: Urban and Regional Change and Conflict in Post-Socialist Societies,* ed. M. Harloe, I. Szelenyi, and G. Andrusz. Oxford, 1996.

Sosnovy, T. *The Housing Problem in the Soviet Union.* New York, 1954.

Springis, E. "Moskovskie zhiteli v sele Ostankine: K istorii dachnoi zhizni stolitsy serediny—vtoroi poloviny XIX veka." *Russkaia usad'ba* 5 (21) (1999).

Steklova, I. "Fenomen uveselitel'nykh sadov v formirovanii kul'turnoi sredy Peterburga-Petrograda." Dissertation, Leningrad, 1991.

——. "'Neskuchnye' sady Peterburga." *Leningradskaia panorama* 4 (1989): 36–37.

Sternin, G. Iu. *Russkaia khudozhestvennaia kul'tura vtoroi poloviny XIX–nachala XX veka.* Moscow, 1984.

Stolpianskii, P. N. *Dachnye okrestnosti Petrograda.* Petrograd and Moscow, 1923.

——. *Peterburg.* St. Petersburg, 1995.

——. *Petergofskaia pershpektiva: Istoricheskii ocherk.* Petrograd, 1923.

——. *Staryi Peterburg: Aptekarskii, Petrovskii, Krestovskii ostrova.* Petrograd, 1916.

Struyk, R., and K. Angelici. "The Russian Dacha Phenomenon." *Housing Studies* 11 (1996): 233–50.

Toporov, V. N. "Aptekarskii ostrov kak gorodskoe urochishche (obshchii vzgliad)." In *Noosfera i khudozhestvennoe tvorchestvo.* Moscow, 1991.

Trifonov, A. A. "Formirovanie seti gorodskikh poselenii na territorii Moskovskoi oblasti (seredina XIX v.–1976 g.)." *Russkii gorod* 5 (1982).

Vagin, V. V. "Russkii provintsial'nyi gorod: Kliuchevye elementy zhizneustroistva." *Mir Rossii* 4 (1997): 53–88.

Vergunov, A. P., and V. A. Gorokhov. *Russkie sady i parki.* Moscow, 1988.

Vihavainen, T., ed. *Normy i tsennosti povsednevnoi zhizni: Stanovlenie sotsialisticheskogo obraza zhizni v Rossii, 1920–30-e gody.* St. Petersburg, 2000.

Vitiazeva, V. A. *Kamennyi ostrov.* Leningrad, 1991.

——. *Nevskie ostrova.* Leningrad, 1986.

Wegren, S. K. *Agriculture and the State in Soviet and Post-Soviet Russia.* Pittsburgh, 1998.

Zima, V. F. *Golod v SSSR, 1946–1947 godov: Proiskhozhdenie i posledstviia.* Moscow, 1996.

# Index